TEPHIYLAH YHWH
"THE LORD'S PRAYER"

אָבִינוּ שֶׁבַּשָּׁמַיִם יִתְקַדֵּשׁ שְׁמֶךָ, תָּבוֹא מַלְכוּתֶךָ, יֵאָשֶׂה רְצוֹנְךָ כְּבַשָּׁמַיִם

AVINU SHAY-BA-SHAMAYIM, YIT-QADESH SHEM-KA, TABO MALKUT-KA,
YAY'ASEH RETZON-KA. KE-BA-SHAMAYIM

גַם בָּאָרֶץ. תֵּן לָנוּ אֶת לֶחֶם צָרְכֵּנוּ הַיוֹם, וּמְחַל לָנוּ אֶת חוֹבוֹתֵינוּ כְּמוֹ

GAM BA-ARETZ. TAYN LANU ET LEKHEM TZARKENU HA-YOM, U'MEKHAL LANU
ET KHOVOTAYNU KEMO

שֶׁגַם אֲנַחְנוּ מָחַלְנוּ לְחַיָּבֵנוּ. וְאַל תְּבִיאֵנוּ לִידֵי נִסָּיוֹן, אֶלָּא הַצִּילֵנוּ מִן

SHE-GAM ANAKHNU MAKHALNU LE'KHAYA'VAYNU. W' AL TEVIAYNU LIDAY
NISAYON, ELA HATZILAYNU MIN

הָרָע. כִּי שֶׁלְּךָ הִי הַמָּלְכוּת וְהַגְּבוּרָה וְהַתִּפְאָרָה לְעוֹלְמֵי עוֹלָמִים.

HA-RA. KI SHEL-KA HEE HA-MALKUT, W' HA-GAVURAH, W' HA-TIPHERAH
L' OLMAY OLAMIM.

Shalom Brothers and Sisters. Here is YAHOWAH'S PRAYER translated from the original
Hebrew/Aramaic Peshitta text. MattitYAHU (Matthew) 6:9-13.
HALLELUYAH!

H.I.S.
WORD
RESTORED HEBREW KJV
APOCRYPHA

A MESSAGE FROM KHAI YASHUA PRESS

We are grateful for the support you've shown to Khai Yashua Press by purchasing this Bible translation. One of our goals for the "RESTORED HEBREW KJV APOCRYPHA" is to highlight the original Hebraic faith of the Holy Bible and Apocrypha. We strive to reveal the hidden history and forgotten heritage and LANGUAGE to the Lost Tribes of Israel who were sold into slavery for their disobedience to YAHOWAH.

DEUTERONOMY 28:68
"AND YAHOWAH SHALL BRING THEE INTO EGYPT (BONDAGE) AGAIN WITH SHIPS (CARGO SLAVE SHIPS), by the way whereof I spake unto thee, Thou shalt see it no more again: AND THERE YE SHALL BE SOLD UNTO YOUR ENEMIES FOR BONDMEN AND BONDWOMEN, AND NO MAN SHALL BUY (REDEEM) YOU."

"H.I.S. WORD" clearly tells us (Hebrew Israelites) that we must return back to the covenant for our Father YAHOWAH to remember us and redeem/save us when YAHOSHUA returns.

2 CHRONICLES 7:14
If my people, which are called by my name, shall humble themselves, and pray, and seek my face, and turn from their wicked ways; then will I hear from heaven, and will forgive their sin, and will heal their land.

Will you answer this question?... How can you turn back to the covenant if you have not read it ALL YOURSELF?

REVELATIONS 10:8-9
8 And the voice which I heard from heaven spake unto me again, and said, Go and take the little book which is open in the hand of the angel which standeth upon the sea and upon the earth.
9 And I went unto the angel, and said unto him, Give me the little book. And he said unto me, Take it, and eat it up; and it shall make thy belly bitter, but it shall be in thy mouth sweet as honey.

Our MESHIAKH sent an angel to tell us to eat this scroll/book up!

We're excited to introduce to you several EXCLUSIVE FEATURES that help meet our goals of showcasing our History, Heritage and Language. The purpose of these EXCLUSIVE FEATURES is to highlight our original Hebraic faith. These EXCLUSIVE FEATURES are designed to make "H.I.S. WORD" easier to study and understand!

PROVERBS 4:7
Wisdom is the principal thing; therefore get wisdom: and with all thy getting get understanding.

2 Timothy 2:15
Study to shew thyself approved unto ELOHIM, a workman that needeth not to be ashamed, rightly dividing the word of truth.

These EXCLUSIVE FEATURES are only available in "H.I.S. WORD Hebrew Israelite Scriptures"!

Our prayer is that you will pick up "H.I.S. WORD" and read it all... because HIS WORDS are LIFE!

PROVERBS 4:20-22
My son, attend to my words; incline thine ear unto my sayings.
Let them not depart from thine eyes; keep them in the midst of thine heart.
For they are life unto those that find them, and health to all their flesh.

On the following pages we have explained all of the features and marked them with this marker so you can easily find the "EXCLUSIVE FEATURE" descriptions.

EF

Also found on the following pages, in "About this translation," we ask that you pay attention to how important the Hebrew language is to our heritage. We can see that OUR HEBREW LANGUAGE is a unique identifier of our NATION, and it defines Our CULTURE and our CUSTOMS!

In closing, we hope that you will seek YAHOWAH's face, remember your HERITAGE and your LANGUAGE.

We have plans to make available many Hebrew language and study tools! We invite you to come visit our website to register your email so that you can stay informed. You will find us at HebrewIsraeliteScriptures.com

ABOUT THIS TRANSLATION

Mark 1:3 & Isaiah 40:3
"The voice of him that crieth in the wilderness, Prepare ye the way of YAHOWAH, make straight in the desert a highway for our ELOHIM."

We love, respect and recognize the power of the (1611) King James Bible. King James, who was a Hebrew Israelite himself, suffered assassination attempts because he defied the power of the Catholic Church by authorizing the translation of the Sacred Text into English for the masses.

The Catholic Church was unsuccessful at their assassination attempts so instead they sought to assassinate his personal character.

John 1:1
"In the beginning was the Word, and the Word was with Elohim, and the Word was Elohim."

The Old and New Testaments were written in the tongue in which it was inspired, (which the Apostles spoke). That language was Hebrew/ Aramaic.

Prologue to The Book of Sirach (Page 645)
"For the same things uttered in Hebrew, and translated into another tongue, have not the same force in them..."

We understand that according to Sirach some words when translated to another tongue, "have not the same force in them". So we have restored selected words (by careful comparison to the original Masoretic Hebrew Text & Aramaic Peshitta) with the intention of restoring the powerful force and meaning of the words from the Original Text and removing all of the Greek influences.

Here, Josephus Flavius, the Hebrew historian who lived in that time, proved that the Hellenic (Greek) culture was not accepted by Hebrew Israelites. They fiercely guarded

Hebrew/Aramaic which was the language of the people.

Wars of the Jews," Josephus in his preface, Section I
"I have proposed to myself for the sake of such as live under the Roman Government, to translate those books into the Greek tongue, which I formally composed in the LANGUAGE OF OUR COUNTRY..." (common Hebrew, otherwise known as Aramaic)."

The Antiquities of the Jews, Book 20, Chapter XI, Section 2
"I also have taken a great deal of pains to obtain the learning of the Greeks, and understand the elements of the Greek language, although I have so long accustomed myself to speak our own tongue, that I cannot pronounce the Greek with sufficient exactness, for our own nation DOES NOT ENCOURAGE THOSE THAT LEARN THE LANGUAGES OF MANY NATIONS...because they look upon this sort of accomplishment as common (profane)... there have yet hardly been so many as two or three that have succeeded (in learning Greek) therein who were immediately rewarded for their pains"

Furthermore, in the book of Maccabees we can see that when the wicked men of Yisra'EL decided to make a covenant with the Greeks, we had "MUCH SORROW"

Maccabees 1:11
"In those days went there out of Yisra'EL wicked men, who persuaded many, saying, Let us go and make a covenant with the heathen (Greeks) that are round about us: for since we departed from them we have had much sorrow."

The book of Maccabees also describes how the Greeks made laws stating that "all should be one people" and "many also of the children of Yisra'EL consented to his "CUSTOMS". This is also true here in this captivity!

Maccabees 1:41- 49
"Moreover king Antiyokos wrote to his whole kingdom, that all should be one people, And every one should leave his laws: so all the heathen (Greeks) agreed according to the commandment of the king. Yea, many also of the children of Yisra'EL consented to his CUSTOMS, and sacrificed unto idols, and profaned the sabbath. For the king had sent letters by messengers unto Yerushalem and the cities of Yehudah that they should follow the strange laws of the land, And forbid burnt offerings, and sacrifice, and drink offerings, in the temple; and that they should profane the sabbaths and festival days: And pollute the sanctuary and holy people: Set up altars, and groves, and chapels of idols, and sacrifice swine's flesh, and unclean beasts: That they should also leave their children uncircumcised, and make their souls abominable with all manner of uncleanness and profanation: TO THE END THEY MIGHT FORGET THE LAW, AND CHANGE ALL THE ORDINANCES."

ABOUT THIS TRANSLATION

Now we can see that the HEATHEN knows that when we take on their "CUSTOMS", the end result is that we "FORGET THE LAW, AND CHANGE ALL THE ORDINANCES".

When you look up the definition of "CUSTOM" on Dictionary.com, here is what you find:

> CUSTOM
> - A habitual practice; the usual way of acting in given circumstances.
> - Habits or usages collectively; convention.
> - A practice so long established that it has the force of law.
> - Such practices collectively.
> - Sociology: a group pattern of habitual activity usually transmitted from one generation to another.

...When you look up the word "CULTURE" in the Oxford American Dictionary and Thesaurus, it says that the words "CUSTOMS" and "CULTURE" are synonymous or exactly the same. They define Culture as "the arts, customs and institutions of a nation, people, or group."

We can tie this all together by looking up the definition of the word "NATION". On Wikipedia.com, we can see that the HEBREW LANGUAGE is a unique identifier of our NATION, and it defines our CULTURE and our CUSTOMS!

A nation (from Latin: natio, "people, tribe, kin, genus, class, flock") is a large group or collective of people with common characteristics attributed to them — including LANGUAGE, traditions, mores (customs), habitus (habits), and ethnicity.

Again, we can see here in the book of Maccabees that MattitYAHU said: "We will not hearken to the king's words, to go from our CUSTOMS"

> Maccabees 2:17- 22
> "Then answered the king's officers, and said to MattitYAHU on this wise, Thou art a ruler, and an honourable and great man in this city, and strengthened with sons and brethren: Now therefore come thou first, and fulfil the king's commandment, like as all the heathen (Greeks) have done, yea, and the men of Yehudah also, and such as remain at Yerushalem: so shalt thou and thy house be in the number of the king's friends, and thou and thy children shall be honoured with silver and gold, and many rewards. Then MattitYAHU answered and spake with a loud voice, Though all the Gentiles that are under the king's dominion obey him, and fall away every one from the CUSTOMS of their fathers, and

give consent to his commandments: Yet will I and my sons and my brethren walk in the covenant of our fathers. ELOHIM forbid that we should forsake the commandments of YAHOWAH our ELOHIM and for us to break his covenant. WE WILL NOT HARKEN TO THE KING'S WORDS, TO GO FROM OUR CUSTOMS, either on the right hand, or the left.

With much prayer, reverence and respect for YAHOWAH's WORD, we've restored and highlighted the names of YAHOWAH, YAHOSHUA and the RUACH HA' QODESH in brilliant GOLD.

Malachi 3:16
"a book of remembrance was written before him for them that feared YAHOWAH, and that thought upon HIS NAME."

EF

It has been recently discovered that the original translators of the Old Testament into the Greek (by the seventy Jewish scholars at the request of Ptolomy-Philadelphius) did not translate nor transliterate the Name of YAHOWAH. Instead, they blocked off a space, and then, in GOLD, they inscribed YAHOWAH every place where YAH's Name was written.

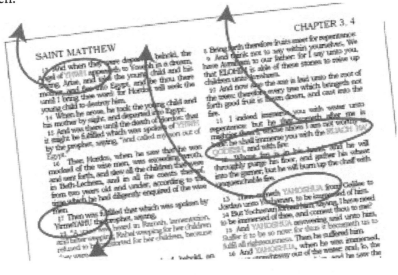

We have also done much research and restored the proper Hebrew names of all the saints of YAH in the Old and New Testaments and Apocrypha.

ABOUT THIS TRANSLATION

Bar-Hebrews, the famous Eastern historian of the Twelfth Century, noted the fact that the Greeks Hellenized many Aramaic-Hebrew names, and stated that they changed the form of many nouns and did not pronounce them as given in the original text.

> Psalms 12: 6-7
> "The words of YAHOWAH are pure words: as silver tried in a furnace of earth, purified seven times. Thou shalt keep them, O YAHOWAH, thou shalt preserve them from this generation for ever."

EF

The WORDS of the Old Testament that are quoted in the New Testament are highlighted in Royal Blue! It is now EASY to see YAHOSHUA revealed in the volume of the book!

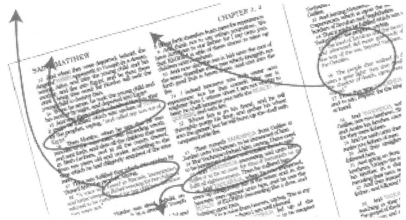

EF

The WORDS of our MESHIACH are highlighted in Red!

> Psalms 40:7 & Hebrews 10:7
> "Then said I, Lo, I come: in the volume of the book it is written of me"

EF

The HOLY DAYS and SHABBATS are highlighted in Purple!

according to the
...any also of the children
...to his customs, and sacr...
...d profaned the Shabbath.
...the king had sent letters by m...
...rushalem and the cities of Yehu...
...ould follow the strange laws of th...
...d forbid burnt offerings, and...
...k offerings, in the temple; and...
...fane the Shabbaths and fest...
...llute the sanctuary and h...
...nd groves...

HalleluYAH!

TESTAMENT OF THE 12 PATRIARCH

THE BOOK OF THE 12 SONS OF JACOB (ISRAE

APOCRYPHA BOOK

HA' SEPHERIM HA' KHITZON

WORD COLOR CHART

EF

To enhance your reading experience and to open the vail of your understanding of the scriptures, we have color coded the text to macth the colors used within YAHOWAH's TEMPLE and of the priestly garments.

The Inner Vail Of Understanding

Exodus.26:31-32

31 And thou shalt make a vail of blue, and purple, and scarlet, and fine twined linen (white) of cunning work: with cherubims shall it be made:

32 And thou shalt hang it upon four pillars of shittim wood overlaid with gold: their hooks shall be of gold, upon the four sockets of silver.

 BRILLIANT GOLD
The names of YAHOWAH, and the RUACH HA' QODESH highlighted in brilliant GOLD

 PURPLE
The WORDS of the Hebrew Concordance, Sabbaths and Holy Days of YAHOWAH are highlighted in Purple.

KHAI YASHUA ASSEMBLY

ISAIAH 36:16
Seek ye out of the book of YAHOWAH, and read: no one of these shall fail, none shall want her mate: for my mouth it hath commanded, and his RUAKH it hath gathered them.

Shalom w'ahavah (peace and love) to all! Welcome to Khai Yashua ministries. Our mission is to help the 12 Tribes of Israel arise from their slumber and return back to YAHOWAH.

Mar 2:11 I say unto thee, Arise, and take up thy bed, and go thy way into thine house.

We hope that through our new and innovative biblical teachings that you will experience exciting revelations that you never have before!

Mar 2:12 And immediately he arose, took up the bed, and went forth before them all; insomuch that they were all amazed, and glorified ELOHIM, saying, WE NEVER SAW IT ON THIS FASHION!

Author, Hebrew instructor and translator, bible teacher JediYah Melek has taught hundreds of thousands of people across the globe about the salvation and redemptive covenant of YAHOSHUA HA' MESHIAKH.

Mar 2:13 And He went forth again by the sea side; and all the multitude resorted unto Him, AND HE TAUGHT THEM.

May The RUAKH HA' QADOSH open your heart to receive eternal life – the Life of YASHUA – KHAI YASHUA!!!

NOTES

THE
APOCRYPHA

The Apocrypha is a collection of 14 ancient books spanning the time period between both the Old and New Testaments. The Hebrew word for Apocrypha is: Ha' Khitzonim. The Apocrypha in the 1611 KJV was translated from Greek and Latin manuscripts (i.e. Codex Vaticanus, Codex Siniticus and Codex Alexandrinus). However, much earlier original Hebrew versions have been discovered within the Dead Sea Scrolls in the Qumran Caves of the West Bank, Israel.

THE HEBREW WORD FOR APOCRYPHA IS: HA' KHITZONIM

The Hebrew Apocrypha includes additional Scriptures missing from the Greek Apocryphal manuscripts. Some of these books include: The Book of Enoch, the Book of Adam and Eve, Testimony of the 12 Patriarchs and the Book of Jubilees.

Qumran Caves where the Dead Sea Scrolls were discovered in West Bank, Israel

THE TESTAMENT OF
REUBEN

1 The copy of the Testament of Reuben even the commands which he gave his sons before he died in the hundred and twenty-fifth year of his life.

2 Two years after the death of Yoseph (Joseph) his brother, when Reuben fell ill, his sons and his sons' sons were gathered together to visit him.

3 And he said to them: My children, behold I am dying, and go the way of my fathers.

4 And seeing there Yehudah, and Gad, and Asher, his brethren, he said to them: Raise me up, that I may tell to my brethren and to my children what things I have hidden in my heart, for behold now at length I am passing away.

5 And he arose and kissed them, and said unto them: Hear, my brethren, and do ye, my children, give ear to Reuben your father in the commands which I give unto you.

6 And behold I call to witness against you this day the ELOHIM (God) of heaven, that ye walk not in the sins of youth and fornication, wherein I was poured out, and defiled the bed of my father Ya'aqob (Jacob).

7 And I tell you that YAHOWAH (The LORD) smote me with a sore plague in my loins for seven months; and had not my father Ya'aqob prayed for me to YAHOWAH, YAHOWAH would have destroyed me.

8 For I was thirty years old when I wrought the evil thing before YAHOWAH, and for seven months I was sick unto death.

9 And after this I repented with set purpose of my soul for seven years before YAHOWAH.

10 And wine and strong drink I drank not, and flesh entered not into my mouth, and I ate no pleasant food; but I mourned over my sin, for it was great, such as had not been in Yisra'EL.

2 And now hear me, my children, what things I saw concerning the seven rukhoth (rukhoth) of deceit, when I repented.

2 Seven rukhoth therefore are appointed against man, and they are the leaders in the works of youth.

3 And seven other rukhoth are given to him at his creation, that through them should be done every work of man.

4 The first is the ruakh (spirit) of life, with which the constitution (of man) is created. The second is the sense of sight, with which ariseth desire.

5 The third is the sense of hearing, with which cometh teaching. The fourth is the sense of smell, with which tastes are given to draw air and breath.

6 The fifth is the power of speech, with which cometh knowledge.

7 The sixth is the sense' of taste, with which cometh the eating of meats and drinks; and by it strength is produced, for in food is the foundation of strength.

8 The seventh is the power of procreation and sexual intercourse, with which through love of pleasure sins enter in.

9 Wherefore it is the last in order of creation, and the first in that of youth, because it is filled with ignorance, and leadeth the youth as a blind man to a pit, and as a beast to a precipice.

3 Besides all these there is an eighth ruakh of sleep, with which is brought about the trance of nature and the image of death.

2 With these rukhoth are mingled the rukhoth of error.

3 First, the ruakh of fornication is seated in the nature and in the senses; the second, the ruakh of insatiableness, in the belly;

4 The third, the ruakh of fighting, in the liver and gall. The fourth is the ruakh of obsequiousness and chicanery, that through officious attention one may be fair in seeming.

5 The fifth is the ruakh of pride, that one may be boastful and arrogant. The sixth is the ruakh of lying, in perdition and in jealousy to practise deceits, and concealments from kindred and friends.

6 The seventh is the ruakh of injustice, with which are thefts and acts of rapacity, that a man may fulfil the desire of his heart; for injustice worketh together with the other rukhoth by the taking of gifts.

7 And with all these the ruakh of sleep is joined which is (that) of error and fantasy.

8 And so perisheth every young man, darkening his mind from the truth, and not understanding the statutes (laws) of YAHOWAH (ELOHIM), nor obeying the admonitions of his fathers, as befell me also in my youth.

9 And now, my children, love the truth, and it will preserve you: hear ye the words of Reuben your father.

10 Pay no heed to the face of a woman, Nor associate with another man's wife, Nor meddle with affairs of womankind.

11 For had I not seen Bilhah bathing in a covered place, I had not fallen into this great iniquity.

12 For my mind taking in the thought of the woman's nakedness, suffered me not to sleep until I had wrought the abominable thing.

13 For while Ya'aqob our father had gone to Yitzkhaq (Isaac) his father, when we were in the tower of Eder, near to Ephrath in Bethlekhem

(Bethlehem), Bilhah became drunk and was asleep uncovered in her chamber.

14 Having therefore gone in and beheld her nakedness, I wrought the impiety without her perceiving it, and leaving her sleeping I departed.

15 And forthwith an Angel of ELOHIM revealed to my father concerning my impiety, and he came and mourned over me, and touched her no more.

4 Pay no heed, therefore, my children, to the beauty of women, nor set your mind on their affairs; but walk in singleness of heart in the fear of YAHOWAH, and expend labour on good works, and on study and on your flocks, until YAHOWAH give you a wife, whom He will, that ye suffer not as I did.

2 For until my father's death I had not boldness to look in his face, or to speak to any of my brethren, because of the reproach.

3 Even until now my conscience causeth me anguish on account of my impiety.

4 And yet my father comforted me much, and prayed for me unto YAHOWAH, that the anger of YAHOWAH might pass from me, even as YAHOWAH showed. And thenceforth until now I have been on my guard and sinned not.

5 Therefore, my children, I say unto you, observe all things whatsoever I command you, and ye shall not sin.

6 For a pit unto the soul is the sin of fornication, separating it from YAHOWAH (ELOHIM), and bringing it near to idols, because it deceiveth the mind and understanding, and leadeth down young men into Sheol (Hell/Hades) before their time.

7 For many hath fornication destroyed; because, though a man be old or noble, or rich or poor, he bringeth reproach upon himself with the sons of men and derision with Beliya'al (Beliar/Belial).

8 For hear ye regarding Yoseph how he guarded himself from a woman, and purged his thoughts from all fornication, and found favour in the sight of ELOHIM and men.

9 For the Mitzrim (Egyptian) woman did many things unto him, and summoned magicians, and offered him love potions, but the purpose of his soul admitted no evil desire.

10 Therefore the ELOHIM of your fathers delivered him from every evil (and) hidden death.

11 For if fornication overcomes not your mind, neither can Beliya'al overcome you.

5 For evil are women, my children; and since they have no power or strength over man, they use wiles by outward attractions that they may draw him to themselves.

2 And whom they cannot bewitch by outward attractions, him they overcome by craft.

3 For moreover, concerning them, the Angel of YAHOWAH told me, and taught me, that women are overcome by the ruakh of fornication more than men, and in their heart they plot against men; and by means of their adornment they deceive first their minds, and by the glance of the eye instil the poison, and then through the accomplished act they take them captive.

4 For a woman cannot force a man openly, but by a harlot's bearing she beguiles him.

5 Flee, therefore, fornication, my children, and command your wives and your daughters, that they adorn not their heads and faces to deceive the mind; because every woman who useth these wiles hath been reserved for eternal punishment.

6 For thus they allured the Watchers who were before the flood; for as these continually beheld them, they lusted after them, and they conceived the act in their mind; for they changed themselves into the shape of men, and appeared to them when they were with their husbands.

7 And the women lusting in their minds after their forms, gave birth to Nephilim (Giants), for the Watchers appeared to them as reaching even unto heaven.

6 Beware, therefore, of fornication; and if you wish to be pure in mind, guard your senses from every woman.

2 And command the women likewise not to associate with men, that they also may be pure in mind.

3 For constant meetings, even though the ungodly deed be not wrought, are to them an irremediable disease, and to us a destruction of Beliya'al and an eternal reproach.

4 For in fornication there is neither understanding nor godliness, and all jealousy dwelleth in the lust thereof.

5 Therefore, then, I say unto you, ye will be jealous against the sons of Lewy (Levi), and will seek to be exalted over them; but ye shall not be able.

6 For ELOHIM will avenge them and ye shall die by an evil death.

7 For to Lewy ELOHIM gave the sovereignty and to Yehudah with him and to me also, and to Dan and Yoseph, that we should be for rulers.

8 Therefore I command you to hearken to Lewy, because he shall know the statutes (laws) of YAHOWAH, and shall give ordinances for judgement and shall sacrifice for all Yisra'EL (Israel) until the consummation of the times, as HA' MESHIAKH (The Anointed One) the Priest, of whom YAHOWAH spake.

9 I adjure you by the ELOHIM of heaven to do truth each one unto his neighbour and to entertain love each for his brother.

10 And draw ye near to Lewy in humbleness of heart, that ye may receive a blessing from his mouth.

11 For he shall bless Yisra'EL and Yehudah, because him hath YAHOWAH chosen to be king over all the nation.

12 And bow down before his seed, for on our behalf it will die in wars visible and invisible, and will be among you an eternal king.

7 And Reuben died, having given these commands to his sons.

2 And they placed him in a coffin until they carried him up from Mitzraim (Egypt), and buried him in Khebron (Hebron) in the cave where his father was.

THE TESTAMENT OF
SIMEON

1 THE copy of the words of Shimon (Simeon), the things which he spake to his sons before he died, in the hundred and twentieth year of his life, at which time Yoseph, his brother, died.

2 For when Shimon was sick, his sons came to visit him. and he strengthened himself and sat up and kissed them, and said:--

2 Hearken, my children, to Shimon your father and I will declare unto you what things I have in my heart.

2 I was born of Ya'aqob as my father's second son; and my mother Leah called me Shimon, because ELOHIM had heard her prayer.

3 Moreover, I became strong exceedingly; I shrank from no achievement nor was I afraid of ought.

4 For my heart was hard, and my liver was immovable, and my bowels without compassion.

5 Because valour also has been given from the Most High to men in soul and body.

6 For in the time of my youth I was jealous in many things of Yoseph, because my father loved him beyond all.

7 And I set my mind against him to destroy him because the prince of deceit sent forth the ruakh of jealousy and blinded my mind, so that I regarded him not as a brother, nor did I spare even Ya'aqob my father.

8 But his ELOHIM and the ELOHIM of his fathers sent forth His Angel, and delivered him out of my hands.

9 For when I went to Shekem (Shechem) to bring ointment for the flocks, and Reuben to Dothan, where were our necessaries and all our stores, Yehudah my brother sold him to the Yishmaelim (Ishmaelites).

10 And when Reuben heard these things he was grieved, for he wished to restore him to his father.

11 But on hearing this I was exceedingly wroth against Yehudah in that he let him go away alive, and for five months I continued wrathful against him.

12 But YAHOWAH restrained me, and withheld from me the power of my hands; for my right hand was half withered for seven days.

13 And I knew, my children, that because of Yoseph this had befallen me, and I repented and wept; and I besought YAHOWAH ELOHIM that my hand might be restored and that I might hold aloof from all pollution and envy and from all folly.

14 For I knew that I had devised an evil thing before YAHOWAH and Ya'aqob my father, on account of Yoseph my brother, in that I envied him.

3 And now, my children, hearken unto me and beware of the ruakh of deceit and envy.

2 For envy ruleth over the whole mind of a man, and suffereth him neither to eat nor to drink, nor to do any good thing.

3 But it ever suggesteth to him to destroy him that he envieth; and so long as he that is envied flourisheth, he that envieth fadeth away.

4 Two years therefore I afflicted my soul with fasting in the fear of YAHOWAH, and I learnt that deliverance from envy cometh by the fear of ELOHIM.

5 For if a man flee to YAHOWAH, the evil ruakh runneth away from him and his mind is lightened.

6 And henceforward he sympathiseth with him whom he envied and forgiveth those who are hostile to him, and so ceaseth from his envy.

4 And my father asked concerning me, because he saw that I was sad; and I said unto him, I am pained in my liver.

2 For I mourned more than they all, because I was guilty of the selling of Yoseph.

3 And when we went down into Mitzraim, and he bound me as a spy, I knew that I was suffering justly, and I grieved not.

4 Now Yoseph was a good man, and had the RUAKH of ELOHIM within him: being compassionate and pitiful, he bore no malice against me; but loved me even as the rest of his brethren.

5 Beware, therefore, my children, of all jealousy and envy, and walk in singleness of heart, that ELOHIM may give you also grace and glory, and blessing upon your heads, even as ye saw in Yoseph's case.

6 All his days he reproached us not concerning this thing, but loved us as his own soul, and beyond his own sons glorified us, and gave us riches, and cattle and fruits.

7 Do ye also, my children, love each one his brother with a good heart, and the ruakh of envy will withdraw from you.

8 For this maketh savage the soul and destroyeth the body; it causes anger and war in the mind, and stirreth up unto deeds of blood, and leadeth the mind into frenzy, and causeth tumult to the soul and trembling to the body.

9 For even in sleep some malicious jealousy, deluding him, gnaweth, and with wicked rukhoth disturbeth his soul, and causeth the body to be troubled, and waketh the mind from sleep in confusion; and as a wicked and poisonous ruakh, so appeareth it to men.

5 Therefore was Yoseph comely in appearance, and goodly to look upon, because no wickedness dwelt in him; for some of the trouble of the ruakh the face manifesteth.

2 And now, my children, Make your hearts good before YAHOWAH, And your ways straight before men, And ye shall find grace before YAHOWAH and men.

3 Beware, therefore, of fornication, For fornication is mother of all evils, Separating from ELOHIM, and bringing near to Beliya'al.

4 I have seen it inscribed in the writing of **Khanok (Enoch)** that your sons shall be corrupted in fornication, and shall do harm to the sons of Lewy with the sword.

5 But they shall not be able to withstand Lewy; for he shall wage the war of YAHOWAH, and shall conquer all your hosts.

6 And they shall be few in number, divided in Lewy and Yehudah, and there shall be none of you for sovereignty, even as also our father prophesied in his blessings.

6 Behold I have told you all things, that I may be acquitted of your sin.

2 Now, if ye remove from you your envy and all stiff-neckedness, as a rose shall my bones flourish in Yisra'EL, and as a lily my flesh in Ya'aqob, and my odour shall be as the odour of Libanus; and as cedars shall holy ones be multiplied from me for ever, and their branches shall stretch afar off.

3 Then shall perish the seed of **Kena'an (Canaan)**, and a remnant shall not be unto **Amaleq (Amalek)**, and all the **Kittim (Cappadocians/ Romans)** shall perish, and all the **Khittim (Hittites)** shall be utterly destroyed.

4 Then shall fail the land of Ham, and all the people shall perish. Then shall all the earth rest from trouble, and all the world under heaven from war.

5 Then shall a sign be glorified greatly unto Yisra'EL, for YAHOWAH ELOHIM appear ing on earth shall come [as man], and saving through him man.

6 Then shall all the rukhoth of deceit be given to be trodden under foot, And men shall rule over wicked rukhoth.

7 Then shall I arise in joy, and will bless the Most High because of His marvellous works, because ELOHIM hath taken a body and eaten with men and saved men.

7 And now, my children, obey Lewy and Yehudah, and be not lifted up against these two tribes, for from them shall arise unto you the salvation of ELOHIM.

2 For YAHOWAH shall raise up from Lewy as it were a High-priest, and from Yehudah as it were a King, ELOHIM and man, He shall save all the Gentiles and (the family (race) of) Yisra'EL.

3 Therefore I give, you these commands that ye also may command your children, that they may observe them throughout their generations.

8 And when Shimon had made an end of commanding his sons, he slept with his fathers, being an hundred and twenty years old.

2 And they laid him in a wooden coffin, to take up his bones to Khebron. And they took them up secretly during a war of the **Mitzrim (Egyptians)**.

3 For the bones of Yoseph the Mitzrim guarded in the tombs of the Kings.

4 For the sorcerers told them, that on the departure of the bones of Yoseph there should be throughout all the land darkness and gloom, and an exceeding great plague to the Mitzrim, so that even with a lamp a man should not recognise his brother.

9 And the sons of Shimon bewailed their father.

2 And they were in Mitzraim until the day of their departure by the hand of **Mosheh (Moses)**.

THE TESTAMENT OF
LEVI

1 The copy of the words of Lewy (Levi), the things which he ordained unto his sons, according to all that they should do, and what things should befall them until the day of judgement

2 He was sound in health when he called them to him; for it had been revealed to him that he should die. And when they were gathered together he said to them:

2 I, Lewy, was born in Haran, and I came with my father to Shekem.

2 And I was young, about twenty years of age, when, with Shimon, I wrought vengeance on Khamor (Hamor) for our sister Dinah.

3 And when I was feeding the flocks in Abel-Mekholah (Abel-Maul), the RUAKH of understanding of YAHOWAH came upon me, and I saw all men corrupting their way, and that unrighteousness had built for itself walls, and lawlessness sat upon towers.

4 And I was grieving for the family (race) of the sons of men, and I prayed to YAHOWAH that I might be saved.

5 Then there fell upon me a sleep, and I beheld a high mountain, and I was upon it.

6 And behold the heavens were opened, and an Angel of ELOHIM said to me, Lewy, enter.

7 And I entered from the first heaven, and I saw there a great sea hanging.

8 And further, I saw a second heaven far brighter and more brilliant, for there was a boundless height also therein.

9 And I said to the Angel, Why is this so ? And the Angel said to me, Marvel not at this, for thou shalt see another heaven more brilliant and incomparable.

10 And when thou hast ascended thither, Thou shalt stand near YAHOWAH, And shalt be His minister, And shalt declare His mysteries to men, And shaft proclaim concerning Him that shall redeem Yisra'EL.

11 And by thee and Yehudah shall YAHOWAH appear among men, Saving every family (race) of men.

12 And from YAHOWAH'S portion shall be thy life, And He shall be thy field and vineyard, And fruits, gold, and silver.

3 Hear, therefore, regarding the heavens widen have been shown to thee. The lowest is for this cause gloomy unto thee, in that it beholds all the unrighteous deeds of men.

2 And it has fire, snow, and ice made ready for the day of judgement, in the righteous judge-ment of ELOHIM; for in it are all the rukhoth of the retributions for vengeance on men.

3 And in the second are the hosts of the armies which are ordained for the day of judgement, to work vengeance on the rukhoth of deceit and of Beliya'al. And above them are the holy ones.

4 And in the highest of all dwelleth the Great Glory, far above all holiness

5 In the heaven next to it are the archangels, who minister and make propitiation to YAHOWAH for all the sins of ignorance of the righteous;

6 Offering to YAHOWAH a sweet-smelling savour, a reasonable and a bloodless offering.

7 And in the heaven below this are the Angels who bear answers to the Angels of the Presence of YAHOWAH.

8 And in the heaven next to this are thrones and dominions, in which always they offer praise to ELOHIM.

9 When, therefore, YAHOWAH looketh upon us, all of us are shaken; yea, the heavens, and the earth, and the abysses are shaken at the Presence of His Majesty.

10 But the sons of men, having no perception of these things, sin and provoke the Most High.

4 Now, therefore, know that YAHOWAH shall execute judgement upon the sons of men. Because when the rocks are being rent, and the sun quenched, and the waters dried up, and the fire cowering, and all creation troubled, and the invisible rukhoth melting away, and Sheol taketh spoils through the visitations of the Most High, men will be unbelieving and persist in their iniquity. On this account with punishment shall they be judged.

2 Therefore, the Most High hath heard thy prayer, to separate thee from iniquity, and that thou shouldest become to Him a son, and a servant, and a minister of His Presence.

3 The light of knowledge shalt thou light up in Ya'aqob, and as the sun shalt thou be to all the seed of Yisra'EL.

4 And there shall be given to thee a blessing, and to all thy seed, until YAHOWAH shall visit all the Gentiles in His tender mercies for ever.

5 And therefore there have been given to thee counsel and understanding, that thou mightest instruct thy sons concerning this;

6 Because they that bless Him shall be blessed, And they that curse Him shall perish.

5 And thereupon the Angel opened to me the gates of heaven, and I saw the holy temple, and upon a throne of glory the Most High.

2 And He said to me: Lewy, I have given thee the blessings of the priesthood until I come and sojourn in the midst of Yisra'EL.

3 Then the Angel brought me down to the earth, and gave me a shield and a sword, and said to me: Execute vengeance on Shekem because of Dinah, thy sister, and I will be with thee because YAHOWAH hath sent me.

4 And I destroyed at that time the sons of Khamor, as it is written in the heavenly tablets.

5 And I said to him: I pray Thee, O YAHOWAH, tell me Thy name, that I may call upon Thee in a day of tribulation.

6 And he said: I am the Angel who intercedeth for the nation of Yisra'EL that they may not be smitten utterly, for every evil ruakh attacketh it.

7 And after these things I awaked, and blessed the Most High, and the Angel who intercedeth for the nation of Yisra'EL and for all the righteous

6 And when I was going to my father, I found a brazen shield; wherefore also the name of the mountain is Siryon (Aspis), which is near Gebal, to the south of Abelah.

2 And I kept these words in my heart. And after this I counselled my father, and Reuben my brother, to bid the sons of Khamor not to be circumcised; for I was jealous because of the abomination which they had wrought on my sister.

3 And I slew Shekem first, and Shimon slew Khamor.

4 And after this my brothers came and smote that city with the edge of the sword.

5 And my father heard these things and was wroth; and he was grieved in that they had received the circumcision, and after that had been put to death, and in his blessings he looked amiss upon us.

6 For we sinned because we had done this thing against his will, and he was sick on that day.

7 But I saw that the sentence of ELOHIM was for evil upon Shekem; for they sought to do to Sarah and Ribqah as they had done to Dinah our sister, but YAHOWAH prevented them.

8 And they persecuted Abraham our father when he was a stranger, and they vexed his flocks when they were big with young; and Yubel (Eblaen), who was born in his house, they most shamefully handled.

9 And thus they did to all strangers, taking away their wives by force, and they banished them.

10 But the wrath of YAHOWAH came upon them to the uttermost.

7 And I said to my father Ya'aqob: By thee will YAHOWAH destroy the Kena'anim (Canaanites), and will give their land to thee and to thy seed after thee.

2 For from this day forward shall Shekem be called a city of imbeciles; for as a man mocketh a fool, so did we mock them

3 Because also they had wrought folly in Yisra'EL by defiling my sister. And we departed and came to Beth'EL.

8 And there again I saw a vision even as the former, after we had spent there seventy days.

2 And I saw seven men in white raiment saying unto me: Arise, put on the robe of the priesthood, and the crown of righteousness, and the breastplate of understanding, and the garment of truth, and the plate of faith, and the turban of the head, and the ephod of prophecy.

3 And they severally carried (these things) and put (them) on me, and said unto me: From henceforth become a priest of YAHOWAH, thou and thy seed for ever.

4 And the first anointed me with holy oil, and gave to me the staff of judgement.

5 The second washed me with pure water, and fed me with bread and wine (even) the most holy things, and clad me with a holy and glorious robe.

6 The third clothed me with a linen vestment like an ephod.

7 The fourth put round me a girdle like unto purple.

8 The fifth gave me a branch of rich olive.

9 The sixth placed a crown on my head.

10 The seventh placed on my head a diadem of priesthood, and filled my hands with incense, that I might serve as priest to YAHOWAH ELOHIM.

11 And they said to me: Lewy, thy seed shall be divided into three offices, for a sign of the glory of YAHOWAH who is to come

12 And the first portion shall be great; yea, greater than it shall none be.

13 The second shall be in the priesthood.

14 And the third shall be called by a new name, because a king shall arise in Yehudah, and shall establish a new priesthood, after the fashion of the Gentiles to all the Gentiles.

15 And his Presence is beloved, as a prophet of the Most High, of the seed of Abraham our father.

16 Therefore, every desirable thing in Yisra'EL shall be for thee and for thy seed, And ye shall eat everything fair to look upon, And the table of YAHOWAH shall thy seed apportion.

17 And some of them shall be high priests, and judges, and scribes; for by their mouth shall the holy place be guarded

18 And when I awoke, I understood that this (dream) was like the first dream.

19 And I hid this also in my heart, and told it not to any man upon the earth.

9 And after two days I and Yehudah went up with our father Ya'aqob to Yitzkhaq our father's father.

2 And my father's father blessed me according to all the words of the visions which I had seen. And he would not come with us to Beth'EL.

3 And when we came to Beth'EL, my father Ya'aqob saw a vision concerning me, that I should be their priest unto ELOHIM.

4 And he rose up early in the morning, and paid tithes of all to YAHOWAH through me.

5 And so we came to Khebron to dwell there.

6 And Yitzkhaq called me continually to put me in remembrance of the statutes (laws) of YAHOWAH, even as the Angel of YAHOWAH showed unto me

7 And he taught me the judgements (laws) of the priesthood, of sacrifices, whole burnt-offerings, first-fruits, freewill-offerings, shalom-offerings.

8 And each day he was instructing me, and was busied on my behalf before YAHOWAH, and said to me:

9 Beware of the ruakh of fornication; for this shall continue and shall by thy seed pollute the holy place.

10 Take, therefore, to thyself a wife without blemish or pollution, while yet thou art young, and not of the family (race) of strange nations,

11 And before entering into the holy place, bathe; and when thou offerest the sacrifice, wash; and again, when thou finishest the sacrifice, wash.

12 Of twelve trees having leaves offer to YAHOWAH, as Abraham taught me also.

13 And of every clean beast and bird offer a sacrifice to YAHOWAH.

14 And of all thy first-fruits and of wine offer the first, as a sacrifice to YAHOWAH ELOHIM; and every sacrifice thou shalt salt with salt.

10 Now, therefore, observe whatsoever I command you, children; for whatsoever things I have heard from my fathers I have declared unto you.

2 And behold, I am clear from your ungodliness and transgression, which ye shall commit in the end of the ages, acting godlessly, deceiving Yisra'EL, and stirring up against it great evils from YAHOWAH.

3 And ye shall deal lawlessly together with Yisra'EL, so He shall not bear with Yerushalem (Jerusalem) because of your wickedness; but the veil of the temple shall be rent, so as not to cover your shame.

4 And ye shall be scattered as captives among the Gentiles, and shall be for a reproach and for a curse there.

5 For the house which YAHOWAH shall choose shall be called Yerushalem, as is contained in the book of Khanok the righteous.

11 : Therefore when I took a wife I was twenty-eight years old, and her name was Milkah (Melcha).

2 And she conceived and bare a son, and I called his name Gershom (Gersam), for we were sojourners in our land.

3 And I saw concerning him, that he would not be in the first rank

4 And Qehath (Kohath) was born in the thirty-fifth year of my life, towards sunrise.

5 And I saw in a vision that he was standing on high in the midst of all the congregation.

6 Therefore I called his name Qehath, which is, beginning of majesty and instruction.

7 And she bare me a third son, Merari, in the fortieth year of my life ; and since his mother bare him with difficulty, I called him Merari, that is my bitterness, because he also was like to die.

8 And Yokhebed (Jochebed) was born in Mitzraim, in my sixty-fourth year, for I was renowned then in the midst of my brethren.

12 And Gershom took a wife, and she bare to him Libni (Lomni) and Shimee (Semei).

2 And the sons of Qehath, Amram (Ambram), Yitzhar (Izhar), Khebron, and Uzzi'EL (Ozeel).

3 And the sons of Merari, Makhli (Mooli) and Mushi (Mouses).

4 And in my ninety-fourth year Amram took Yokhebed (Jochebed) my daughter to him to wife, for they were born in one day, he and my daughter.

5 Eight years old was I when I went into the land of Kena'an, and eighteen years when I slew Shekem, and at nineteen years I became priest, and at twenty-eight years I took a wife, and at forty-eight I went into Mitzraim.

6 And behold, my children, ye are a third generation

7 In my hundred-and-eighteenth year Yoseph died

13 And now, my children, I command you: Fear YAHOWAH your ELOHIM with your whole heart, and walk in simplicity according to all His commandments (laws).

2 And do ye also teach your children letters, that they may have understanding all their life, reading unceasingly the Torah (Law) of ELOHIM.

3 For every one that knoweth the Torah of YAHOWAH shall be honoured, and shall not be a stranger whithersoever he goeth.

4 Yea, many friends shall he gain more than his parents, and many men shall desire to serve him, and to hear the Torah from his mouth.

5 Work righteousness, therefore, my children, upon the earth, That ye may have (it) as a treasure in heaven.

6 And sow good things in your souls, that ye may find them in your life. But if ye sow evil things, ye shall reap every trouble and affliction.

7 Get wisdom in the tear of ELOHIM with diligence; For though there be a leading into captivity, and cities and lands be destroyed, and gold and silver and every possession perish, the wisdom of the wise naught can take away, save the blindness of ungodliness, and the callousness (that comes) of sin.

8 For if one keep oneself from these evil things, then even among his enemies shall wisdom be a glory to him, and in a strange country a fatherland, And in the midst of foes shall prove a friend.

9 Whosoever teacheth noble things and doeth them, shall be enthroned with kings, as was also Yoseph my brother.

14 Therefore, my brethren (children), I (have learnt) know from the book of Khanok that at the end of the ages ye will transgress against YAHOWAH, stretching out hands to wickedness against Him; and to all the Gentiles shall ye become a scorn.

2 For our father Ya'aqob (Yisra'EL) is pure from the transgressions of the high priests (chief priests who shall lay their hands upon the Saviour of the world).

3 My sons, as the heaven is purer (in the Lord's sight) than the earth, so also be ye, the lights of Yisra'EL, (purer) than all the Gentiles.

4 But if ye be darkened through transgressions, what, therefore, will all the Gentiles do living in blindness? Yea, ye shall bring a curse upon our family (race), because the light of the Torah which was given for to lighten every man, this ye desire to destroy by teaching commandments contrary to the ordinances of ELOHIM.

5 The offerings of YAHOWAH ye shall rob, and from His portion shall ye steal choice portions, eating (them) contemptuously with harlots.

6 And out of covetousness ye shall teach the commandments of YAHOWAH, wedded women shall ye pollute, and the virgins of Yerushalem shall ye defile; and with harlots and adulteresses shall ye be joined, and the daughters of the Gentiles shall ye take to wife, purifying them with an unlawful purification; and your union shall be like unto **Sedom (Sodom)** and **Amorrah (Gomorrah)**.

7 And ye shall be puffed up because of your priesthood, lifting yourselves up against men, and not only so, but also against the commands of ELOHIM.

8 For ye shall contemn the holy things with jests and laughter.

15 Therefore the temple, which YAHOWAH shall choose, shall be laid waste through your uncleanness, and ye shall be captives throughout all nations.

2 And ye shall be an abomination unto them, and ye shall receive reproach and everlasting shame from the righteous judgement of ELOHIM.

3 And all who hate you shall rejoice at your destruction.

4 And if you were not to receive mercy through Abraham, Yitzhaq, and Ya'aqob, our fathers, not one of our seed should be left upon the earth.

16 And now I have learnt that for seventy weeks ye shall go astray, and profane the priesthood, and pollute the sacrifices.

2 And ye shall make void the Torah, and set at nought the words of the prophets by evil perverseness. And ye shall persecute righteous men, and hate the godly; the words of the faithful shall ye abhor.

3 And a man who reneweth the Torah in the power of the Most High, ye shall call a deceiver; and at last ye shall rush (upon him) to slay him, not knowing his dignity, taking innocent blood through wickedness upon your heads.

4 And your holy places shall be laid waste even to the ground because of him.

5 And ye shall have no place that is clean; but ye shall be among the Gentiles a curse and a dispersion until He shall again visit you, and in pity shall receive you through faith and water.

17 And whereas ye have heard concerning the seventy weeks, hear also concerning the priesthood.

2 For in each **Yobel (Jubilee)** there shall be a priesthood. And in the first Yobel, the first who is anointed to the priesthood shall be great, and shall speak to ELOHIM as to a father. And his priesthood shall be perfect with YAHOWAH, and in the day of his gladness shall he arise for the judgement (salvation) of the world.

3 In the second Yobel, he that is anointed shall be conceived in the sorrow of beloved ones; and his priesthood shall be honoured and shall be glorified by all.

4 And the third priest shall be taken hold of by sorrow.

5 And the fourth shall be in pain, because unrighteousness shall gather itself against him exceedingly, and all Yisra'EL shall hate each one his neighbour.

6 The fifth shall be taken hold of by darkness.

7 Likewise also the sixth and the seventh.

8 And in the seventh shall be such pollution as I cannot express before men, for they shall know it who do these things.

9 Therefore shall they be taken captive and become a prey, and their land and their substance shall be destroyed.

10 And in the fifth week they shall return to their desolate country, and shall renew the house of YAHOWAH.

11 And in the seventh week shall come priests, (who are) idolaters, adulterers, lovers of money, proud, lawless, lascivious, abusers of children and beasts.

18 And after their punishment shall have come from YAHOWAH, the priesthood shall fail.

2 Then shall YAHOWAH raise up a new priest. And to him all the words of YAHOWAH shall be revealed; And he shall execute a righteous judgement upon the earth for a multitude of days.

3 And his star shall arise in heaven as of a king, Lighting up the light of knowledge as the sun the day, And he shall be magnified in the world.

4 He shall shine forth as the sun on the earth, And shall remove all darkness from under heaven, And there shall be **shalom (peace)** in all the earth.

5 The heavens shall exult in his days, And the earth shall be glad, And the clouds shall rejoice ; And the knowledge of YAHOWAH shall be poured forth upon the earth, as the water of the seas ; And the Angels of the glory of the Presence of YAHOWAH shall be glad in him.

6 The heavens shall be opened, And from the temple of glory shall come upon him sanctification, With the Father's voice as from Abraham to Yitzkhaq.

7 And the glory of the Most High shall be uttered over him, And the RUAKH of understanding and sanctification shall rest upon him in the water.

8 For he shall give the majesty of YAHOWAH to His sons in truth for evermore ; And there shall none succeed him for all generations for ever

9 And in his priesthood the Gentiles shall be multiplied in knowledge upon the earth, And enlightened through the grace of YAHOWAH: In his priesthood shall sin come to an end, And the lawless shall cease to do evil. And the just shall rest in him.

10 And he shall open the gates of the Garden of Eden (Paradise), And shall remove the threatening sword against Adam.

11 And he shall give to the saints to eat from the tree of life, And the RUAKH of holiness shall be on them.

12 And Beliya'al shall be bound by him, And he shall give power to His children to tread upon the evil rukhoth.

13 And YAHOWAH shall rejoice in His children, And be well pleased in His beloved ones for ever.

14 Then shall Abraham and Yitzkhaq and Ya'aqob exult, And I will be glad, And all the saints shall clothe themselves with joy.

19 And now, my children, ye have heard all; choose, therefore, for yourselves either the light or the darkness, either the Torah of YAHOWAH or the works of Beliya'al.

2 And his sons answered him, saying, Before YAHOWAH we will walk according to His Torah.

3 And their father said unto them, YAHOWAH is witness, and His Angels are witnesses, and ye are witnesses, and I am witness, concerning the word of your mouth. And his sons said unto him : We are witnesses.

4 And thus Lewy ceased commanding his sons; and he stretched out his feet on the bed, and was gathered to his fathers, after he had lived a hundred and thirty-seven years.

5 And they laid him in a coffin, and afterwards they buried him in Khebron, with Abraham, Yitzkhaq, and Ya'aqob,

THE TESTAMENT OF
JUDAH

1 The copy of the words of Yehudah, what things he spake to his sons before he died.

2 They gathered themselves together, therefore, and came to him, and he said to them:

3 Hearken, my children, to Yehudah your father. I was the fourth son born to my father Ya'aqob; and Leah my mother named me Yehudah, saying, I give thanks to YAHOWAH, because He hath given me a fourth son ralso.

4 I was swift in my youth, and obedient to my father in everything.

5 And I honoured my mother and my mother's sister.

6 And it came to pass, when I became a man, that my father blessed me, saying, Thou shalt be a king, prospering in all things.

2 And YAHOWAH showed me favour in all my works both in, the field and in the house.

2 I know that I raced a hind, and caught it, and prepared the meat for my father, and he did eat.

3 And the roes I used to master in the chase, and overtake all that was in the plains. A wild mare I overtook, and caught it and tamed it.

4 I slew a lion and plucked a kid out of its mouth. I took a bear by its paw and hurled it down the cliff, and it was crushed.

5 I outran the wild boar, and seizing it as I ran, I tare it in sunder.

6 A leopard in Khebron leaped upon my dog, and I caught it by the tail, and hurled it on the rocks, and it was broken in twain.

7 I found a wild ox feeding in the fields, and seizing it by the horns, and whirling it round and stunning it, I cast it from me and slew it.

3 And when the two kings of the Kena'anim came, sheathed in armour, against our flocks, and much people with them, single-handed I rushed upon the king of **Khatzor (Hazor)**, and smote him on the greaves and dragged him down, and so I slew him.

2 And the other, the king of **Tappuakh (Tappuah)**, as he sat upon his horse, I slew, and so I scattered all his people.

3 **Akor (Achor)**, the king a man of Anaq (giant stature) I found, hurling javelins before and behind as he sat on horseback, and I took up a stone of sixty pounds weight, and hurled it and smote his horse, and killed it.

4 And I fought with (this) other for two hours; and I clave his shield in twain, and I chopped off his feet, and killed him.

5 And as I was stripping off his breastplate, behold nine men, his companions, began to fight with me.

6 And I wound my garment on my hand; and I slung stones at them, and killed four of them, and the rest fled.

7 And Ya'aqob my father slew **Baal Shiloh (Beelesath)**, king of all the kings, an Anaq (giant) in strength, twelve cubits high.

8 And fear fell upon them, and they ceased warring against us.

9 Therefore my father was free from anxiety in the wars when I was with my brethren.

10 For he saw in a vision concerning me that an Angel of might followed me everywhere, that I should not be overcome.

4 And in the south there came upon us a greater war than that in Shekem; and I joined in battle array with my brethren, and pursued a thousand men, and slew of them two hundred men and four kings.

2 And I went up upon the wall, and I slew four mighty men.

3 And so we captured Khatzor, and took all the spoil

5 On the next day we departed to **Martan (Aretan)**, a city strong and walled and inaccessible, threatening us with death.

2 But I and Gad approached on the east side of the city, and Reuben and Lewy on the west.

3 And they that were upon the wall, thinking that we were alone, were drawn down against us.

4 And so my brothers secretly climbed up the wall on both sides by stakes, and entered the city, while the men knew it not.

5 And we took it with the edge of the sword. And as for those who had taken refuge in the tower, we set fire to the tower and took both it and them.

6 And as we were departing the men of Tappuakh seized our spoil, and seeing (this) we fought with them.

7 And we slew them all and recovered our spoil.

6 And when I was at the waters of Kozaba, the men of **Arbel (Jobel)** came against us to battle.

2 And we fought with them and routed them; and their allies from **Shiloakh (Shiloh)** we slew, and we did not leave them power to come in against us.

3 And the men of Makir came upon us the fifth day, to seize our spoil; and we attacked them and overcame them in fierce battle: for there was a host of mighty men amongst them, and we slew them before they had gone up the ascent.

4 And when we came to their city their women rolled upon us stones from the brow

of the hill on which the city stood.

5 And I and Shimon hid ourselves behind the town, and seized upon the heights and destroyed this city also.

7 And the next day it was told us that the king of the city of Gaash with a mighty host was coming against us.

2 I, therefore, and Dan feigned ourselves to be Emorim (Amorites), and as allies went into their city.

3 And in the depth of night our brethren came and we opened to them the gates; and we destroyed all the men and their substance, and we took for a prey all that, was theirs and their three walls we cast down.

4 And we drew near to Timnah, where was all the substance of the hostile kings.

5 Then being insulted by them, I was therefore wroth, and rushed against them to the summit; and they kept slinging against me stones and darts.

6 And had not Dan my brother aided me, they would have slain me.

7 We came upon them, therefore, with wrath, and they all fled; and passing by another way, they besought my father, and he made shalom with them.

8 And we did to them no hurt, and they became tributary to us, and we restored to them their spoil.

9 And I built Timnah, and my father built Arbal (Rabael)

10 I was twenty years old when this war befell.

11 And the Kena'anim feared me and my brethren.

8 And I had much cattle, and I had for chief herdsman Khiram (Iram) the Adullamim.

2 And when I went to him I saw Ben-Shua (Barsaba), king of Adullam; and he spake unto us, and he made us a feast; and when I was heated he gave me his daughter Bathshua to wife.

3 She bare me Er, and Onan, and Shelah; and two of them YAHOWAH smote: for Shelah lived, and his children are ye.

9 And eighteen years my father abode at shalom with his brother Esaw (Esau), and his sons with us, after that we came from Aram-Naharaim (Mesopotamia), from Laban.

2 And when eighteen years were fulfilled, in the fortieth year of my life, Esaw, the brother of my father, came upon us with a mighty and strong people.

3 And Ya'aqob smote Esaw with an arrow, and he was taken up wounded on Mount Seir, and as he went he died at Anoniram.

4 And we pursued after the sons of Esaw. Now they had a city with walls of iron and gates of brass; and we could not enter into it, and we encamped around, and besieged it.

5 And when they opened not to us in twenty days, I set up a ladder in the sight of all, and with my shield upon my head I went up, sustaining the as-

saults of stones, upwards of three talents weight; and I slew four of their mighty men.

6 And Reuben and Gad slew six others.

7 Then they asked from us terms of shalom; and having taken counsel with our father, we received them as tributaries.

8 And they gave us five hundred cors of wheat, five hundred baths of oil, five hundred measures of wine, until the famine, when we went down into Mitzraim.

10 And after these things my son Er took to wife Tamar, from Aram-Naharaim, a daughter of Aram.

2 Now Er was wicked, and he was in need concerning Tamar, because she was not of the land of Kena'an. And on the third night an Angel of YAHOWAH smote him.

3 And he had not known her according to the evil craftiness of his mother, for he did not wish to have children by her.

4 In the days of the wedding-feast I gave Onan to her in marriage; and he also in wickedness knew her not, though he spent with her a year.

5 And when I threatened him he went in unto her, but he spilled the seed on the ground, according to the command of his mother, and he also died through wickedness.

6 And I wished to give Shelah also to her, but his mother did not permit it; for she wrought evil against Tamar, because she was not of the daughters of Kena'an, as she also herself was.

11 And I knew that the family (race) of the Kena'anim was wicked, but the impulse of youth blinded my mind.

2 And when I saw her pouring out wine, owing to the intoxication of wine was I deceived, and took her although my father had not counselled (it).

3 And while I was away she went and took for Shelah a wife from Kena'an.

4 And when I knew what she had done, I cursed her in the anguish of my soul.

5 And she also died through her wickedness together with her sons.

12 And after these things, while Tamar was a widow, she heard after two years that I was going up to shear my sheep, and adorned herself in bridal array, and sat in the city Enaim by the gate.

2 For it was a statute (law) of the Emorim, that she who was about to marry should sit in fornication seven days by the gate.

3 Therefore being drunk with wine, I did not recognise her; and her beauty deceived me, through the fashion of her adorning.

4 And I turned aside to her, and said: Let me go in unto thee. And she said: What wilt thou give me? And I gave her my staff, and my girdle, and the diadem of my kingdom in pledge. And I went in unto her, and she conceived.

5 And not knowing what I had done, wished to slay her; but she privily sent my pledges,

JUDAH

and put me to shame.

6 And when I called her, I heard also the secret words which I spoke when lying with her in my drunkenness; and I could not slay her, because it was from YAHOWAH.

7 For I said, Lest haply she did it in subtlety, having received the pledge from another woman.

8 But I came not again near her while I lived, because I had done this abomination in all Yisra'EL.

9 Moreover, they who were in the city said that there was no harlot in the gate, because she came from another place, and sat for a while in the gate.

10 And I thought that no one knew that I had gone in to her.

11 And after this we came into Mitzraim to Yoseph, because of the famine

12 And I was forty and six years old, and seventy and three years lived I in Mitzraim.

13And now I command you, my children, hearken to Yehudah your father, and keep my sayings to perform all the ordinances of YAHOWAH, and to obey the commands of ELOHIM.

2 And walk not after your lusts, nor in the imaginations of your thoughts in haughtiness of heart; and glory not in the deeds and strength of your youth, for this also is evil in the eyes of YAHOWAH.

3 Since I also gloried that in wars no comely woman's face ever enticed me, and reproved Reuben my brother concerning Bilhah, the wife of my father, the rukhoth of jealousy and of fornication arrayed themselves against me, until I lay with Bathshua the Kena'anim, and Tamar, who was espoused to my sons.

4 For I said to my father-in-law: I will take counsel with my father, and so will I take thy daughter. And he was unwilling, but he showed me a boundless store of gold in his daughter's behalf; for he was a king.

5 And he adorned her with gold and pearls, and caused her to pour out wine for us at the feast with the beauty of women.

6 And the wine turned aside my eyes, and pleasure blinded my heart.

7 And I became enamoured of and I lay with her, and transgressed the commandment of YAHOWAH and the commandment of my fathers, and I took her to wife.

8 And YAHOWAH rewarded me according to the imagination of my heart, inasmuch as I had no joy in her children.

14And now, my children, I say unto you, be not drunk with wine; for wine turneth the mind away from the truth, and inspires the passion of lust, and leadeth the eyes into error.

2 For the ruakh of fornication hath wine as a minister to give pleasure to the mind; for these two also take away the mind of man.

3 For if a man drink wine to drunkenness, it disturbeth the mind with filthy thoughts leading to fornication, and heateth the body to carnal union;

and if the occasion of the lust be present, he worketh the sin, and is not ashamed.

4 Such is the inebriated man, my children; for he who is drunken reverenceth no man.

5 For, lo, it made me also to err, so that I was not ashamed of the multitude in the city, in that before the eyes of all I turned aside unto Tamar, and I wrought a great sin, and I uncovered the covering of my sons' shame.

6 After I had drunk wine I reverenced not the commandment of ELOHIM, and I took a woman of Kena'an to wife.

7 For much discretion needeth the man who drinketh wine, my children; and herein is discretion in drinking wine, a man may drink so long as he preserveth modesty.

8 But if he go beyond this limit the ruakh of deceit attacketh his mind, and it maketh the drunkard to talk filthily, and to transgress and not to be ashamed, but even to glory in his shame, and account himself honourable.

15He that committeth fornication is not aware when he suffers loss, and is not ashamed when put to dishonour.

2 For even though a man be a king and commit fornication, he is stripped of his kingship by becoming the slave of fornication, as I myself also suffered.

3 For I gave my staff, that is, the stay of my tribe; and my girdle, that is, my power; and my diadem, that is, the glory of my kingdom.

4 And indeed I repented of these things; wine and flesh I eat not until my old age, nor did I behold any joy.

5 And the Angel of ELOHIM showed me that for ever do women bear rule over king and beggar alike.

6 And from the king they take away his glory, and from the valiant man his might, and from the beggar even that little which is the stay of his poverty.

16Observe, therefore, my children, the (right) limit in wine; for there are in it four evil rukhoth— of lust, of hot desire, of profligacy, of filthy lucre.

2 If ye drink wine in gladness, be ye modest with the fear of ELOHIM. For if in (your) gladness the fear of ELOHIM departeth, then drunkenness ariseth and shamelessness stealeth in.

3 But if you would live soberly do not touch wine at all, lest ye sin in words of outrage, and in fightings and slanders, and transgressions of the commandments of ELOHIM, and ye perish before your time.

4 Moreover, wine revealeth the mysteries of ELOHIM and men, even as I also revealed the commandments of ELOHIM and the mysteries of Ya'aqob my father to the **Kena'anith (Canaanitish)** woman Bathshua, which ELOHIM bade me not to reveal.

5 And wine is a cause both of war and confusion.

17 And now I command you, my children, not to love money, nor to gaze upon the beauty of women; because for the sake of money and beauty I was led astray to Bathshua the Kena'anim.

2 For I know that because of these two things shall my family (race) fall into wickedness.

3 For even wise men among my sons shall they mar, and shall cause the kingdom of Yehudah to be diminished, which YAHOWAH gave me because of my obedience to my father.

4 For I never caused grief to Ya'aqob, my father; for all things whatsoever he commanded I did.

5 And Yitzkhaq, the father of my father, blessed me to be king in Yisra'EL, and Ya'aqob further blessed me in like manner.

6 And I know that from me shall the kingdom be established.

18 And I know what evils ye will do in the last days. 2 Beware, therefore, my children, of fornication and the love of money, and hearken to Yehudah your father.

3 For these things withdraw you from the Torah of ELOHIM, And blind the inclination of the soul, And teach arrogance, And suffer not a man to have compassion upon his neighbour.

4 They rob his soul of all goodness, And oppress him with toils and troubles, And drive away sleep from him, And devour his flesh.

5 And he hindereth the sacrifices of ELOHIM; And he remembereth not the blessing of ELOHIM, He hearkeneth not to a prophet when he speaketh, And resenteth the words of godliness.

6 For he is a slave to two contrary passions, And cannot obey ELOHIM, Because they have blinded his soul, And he walketh in the day as in the night.

19 My children, the love of money leadeth to idolatry; because, when led astray through money, men name as gods those who are not gods, and it causeth him who hath it to fall into madness.

2 For the sake of money I lost my children, and had not my repentance, and my humiliation, and the prayers of my father been accepted, I should have died childless.

3 But the ELOHIM of my fathers had mercy on me, because I did it in ignorance.

4 And the prince of deceit blinded me, and I was ignorant as a man and as flesh, being corrupted through sins; and I learnt my own weakness while thinking myself invincible.

20 Know, therefore, my children, that two rukhoth wait upon man— the RUAKH of truth and the ruakh of deceit.

2 And in the midst is the RUAKH of the understanding of the mind, to which it belongeth to turn whithersoever it will.

3 And the works of truth and the works of deceit are written upon the hearts of men, and each one of them YAHOWAH knoweth.

4 And there is no time at which the works of men can be hid; for on the heart itself have they been written down before YAHOWAH.

5 And the RUAKH of truth testifieth all things, and accuseth all; and the sinner is burnt up by his own heart, and cannot raise his face to the judge.

21 And now, my children, I command you, love Lewy, that ye may abide, and exalt not yourselves against him, lest ye be utterly destroyed.

2 For to me YAHOWAH gave the kingdom, and to him the priesthood, and He set the kingdom beneath the priesthood.

3 To me He gave the things upon the earth; to him the things in the heavens.

4 As the heaven is higher than the earth, so is the priesthood of ELOHIM higher than the earthly kingdom, unless it falleth away through sin from YAHOWAH and is dominated by the earthly kingdom.

5 For the Angel of YAHOWAH said unto me: YAHOWAH chose him rather than thee, to draw near to Him, and to eat of His table and to offer Him the first-fruits of the choice things of the sons of Yisra'EL; but thou shalt be king of Ya'aqob.

6 And thou shalt be amongst them as the sea. For as, on the sea, just and unjust are tossed about, some taken into captivity while some are enriched, so also shall every family of men be in thee: some shall be impoverished, being taken captive, and others grow rich by plundering the possessions of others.

7 For the kings shall be as sea-monsters. They shall swallow men like fishes: The sons and daughters of freemen shall they enslave; Houses, lands, flocks, money shall they plunder:

8 And with the flesh of many shall they wrongfully feed the ravens and the cranes; And they shall advance in evil, in covetousness uplifted,

9 And there shall be false prophets like tempests, And they shall persecute all righteous men.

22 And YAHOWAH shall bring upon them divisions one against another. And there shall be continually wars in Yisra'EL;

2 And among men of another family shall my kingdom be brought to an end, Until the salvation of Yisra'EL shall come, Until the appearing of the ELOHIM of righteousness, That Ya'aqob and all the Gentiles may rest in shalom.

3 And He shall guard the might of my kingdom for ever; For YAHOWAH sware to me with an oath that He would not destroy the kingdom from my seed for ever.

23 Now I have much grief, my children, because of your lewdness and witchcrafts, and idolatries which ye shall practise against the kingdom, following them that have familiar rukhoth, diviners, and demons of error.

2 Ye shall make your daughters singing girls and harlots, and ye shall mingle in the abominations of the Gentiles.

3 For which things' sake YAHOWAH shall bring upon you famine and pestilence, death and the sword, beleaguering by enemies, and revilings of friends, the slaughter of children, the rape of wives, the plundering of possessions, the burning of the temple of ELOHIM, the laying waste of the land, the enslavement of yourselves among the Gentiles.

4 And they shall make some of you eunuchs for their wives.

5 Until YAHOWAH visit you, when with perfect heart ye repent and walk in all His commandments, and He bring you up from captivity among the Gentiles.

24 And after these things shall a star arise to you from Ya'aqob in shalom, And a man shall arise from my seed, like the sun of righteousness, Walking with the sons of men in meekness and righteousness; And no sin shall be found in him.

2 And the heavens shall be opened unto him, To pour out the RUAKH, (even) the blessing of the Holy Father;

3 And He shall pour out the RUAKH of grace upon you; And ye shall be unto Him sons in truth, And ye shall walk in His commandments first and last.

4 This Branch of ELOHIM Most High, And this Fountain giving life unto all.

5 Then shall the sceptre of my kingdom shine forth; And from your root shall arise a stem;

6 And from it shall grow a rod of righteousness to the Gentiles, To judge and to save all that call upon YAHOWAH.

25 And after these things shall Abraham and Yitzkhaq and Ya'aqob arise unto life, and I and my brethren shall be chiefs of the tribes of Yisra'EL: Lewy first, I the second, Yoseph third, Benyamin (Benjamin) fourth, Shimon fifth, Yissaskar (Issachar) sixth, and so all in order.

2 And YAHOWAH blessed Lewy, and the Angel of the Presence, me; the powers of glory, Shimon; the heaven, Reuben; the earth, Yissaskar; the sea, Zebulun; the mountains, Yoseph; the tabernacle, Benjamin; the luminaries, Dan; Eden, Naphtali; the sun, Gad; the moon, Asher.

3 And ye shall be the people of YAHOWAH, and have one tongue; And there shall be there no ruakh of deceit of Beliya'al, For he shall be cast into the fire for ever.

4 And they who have died in grief shall arise in joy, And they who were poor for YAHOWAH'S sake shall be made rich, And they who are put to death for YAHOWAH'S sake shall awake to life.

5 And the harts of Ya'aqob shall run in joyfulness, And the eagles of Yisra'EL shall fly in gladness; And all the peoples shall glorify YAHOWAH for ever.

26 Observe, therefore, my children, all the Torah of YAHOWAH, for there is hope for all them who hold fast unto His ways.

2 And he said to them: Behold, I die before your eyes this day, a hundred and nineteen years old.

3 Let no one bury me in costly apparel, nor tear open my bowels, for this shall they who are kings do; and carry me up to Khebron with you.

4 And Yehudah, when he had said these things, fell asleep; and his sons did according to all whatsoever he commanded them, and they buried him in Khebron with his fathers.

THE TESTAMENT OF
ISSACHAR

1 The copy of the words of Yissaskar. For he called his sons and said to them: Hearken, my children, to Yissaskar your father; Give ear to the words of him who is beloved of YAHOWAH.

2 I was born the fifth son to Ya'aqob, by way of hire for the mandrakes.

3 For Reuben my brother brought in mandrakes from the field, and Rakhel (Rachel) met him and took them.

4 And Reuben wept, and at his voice Leah my mother came forth.

5 Now these (mandrakes) were sweet-smelling apples which were produced in the land of Aram (Haran) below a ravine of water.

6 And Rakhel said: I will not give them to thee, but they shall be to me instead of children. For YAHOWAH hath despised me, and I have not borne children to Ya'aqob.

7 Now there were two apples; and Leah said to Rakhel: Let it suffice thee that thou hast taken my husband: wilt thou take these also?

8 And Rakhel said to her: Thou shalt have Ya'aqob this night for the mandrakes of thy son.

9 And Leah said to her: Ya'aqob is mine, for I am the wife of his youth.

10 But Rakhel said: Boast not, and vaunt not thyself; for he espoused me before thee, and for my sake he served our father fourteen years.

11 And had not craft increased on the earth and the wickedness of men prospered, thou wouldest not now see the face of Ya'aqob.

12 For thou art not his wife, but in craft wert taken to him in my stead.

13 And my father deceived me, and removed me on that night, and did not suffer Ya'aqob to see me; for had I been there, this had not happened to him.

14 Nevertheless, for the mandrakes I am hiring Ya'aqob to thee for one night.

15 And Ya'aqob knew Leah, and she conceived and bare me, and on account of the hire I was called Yissaskar.

2 Then appeared to Ya'aqob an Angel of YAHOWAH, saying: Two children shall Rakhel bear, inasmuch as she hath refused company with her husband, and hath chosen continency.

2 And had not Leah my mother paid the two apples for the sake of his company, she would have borne eight sons; for this reason she bare six, and Rakhel bare the two: for on account of the mandrakes YAHOWAH visited her.

3 For He knew that for the sake of children she wished to company with Ya'aqob, and not for lust of pleasure.

4 For on the morrow also she again gave up Ya'aqob. Because of the mandrakes, therefore, YAHOWAH hearkened to Rakhel.

5 For though she desired them, she ate them not, but offered them in the house of YAHOWAH, presenting them to the priest of the Most High who was at that time.

3 When, therefore, I grew up, my children, I walked in uprightness of heart, and I became a husbandman for my father and my brethren, and I brought in fruits from the field according to their season.

2 And my father blessed me, for he saw that I walked in rectitude before him.

3 And I was not a busybody in my doings, nor envious and malicious against my neighbour.

4 I never slandered any one, nor did I censure the life of any man, walking as I did in singleness of eye.

5 Therefore, when I was thirty-five years old, I took to myself a wife, for my labour wore away my strength, and I never thought upon pleasure with women; but owing to my toil, sleep overcame me.

6 And my father always rejoiced in my rectitude, because I offered through the priest to YAHOWAH all first-fruits; then to my father also.

7 And YAHOWAH increased ten thousandfold His benefits in my hands; and also Ya'aqob, my father, knew that ELOHIM aided my singleness.

8 For on all the poor and oppressed I bestowed the good things of the earth in the singleness of my heart.

4 And now, hearken to me, my children,

2 The single-(minded) man coveteth not gold, He overreacheth not his neighbour, He longeth not after manifold dainties, He delighteth not in varied apparel.

3 He doth not desire to live a long life, But only waiteth for the will of ELOHIM.

4 And the rukhoth of deceit have no power against him, For he looketh not on the beauty of women, Lest he should pollute his mind with corruption.

5 There is no envy in his thoughts, Nor malicious person maketh his soul to pine away, Nor worry with insatiable desire in his mind.

6 For he walketh in singleness rof soul, And beholdeth all things in uprightness of heart, Shunning eyes (made) evil through the error of the world, Lest he should see the perversion of any of the commandments of YAHOWAH.

5 Keep, therefore, my children, the Torah of ELOHIM, And get singleness, rAnd walk in guilelessness, Not playing the busybody with the business of your neighbour.

2 But love YAHOWAH and your neighbour, Have compassion on the poor and weak.

3 Bow down your back unto husbandry, And toil in labours rin all manner of husbandry, offering gifts to YAHOWAH with thanksgiving.

4 For with the first-fruits of the earth will YAHOWAH bless you, even as He blessed all the saints from Hebel even until now.

5 For no other portion is given to you than of the fatness of the earth, whose fruits are raised by toil.

6 For our father Ya'aqob blessed me with blessings of the earth and of first-fruits.

7 And Lewy and Yehudah were glorified by YAHOWAH even among the sons of Ya'aqob; for YAHOWAH gave them an inheritance, and to Lewy He gave the priesthood, and to Yehudah the kingdom.

8 And do ye therefore obey them, and walk in the singleness of your father; for unto Gad hath it been given to destroy the troops that are coming upon Yisra'EL.

6 Know ye, therefore, my children, that in the last times Your sons will forsake singleness, And will cleave unto insatiable desire; And leaving guilelessness, will draw near to malice;And forsaking the commandments of YAHOWAH, They will cleave unto Beliya'al;

2 And leaving husbandry, They will follow after their own wicked devices, And they shall be dispersed among the Gentiles, And shall serve their enemies.

3 And do ye therefore give these commands to your children, that, if they sin, they may the more quickly return to YAHOWAH;

4 For He is merciful, and will deliver them, even to bring them back into their land.

7 Behold, therefore, as ye see, I am a hundred and twenty-six years old and am not conscious of committing any sin.

2 Except my wife I have not known any woman. I never committed fornication by the uplifting of my eyes.

3 I drank not wine, to be led astray thereby; I coveted not any desirable thing that was my neighbour's.

4 Guile arose not in my heart; A lie passed not through my lips.

5 If any man were in distress I joined my sighs with his, And I shared my bread with the poor. I wrought godliness, all my days I kept truth.

6 I loved YAHOWAH; Likewise also every man with all my heart.

7 So do ye also these things, my children, And every ruakh of Beliya'al shall flee from you, And no deed of wicked men shall rule over you; And every wild beast shall ye subdue, Since ye have with you the ELOHIM of heaven and earth (And) walk with men in singleness of heart.

8 And having said these things, he commanded his sons that they should carry him up to Khebron, and bury him there in the cave with his fathers.

9 And he stretched out his feet and died, the fifth son of Ya'aqob, at a good old age; with every limb sound, and with strength unabated, he slept the eternal sleep.

THE TESTAMENT OF
ZEBULUN

1 The copy of the words of Zebulun, which he enjoined on his sons before he died in the hundred and fourteenth year of his life, two years after the death of Yoseph.

2 And he said to them : Hearken to me, ye sons of Zebulun, attend to the words of your father.

3 I, Zebulun, was born a good gift to my parents. For when I was born my father was increased very exceedingly, both in flocks and herds, when with the straked rods he had his portion.

4 I am not conscious that I have sinned all my days, save in thought.

5 Nor yet do I remember that I have done any iniquity, except the sin of ignorance which I committed against Yoseph ; for I covenanted with my brethren not to tell my father what had been done.

6 But I wept in secret many days on account of Yoseph, for I feared my brethren, because they had all agreed, that if any one should declare the secret, he should be slain.

7 But when they wished to kill him, I adjured them much with tears not to be guilty of this sin.

2 For Shimon and Gad came against Yoseph to kill him, and he said unto them with tears:

2 Pity me, my brethren, have mercy upon the bowels of Ya'aqob our father: lay not upon me your hands to shed innocent blood, for I have not sinned against you.

3 And if indeed I have sinned, with chastening chastise me, my brethren, but lay not upon me your hand, for the sake of Ya'aqob our father.

4 And as he spoke these words, wailing as he did so, I was unable to bear his lamentatioms, and began to weep, and my liver was poured out, and all the substance of my bowels was loosened.

5 And I wept with Yoseph, and my heart sounded, and the joints of my body trembled, and I was not able to stand.

6 And when Yoseph saw me weeping with him, and them coming against him to slay him, he fled behind me, beseeching them.

7 But meanwhile Reuben rose and said: Come, my brethren, let us not slay him, but let us cast him into one of these dry pits, which our fathers digged and found no water.

8 For for this cause YAHOWAH forbade that water should rise up in them, in order that Yoseph should be preserved.

9 And they did so, until they sold him to the Yishmaelim.

3 For in his price I had no share, my children.

2 But Shimon and Gad and six other of our brethren took the price of Yoseph, and bought sandals for themselves, and their wives, and their children, saying:

3 We will not eat of it, for it is the price of our brother's blood, but we will assuredly tread it under foot, because he said that he would be king over us, and so let us see what will become of his dreams.

4 Therefore it is written in the book of Khanok (writing of the law of Moses), that whosoever will not raise up seed to his brother, his sandal should be unloosed, and they should spit into his face.

5 And the brethren of Yoseph wished not that their brother should live, and YAHOWAH loosed from them the sandal which they wore against Yoseph their brother.

6 For when they came into Mitzraim they were unloosed by the servants of Yoseph outside the gate, and so they made obeisance to Yoseph after the fashion of King Phar'oh (Pharaoh).

7 And not only did they make obeisance to him, but were spit upon also, falling down before him forthwith, and so they were put to shame before the Mitzrim.

8 For after this the Mitzrim heard all the evils that they had done to Yoseph.

4 And after he was sold my brothers sat down to eat and drink.

2 But I, through pity for Yoseph, did not eat, but watched the pit, since Ychudah feared lest Shimon, Dan, and Gad should rush off and slay him.

3 But when they saw that I did not eat, they set me to watch him, till he was sold (to the Yishmaelim)

4 And he was in the pit three days and three nights hungered, and so he was sold.

5 And when Reuben came and heard that while he was away (Yoseph) had been sold, he rent his garments, (and) mourning, said: How shall I look on the face of my father Ya'aqob?

6 And he took the money and ran after the merchants, but as he failed to find them he returned grieving. But the merchants had left the broad road and marched through the Troglodytes by a short cut.

7 But Reuben was grieved, and ate no food that day. Dan therefore came to him and said:

8 Weep not, neither grieve; for we have found what we can say to our father Ya'aqob.

9 Let us slay a kid of the goats, and dip in it the coat of Yoseph; and let us send it to Ya'aqob, saying : Know, is this the coat of

thy son? And they did so.

10 For they stripped off from Yoseph his coat when they were selling him, and put upon him the garment of a slave.

11 Now Shimon took the coat, and would not give it up, for he wished to rend it with his sword, as he was angry that Yoseph lived and that he had not slain him.

12 Then we all rose up and said unto him: If thou givest not up the coat, we will say to our father that thou alone didst this evil thing in Yisra'EL.

13 And so he gave it unto them, and they did even as Dan had said.

5 And now, my children, I bid you to keep the commands of YAHOWAH, and to show mercy to your neighbours, and to have compassion towards all, not towards men only, but also towards beasts.

2 For, for this thing's sake YAHOWAH blessed me, and when all my brethren were sick, I escaped without sickness, for YAHOWAH knoweth the purposes of each.

3 Have, therefore, compassion in your hearts, my children, because even as a man doeth to his neighbour, even so also will YAHOWAH do to him.

4 For the sons of my brethren were sickening and were dying on account of Yoseph, because they showed not mercy in their hearts; but my sons were preserved without sickness, as ye know.

5 And when I was in the land of Kena'an, by the sea-coast, I made a catch of fish for Ya'aqob my father; and when many were choked in the sea, I continued unhurt.

6 I was the first to make a boat to sail upon the sea, for YAHOWAH gave me understanding and wisdom therein.

2 And I let down a rudder behind it, and I stretched a sail upon another upright piece of wood in the midst.

3 And I sailed therein along the shores, catching fish for the house of my father until we came to Mitzraim.

4 And through compassion I shared my catch with every stranger.

5 And if a man were a stranger, or sick, or aged, I boiled the fish, and dressed them well, and offered them to all men, as every man had need, grieving with and having compassion upon them.

6 Wherefore also YAHOWAH satisfied me with abundance of fish when catching fish; for he that shareth with his neighbour receiveth manifold more from YAHOWAH.

7 For five years I caught fish, and gave thereof to every man whom I saw, and sufficed for all the house of my father.

8 And in the summer I caught fish, and in the winter I kept sheep with my brethren.

7 Now I will declare unto you what I did. I saw a man in distress through nakedness in wintertime, and had compassion upon him, and stole away a garment secretly from my father's house, and gave it to him who was in distress.

2 Do ye, therefore, my children, from that which ELOHIM bestoweth upon you, show compassion and mercy without hesitation to all men, and give to every man with a good heart.

3 And if ye have not the wherewithal to give to him that needeth, have compassion for him in bowels of mercy.

4 I know that my hand found not the wherewithal to give to him that needed, and I walked with him weeping for seven furlongs, and my bowels yearned towards him in compassion.

8 Have, therefore, yourselves also, my children, compassion towards every man with mercy, that YAHOWAH also may have compassion and mercy upon you.

2 Because also in the last days ELOHIM will send His compassion on the earth, and wheresoever He findeth bowels of mercy He dwelleth in him.

3 For in the degree in which a man hath compassion upon his neighbours, in the same degree hath YAHOWAH also upon him.

4 And when we went down into Mitzraim, Yoseph bore no malice against us.

5 To whom taking heed, do ye also, my children, approve yourselves without malice, and love one another; and do not set down in account, each one of you, evil against his brother.

6 For this breaketh unity and divideth all kindred, and troubleth the soul, and weareth away the countenance.

9 Observe, therefore, the waters, and know when they flow together, they sweep along stones, trees, earth, and other things.

2 But if they are divided into many streams, the earth swalloweth them up, and they become of no account.

3 So shall ye also be if ye be divided.

4 Be not ye, therefore, divided into two heads, for everything which YAHOWAH made hath but one head, and two shoulders, two hands, two feet, but all the remaining members.

5 For I have learnt in the writing of my fathers, that Ye shall be divided in Yisra'EL, And ye shall follow two kings, And shall work every abomination.

6 And your enemies shall lead you captive, And ye shall be evil entreated among the Gentiles, With many infirmities and tribulations.

7 And after these things ye shall remember YAHOWAH and repent, And He shall have mercy upon you, for He is merciful and compassionate. And He setteth not down in account evil against the sons of men, Because they are flesh, and are deceived through their own wicked deeds.

8 And after these things shall there arise unto you YAHOWAH Himself, the light of righteousness, And ye shall return unto your own land. And ye shall see Him in Yerushalem, for His name's sake.

9 And again through the wickedness of your works shall ye provoke Him to anger, And ye shall

be cast away by Him unto the time of consummation.

10 And now, my children, grieve not that I am dying, nor be cast down in that I am coming to my end.

2 For I shall rise again in the midst of you, as a ruler in the midst of his sons; and I shall rejoice in the midst of my tribe, as many as shall keep the Torah of YAHOWAH, and the commandments of Zebulun their father.

3 But upon the ungodly shall YAHOWAH bring eternal fire, and destroy them throughout all generations.

4 But I am now hastening away to my rest, as did also my fathers.

5 But do ye fear YAHOWAH your ELOHIM with all your strength all the days of your life.

6 And when he had said these things he fell asleep, at a good old age. And his sons laid him in a wooden coffin.

7 And afterwards they carried him up and buried him in Khebron, with his fathers.

THE TESTAMENT OF
DAN

1 The copy of the words of Dan, which he spake to his sons in his last days, in the hundred and twenty-fifth year of his life.

2 For he called together his family, and said: Hearken to my words, ye sons of Dan; and give heed to the words of your father.

3 I have proved in my heart, and in my whole life, that truth with just dealing is good and well-pleasing to ELOHIM, and that lying and anger are evil, because they teach man all wickedness.

4 I confess, therefore, this day to you, my children, that in my heart I resolved on the death of Yoseph my brother, the true and good man.

5 And I rejoiced that he was sold, because his father loved him more than us.

6 For the ruakh of jealousy and vain-glory said to me: Thou thyself also art his son.

7 And one of the rukhoth of Beliya'al stirred me up, saying: Take this sword, and with it slay Yoseph; so shall thy father love thee when he is dead.

8 Now this was the ruakh of anger that persuaded me to crush Yoseph as a leopard crusheth a kid.

9 But the ELOHIM of my fathers did not suffer him to fall into my hands, so that I should find him alone and slay him, and cause a second tribe to be destroyed in Yisra'EL.

2 And now, my children, behold I am dying, and I tell you of a truth, that unless ye keep yourselves from the ruakh of lying and of anger, and love truth and long-suffering, ye shall perish.

2 For anger is blindness, and doth not suffer one to see the face of any man with truth.

3 For though it be a father or a mother, he behaveth towards them as enemies; though it be a brother, he knoweth him not; though it be a prophet of YAHOWAH, he disobeyeth him; though a righteous man, he regardeth him not; though a friend, he doth not acknowledge him.

4 For the ruakh of anger encompasseth him with the net of deceit, and blindeth his eyes, and through lying darkeneth his mind, and giveth him its own peculiar vision.

5 And wherewith encompasseth it his eyes? With hatred of heart, so as to be envious of his brother.

3 For anger is an evil thing, my children, for it troubleth even the soul itself.

2 And the body of the angry man it maketh its own, and over his soul it getteth the mastery, and it bestoweth upon the body power that it may work all iniquity.

3 And when the body doeth all these things, the soul justifieth what is done, since it seeth not aright.

4 Therefore he who is wrathful, if he be a mighty man, hath a threefold power in his anger: one by the help of his servants; and a second by his wealth, whereby he persuadeth and overcometh wrongfully; and thirdly, having his own natural power he worketh thereby the evil.

5 And though the wrathful man be weak, yet hath he a power twofold of that which is by nature; for wrath ever aideth such in lawlessness.

6 This ruakh goeth always with lying at the right hand of Satan, that with cruelty and lying his works may be wrought.

4 Understand ye, therefore, the power of wrath, that it is vain.

2 For it first of all giveth provocation by word; then by deeds it strengtheneth him who is angry, and with sharp losses disturbeth his mind, and so stirreth up with great wrath his soul.

3 Therefore, when any one speaketh against you, be not ye moved to anger, and if any man praiseth you as holy men, be not uplifted: be not moved either to delight or to disgust.

4 For first it pleaseth the hearing, and so maketh the mind keen to perceive the grounds for provocation; and then being enraged, he thinketh that he is justly angry.

5 If ye fall into any loss or ruin, my children, be not afflicted; for this very ruakh maketh (a man) desire that which is perishable, in order that he may be enraged through the affliction.

6 And if ye suffer loss voluntarily, or involuntarily, be not vexed; for from vexation ariseth wrath with lying.

7 Moreover, a twofold mischief is wrath with lying; and they assist one another in order to disturb the heart; and when the soul is continually disturbed, YAHOWAH departeth from it, and Beliya'al ruleth over it.

5 Observe, therefore, my children, the commandments of YAHOWAH, And keep His Torah; Depart from wrath, And hate lying, That YAHOWAH may dwell among you, And Beliya'al may flee from you.

2 Speak truth each one with his neighbour, So shall ye not fall into wrath and confusion; But ye shall be in shalom, having the ELOHIM of shalom, So shall no war prevail over you.

3 Love YAHOWAH through all your life, And one another with a true heart.

4 I know that in the last days ye shall depart from YAHOWAH, And ye shall provoke Lewy unto anger, And fight against Yehudah; But ye shall not prevail against them, For an Angel of YAHOWAH shall guide them both; For by them shall Yisra'EL stand.

5 And whensoever ye depart from YAHOWAH, ye shall walk in all evil and work the abominations of the Gentiles, going a-whoring after women of the lawless ones, while with all wickedness the rukhoth of wickedness work in you.

6 For I have read in the book of Khanok, the righteous, that your prince is Satan, and that all the rukhoth of wickedness and pride will conspire to attend constantly on the sons of Lewy, to cause them to sin before YAHOWAH.

7 And my sons will draw near to Lewy, And sin with them in all things; And the sons of Yehudah will be covetous, Plundering other men's goods like lions.

8 Therefore shall ye be led away with them into captivity, And there shall ye receive all the plagues of Mitzraim. And all the evils of the Gentiles.

9 And so when ye return to YAHOWAH ye shall obtain mercy, And He shall bring you into His sanctuary, And He shall give you shalom.

10 And there shall arise unto you from the tribe of Yehudah and of Lewy the salvation of YAHOWAH; And he shall make war against Beliya'al, And execute an everlasting vengeance on our enemies:

11 And the captivity shall he take from Beliya'al the souls of the saints, And turn disobedient hearts unto YAHOWAH, And give to them that call upon him eternal shalom.

12 And the saints shall rest in Eden, And in the New Yerushalem will the righteous rejoice, And it shall be unto the glory of ELOHIM for ever.

13 And no longer shall Yerushalem endure desolation, Nor Yisra'EL be led captive; For YAHOWAH shall be in the midst of it living amongst men, And the Holy One of Yisra'EL shall reign over it in humility and in poverty; and he who believeth on Him shall reign amongst men in truth.

6 And now, fear YAHOWAH, my children, and beware of Satan and his rukhoth.

2 Draw near unto ELOHIM and to the Angel that intercedeth for you, for he is a mediator between ELOHIM and man, and for the shalom of Yisra'EL he shall stand up against the kingdom of the enemy.

3 Therefore is the enemy eager to destroy all that call upon YAHOWAH.

4 For he knoweth that on the day on which Yisra'EL shall repent, the kingdom of the enemy shall be brought to an end.

5 For the very Angel of shalom shall strengthen Yisra'EL, that it fall not into the extremity of evil.

6 And it shall be in the time of the lawlessness of Yisra'EL, that YAHOWAH will (not) depart from them, but will transform them into a nation that doeth His will, for none of the Angels will be equal unto him.

7 And His name shall be in every place of Yisra'EL, and among the Gentiles.

8 Keep, therefore, yourselves, my children, from every evil work, And cast away wrath and all lying, And love truth and long-suffering.

9 And the things which ye have heard from your father, do ye also impart to your children that the Saviour of the Gentiles may receive you; for he is true and long-suffering, meek and lowly, and teacheth by his works the Torah of ELOHIM.

10 Depart, therefore, from all unrighteousness, and cleave unto the righteousness of ELOHIM, and your family (race) will be saved for ever.

11 And bury me near my fathers.

7 And when he had said these things he kissed them, and fell asleep at a good old age.

2 And his sons buried him. And after that they carried up rhis bones, and placed them near Abraham, and Yitzkhaq, and Ya'aqob.

3 Nevertheless, Dan prophesied unto them that they should forget their ELOHIM, and should be alienated from the land of their inheritance and from the tribe (race) of Yisra'EL, and from their heritage (the family of their seed).

THE TESTAMENT OF
NAPHTALI

1 The copy of the testament of Naphtali, which he ordained at the time of his death in the hundred and thirtieth year of his life.

2 When his sons were gathered together in the seventh month, on the first day of the month, while still in good health, he made them a feast of food and wine.

3 And after he was awake in the morning, he said to them, I am dying; and they believed him not.

4 And as he glorified YAHOWAH, he grew strong and said that after yesterday's feast he should die.

5 And he began then to say: Hear, my children, ye sons of Naphtali, hear the words of your father.

6 I was born from Bilhah; and because Rakhel dealt craftily, and gave Bilhah in place of herself to Ya'aqob, and she conceived and bare me upon Rakhel's knees, therefore she called my name Naphtali.

7 For Rakhel loved me very much because I was born upon her lap; and when I was still young she was wont to kiss me, and say: May I have a brother of thine from mine own womb, like unto thee.

8 Whence also Yoseph was like unto me in all things, according to the prayers of Rakhel.

9 Now my mother was Bilhah, daughter of **Rutai (Rotheus)** the brother of Deborah, **Ribqah's (Rebecca's)** nurse, who was born on one and the self-same day with Rakhel.

10 And Rutai was of the family of Abraham, a **Kasdim (Chaldean)**, ELOHIM-fearing, free-born, and noble.

11 And he was taken captive and was bought by Laban; and he gave him **Ednah (Euna)** his hand-maid to wife, and she bore a daughter, and called her name Zilpah, after the name of the village in which he had been taken captive.

12 And next she bore Bilhah, saying: My daughter hasteneth after what is new, for immediately that she was born she seized the breast and hastened to suck it.

2 And I was swift on my feet like the deer, and my father Ya'aqob appointed me for all messages, and as a deer did he give me his blessing.

2 For as the potter knoweth the vessel, how much it is to contain, and bringeth clay accordingly, so also doth YAHOWAH make the body after the likeness of the RUAKH, and according to the capacity of the body doth He implant the RUAKH.

3 And the one doth not fall short of the other by a third part of a hair; for by weight, and measure, and rule was all the creation made.

4 And as the potter knoweth the use of each vessel, what it is meet for, so also doth YAHOWAH

know the body, how far it will persist in goodness, and when it beginneth in evil.

5 For there is no inclination or thought which YAHOWAH knoweth not, for He created every man after His own image.

6 For as a man's strength, so also is his work; as his eye, so also is his sleep; as his soul, so also is his word either in the Torah of YAHOWAH or in the works (law) of Beliya'al.

7 And as there is a division between light and darkness, between seeing and hearing, so also is there a division between man and man, and between woman and woman; and it is not to be said that the one is like the other either in face or in mind.

8 For ELOHIM made all things good in their order, the five senses in the head, and He joined on the neck to the head, adding to it the hair also for comeliness and glory, then the heart for understanding, the belly for excrement, and the stomach for grinding, the windpipe for taking in (the breath), the liver for wrath, the gall for bitterness, the spleen for laughter, the reins for prudence, the muscles of the loins for power, the lungs for drawing in, the loins for strength, and so forth.

9 So then, my children, let all your works be done in order with good intent in the fear of ELOHIM, and do nothing disorderly in scorn or out of its due season.

10 For if thou bid the eye to hear, it cannot; so neither while ye are in darkness can ye do the works of light.

3 Be ye, therefore, not eager to corrupt your doings through covetousness or with vain words to, beguile your souls; because if ye keep silence in purity of heart, ye shall understand how to hold fast the will of ELOHIM, and to cast away the will of Beliya'al.

2 Sun and moon and stars change not their order; so do ye also change not the Torah of ELOHIM in the disorderliness of your doings.

3 The Gentiles went astray, and forsook YAHOWAH, and changed their order, and obeyed stocks and stones, rukhoth of deceit.

4 But ye shall not be so, my children, recognising in the firmament, in the earth, and in the sea, and in all created things, YAHOWAH Who made all things, that ye become not as Sedom, which changed the order of nature.

5 In like manner the Watchers also change the order of their nature, whom YAHOWAH cursed at the flood, on whose account He made the earth without inhabitant and fruitless.

4 These things I say unto you, my children, for I have read in the writing of Khanok that ye yourselves also shall depart from YAHOWAH, walking according to all the lawlessness of the Gentiles, and ye shall do according to all the wickedness of Sedom.

2 And YAHOWAH shall bring captivity upon you, and there shall ye serve your enemies, and ye shall be bowed down with every affliction and tribulation, until YAHOWAH have consumed you all.

3 And after ye have become minished and made few, ye shall return and acknowledge YAHOWAH your ELOHIM; and He shall bring you back into your own land, according to His abundant mercy.

4 And it shall be, that after that they come into the land of their fathers, they shall again forget YAHOWAH and become ungodly.

5 And YAHOWAH shall scatter them upon the face of all the earth, until the compassion of YAHOWAH shall come, a man working righteousness and working mercy unto all them that are afar off, and to them that are near.

5 For in the fortieth year of my life, I saw a vision on the Mount of Olives, on the east of Yerushalem, that the sun and the moon were standing still.

2 And behold Yitzkhaq, the father of my father, said to us: Run and lay hold of them, each one according to his strength; and to him that seizeth them will the sun and moon belong.

3 And we all of us ran together, and Lewy laid hold of the sun, and Yehudah outstripped the others and seized the moon, and they were both of them lifted up with them.

4 And when Lewy became as a sun, lo, a certain young man gave to him twelve branches of palm; and Yehudah was bright as the moon, and under their feet were twelve rays.

5 And the two, Lewy and Yehudah, ran, and laid hold of them.

6 And lo, a bull upon the earth, with two great horns, and an eagle's wings upon his back; and we wished to seize him, but could not.

7 But Yoseph came, and seized him, and ascended up with him on high.

8 And I saw, for I was there, and behold a holy writing appeared to us, saying: **Asshurim (Assyrians), Madim (Medes), Parsim (Persians), Kasdim (Chaldeans), Surim (Syrians)**, shall possess in captivity the twelve tribes of Yisra'EL.

6 And again, after seven days, I saw our father Ya'aqob standing by the sea of **Yamniyah (Jamnia)**, and we were with him.

2 And, behold, there came a ship sailing by, without sailors or pilot; and there was written upon the ship, The ship of Ya'aqob.

3 And our father saith to us: Come let us embark on our ship.

4 And when we had gone on board, there arose a vehement storm, and a mighty tempest of wind; and our father, who was holding the helm, departed from us.

5 And we, being tost with the tempest, were borne along over the sea; and the ship was filled with water, (and was) pounded by mighty waves, until it was broken up.

6 And Yoseph fled away upon a little boat, and we all were divided upon nine planks, and Lewy and Yehudah were together.

7 And we were all scattered unto the ends of the earth.

8 Then Lewy, girt about with sackcloth, prayed for us all unto YAHOWAH.

9 And when the storm ceased, the ship reached the land, as it were in shalom.

10 And, lo, our father came, and we all rejoiced with one accord.

7 These two dreams I told to my father; and he said to me: These things must be fulfilled in their season, after that Yisra'EL hath endured many things.

2 Then my father saith unto me: I believe ELOHIM that Yoseph liveth, for I see always that YAHOWAH numbereth him with you.

3 And he said, weeping: Ah me, my son, Yoseph, thou livest, though I behold thee not, and thou seest not Ya'aqob that begat thee.

4 He caused me also, therefore, to weep by these words, and I burned in my heart to declare that Yoseph had been sold, but I feared my brethren.

8 And lo! my children, I have shown unto you the last times, how everything shall come to pass in Yisra'EL.

2 Do ye also, therefore, charge your children that they be united to Lewy and to Yehudah; For through them shall salvation arise unto Yisra'EL, And in them shall Ya'aqob be blessed.

3 For through their tribes shall ELOHIM appear dwelling among men on earth, To save the family of Yisra'EL, And to gather together the righteous from amongst the Gentiles.

4 If ye work that which is good, my children, Both men and Angels shall bless you; And ELOHIM shall be glorified among the Gentiles through you, And the devil shall flee from you, And the wild beasts shall fear you, And YAHOWAH shall love you, And the Angels shall cleave to you.

5 As a man who has trained a child well is kept in kindly remembrance; So also for a good work there is a good remembrance before ELOHIM.

6 But him who doeth not that which is good, Both Angels and men shall curse, And ELOHIM shall be dishonoured among the Gentiles through him, And the devil shall make him as his own peculiar instrument, And every wild beast shall master him, And YAHOWAH shall hate him.

7 For the commandments of the Torah are twofold, And through prudence must they be fulfilled.

8 For there is a season for a man to embrace his wife, And a season to abstain therefrom for his prayer.

9 So, then, there are two commandments; and, unless they be done in due order, they bring very great sin upon men. So also is it with the other commandments.

10 Be ye therefore wise in ELOHIM, my children, and prudent, understanding the order of His commandments, and the laws of every word, that YAHOWAH may love you.

9 And when he had charged them with many such words, he exhorted them that they should remove his bones to Khebron, and that they should bury him with his fathers.

2 And when he had eaten and drunken with a merry heart, he covered his face and died.

3 And his sons did according to all that Naphtali their father had commanded them.

THE TESTAMENT OF
GAD

1 The copy of the testament of Gad, what things he spake unto his sons, in the hundred and twenty-fifth year of his life, saying unto them:

2 Hearken, my children, I was the ninth son born to Ya'aqob, and I was valiant in keeping the flocks

3 Accordingly I guarded at night the flock; and whenever the lion came, or the wolf, or any wild beast against the fold, I pursued it, and overtaking (it) I seized its foot with my hand and hurled it about a stone's throw, and so killed it.

4 Now Yoseph my brother was feeding the flock with us for upwards of thirty days, and being young, he fell sick by reason of the heat.

5 And he returned to Khebron to our father, who made him lie down near him, because he loved him greatly.

6 And Yoseph told our father that the sons of Zilpah and Bilhah were slaying the best of the flock and eating them against the judgement of Reuben and Yehudah.

7 For he saw that I had delivered a lamb out of the mouth of the bear, and put the bear to death; but had slain the lamb, being grieved concerning it that it could not live, and that we had eaten it.

8 And regarding this matter I was wroth with Yoseph until the day that he was sold.

9 And the ruakh of hatred was in me, and I wished not either to hear of Yoseph with the ears, or to see him with the eyes, because he rebuked us to our faces saying that we were eating of the flock without Yehudah. For whatsoever things he told our father, he believed him.

2 I confess now my sin, my children, that oftentimes I wished to kill him, because I hated him from my heart.

2 Moreover, I hated him yet more for his dreams; and I wished to lick him out of the land of the living, even as an ox licketh up the grass of the field.

3 And Yehudah sold him secretly to the Yishmaelim.

4 And thus through covetousness we were bent on slaying him.

5 Thus the ELOHIM of our fathers delivered him from our hands, that we should not work great lawlessness in Yisra'EL.

3 And now, my children, hearken to the words of truth to work righteousness, and all the Torah of the Most High, and go not astray through the ruakh of hatred, for it is evil in all the doings of men.

2 Whatsoever a man doeth the hater abominateth him: and though a man worketh the Torah of YAHOWAH, he praiseth him not; though a man feareth YAHOWAH, and taketh pleasure in that which is righteous, he loveth him not.

3 He despiseth the truth, he envieth him that prospereth, he welcometh evil-speaking, he loveth arrogance, for hatred blindeth his soul; as I also then looked on Yoseph.

4 Beware, therefore, my children, of hatred; for it worketh lawlessness even against YAHOWAH Himself.

2 For it will not hear rthe words of His commandments concerning the loving of one's neighbour, and it sinneth against ELOHIM.

3 For if a brother stumble, it delighteth immediately to proclaim it to all men, and is urgent that he should be judged for it, and be punished and be put to death.

4 And if it be a servant it stirs him up against his master, and with every affliction it deviseth against him, if possibly he can be put to death.

5 For hatred worketh with envy also against them that prosper: so long as it heareth of or seeth their success, it always languisheth.

6 For as love would quicken even the dead, and would call back them that are condemned to die, so hatred would slay the living, and those that had sinned venially it would not suffer to live.

7 For the ruakh of hatred worketh together with Satan, through hastiness of ruakh, in all things unto men's death; but the RUAKH of love worketh together with the Torah of ELOHIM in long-suffering unto the salvation of men.

5 Hatred, therefore, is evil, for it constantly mateth with lying, speaking against the truth; and it maketh small things to be great, and causeth the light to be darkness, and calleth the sweet bitter, and teacheth slander, and kindleth wrath, and stirreth up war, and violence, and all covetousness; it filleth the heart with evils and devilish poison.

2 These things, therefore, I say to you from experience, my children, that ye may drive forth hatred, which is of the devil, and cleave to the love of ELOHIM.

3 Righteousness casteth out hatred, humility destroyeth envy. For he that is just and humble is ashamed to do what is unjust, being reproved not of another, but of his own heart, because YAHOWAH looketh on his inclination.

4 He speaketh not against a holy man, because the fear of ELOHIM overcometh hatred.

5 For fearing lest he should offend YAHOWAH, he will not do wrong to any man, even in thought.

6 These things I learnt at last, after I had repented concerning Yoseph.

7 For true repentance after a godly sort destroyeth ignorance, and driveth away the darkness, and enlighteneth the eyes, and giveth knowledge to the soul, and leadeth the mind to salvation.

8 And those things which it hath not learnt from man, it knoweth through repentance.

9 For ELOHIM brought upon me a disease of the liver; and had not the prayers of Ya'aqob my father succoured me, it had hardly failed but my ruakh had departed.

10 For by what things a man transgresseth, by the same also is he punished,

11 Since, therefore, my liver was set mercilessly against Yoseph, in my liver too I suffered mercilessly, and was judged for eleven months, for so long a time as I had been angry against Yoseph.

6 And now, my children, I exhort you, love ye each one his brother, and put away hatred from your hearts, love one another in deed, and in word, and in the inclination of the soul.

2 For in the presence of my father I spake peaceably to Yoseph; and when I had gone out, the ruakh of hatred darkened my mind, and stirred up my soul to slay him.

3 Love ye one another from the heart; and if a man sin against thee, speak peaceably to him, and in thy soul hold not guile; and if he repent and confess, forgive him.

4 But if he deny it, do not get into a passion with him, lest catching the poison from thee he take to swearing and so thou sin doubly.

5 Let not another man hear thy secrets when engaged in legal strife, lest he come to hate thee and become thy enemy, and commit a great sin against thee; for ofttimes he addresseth thee guilefully or busieth himself about thee with wicked intent.

6 And though he deny it and yet have a sense of shame when reproved, give over reproving him. For he who denieth may repent so as not to wrong

thee again; yea, he may also honour thee, and fear and be at shalom with thee.

7 But if he be shameless and persisteth in his wrongdoing, even so forgive him from the heart, and leave to ELOHIM the avenging.

7 If a man prosper more than you, do not be vexed, but pray also for him, that he may have perfect prosperity. For so it is expedient for you.

2 And if he be further exalted, be not envious of him, remembering that all flesh shall die; and offer praise to ELOHIM, who giveth things good and profitable to all men.

3 Seek out the judgements of YAHOWAH, and thy mind will rest and be at shalom.

4 And though a man become rich by evil means, even as Esaw, the brother of my father, be not jealous; but wait for the end of YAHOWAH.

5 For if He take away (from a man) wealth gotten by evil means He forgiveth him if he repent, but the unrepentant is reserved for eternal punishment.

6 For the poor man, if free from envy he pleaseth YAHOWAH in all things, is blessed beyond all men, because he hath not the travail of vain men.

7 Put away, therefore, jealousy from your souls, and love one another with uprightness of heart.

8 Do ye also, therefore, tell these things to your children, that they honour Yehudah and Lewy, for from them shall YAHOWAH raise up salvation to Yisra'EL.

2 For I know that at the last your children shall depart from Him, and shall walk in all wickedness, and affliction, and corruption before YAHOWAH.

3 And when he had rested for a little while, he said again: My children, obey your father, and bury me near to my fathers.

4 And he drew up his feet, and fell asleep in shalom.

5 And after five years they carried him up to Khebron, and laid him with his fathers.

THE TESTAMENT OF
ASHER

1 The copy of the testament of Asher, what things he spake to his sons in the hundred and twenty-fifth year of his life.

2 For while he was still in health, he said to them: Hearken, ye children of Asher, to your father, and I will declare to you all that is upright in the sight of ELOHIM.

3 Two ways hath ELOHIM given to the sons of men, and two inclinations, and two kinds of action, and two modes (of action), and two issues.

4 Therefore all things are by twos, one over against the other.

5 For there are two ways of good and evil, and with these are the two inclinations in our breasts discriminating them.

6 Therefore if the soul take pleasure in the good (inclination), all its actions are in righteousness; and if it sin it straightway repenteth.

7 For, having its thoughts set upon righteousness, and casting away wickedness, it straightway overthroweth the evil, and uprooteth the sin.

8 But if it incline to the evil inclination, all its actions are in wickedness, and it driveth away the good, and cleaveth to the evil, and is ruled by Beliya'al; even though it work what is good, he perverteth it to evil.

9 For whenever it beginneth to do good, he forceth the issue of the action into evil for him, seeing that the treasure of the inclination is filled with an evil ruakh.

2 A person, then, may with words help the good for the sake of the evil, yet the issue of the action leadeth to mischief.

2 There is a man who showeth no compassion upon him who serveth his turn in evil; and this thing hath two aspects, but the whole is evil.

3 And there is a man that loveth him that worketh evil, because he would prefer even to die in evil for his sake; and concerning this it is clear that it hath two aspects, but the whole is an evil work.

4 Though, indeed, he have love, yet is he wicked who concealeth what is evil for the sake of the good name, but the end of the action tendeth unto evil.

5 Another stealeth, doeth unjustly, plundereth, defraudeth, and withal pitieth the poor: this too hath a twofold aspect, but the whole is evil.

6 He who defraudeth his neighbour provoketh ELOHIM, and sweareth falsely against the Most High, and yet pitieth the poor: YAHOWAH Who commandeth the Torah he setteth at nought and provoketh, and yet he refresheth the poor.

7 He defileth the soul, and maketh gay the body; he killeth many, and pitieth a few: this, too, hath a twofold aspect, but the whole is evil.

8 Another committeth adultery and fornication, and abstaineth from meats, and when he fasteth he doeth evil, and by the power of his wealth overwhelmeth many; and notwithstanding his excessive wickedness he doeth then commandments: this, too, hath a twofold aspect, but the whole is evil.

9 Such men are hares; for they are half clean, but in very deed are unclean.

10 For ELOHIM in the tables of the commandments hath thus declared.

3 But do not ye, my children, wear two faces like unto them, of goodness and of wickedness; but cleave unto goodness only, for ELOHIM hath His habitation therein, and men desire it.

2 But from wickedness flee away, destroying the (evil) inclination by your good works; for they that are double-faced serve not ELOHIM, but their own lusts, so that they may please Beliya'al and men like unto themselves.

4 For good men, even they that are of single face, though they be thought by them that are double-faced to sin, are just before ELOHIM.

2 For many in killing the wicked do two works, of good and evil; but the whole is good, because he hath uprooted and destroyed that which is evil.

3 One man hateth the merciful and unjust man, and the man who committeth adultery and fasteth: this, too, has a twofold aspect, but the whole work is good, because he followeth YAHOWAH'S example, in that he accepteth not the seeming good as the genuine good.

4 Another desireth not to see a good day with them that riot, lest he defile his body and pollute his soul: this, too, is double-faced, but the whole is good.

5 For such men are like to stags and to hinds, because in the manner of wild animals they seem to be unclean, but they are altogether clean; because they walk in zeal for YAHOWAH and abstain from what ELOHIM also hateth and forbiddeth by His commandments, warding off the evil from the good.

5 Ye see, my children, how that there are two in all things, one against the other, and the one is hidden by the other: in wealth (is hidden) covetousness, in conviviality drunkenness, in laughter grief, in wedlock profligacy.

2 Death succeedeth to life, dishonour to glory, night to day, and darkness to light; and all things are under the day, just things under life, unjust things under death; wherefore also eternal life awaiteth death.

3 Nor may it be said that truth is a lie, nor right wrong; for all truth is under the light, even as all things are under ELOHIM.

4 All these things, therefore, I proved in my life, and I wandered not from the truth of YAHOWAH, and I searched out the commandments of the Most High, walking according to all my strength with singleness of face unto that which is good.

6 Take heed, therefore, ye also, my children, to the commandments of YAHOWAH, following the truth with singleness of face.

2 For they that are double-faced are guilty of a twofold sin; for they both do the evil thing and they have pleasure in them that do it, following the example of the rukhoth of deceit, and striving against mankind.

3 Do ye, therefore, my children, keep the Torah of YAHOWAH, and give not heed unto evil as unto good; but look unto the thing that is really good, and keep it in all commandments of YAHOWAH, having your conversation therein, and resting therein.

4 For the latter ends of men do show their righteousness (or unrighteousness), when they meet the Angels of YAHOWAH and of Satan.

5 For when the soul departeth troubled, it is tormented by the evil ruakh which also it served in lusts and evil works.

6 But if he is peaceful with joy he meeteth the Angel of shalom, and he leadeth him into eternal life.

7 Become not, my children, as Sedom, which knew not the Angels of YAHOWAH, and perished for ever.

2 For I know that ye shall sin, and be delivered into the hands of your enemies; and your land shall be made desolate, and your holy places destroyed, and ye shall be scattered unto the four corners of the earth. And ye shall be set at nought in the Dispersion as useless water,

3 Until the Most High shall visit the earth, coming Himself as man, with men eating and drinking, and breaking the head of the dragon in the water. He shall save Yisra'EL and all the Gentiles ELOHIM speaking in the person of man.

4 Therefore do ye also, my children, tell these things to your children, that they disobey Him not.

5 For I have known that ye shall assuredly be disobedient, and assuredly act ungodly, not giving heed to the Torah of ELOHIM, but to the commandments of men, being corrupted through wickedness.

6 And therefore shall ye be scattered as Gad and Dan my brethren, and ye shall know not your own lands, tribe, and tongue.

7 But YAHOWAH will gather you together in faith through His tender mercy, and for the sake of Abraham, Yitzkhaq, and Ya'aqob.

8 And when he had said these things unto them, he commanded saying: Bury me in Khebron. And he fell asleep and died at a good old age.

2 And his sons did as he had commanded them, and they carried him up to Khebron, and buried him with his fathers.

THE TESTAMENT OF
JOSEPH

1 The copy of the testament of Yoseph. When he was about to die he called his sons and his brethren together, and said to them:

2 My brethren and my children, Hearken to Yoseph the beloved of Yisra'EL; Give ear, my sons, unto your father.

3 I have seen in my life envy and death, Yet I went not astray, but persevered in the truth of YAHOWAH.

4 These my brethren hated me, but YAHOWAH loved me: They wished to slay me, but the ELOHIM of my fathers guarded me: They let me down into a pit, and the Most High brought me up again.

5 I was sold into slavery, and YAHOWAH of all made me free: I was taken into captivity, and His strong hand succoured me. I was beset with hunger, and YAHOWAH Himself nourished me.

6 I was alone, and ELOHIM comforted me: I was sick, and YAHOWAH visited me: I was in prison, and my ELOHIM showed favour unto me; In bonds, and He released me;

7 Slandered, and He pleaded my cause; Bitterly spoken against by the Mitzrim, and He delivered me; Envied by my fellow-slaves, and He exalted me.

2 And this chief captain of Phar'oh entrusted to me his house.

2 And I struggled against a shameless woman, urging me to transgress with her; but the ELOHIM of Yisra'EL my father delivered me from the burning flame.

3 I was cast into prison, I was beaten, I was mocked; but YAHOWAH granted me to find mercy in the sight of the keeper of the prison.

4 For YAHOWAH doth not forsake them that fear Him. Neither in darkness, nor in bonds, nor in tribulations, nor in necessities.

5 For ELOHIM is not put to shame as a man, Nor as the son of man is He afraid, Nor as one that is earth-born is He weak or affrighted.

6 But in all these things doth He give protection, And in divers ways doth He comfort, (Though) for a little space He departeth to try the inclination of the soul.

7 In ten temptations He showed me approved, And in all of them I endured; For endurance is a mighty charm, And patience giveth many good things.

3 How often did the Mitzrim woman threaten me with death! How often did she give me over to punishment, and then call me back and threaten me, and when I was unwilling to company with her, she said to me:

2 Thou shalt be lord of me, and all that is in mine house, if thou wilt give thyself unto me, and thou shalt be as our master.

3 But I remembered the words of my father, and going into my chamber, I wept and prayed unto YAHOWAH.

4 And I fasted in those seven years, and I appeared to the Mitzrim as one living delicately, for they that fast for ELOHIM's sake receive beauty of face.

5 And if Adoni (my lord) were away from home, I drank no wine; nor for three days did I take my food, but I gave it to the poor and sick.

6 And I sought YAHOWAH early, and I wept for the Mitzrim woman of Moph (Memphis), for very unceasingly did she trouble me, for also at night she came to me under pretence of visiting me.

7 And because she had no male child she pretended to regard me as a son.

8 And for a time she embraced me as a son, and I knew it not; but later, she sought to draw me into fornication.

9 And when I perceived it I sorrowed unto death; and when she had gone out, I came to myself, and I lamented for her many days, because I recognised her guile and her deceit.

10 And I declared unto her the words of the Most High, if haply she would turn from her evil lust.

4 Often, therefore, did she flatter me with words as a holy man, and guilefully in her talk praise my chastity before her husband, while desiring to ensnare me when we were alone.

2 For she lauded me openly as chaste, and in secret she said unto me: Fear not my husband; for he is persuaded concerning thy chastity: for even should one tell him concerning us, he would not believe.

3 Owing to all these things I lay upon the ground, and besought ELOHIM that YAHOWAH would deliver me from her deceit.

4 And when she prevailed nothing thereby, she came again to me under the plea of instruction, that she might learn the word of ELOHIM.

5 And she said unto me: If thou willest that I should leave my idols, lie with me, and I will persuade my husband to depart from his idols, and we will walk in the statutes (law) of YAHOWAH thy ELOHIM.

6 And I said unto her: YAHOWAH willeth not that those that reverence Him should be in uncleanness, nor doth He take pleasure in them that commit adultery, but in those that approach Him with a pure heart and undefiled lips.

7 But she held her shalom, longing to accomplish her evil desire.

8 And I gave myself yet more to fasting and prayer, that YAHOWAH might deliver me from her.

5 And again, at another time she said unto me: If thou wilt not commit adultery, I will kill my husband by poison, and take thee to be my husband.

2 I therefore, when I heard this, rent my garments, and said unto her: Woman, reverence ELOHIM, and do not this evil deed, lest thou be destroyed; for know indeed that I will declare this thy device unto all men.

3 She therefore, being afraid, besought that I would not declare this device.

4 And she departed, soothing me with gifts, and sending to me every delight of the sons of men.

6 And afterwards she sent me food mingled with enchantments.

2 And when the eunuch who brought it came, I looked up and beheld a terrible man giving me with the dish a sword, and I perceived that (her) scheme was to beguile me.

3 And when he had gone out I wept, nor did I taste that nor any other of her food.

4 So then after one day she came to me and observed the food, and said unto me: Why is it that thou hast not eaten of the food?

5 And I said unto her: It is because thou hast filled it with deadly enchantments; and how saidst thou: I come not near to idols, but to YAHOWAH alone?

6 Now therefore know that the ELOHIM of my father hath revealed unto me by His Angel thy wickedness, and I have kept it to convict thee, if haply thou mayest see and repent.

7 But that thou mayest learn that the wickedness of the ungodly hath no power over them that worship ELOHIM with chastity, behold I will take of it and eat before thee. And having so said, I prayed thus: The ELOHIM of my fathers and the Angel of Abraham, be with me; and ate.

8 And when she saw this she fell upon her face at my feet, weeping; and I raised her up and admonished her.

9 And she promised to do this iniquity no more.

7 But her heart was still set upon evil, and she looked around how to ensnare me, and sighing deeply she became downcast, though she was not sick.

2 And when her husband saw her, he said unto her: Why is thy countenance fallen? And she said unto him: I have a pain at my heart, and the groanings of my ruakh oppress me; and so he comforted her who was not sick.

3 Then accordingly seizing an opportunity she rushed unto me while her husband was yet without, and said unto me: I will hang myself, or cast myself over a cliff, if thou wilt not lie with me.

4 And when I saw the ruakh of Beliya'al was troubling her, I prayed unto YAHOWAH, and said unto her:

5 Why, wretched woman, art thou troubled and disturbed, blinded through sins? Remember that if thou kill thyself, Asteho, the concubine of thy husband, thy rival, will beat thy children, and thou wilt destroy thy memorial from off the earth.

6 And she said unto me: Lo, then thou lovest me; let this suffice me: only strive for my life and my children, and I expect that I shall enjoy my desire also.

7 But she knew not that because of Adoni I spake thus, and not because of her.

8 For if a man hath fallen before the passion of a wicked desire and become enslaved by it, even as she, whatever good thing he may hear with regard to that passion, he receiveth it with a view to his wicked desire.

8 I declare, therefore, unto you, my children, that it was about the sixth hour when she departed from me; and I knelt before YAHOWAH all the day, and all the night; and about dawn I rose up, weeping the while and praying for a release from her.

2 At last, then, she laid hold of my garments, forcibly dragging me to have connection with her.

3 When, therefore, I saw that in her madness she was holding fast to my garment, I left it behind, and fled away naked.

4 And holding fast to the garment she falsely accused me, and when her husband came he cast me into prison in his house; and on the morrow he scourged me and sent me into Phar'oh's prison.

5 And when I was in bonds, the Mitzrim woman was oppressed with grief, and she came and heard how I gave thanks unto YAHOWAH and sang praises in the abode of darkness, and with glad voice rejoiced, glorifying my ELOHIM that I was delivered from the lustful desire of the Mitzrim woman.

9 And often hath she sent unto me saying: Consent to fulfil my desire, and I will release thee from thy bonds, and I will free thee from the darkness.

2 And not even in thought did I incline unto her. For ELOHIM loveth him who in a den of darkness combineth fasting with chastity, rather than the man who in kings' chambers combineth luxury with licence.

3 And if a man liveth in chastity, and desireth also glory, and the Most High knoweth that it is expedient for him, He bestoweth this also upon him, even as upon me.

4 How often, though she were sick, did she come down to me at unlooked-for times, and listened to my voice as I prayed! And when I heard her groanings I held my shalom.

5 For when I was in her house she was wont to bare her arms, and breasts, and legs, that I might lie with her; for she was very beautiful, splendidly adorned in order to beguile me. And YAHOWAH guarded me from her devices.

10 Ye see, therefore, my children, how great things patience worketh, and prayer with fasting.

2 So ye too, if ye follow after chastity and purity with patience and prayer with fasting in humility of heart, YAHOWAH will dwell among you, because He loveth chastity.

3 And wheresoever the Most High dwelleth, even though envy, or slavery, or slander befalleth (a man), YAHOWAH who dwelleth in him, for the sake of his chastity not only delivereth him from evil, but also exalteth him even as me.

4 For in every way the man is lifted up, whether in deed, or in word, or in thought.

5 My brethren knew how my father loved me, and yet I did not exalt myself in my mind: although I was a child, I had the fear of ELOHIM in my heart; for I knew that all things would pass away.

6 And I did not raise myself (against them) with evil intent, but I honoured my brethren; and out of respect for them, even when I was being sold, I refrained from telling the Yishmaelim that I was the son of Ya'aqob, a great man and a mighty.

11 Do ye also, therefore, my children, have the fear of ELOHIM in all your works before your eyes, and honour your brethren. For every one who doeth the statutes of YAHOWAH shall be loved by YAHOWAH.

2 And when I came (to the Indocolpita) with the Yishmaelim, they asked me, saying: Art thou a slave? And I said that I was a home-born slave, that I might not put my brethren to shame.

3 And the eldest of them said unto me: Thou art not a slave, for even thy appearance doth make it manifest. But I said that I was their slave.. Now when we came into Mitzraim they strove concerning me, which of them should buy me and take me.

4 Therefore it seemed good to all that I should remain in Mitzraim with the merchant of their trade, until they should return bringing merchandise.

5 And YAHOWAH gave me favour in the eyes of the merchant, and he entrusted unto me his house.

6 And ELOHIM blessed him by my means, and increased him in gold and silver and in household servants.

7 And I was with him three months and five days.

12 And about that time the Mophian (Memphian) woman, the wife of Potiphar (Pentephris), came down in a chariot, with great pomp, because she had heard from her eunuchs concerning me.

2 And she told her husband that the merchant had become rich by means of a young Hebrew, and they say that he had assuredly been stolen out of the land of Kena'an.

3 Now, therefore, render justice unto him, and take away the youth to thy house; so shall the ELOHIM of the Hebrews bless thee, for grace from heaven is upon him.

13 And Potiphar was persuaded by her words, and commanded the merchant to be brought, and said unto him: What is this that I hear concerning thee, that thou stealest persons out of the land of Kena'an, and sellest them for slaves?

2 But the merchant fell at his feet, and besought him, saying: I beseech thee, my lord, I know not what thou sayest.

3 And Potiphar said unto him: Whence, then, is the Hebrew slave? And he said: The Yishmaelim entrusted him to me until they should return.

4 But he believed him not, but commanded him to be stripped and beaten. And when he persisted in this statement, Potiphar said: Let the youth be brought.

5 And when I was brought in, I did obeisance to Potiphar (for he was third in rank of the officers of Phar'oh).

6 And he took me apart from him, and said unto me: Art thou a slave or free? And I said: A slave.

7 And he said: Whose? And I said: The Yishmaelim'.

8 And he said: How didst thou become their slave? And I said: They bought me out of the land of Kena'an.

9 And he said unto me: Truly thou liest; and straightway he commanded me to be stripped and beaten.

14 Now the Mophian woman was looking through a window at me while I was being beaten, for her house was near, and she sent unto him, saying: Thy judgement is unjust; for thou dost punish a free man who hath been stolen, as though he were a transgressor.

2 And when I made no change in my statement, though I was beaten, he ordered me to be imprisoned, until, he said, the owners of the boy should come.

3 And the woman said unto her husband: Wherefore dost thou detain the captive and well-born lad in bonds, who ought rather to be set at liberty, and be waited upon?

4 For she wished to see me out of a desire of sin, but I was ignorant concerning all these things.

5 And he said to her: It is not the custom of the Mitzrim to take away that which belongeth to others before proof is given.

6 This, therefore, he said concerning the merchant; but as for the lad, he must be imprisoned.

15 Now after four and twenty days came the Yishmaelim; for they had heard that Ya'aqob my father was mourning much concerning me. And they came and said unto me:

2 How is it that thou saidst that thou wast a slave? and lo, we have learnt that thou art the son of a mighty man in the land of Kena'an, and thy father still mourneth for thee in sackcloth and ashes.

3 When I heard this my bowels were dissolved and my heart melted, and I desired greatly to weep, but I restrained myself, that I should not put my brethren to shame. And I said unto them, I know not, I am a slave.

4 Then, therefore, they took counsel to sell me, that I should not be found in their hands.

5 For they feared my father, lest he should come and execute upon them a grievous vengeance. For they had heard that he was mighty with ELOHIM and with men.

6 Then said the merchant unto them: Release me from the judgement of Potiphar.

7 And they came and requested me, saying: Say that thou wast bought by us with money, and he will set us free.

16 Now the Mophian woman said to her husband: Buy the youth; for I hear, said she, that they are selling him.

2 And straightway she sent a eunuch to the Yishmaelim, and asked them to sell me.

3 But since the eunuch would not agree to buy me (at their price) he returned, having made trial of them, and he made known to his mistress that they asked a large price for their slave.

4 And she sent another eunuch, saying: Even though they demand two minae, give them, do not spare the gold; only buy the boy, and bring him to me.

5 The eunuch therefore went and gave them eighty pieces of gold, and he received me; but to the Mitzrim woman he said: I have given a hundred.

6 And though I knew (this) I held my shalom, lest the eunuch should be put to shame.

17 Ye see, therefore, my children, what great things I endured that I should not put my brethren to shame.

2 Do ye also, therefore, love one another, and with long-suffering hide ye one another's faults.

3 For ELOHIM delighteth in the unity of brethren, and in the purpose of a heart that taketh pleasure in love.

4 And when my brethren came into Mitzraim they learnt that I had returned their money unto them, and upbraided them not, and comforted them.

5 And after the death of Ya'aqob my father I loved them more abundantly, and all things whatsoever he commanded I did very abundantly for them.

6 And I suffered them not to be afflicted even in the smallest matter; and all that was in my hand I gave unto them.

7 And their children were my children, and my children as their servants; and their life was my life, and all their suffering was my suffering, and all their sickness was my infirmity. My land was their land, and their counsel my counsel.

8 And I exalted not myself among them in arrogance because of my worldly glory, but I was among them as one of the least.

18 If ye also, therefore, walk in the commandments of YAHOWAH, my children, He will exalt you there, and will bless you with good things for ever and ever.

2 And if any one seeketh to do evil unto you, do well unto him, and pray for him, and ye shall be redeemed of YAHOWAH from all evil.

3 For, behold, ye see that out of my humility and long-suffering I took unto wife the daughter of the priest of Ayr-Shemesh (Heliopolis). And a hundred talents of gold were given me with her, and YAHOWAH made them to serve me.

4 And He gave me also beauty as a flower beyond the beautiful ones of Yisra'EL; and He preserved me unto old age in strength and in beauty, because I was like in all things to Ya'aqob.

19 Hear ye, therefore, the vision which I saw.

2 I saw twelve harts feeding. And nine of them were dispersed. Now the three were preserved, but on the following day they also were dispersed,

3 And I saw that the three harts became three lambs, and they cried tp YAHOWAH, and He brought them forth into a flourishing and well-watered place, yea He brought them out of darkness into light.

4 And there they cried unto YAHOWAH until there gathered together to them the nine harts, and they became as twelve sheep, and after a little time they increased and became many flocks.

5 And after these things I saw and behold, twelve bulls were sucking one cow, which produced a sea of milk, and there drank thereof the twelve flocks and innumerable herds.

6 And the horns of the fourth bull went up unto heaven and became as a wall for the flocks, and in the midst of the two horns there grew another horn.

7 And I saw a bull calf which surrounded them twelve times, and it became a help to the bulls wholly.

8 (And I saw in the midst of the horns a virgin wearing a many-coloured garment, and from her went forth a lamb; and on his right (was as it were a lion; and) all the beasts and all the reptiles rushed (against him), and the lamb overcame them and destroyed them.

9 And the bulls rejoiced because of him, and the cow and the harts exulted together with them.)

10 And these things must come to pass in their season.

11 And do ye, my children, honour Lewy and Yehudah, for from them shall arise the salvation of Yisra'EL.

12 For my kingdom which is among you shall come to an end as a watcher's hammock, which will not appear after the summer.

20 For I know that after my death the Mitzrim will afflict you, but ELOHIM will avenge you, and will bring you into that which He promised to your fathers.

2 But ye shall carry up my bones with you; for when my bones are being taken up thither, YAHOWAH shall be with you in light, and Beliya'al shall be in darkness with the Mitzrim

3 And carry ye up Asenath your mother to Ephratah (Hippodrome), and near Rakhel

your mother bury her.

4 And when he had said these things he stretched out his feet, and died at a good old age.

5 And all Yisra'EL mourned for him, and all Mitzraim, with a great mourning.

6 And when the children of Yisra'EL went out of Mitzraim, they took with them the bones of Yoseph, and they buried him in Khebron with his fathers, and the years of his life were one hundred and ten years.

THE TESTAMENT OF
BENJAMIN

1 The copy of the words of Benyamin, which he commanded his sons to observe, after he had lived a hundred and twenty-five years.

2 And he kissed them, and said: As Yitzkhaq was born to Abraham in his old age, so also was I to Ya'aqob.

3 And since Rakhel my mother died in giving me birth, I had no milk; therefore I was suckled by Bilhah her handmaid.

4 For Rakhel remained barren for twelve years after she had borne Yoseph; and she prayed YAHOWAH with fasting twelve days, and she conceived and bare me.

5 For my father loved Rakhel dearly, and prayed that he might see two sons born from her.

6 Therefore was I called Benyamin, that is, a son of days.

2 And when I went into Mitzraim, to Yoseph, and my brother recognised me, he said unto me: What did they tell my father when they sold me?

2 And I said unto him, They dabbled thy coat with blood and sent it, and said: Know whether this be thy son's coat?

3 And he said unto me: Even so, brother, when they had stripped me of my coat they gave me to the Yishmaelim, and they gave me a loin cloth, and scourged me, and bade me run.

4 And as for one of them that had beaten me with a rod, a lion met him and slew him.

5 And so his associates were affrighted.

3 Do ye also, therefore, my children, love YAHOWAH ELOHIM of heaven and earth, and keep His commandments, following the example of the good and holy man Yoseph.

2 And let your mind be unto good, even as ye know me; for he that hath his mind right, seeth all things rightly.

3 Fear ye YAHOWAH, and love your neighbour; and even though the rukhoth of Beliya'al claim you to afflict you with every evil, yet shall they not have dominion over you, even as they had not over Yoseph my brother.

4 How many men wished to slay him, and ELOHIM shielded him! For he that feareth ELOHIM and loveth his neighbour cannot be smitten by the ruakh of Beliya'al, being shielded by the fear of ELOHIM.

5 Nor can he be ruled over by the device of men or beasts, for he is helped by YAHOWAH through the love which he hath towards his neighbour.

6 For Yoseph also besought our father that he would pray for his brethren, that YAHOWAH would not impute to them as sin whatever evil they had done unto him.

7 And thus Ya'aqob cried out: My good child Yoseph, thou hast prevailed over the bowels of thy father Ya'aqob. And he embraced him, and kissed him for two hours (saying:

8 In thee shall be fulfilled the prophecy of heaven concerning the Lamb of ELOHIM, and Saviour of the world, that a blameless one shall be delivered up for lawless men, and a sinless shall die for ungodly men in the blood of the covenant, for the salvation of the Gentiles and of Yisra'EL, and shall destroy Beliya'al and. his servants.)

4 See ye, therefore, my children, the end of the good man Yoseph? Be followers of his compassion, therefore, with a good mind, that ye also may wear crowns of glory.

2 For the good man hath not a dark eye; for he showeth mercy to all men, even though they be sinners.

3 And though they devise with evil intent concerning him, by doing good he overcometh evil, being shielded by ELOHIM; and he loveth the righteous as his own soul.

4 If any one is glorified, he envieth him not; if any one is enriched, he is not jealous; if any one is valiant, he praiseth him; the virtuous man he laudeth; on the poor man he hath mercy; on the weak he hath compassion; unto YAHOWAH (ELOHIM) he singeth praises.

5 To him who has the fear of YAHOWAH, he shields; him that loves ELOHIM he aids; him that rejects the Most High he admonishes and turns back; and him that has the grace of a good ruakh, he loves even as his own soul.

5 If, therefore, ye also have a good mind, then will both wicked men be at shalom with you, and the profligate will reverence you and turn unto good; and the covetous will not only cease from their inordinate desire, but even give the objects of their covetousness to them that are afflicted.

2 If ye do well, even the unclean rukhoth will flee from you; and the beasts will dread you.

3 For where there is reverence for good works and light in the mind, even darkness fleeth away from him.

4 For if any one doeth violence to a holy man, he repenteth; for the holy man is merciful to his reviler, and holdeth his shalom.

5 And if any one betrayeth a righteous man, the righteous man prayeth: though for a little he be humbled, yet not long after he appeareth far more

glorious, as was Yoseph my brother.

6 The inclination of the good man is not in the power of the deceit of the ruakh of Beliya'al, for the Angel of shalom guideth his soul.

2 And he gazeth not passionately upon corruptible things, nor gathereth together riches through a desire of pleasure.

3 He delighteth not in pleasure, he grieveth not his neighbour, he sateth not himself with luxuries, he erreth not in the uplifting of the eyes, for YAHOWAH is his portion.

4 The good inclination receiveth not glory nor dishonour from men, and it knoweth not any guile, or lie, or fighting, or reviling; for YAHOWAH dwelleth in him and lighteth up his soul, and he rejoiceth towards all men alway.

5 The good mind hath not two tongues, of blessing and of cursing, of contumely and of honour, of sorrow and of joy, of quietness and of confusion, of hypocrisy and of truth, of poverty and of wealth; but it hath one disposition, uncorrupt and pure, concerning all men.

6 It hath no double sight, nor double hearing; for in everything which he doeth, or speaketh, or seeth, he knoweth that YAHOWAH looketh on his soul.

7 And he cleanseth his mind that he be not condemned by men as well as by ELOHIM. And in like manner the works of Beliya'al are twofold, and there is no singleness in them.

7 Therefore, my children, I tell you, flee the malice of Beliya'al; for he giveth a sword to them that obey him.

2 And the sword is the mother of seven evils. First the mind conceiveth through Beliya'al, and first there is bloodshed; secondly, ruin; thirdly, tribulation ; fourthly, exile ; fifthly, dearth; sixthly, panic; seventhly, destruction.

3 Therefore was Qayin (Cain) also delivered over to seven vengeances by ELOHIM, for in every hundred years YAHOWAH brought one plague upon him.

4 And when he was two hundred years old he began to suffer, and in the nine-hundredth year he was destroyed. For on account of Hebel (Abel), his brother, with all the evils was he judged, but Lemek (Lemech) with seventy times seven.

5 Because forever those who are like unto Qayin in envy and hatred of brethren, shall be punished with the same judgement.

8 And do ye, my children, flee evil-doing, envy, and hatred of brethren, and cleave to goodness and love.

2 He that hath a pure mind in love, looketh not after a woman with a view to fornication; for he hath no defilement in his heart, because the RUAKH of ELOHIM resteth upon him.

3 For as the sun is not defiled by shining on dung and mire, but rather drieth up both and driveth away the evil smell; so also the pure mind, though encompassed by the defilements of earth, rather cleanseth (them), and is not itself defiled.

9 And I believe that there will be also evil-doings among you, from the words of Khanok the righteous: that ye shall commit fornication with the fornication of Sedom, and shall perish, all save a few, and shall renew wanton deeds with women; and the kingdom of YAHOWAH shall not be among you, for straightway He shall take it away.

2 Nevertheless the temple of ELOHIM shall be in your portion, and the last (temple) shall be more glorious than the first. And the twelve tribes shall be gathered together there, and all the Gentiles, until the Most High shall send forth His salvation in the visitation of an only-begotten prophet.

3 And He shall enter into the first temple, and there shall YAHOWAH be treated with outrage, and He shall be lifted up upon a tree.

4 And the veil of the temple shall be rent, and the RUAKH of ELOHIM shall pass on to the Gentiles as fire poured forth.

5 And He shall ascend from Sheol and shall pass from earth into heaven. And I know how lowly He shall be upon earth, and how glorious in heaven.

10 Now when Yoseph was in Mitzraim, I longed to see his figure and the form of his countenance; and through the prayers of Ya'aqob my father I saw him, while awake in the day-time, even his entire figure exactly, as he was.

2 And when he had said these things, he said unto them: Know ye, therefore, my children, that I am dying.

3 Do ye, therefore, truth each one to his neighbour, and keep the Torah of YAHOWAH and His commandments

4 For these things do I leave you instead of inheritance. Do ye also, therefore, give them to your children for an everlasting possession; for so did both Abraham, and Yitzkhaq, and Ya'aqob.

5 For all these things they gave us for an inheritance, saying: Keep the commandments of ELOHIM, until YAHOWAH shall reveal His salvation to all Gentiles.

6 And then shall ye see Khanok, Noakh (Noah), and Shem, and Abraham, and Yitzkhaq, and Ya'aqob, rising on the right hand in gladness

7 Then shall we also rise, each one over our tribe, worshipping the King of heaven, Who appeared upon earth in the form of a man in humility. And as many as believe on Him on the earth shall rejoice with Him.

8 Then also all men shall rise, some unto glory and some unto shame. And YAHOWAH shall judge Yisra'EL first, for their unrighteousness; for when He appeared as ELOHIM in the flesh to deliver them they believed Him not.

9 And then shall He judge all the Gentiles, as many as believed Him not when He appeared upon earth.

10 And He shall convict Yisra'EL through the chosen ones of the Gentiles, even as he reproved Esaw through the **Medanim (Midianites)**, who deceived their brethren, so that they fell into fornication, and idolatry; and they were alienated from ELOHIM, becoming therefore children in the portion of them that fear not YAHOWAH.

11 If ye therefore, my children, walk in holiness according to the commandments of YAHOWAH, ye shall again dwell securely with me, and all Yisra'EL shall be gathered unto YAHOWAH.

11 And I shall no longer be called a ravening wolf on account of your ravages, but a worker of YAHOWAH distributing food to them that work what is good.

2 And there shall arise in the latter days one beloved of YAHOWAH, of the tribe of Yehudah and Lewy, a doer of His good pleasure in his mouth, with new knowledge enlightening the Gentiles.

3 Until the consummation of the age shall he be in the Congregations of the Gentiles, and among their rulers, as a strain of music in the mouth of all.

4 And he shall be inscribed in the holy books, both his work and his word, and he shall be a chosen one of ELOHIM for ever.

5 And through them he shall go to and fro as Ya'aqob my father, saying: He shall fill up that which lacketh of thy tribe.

12 And when he had said these things he stretched out his feet,

2 And died in a beautiful and good sleep.

3 And his sons did as he had enjoined them, and they took up his body and buried it in Khebron with his fathers.

4 And the number (of the days) of his life were a hundred and twenty-five years.

BLESSINGS OF THE
12 TRIBES of ISRAEL

And Ya'aqob called unto his sons, and said, Gather yourselves together, that I may tell you that which shall befall you in the last days. Gather yourselves together, and hear, ye sons of Ya'aqob; and hearken unto Yisra'EL your father.

REUBEN, thou art my firstborn, my might, and the beginning of my strength, the excellency of dignity, and the excellency of power: Unstable as water, thou shalt not excel; because thou wentest up to thy father's bed; then defiledst thou it: he went up to my couch.

SHIMON and LEWI are brethren; instruments of cruelty are in their habitations. O my soul, come not thou into their secret; unto their assembly, mine honour, be not thou united: for in their anger they slew a man, and in their selfwill they digged down a wall. Cursed be their anger, for it was fierce; and their wrath, for it was cruel: I will divide them in Ya'aqob, and scatter them in Yisra'EL.

YEHUDAH, thou art he whom thy brethren shall praise: thy hand shall be in the neck of thine enemies; thy father's children shall bow down before thee. Yehudah is a lion's whelp: from the prey, my son, thou art gone up: he stooped down, he couched as a lion, and as an old lion; who shall rouse him up? The sceptre shall not depart from Yehudah, nor a lawgiver from between his feet, until Shiloh come; and unto him shall the gathering of the people be. Binding his foal unto the vine, and his ass's colt unto the choice vine; he washed his garments in wine, and his clothes in the blood of grapes: His eyes shall be red with wine, and his teeth white with milk.

ZEBULON shall dwell at the haven of the sea; and he shall be for an haven of ships; and his border shall be unto Tzidon.

YISSASKAR is a strong ass couching down between two burdens: And he saw that rest was good, and the land that it was pleasant; and bowed his shoulder to bear, and became a servant unto tribute.

DAN shall judge his people, as one of the tribes of Yisra'EL. Dan shall be a serpent by the way, an adder in the path, that biteth the horse heels, so that his rider shall fall backward. I have waited for thy salvation, O YAHOWAH.

GAD, a troop shall overcome him: but he shall overcome at the last.

ASHER Out of his bread shall be fat, and he shall yield royal dainties.

NAPHTALI is a hind let loose: he giveth goodly words.

YOSEPH is a fruitful bough, even a fruitful bough by a well; whose branches run over the wall: The archers have sorely grieved him, and shot at him, and hated him: But his bow abode in strength, and the arms of his hands were made strong by the hands of the mighty ELOHIM of Ya'aqob; (from thence is the shepherd, the stone of Yisra'EL: Even by the ELOHIM of thy father, who shall help thee; and by the Almighty, who shall bless thee with blessings of heaven above, blessings of the deep that lieth under, blessings of the breasts, and of the womb: The blessings of thy father have prevailed above the blessings of my progenitors unto the utmost bound of the everlasting hills: they shall be on the head of Yoseph, and on the crown of the head of him that was separate from his brethren.

BENYAMIN shall ravin as a wolf: in the morning he shall devour the prey, and at night he shall divide the spoil.

All these are the twelve tribes of Yisra'EL: and this is it that their father spake unto them, and blessed them; every one according to his blessing he blessed them.

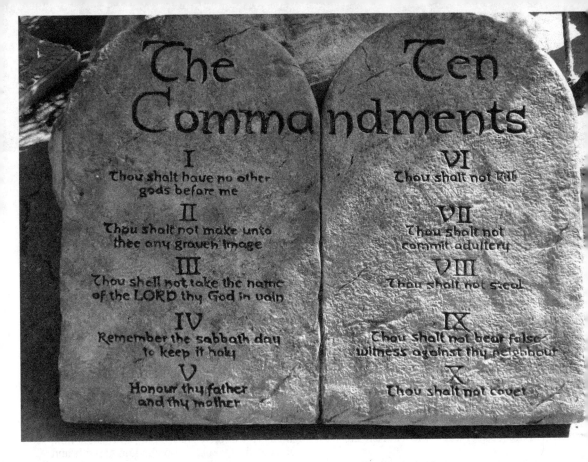

TEN COMMANDMENTS IN BIBLICAL HEBREW

אנכי יהוה אלהיך אשר הוצאתיך מארץ מצרים מבית עבדים:

לא יהיה–לך אלהים אחרים על פני:

1. ANOKI YAHOWAH ELOHAY-KA
ASHER HOTZAYTI-KA M'ARETZ MITZRAYIM M'BAYT ABADIM: LO YIYEH-LEKA ELOHIM
AKHARIM AL-PANAI

לא תעשה–לך פסל וכל–תמונה אשר בשמים ממעל ואשר
בארץ מתחת ואשר במים מתחת לארץ: לא–תשתחוה להם ולא
תעבדם כי אנכי יהוה אלהיך אל קנא פקד עון אבת על–בנים
על–שלשים ועל–רבעים לשנאי: ועשה חסד לאלפים לאהבי
ולשמרי מצותי:

2. LO TA'ASEH-LEKA PHESEL W'KAL-TEMUNAH ASHER
BA-SHAMAYIM MI-MA'AL WA-ASHER BA-ARETZ MI-TAKHAT WA-ASHER BA-MAYIM
MI-TAKHAT LA-ARETZ: LO-TISHTAKHEWEH LAHEM W'LO TA'ABDEM KI ANOKI
YAHOWAH ELOHAY-KA EL QANA POQED AON ABOTE AL-BANIM AL-SHILESHIM
W'AL-RIBAYIM L-SONAI: W'OSEH KHESED LA-ALAPHIM L'OHABAI UL-SHOMRAY
MITZWOTAI:

TEN COMMANDMENTS IN BIBLICAL HEBREW

לא תשא את–שם–יהוה אלהיך לשוא כי לא ינקה יהוה את
אשר–ישא את–שמו לשוא:

3. LO TISA ET-SHEM-YAHOWAH ELOHAY-KA:
LA-SHAW KI LO YENAQEH YAHOWAH ET ASHER-YISA ET-SHEMO LA-SHAW:

זכור את–יום השבת לקדשו: ששת ימים תעבד ועשית
כל–מלאכתך: ויום השביעי שבת ליהוה אלהיך לא–תעשה
כל–מלאכה אתה ובנך–ובתך עבדך ואמתך ובהמתך וגרך אשר
בשעריך: כי ששת–ימים עשה יהוה את–השמים ואת–הארץ
את–הים ואת–כל–אשר–בם וינח ביום השביעי על–כן ברך
יהוה את–יום השבת ויקדשהו:

4. ZAKOR ET-YOM HA-SHABBAT:
LE-QADSHO: SHESHET YAMIM TA'ABODE W'ASITA KAL-ME-LAK-TEKA: W'YOM
HA-SHEBI'EE SHABBAT LA-YAHOWAH ELOHAY-KA LO-TA'ASEH KAL-MELAKAH ATAH
UBIN-KA- UBITEKA ABDE-KA WA-AMAT-KA U'BEHEM-TEKA W'GER-KA ASHER
BISHARAY-KA: KI SHESHET - YAMIM ASAH YAHOWAH ET-HA-SHAMAYIM
W'ET-HA-ARETZ ET-HA-YAM W'ET - KAL - ASHER - BAM WA-YANAKH BA-YOM
HA-SHEBIEE AL-KEN BERAK YAHOWAH ET-YOM HA-SHABBAT WAI-QADSHEHU:

כבד את–אביך ואת–אמך למען יארכון ימיך על האדמה
אשר–יהוה אלהיך נתן לך:

5. KABED ET - ABI-KA W'ET-IMEKA LE-MA'AN
YA'ARIKUN YAMEY-KA AL HA-ADAMAH ASHER-YAHOWAH ELOHAY-KA NOTEN LAK:

לא תרצח:

6. LO TIRTZAKH:

לא תנאף:

7. LO TINAPH:

לו תגנב:

8. LO TIGNOB:

לא–תענה ברעך עד שקר:

9. LO - TA'ANEH BEREA-KA ED SHAQER:

לא תחמד בית רעך לא–תחמד אשת רעך ועבדו ואמתו ושורו
וחמרו וכל אשר לרעך:

10. LO TAKHMOD BAYT RE'EKA LO - TAKHMODE ESHET:
RE'EKA W'ABDO WA-AMATO W'SHORO WA-KHAMORO W'KOL ASHER LE-RE'EKA:

THE FIRST BOOK OF
EDRAS
ALSO KNOWN AS THE THIRD BOOK OF EZRA

1 And YoshiYAH held the feast of the Pesakh in Yerushalem unto YAHOWAH his ELOHIM, and offered the Pesakh the fourteenth day of the first month;

2 Having set the priests according to their daily courses, being arrayed in long garments, in the temple of YAHOWAH.

3 And he spake unto the Lewy'im, the holy ministers of Yisra'EL, that they should hallow themselves unto YAHOWAH, to set the holy ark of YAHOWAH in the house that king Shelomoh the son of Dawid had built:

4 And said, Ye shall no more bear the ark upon your shoulders: now therefore serve YAHOWAH your ELOHIM, and minister unto his people Yisra'EL, and prepare you after your families and kindreds,

5 According as Dawid the king of Yisra'EL prescribed, and according to the magnificence of Shelomoh his son: and standing in the temple according to the several dignity of the families of you the Lewy'im, who minister in the presence of your brethren the children of Yisra'EL,

6 Offer the Pesakh in order, and make ready the sacrifices for your brethren, and keep the Pesakh according to the commandment of YAHOWAH, which was given unto Mosheh.

7 And unto the people that was found there YoshiYAH gave thirty thousand lambs and kids, and three thousand calves: these things were given of the king's allowance, according as he promised, to the people, to the priests, and to the Lewy'im.

8 And KhilqiYAH, ZekarYAHU, and Yekhi'EL, the governors of the temple, gave to the priests for the Pesakh two thousand and six hundred sheep, and three hundred calves.

9 And YekonYAH, and ShemaYAH, and Nathan'EL his brother, and KhashabYAHU, and Yay'EL, and Yozabad, captains over thousands, gave to the Lewy'im for the Pesakh five thousand sheep, and seven hundred calves.

10 And when these things were done, the priests and Lewy'im, having the unleavened bread, stood in very comely order according to the kindreds,

11 And according to the several dignities of the fathers, before the people, to offer to YAHOWAH, as it is written in the book of Mosheh: and thus did they in the morning.

12 And they roasted the Pesakh with fire, as appertaineth: as for the sacrifices, they sod them in brass pots and pans with a good savour,

13 And set them before all the people: and afterward they prepared for themselves, and for the priests their brethren, the sons of Aharon.

14 For the priests offered the fat until night: and the Lewy'im prepared for themselves, and the priests their brethren, the sons of Aharon.

15 The holy singers also, the sons of Asaph, were in their order, according to the appointment of Dawid, to wit, Asaph, ZekarYAHU, and Yeduthun, who was of the king's retinue.

16 Moreover the porters were at every gate; it was not lawful for any to go from his ordinary service: for their brethren the Lewy'im prepared for them.

17 Thus were the things that belonged to the sacrifices of YAHOWAH accomplished in that day, that they might hold the Pesakh,

18 And offer sacrifices upon the altar of YAHOWAH, according to the commandment of king YoshiYAH.

19 So the children of Yisra'EL which were present held the Pesakh at that time, and the feast of sweet bread seven days.

20 And such a Pesakh was not kept in Yisra'EL since the time of the prophet Shemu'EL.

21 Yea, all the kings of Yisra'EL held not such a Pesakh as YoshiYAH, and the priests, and the Lewy'im, and the Yehudim, held with all Yisra'EL that were found dwelling at Yerushalem.

22 In the eighteenth year of the reign of YoshiYAH was this Pesakh kept.

23 And the works of YoshiYAH were upright before YAHOWAH his ELOHIM with an heart full of godliness.

24 As for the things that came to pass in his time, they were written in former times, concerning those that sinned, and did wickedly against YAHOWAH above all people and kingdoms, and how they grieved him exceedingly, so that the words of YAHOWAH rose up against Yisra'EL.

25 Now after all these acts of YoshiYAH it came to pass, that Pharaoh the king of Mitzraim came to raise war at Carchamis upon Perath: and YoshiYAH went out against him.

26 But the king of Mitzraim sent to him, saying, What have I to do with thee, O king of Yehudah?

27 I am not sent out from YAHOWAH ELOHIM against thee; for my war is upon Perath: and now YAHOWAH is with me, yea, YAHOWAH is with me hasting me forward: depart from me, and be not against YAHOWAH.

28 Howbeit YoshiYAH did not turn back his chariot from him, but undertook to fight with him, not regarding the words of the prophet YirmeYAHU spoken by the mouth of YAHOWAH:

29 But joined battle with him in the plain of Magiddo, and the princes came against king YoshiYAH.

30 Then said the king unto his servants, Carry me away out of the battle; for I am very weak. And immediately his servants took him away out of the battle.

31 Then gat he up upon his second chariot; and being brought back to Yerushalem died, and was buried in his father's sepulchre.

32 And in all Yehudah they mourned for Yoshi-YAH, yea, YirmeYAHU the prophet lamented for YoshiYAH, and the chief men with the women made lamentation for him unto this day: and this was given out for an ordinance to be done continually in all the nation of Yisra'EL.

33 These things are written in the book of the stories of the kings of Yehudah, and every one of the acts that YoshiYAH did, and his glory, and his understanding in the Torah (Law) of YAHOWAH, and the things that he had done before, and the things now recited, are reported in the book of the kings of Yisra'EL and Yehudah.

34 And the people took Yoakhaz the son of Yoshi-YAH, and made him king instead of YoshiYAH his father, when he was twenty and three years old.

35 And he reigned in Yehudah and in Yerushalem three months: and then the king of Mitzraim deposed him from reigning in Yerushalem.

36 And he set a tax upon the land of an hundred talents of silver and one talent of gold.

37 The king of Mitzraim also made king Yaho'yaqim his brother king of Yehudah and Yerushalem.

38 And he bound Yaho'yaqim and the nobles: but Yoakhaz his brother he apprehended, and brought him out of Mitzraim.

39 Five and twenty years old was Yaho'yaqim when he was made king in the land of Yehudah and Yerushalem; and he did evil before YAHOWAH.

40 Wherefore against him Nebukad'netzar the king of Babel came up, and bound him with a chain of brass, and carried him into Babel.

41 Nebukad'netzar also took of the holy vessels of YAHOWAH, and carried them away, and set them in his own temple at Babel.

42 But those things that are recorded of him, and of his uncleaness and impiety, are written in the chronicles of the kings.

43 And Yaho'yaqim his son reigned in his stead: he was made king being eighteen years old;

44 And reigned but three months and ten days in Yerushalem; and did evil before YAHOWAH.

45 So after a year Nebukad'netzar sent and caused him to be brought into Babel with the holy vessels of YAHOWAH.

46 And made TzedeqYAH king of Yehudah and Yerushalem, when he was one and twenty years old; and he reigned eleven years:

47 And he did evil also in the sight of YAHOWAH, and cared not for the words that were spoken unto him by the prophet YirmeYAHU from the mouth of YAHOWAH.

48 And after that king Nebukad'netzar had made him to swear by the name of YAHOWAH, he forswore himself, and rebelled; and hardening his neck, his heart, he transgressed the Torah of YAHOWAH ELOHIM of Yisra'EL.

49 The governors also of the people and of the priests did many things against the Torah, and passed all the pollutions of all Gentiles, and defiled the temple of YAHOWAH, which was sanctified in Yerushalem.

50 Nevertheless the ELOHIM of their fathers sent by his messenger to call them back, because he spared them and his tabernacle also.

51 But they had his messengers in derision; and, look, when YAHOWAH spake unto them, they made a sport of his prophets:

52 So far forth, that he, being wroth with his people for their great ungodliness, commanded the kings of the Chaldees to come up against them;

53 Who slew their young men with the sword, yea, even within the compass of their holy temple, and spared neither young man nor maid, old man nor child, among them; for he delivered all into their hands.

54 And they took all the holy vessels of YAHOWAH, both great and small, with the vessels of the ark of ELOHIM, and the king's treasures, and carried them away into Babel.

55 As for the house of YAHOWAH, they burnt it, and brake down the walls of Yerushalem, and set fire upon her towers:

56 And as for her glorious things, they never ceased till they had consumed and brought them all to nought: and the people that were not slain with the sword he carried unto Babel:

57 Who became servants to him and his children, till the Persians reigned, to fulfil the word of YAHOWAH spoken by the mouth of YirmeYAHU:

58 Until the land had enjoyed her Shabbats, the whole time of her desolation shall she rest, until the full term of seventy years.

2 In the first year of Korash king of the Persians, that the word of YAHOWAH might be accomplished, that he had promised by the mouth of YirmeYAHU;

2 YAHOWAH raised up the ruakh of Korash the king of the Persians, and he made proclamation through all his kingdom, and also by writing,

3 Saying, Thus saith Korash king of the Persians; YAHOWAH of Yisra'EL, the Most High YAHOWAH, hath made me king of the whole world,

4 And commanded me to build him an house at Yerushalem in Yehudah.

5 If therefore there be any of you that are of his people, let YAHOWAH, even YAHOWAH his ELOHIM, be with him, and let him go up to Yerushalem that is in Yehudah, and build the house of YAHOWAH of Yisra'EL: for he is YAHOWAH that dwelleth in Yerushalem.

6 Whosoever then dwell in the places about, let them help him, those, I say, that are his neigh-

bours, with gold, and with silver,

7 With gifts, with horses, and with cattle, and other things, which have been set forth by vow, for the temple of YAHOWAH at Yerushalem.

8 Then the chief of the families of Yehudah and of the tribe of Benyamin stood up; the priests also, and the Lewy'im, and all they whose mind YAHOWAH had moved to go up, and to build an house for YAHOWAH at Yerushalem,

9 And they that dwelt round about them, and helped them in all things with silver and gold, with horses and cattle, and with very many free gifts of a great number whose minds were stirred up thereto.

10 King Korash also brought forth the holy vessels, which Nebukad'netzar had carried away from Yerushalem, and had set up in his temple of idols.

11 Now when Korash king of the Persians had brought them forth, he delivered them to Mithredath his treasurer:

12 And by him they were delivered to Shashbatzar the governor of Yehudah.

13 And this was the number of them; A thousand golden cups, and a thousand of silver, censers of silver twenty nine, vials of gold thirty, and of silver two thousand four hundred and ten, and a thousand other vessels.

14 So all the vessels of gold and of silver, which were carried away, were five thousand four hundred threescore and nine.

15 These were brought back by Shashbatzar, together with them of the captivity, from Babel to Yerushalem.

16 But in the time of Artakh'shasheth (Artaxerxes) king of the Persians Belemus, and Mithredath, and Tab'EL, and Rekhum, and Baal-te'am, and Shimshai the secretary, with others that were in commission with them, dwelling in Shomron and other places, wrote unto him against them that dwelt in Yehudah and Yerushalem these letters following;

17 To king Artakh'shasheth our Adon, Thy servants, Rekhum the storywriter, and Shimshai the scribe, and the rest of their council, and the judges that are in Aram and Kena'an.

18 Be it now known to the Adon king, that the Yehudim that are up from you to us, being come into Yerushalem, that rebellious and wicked city, do build the marketplaces, and repair the walls of it and do lay the foundation of the temple.

19 Now if this city and the walls thereof be made up again, they will not only refuse to give tribute, but also rebel against kings.

20 And forasmuch as the things pertaining to the temple are now in hand, we think it meet not to neglect such a matter,

21 But to speak unto our Adon the king, to the intent that, if it be thy pleasure it may be sought out in the books of thy fathers:

22 And thou shalt find in the chronicles what is written concerning these things, and shalt understand that that city was rebellious,

troubling both kings and cities:

23 And that the Yehudim were rebellious, and raised always wars therein; for the which cause even this city was made desolate.

24 Wherefore now we do declare unto thee, O Adon the king, that if this city be built again, and the walls thereof set up anew, thou shalt from henceforth have no passage into Aram and Kena'an.

25 Then the king wrote back again to Rekhum the storywriter, to Baal-te'am, to Shimshai the scribe, and to the rest that were in commission, and dwellers in Shomron and Aram and Kena'an, after this manner;

26 I have read the epistle which ye have sent unto me: therefore I commanded to make diligent search, and it hath been found that that city was from the beginning practising against kings;

27 And the men therein were given to rebellion and war: and that mighty kings and fierce were in Yerushalem, who reigned and exacted tributes in Aram and Kena'an.

28 Now therefore I have commanded to hinder those men from building the city, and heed to be taken that there be no more done in it;

29 And that those wicked workers proceed no further to the annoyance of kings,

30 Then king Artakh'shasheth his letters being read, Rekhum, and Shimshai the scribe, and the rest that were in commission with them, removing in haste toward Yerushalem with a troop of horsemen and a multitude of people in battle array, began to hinder the builders; and the building of the temple in Yerushalem ceased until the second year of the reign of Daryawesh king of the Persians.

3 Now when Daryawesh reigned, he made a great feast unto all his subjects, and unto all his household, and unto all the princes of Madai (Media) and Paras,

2 And to all the governors and captains and lieutenants that were under him, from Hodu unto Kush, of an hundred twenty and seven provinces.

3 And when they had eaten and drunken, and being satisfied were gone home, then Daryawesh the king went into his bedchamber, and slept, and soon after awaked.

4 Then three young men, that were of the guard that kept the king's body, spake one to another;

5 Let every one of us speak a sentence: he that shall overcome, and whose sentence shall seem wiser than the others, unto him shall the king Daryawesh give great gifts, and great things in token of victory:

6 As, to be clothed in purple, to drink in gold, and to sleep upon gold, and a chariot with bridles of gold, and an headtire of fine linen, and a chain about his neck:

7 And he shall sit next to Daryawesh because of his wisdom, and shall be called Daryawesh his cousin.

8 And then every one wrote his sentence, sealed it, and laid it under king Daryawesh his pillow;

9 And said that, when the king is risen, some will give him the writings; and of whose side the king and the three princes of Paras shall judge that his sentence is the wisest, to him shall the victory be given, as was appointed.

10 The first wrote, Wine is the strongest.

11 The second wrote, The king is strongest.

12 The third wrote, Women are strongest: but above all things Truth beareth away the victory.

13 Now when the king was risen up, they took their writings, and delivered them unto him, and so he read them:

14 And sending forth he called all the princes of Paras and Madai, and the governors, and the captains, and the lieutenants, and the chief officers;

15 And sat him down in the royal seat of judgment; and the writings were read before them.

16 And he said, Call the young men, and they shall declare their own sentences. So they were called, and came in.

17 And he said unto them, Declare unto us your mind concerning the writings. Then began the first, who had spoken of the strength of wine;

18 And he said thus, O ye men, how exceeding strong is wine! it causeth all men to err that drink it:

19 It maketh the mind of the king and of the fatherless child to be all one; of the bondman and of the freeman, of the poor man and of the rich:

20 It turneth also every thought into jollity and mirth, so that a man remembereth neither sorrow nor debt:

21 And it maketh every heart rich, so that a man remembereth neither king nor governor; and it maketh to speak all things by talents:

22 And when they are in their cups, they forget their love both to friends and brethren, and a little after draw out swords:

23 But when they are from the wine, they remember not what they have done.

24 O ye men, is not wine the strongest, that enforceth to do thus? And when he had so spoken, he held his shalom.

4 Then the second, that had spoken of the strength of the king, began to say,

2 O ye men, do not men excel in strength that bear rule over sea and land and all things in them?

3 But yet the king is more mighty: for he is Adon of all these things, and hath dominion over them; and whatsoever he commandeth them they do.

4 If he bid them make war the one against the other, they do it: if he send them out against the enemies, they go, and break down mountains walls and towers.

5 They slay and are slain, and transgress not the king's commandment: if they get the victory, they bring all to the king, as well the spoil, as all things else.

6 Likewise for those that are no soldiers, and have not to do with wars, but use husbundry, when they have reaped again that which they had sown, they bring it to the king, and compel one another to pay tribute unto the king.

7 And yet he is but one man: if he command to kill, they kill; if he command to spare, they spare;

8 If he command to smite, they smite; if he command to make desolate, they make desolate; if he command to build, they build;

9 If he command to cut down, they cut down; if he command to plant, they plant.

10 So all his people and his armies obey him: furthermore he lieth down, he eateth and drinketh, and taketh his rest:

11 And these keep watch round about him, neither may any one depart, and do his own business, neither disobey they him in any thing.

12 O ye men, how should not the king be mightiest, when in such sort he is obeyed? And he held his tongue.

13 Then the third, who had spoken of women, and of the truth, (this was Zerubabel) began to speak.

14 O ye men, it is not the great king, nor the multitude of men, neither is it wine, that excelleth; who is it then that ruleth them, or hath the lordship over them? are they not women?

15 Women have borne the king and all the people that bear rule by sea and land.

16 Even of them came they: and they nourished them up that planted the vineyards, from whence the wine cometh.

17 These also make garments for men; these bring glory unto men; and without women cannot men be.

18 Yea, and if men have gathered together gold and silver, or any other goodly thing, do they not love a woman which is comely in favour and beauty?

19 And letting all those things go, do they not gape, and even with open mouth fix their eyes fast on her; and have not all men more desire unto her than unto silver or gold, or any goodly thing whatsoever?

20 A man leaveth his own father that brought him up, and his own country, and cleaveth unto his wife.

21 He sticketh not to spend his life with his wife. and remembereth neither father, nor mother, nor country.

22 By this also ye must know that women have dominion over you: do ye not labour and toil, and give and bring all to the woman?

23 Yea, a man taketh his sword, and goeth his way to rob and to steal, to sail upon the sea and upon rivers;

24 And looketh upon a lion, and goeth in the darkness; and when he hath stolen, spoiled, and robbed, he bringeth it to his love.

25 Wherefore a man loveth his wife better than father or mother.

26 Yea, many there be that have run out of their wits for women, and become servants for their sakes.

27 Many also have perished, have erred, and sinned, for women.

28 And now do ye not believe me? is not the king great in his power? do not all regions fear to touch him?

29 Yet did I see him and Apamah the king's concubine, the daughter of the admirable Bartaq, sitting at the right hand of the king,

30 And taking the crown from the king's head, and setting it upon her own head; she also struck the king with her left hand.

31 And yet for all this the king gaped and gazed upon her with open mouth: if she laughed upon him, he laughed also: but if she took any displeasure at him, the king was fain to flatter, that she might be reconciled to him again.

32 O ye men, how can it be but women should be strong, seeing they do thus?

33 Then the king and the princes looked one upon another: so he began to speak of the truth.

34 O ye men, are not women strong? great is the earth, high is the heaven, swift is the sun in his course, for he compasseth the heavens round about, and fetcheth his course again to his own place in one day.

35 Is he not great that maketh these things? therefore great is the truth, and stronger than all things.

36 All the earth crieth upon the truth, and the heaven blesseth it: all works shake and tremble at it, and with it is no unrighteous thing.

37 Wine is wicked, the king is wicked, women are wicked, all the children of men are wicked, and such are all their wicked works; and there is no truth in them; in their unrighteousness also they shall perish.

38 As for the truth, it endureth, and is alwaYs strong; it liveth and conquereth for evermore.

39 With her there is no accepting of persons or rewards; but she doeth the things that are just, and refraineth from all unjust and wicked things; and all men do well like of her works.

40 Neither in her judgment is any unrighteousness; and she is the strength, kingdom, power, and majesty, of all ages. Blessed be the ELOHIM of truth.

41 And with that he held his shalom. And all the people then shouted, and said, Great is Truth, and mighty above all things.

42 Then said the king unto him, Ask what thou wilt more than is appointed in the writing, and we will give it thee, because thou art found wisest; and thou shalt sit next me, and shalt be called my cousin.

43 Then said he unto the king, Remember thy vow, which thou hast vowed to build Yerushalem, in the day when thou camest to thy kingdom,

44 And to send away all the vessels that were taken away out of Yerushalem, which Korash set apart, when he vowed to destroy Babel, and to send them again thither.

45 Thou also hast vowed to build up the temple, which the Edomim burned when Yehudah was made desolate by the Chaldees.

46 And now, O Adon the king, this is that which I require, and which I desire of thee, and this is the princely liberality proceeding from thyself: I desire therefore that thou make good the vow, the performance whereof with thine own mouth thou hast vowed to the King of heaven.

47 Then Daryawesh the king stood up, and kissed him, and wrote letters for him unto all the treasurers and lieutenants and captains and governors, that they should safely convey on their way both him, and all those that go up with him to build Yerushalem.

48 He wrote letters also unto the lieutenants that were in Aram and Kena'an, and unto them in Lebanon, that they should bring cedar wood from Lebanon unto Yerushalem, and that they should build the city with him.

49 Moreover he wrote for all the Yehudim that went out of his realm up into Yehudah, concerning their freedom, that no officer, no ruler, no lieutenant, nor treasurer, should forcibly enter into their doors;

50 And that all the country which they hold should be free without tribute; and that the Edomim should give over the villages of the Yehudim which then they held:

51 Yea, that there should be yearly given twenty talents to the building of the temple, until the time that it were built;

52 And other ten talents yearly, to maintain the burnt offerings upon the altar every day, as they had a commandment to offer seventeen:

53 And that all they that went from Babel to build the city should have free liberty, as well they as their posterity, and all the priests that went away.

54 He wrote also concerning. the charges, and the priests' vestments wherein they minister;

55 And likewise for the charges of the Lewy'im, to be given them until the day that the house were finished, and Yerushalem builded up.

56 And he commanded to give to all that kept the city pensions and wages.

57 He sent away also all the vessels from Babel, that Korash had set apart; and all that Korash had given in commandment, the same charged he also to be done, and sent unto Yerushalem.

58 Now when this young man was gone forth, he lifted up his face to heaven toward Yerushalem, and praised the King of heaven,

59 And said, From thee cometh victory, from thee cometh wisdom, and thine is the glory, and I am thy servant.

60 Blessed art thou, who hast given me wisdom: for to thee I give thanks, O YAHOWAH of our fathers.

61 And so he took the letters, and went out, and came unto Babel, and told it all his brethren.

62 And they praised the ELOHIM of their fathers, because he had given them freedom and liberty

63 To go up, and to build Yerushalem, and the temple which is called by his name: and they feasted with instruments of musick and gladness seven days.

5 After this were the principal men of the families chosen according to their tribes, to go up with their wives and sons and daughters, with their menservants and maidservants, and their cattle.

2 And Daryawesh sent with them a thousand horsemen, till they had brought them back to Yerushalem safely, and with musical [instruments] tabrets and flutes.

3 And all their brethren played, and he made them go up together with them.

4 And these are the names of the men which went up, according to their families among their tribes, after their several heads.

5 The priests, the sons of Pinkhas the son of Aharon: Yahoshua the son of Yaho-Tzadaq, the son of SeraYAH, and Yaho'yaqim the son of Zerubabel, the son of She'alti'EL, of the house of Dawid, out of the kindred of Peretz, of the tribe of Yehudah;

6 Who spake wise sentences before Daryawesh the king of Paras in the second year of his reign, in the month Nisan, which is the first month.

7 And these are they of Yehudah that came up from the captivity, where they dwelt as strangers, whom Nebukad'netzar the king of Babel had carried away unto Babel.

8 And they returned unto Yerushalem, and to the other parts of Yehudah, every man to his own city, who came with Zerubabel, with Yahoshua, NekhemYAH, and ZekarYAHU, and Ra'amYAH, Nakhamani, Mordekai. Bilshan, Misparath, Bigwai, Rekhum, and Baanah, their guides.

9 The number of them of the nation, and their governors, sons of Parash, two thousand an hundred seventy and two; the sons of ShaphatYAH, four hundred seventy and two:

10 The sons of Arakh, seven hundred fifty and six:

11 The sons of Pakhath Moab (the sons of Yahoshua and Yoab), two thousand eight hundred and twelve:

12 The sons of Ailam, a thousand two hundred fifty and four: the sons of Zathu, nine hundred forty and five: the sons of Zakki, seven hundred and five: the sons of Banai, six hundred forty and eight:

13 The sons of Bebai, six hundred twenty and three: the sons of Azgad, three thousand two hundred twenty and two:

14 The sons of Adoniqam, six hundred sixty and seven: the sons of Bigwai, two thousand sixty and six: the sons of Adin, four hundred fifty and four:

15 The sons of Atar (for ChizqiYAH), ninety and eight: the sons of Qilan and Azathah threescore and seven: the sons of Azur, four hundred thirty and two:

16 The sons of KhananYAH, an hundred and one: the sons of Kharam, thirty two: and the sons of Betzei, three hundred twenty and three: the sons of Khariph, an hundred and twelve:

17 The sons of Gibar, ninety and five: the sons of Bethlekhem, an hundred twenty and three:

18 They of Netophah, fifty and five: they of Anatoth, an hundred fifty and eight: they of Beth-Azmawath, forty and two:

19 They of Qiryath-Yaarim, twenty and five: they of Kephirah and Be'eroth, seven hundred forty and three: they of Pira, seven hundred:

20 They of Khadid and Kharam, four hundred twenty and two: they of Haramah and Gaba, six hundred twenty and one:

21 They of Mikmam, an hundred twenty and two: they of Beth-EL, fifty and two: the sons of Magbis, an hundred fifty and six:

22 The sons of Ailam-Akhar, a thousand two hundred fifty and four and Ono, seven hundred twenty and five: the sons of Yerekho, two hundred forty and five:

23 The sons of Senaah, three thousand three hundred and thirty.

24 The priests: the sons of YedaYAH, the son of Yahoshua among the sons of El'yashib, nine hundred seventy and two: the sons of Imer, a thousand fifty and two:

25 The sons of Pashkhur, a thousand forty and seven: the sons of Charim, a thousand and seventeen.

26 The Lewy'im: the sons of Yeshua, and Qadmi'EL, and Baanah, and HodaYAH, seventy and four.

27 The holy singers: the sons of Asaph, an hundred twenty and eight.

28 The porters: the sons of Shalum, the sons of Atar, the sons of Talmon, the sons of Aqub, the sons of Khatita, the sons of Shobai, in all an hundred thirty and nine.

29 The servants of the temple: the sons of Tzikha, the sons of Khasupha, the sons of Tabaoth, the sons of Qarom, the sons of Siaha, the sons of Padon, the sons of Labanah, the sons of Khagaba,

30 The sons of Aqub, the sons of Uta, the sons of Ketab, the sons of Khagav, the sons of Shamlai, the sons of Khanan, the sons of Gidal, the sons of Gakhar,

31 The sons of ReaYAH, the sons of Retzin, the sons of Neqoda, the sons of Gazam, the sons of Uzza, the sons of Pesaeach, the sons of Basai, the sons of Asnah, the sons of Meunim, the sons of Nephiysim, the sons of Baqbuq, the sons of Chaqupha, the sons of Charchur, the sons of Batzluth,

32 The sons of Mekhida, the sons of Kharsha, the sons of Barqom, the sons of Sisra, the sons of Tamakh, the sons of Netziyakh, the sons of Khatipha.

33 The sons of the servants of Shelomoh: the sons of Hasophereth, the sons of Pheruda, the sons of Yaalah, the sons of Darqon, the sons of Gidal, the sons of ShephatYAH,

34 The sons of Khatil, the sons of Phocarath, the hosts of the sons of Amon.

35 All the ministers of the temple, and the sons of the servants of Shelomoh, were three hundred seventy and two.

36 These came up from Thel-Melakh and Thel-Kharsha, Kerub leading them, Adan and Imer;

37 Neither could they shew their families, nor their stock, how they were of Yisra'EL: the sons of DelaYAH, the son of TobiYAH, the sons of Neqoda, six hundred fifty and two.

38 And of the priests that usurped the office of the priesthood, and were not found: the sons of KhavaiYAH, the sons of Haqotz, the sons of Yadua, who married OgiYAH one of the daughters of Barzilai, and was named after his name.

39 And when the description of the kindred of these men was sought in the register, and was not found, they were removed from executing the office of the priesthood:

40 For unto them said NekhemYAH the governor, that they should not be partakers of the holy things, till there arose up an high priest clothed with doctrine and truth.

41 So of Yisra'EL, from them of twelve years old and upward, they were all in number forty thousand, beside menservants and womenservants two thousand three hundred and sixty.

42 Their menservants and handmaids were seven thousand three hundred forty and seven: the singing men and singing women, two hundred forty and five:

43 Four hundred thirty and five camels, seven thousand thirty and six horses, two hundred forty and five mules, five thousand five hundred twenty and five beasts used to the yoke.

44 And certain of the chief of their families, when they came to the temple of ELOHIM that is in Yerushalem, vowed to set up the house again in his own place according to their ability,

45 And to give into the holy treasury of the works a thousand pounds of gold, five thousand of silver, and an hundred priestly vestments.

46 And so dwelt the priests and the Lewy'im and the people in Yerushalem, and in the country, the singers also and the porters; and all Yisra'EL in their villages.

47 But when the seventh month was at hand, and when the children of Yisra'EL were every man in his own place, they came all together with one consent into the open place of the first gate which is toward the east.

48 Then stood up Yahoshua the son of Yaho-Tzadaq, and his brethren the priests and Zerubabel the son of She'alti'EL, and his brethren, and made ready the altar of the ELOHIM of Yisra'EL,

49 To offer burnt sacrifices upon it, according as it is expressly commanded in the book of Mosheh the man of ELOHIM.

50 And there were gathered unto them out of the other Gentiles of the land, and they erected the altar upon his own place, because all the Gentiles of the land were at enmity with them, and oppressed them; and they offered sacrifices according to the time, and burnt offerings to YAHOWAH both morning and evening.

51 Also they held The Feast of Sukkot, as it is commanded in the Torah, and offered sacrifices daily, as was meet:

52 And after that, the continual oblations, and the sacrifice of the Shabbats, and of the Renewed Months, and of all holy feasts.

53 And all they that had made any vow to ELOHIM began to offer sacrifices to ELOHIM from the first day of the seventh month, although the temple of YAHOWAH was not yet built.

54 And they gave unto the masons and carpenters money, meat, and drink, with cheerfulness.

55 Unto them of Tzidon also and Tzor they gave carrs, that they should bring cedar trees from Lebanon, which should be brought by floats to the haven of Yoppa, according as it was commanded them by Korash king of the Persians.

56 And in the second year and second month after his coming to the temple of ELOHIM at Yerushalem began Zerubabel the son of She'alti'EL, and Yahoshua the son of Yaho-Tzadaq, and their brethren, and the priests, and the Lewy'im, and all they that were come unto Yerushalem out of the captivity:

57 And they laid the foundation of the house of ELOHIM in the first day of the second month, in the second year after they were come to Yehudah and Yerushalem.

58 And they appointed the Lewy'im from twenty years old over the works of YAHOWAH. Then stood up Yahoshua, and his sons and brethren, and Qadmi'EL his brother, and the sons of Yehudah, with the sons of Khenadad with their sons and brethren, all Lewy'im, with one accord setters forward of the business, labouring to advance the works in the house of ELOHIM. So the workmen built the temple of YAHOWAH.

59 And the priests stood arrayed in their vestments with musical instruments and trumpets; and the Lewy'im the sons of Asaph had cymbals,

60 Singing songs of thanksgiving, and praising YAHOWAH, according as Dawid the king of Yisra'EL had ordained.

61 And they sung with loud voices songs to the praise of YAHOWAH, because his mercy and glory is for ever in all Yisra'EL.

62 And all the people sounded trumpets, and shouted with a loud voice, singing songs of thanksgiving unto YAHOWAH for the rearing up of the house of YAHOWAH.

63 Also of the priests and Lewy'im, and of the chief of their families, the ancients who had seen the former house came to the building of this with weeping and great crying.

64 But many with trumpets and joy shouted with loud voice,

65 Insomuch that the trumpets might not be heard for the weeping of the people: yet the multitude sounded marvellously, so that it was heard afar off.

66 Wherefore when the enemies of the tribe of Yehudah and Benyamin heard it, they came to know what that noise of trumpets should mean.

67 And they perceived that they that were of the captivity did build the temple unto YAHOWAH ELOHIM of Yisra'EL.

68 So they went to Zerubabel and Yahoshua, and to the chief of the families, and said unto them, We will build together with you.

69 For we likewise, as ye, do obey your YAHOWAH, and do sacrifice unto him from the

days of Asar-Khadon the king of the Assyrians, who brought us hither.

70 Then Zerubabel and Yahoshua and the chief of the families of Yisra'EL said unto them, It is not for us and you to build together an house unto YAHOWAH our ELOHIM.

71 We ourselves alone will build unto YAHOWAH of Yisra'EL, according as Korash the king of the Persians hath commanded us.

72 But the heathen of the land lying heavy upon the inhabitants of Yehudah, and holding them strait, hindered their building;

73 And by their secret plots, and popular persuasions and commotions, they hindered the finishing of the building all the time that king Korash lived: so they were hindered from building for the space of two years, until the reign of Daryawesh.

6 Now in the second year of the reign of Daryawesh, Khagai and ZekarYAHU the son of Addo, the prophets, prophesied unto the Yehudim in Yehudah and Yerushalem in the name of YAHOWAH ELOHIM of Yisra'EL, which was upon them.

2 Then stood up Zerubabel the son of She'alti'EL, and Yahoshua the son of Yaho-Tzadaq, and began to build the house of YAHOWAH at Yerushalem, the prophets of YAHOWAH being with them, and helping them.

3 At the same time came unto them Shashnai the governor of Aram and Kena'an, with Shethar-Boznai and his companions, and said unto them,

4 By whose appointment do ye build this house and this roof, and perform all the other things? and who are the workmen that perform these things?

5 Nevertheless the elders of the Yehudim obtained favour, because YAHOWAH had visited the captivity;

6 And they were not hindered from building, until such time as signification was given unto Daryawesh concerning them, and an answer received.

7 The copy of the letters which Shashnai, governor of Aram and Kena'an, and Shethar-Boznai, with their companions, rulers in Aram and Kena'an, wrote and sent unto Daryawesh; To king Daryawesh, greeting:

8 Let all things be known unto our Adon the king, that being come into the country of Yehudah, and entered into the city of Yerushalem we found in the city of Yerushalem the ancients of the Yehudim that were of the captivity

9 Building an house unto YAHOWAH, great and new, of hewn and costly stones, and the timber already laid upon the walls.

10 And those works are done with great speed, and the work goeth on prosperously in their hands, and with all glory and diligence is it made.

11 Then asked we these elders, saying, By whose commandment build ye this house, and lay the foundations of these works?

12 Therefore to the intent that we might give knowledge unto thee by writing, we demanded of them who were the chief doers, and we required of them the names in writing of their principal men.

13 So they gave us this answer, We are the servants of YAHOWAH which made heaven and earth.

14 And as for this house, it was builded many years ago by a king of Yisra'EL great and strong, and was finished.

15 But when our fathers provoked ELOHIM unto wrath, and sinned against YAHOWAH of Yisra'EL which is in heaven, he gave them over into the power of Nebukad'netzar king of Babel, of the Chaldees;

16 Who pulled down the house, and burned it, and carried away the people captives unto Babel.

17 But in the first year that king Korash reigned over the country of Babel Korash the king wrote to build up this house.

18 And the holy vessels of gold and of silver, that Nebukad'netzar had carried away out of the house at Yerushalem, and had set them in his own temple those Korash the king brought forth again out of the temple at Babel, and they were delivered to Zerubabel and to Shashbatzar the ruler,

19 With commandment that he should carry away the same vessels, and put them in the temple at Yerushalem; and that the temple of YAHOWAH should be built in his place.

20 Then the same Shashbatzar, being come hither, laid the foundations of the house of YAHOWAH at Yerushalem; and from that time to this being still a building, it is not yet fully ended.

21 Now therefore, if it seem good unto the king, let search be made among the records of king Korash:

22 And if it be found that the building of the house of YAHOWAH at Yerushalem hath been done with the consent of king Korash, and if our Adon the king be so minded, let him signify unto us thereof.

23 Then commanded king Daryawesh to seek among the records at Babel: and so at Ecbatane the palace, which is in the country of Madai, there was found a roll wherein these things were recorded.

24 In the first year of the reign of Korash king Korash commanded that the house of YAHOWAH at Yerushalem should be built again, where they do sacrifice with continual fire:

25 Whose height shall be sixty cubits and the breadth sixty cubits, with three rows of hewn stones, and one row of new wood of that country; and the expences thereof to be given out of the house of king Korash:

26 And that the holy vessels of the house of YAHOWAH, both of gold and silver, that Nebukad'netzar took out of the house at Yerushalem, and brought to Babel, should be restored to the house at Yerushalem, and be set in the place where they were before.

27 And also he commanded that Shashnai the governor of Aram and Kena'an, and Shethar-Boznai, and their companions, and those which were appointed rulers in Aram and Kena'an, should be

careful not to meddle with the place, but suffer Zerubabel, the servant of YAHOWAH, and governor of Yehudah, and the elders of the Yehudim, to build the house of YAHOWAH in that place.

28 I have commanded also to have it built up whole again; and that they look diligently to help those that be of the captivity of the Yehudim, till the house of YAHOWAH be finished:

29 And out of the tribute of Aram and Kena'an a portion carefully to be given these men for the sacrifices of YAHOWAH, that is, to Zerubabel the governor, for bullocks, and rams, and lambs;

30 And also corn, salt, wine, and oil, and that continually every year without further question, according as the priests that be in Yerushalem shall signify to be daily spent:

31 That offerings may be made to the Most High ELOHIM for the king and for his children, and that they may pray for their lives.

32 And he commanded that whosoever should transgress, yea, or make light of any thing afore spoken or written, out of his own house should a tree be taken, and he thereon be hanged, and all his goods seized for the king.

33 YAHOWAH therefore, whose name is there called upon, utterly destroy every king and nation, that stretcheth out his hand to hinder or endamage that house of YAHOWAH in Yerushalem.

34 I Daryawesh the king have ordained that according unto these things it be done with diligence.

7 Then Shashnai the governor of Aram and Kena'an, and Shethar-Boznai, with their companions following the commandments of king Daryawesh,

2 Did very carefully oversee the holy works, assisting the ancients of the Yehudim and governors of the temple.

3 And so the holy works prospered, when Khagai and ZekarYAHU the prophets prophesied.

4 And they finished these things by the commandment of YAHOWAH ELOHIM of Yisra'EL, and with the consent of Korash, Daryawesh, and Artakh'shasheth, kings of Paras.

5 And thus was the holy house finished in the three and twentieth day of the month Adar, in the sixth year of Daryawesh king of the Persians

6 And the children of Yisra'EL, the priests, and the Lewy'im, and others that were of the captivity, that were added unto them, did according to the things written in the book of Mosheh.

7 And to the dedication of the temple of YAHOWAH they offered an hundred bullocks two hundred rams, four hundred lambs;

8 And twelve goats for the sin of all Yisra'EL, according to the number of the chief of the tribes of Yisra'EL.

9 The priests also and the Lewy'im stood arrayed in their vestments, according to their kindreds, in the service of YAHOWAH ELOHIM of Yisra'EL, according to the book of Mosheh: and the porters at every gate.

10 And the children of Yisra'EL that were of the captivity held the Pesakh the fourteenth day of the first month, after that the priests and the Lewy'im were sanctified.

11 They that were of the captivity were not all sanctified together: but the Lewy'im were all sanctified together.

12 And so they offered the Pesakh for all them of the captivity, and for their brethren the priests, and for themselves.

13 And the children of Yisra'EL that came out of the captivity did eat, even all they that had separated themselves from the abominations of the people of the land, and sought YAHOWAH.

14 And they kept The Feast of Matzot seven days, making merry before YAHOWAH,

15 For that he had turned the counsel of the king of Asshur toward them, to strengthen their hands in the works of YAHOWAH ELOHIM of Yisra'EL.

8 And after these things, when Artakh'shasheth the king of the Persians reigned came Ezra the son of SeraYAH, the son of AzarYAH, the son of KhilqiYAH, the son of Shalum,

2 The son of Tzadoq, the son of Akhitub, the son of AmarYAH, the son of AzarYAH, the son of Meraioth, the son of ZerakhYAH, the son of Uzzi, the son of Buqqi, the son of Abishua, the son of Pinkhas, the son of Eleazar, the son of Aharon the chief priest.

3 This Ezra went up from Babel, as a scribe, being very ready in the Torah of Mosheh, that was given by the ELOHIM of Yisra'EL.

4 And the king did him honour: for he found grace in his sight in all his requests.

5 There went up with him also certain of the children of Yisra'EL, of the priest of the Lewy'im, of the holy singers, porters, and ministers of the temple, unto Yerushalem,

6 In the seventh year of the reign of Artakh'shasheth, in the fifth month, this was the king's seventh year; for they went from Babel in the first day of the first month, and came to Yerushalem, according to the prosperous journey which YAHOWAH gave them.

7 For Ezra had very great skill, so that he omitted nothing of the Torah and commandments of YAHOWAH, but taught all Yisra'EL the ordinances and judgments.

8 Now the copy of the commission, which was written from Artakh'shasheth the king, and came to Ezra the priest and reader of the Torah of YAHOWAH, is this that followeth;

9 King Artakh'shasheth unto Ezra the priest and reader of the Torah of YAHOWAH sendeth greeting:

10 Having determined to deal graciously, I have given order, that such of the nation of the Yehudim, and of the priests and Lewy'im being within our realm, as are willing and desirous should go with thee unto Yerushalem.

11 As many therefore as have a mind thereunto, let them depart with thee, as it hath seemed good both to me and my seven friends the counsellors;

12 That they may look unto the affairs of Yehudah and Yerushalem, agreeably to that which is in the Torah of YAHOWAH;

13 And carry the gifts unto YAHOWAH of Yisra'EL to Yerushalem, which I and my friends have vowed, and all the gold and silver that in the country of Babel can be found, to YAHOWAH in Yerushalem,

14 With that also which is given of the people for the temple of YAHOWAH their ELOHIM at Yerushalem: and that silver and gold may be collected for bullocks, rams, and lambs, and things thereunto appertaining;

15 To the end that they may offer sacrifices unto YAHOWAH upon the altar of YAHOWAH their ELOHIM, which is in Yerushalem.

16 And whatsoever thou and thy brethren will do with the silver and gold, that do, according to the will of thy ELOHIM.

17 And the holy vessels of YAHOWAH, which are given thee for the use of the temple of thy ELOHIM, which is in Yerushalem, thou shalt set before thy ELOHIM in Yerushalem.

18 And whatsoever thing else thou shalt remember for the use of the temple of thy ELOHIM, thou shalt give it out of the king's treasury.

19 And I king Artakh'shasheth have also commanded the keepers of the treasures in Aram and Kena'an, that whatsoever Ezra the priest and the reader of the Torah of the Most High ELOHIM shall send for, they should give it him with speed,

20 To the sum of an hundred talents of silver, likewise also of wheat even to an hundred cors, and an hundred pieces of wine, and other things in abundance.

21 Let all things be performed after the Torah of ELOHIM diligently unto the Most High ELOHIM, that wrath come not upon the kingdom of the king and his sons.

22 I command you also, that ye require no tax, nor any other imposition, of any of the priests, or Lewy'im, or holy singers, or porters, or ministers of the temple, or of any that have doings in this temple, and that no man have authority to impose any thing upon them.

23 And thou, Ezra, according to the wisdom of ELOHIM ordain judges and justices, that they may judge in all Aram and Kena'an all those that know the Torah of thy ELOHIM; and those that know it not thou shalt teach.

24 And whosoever shall transgress the Torah of thy ELOHIM, and of the king, shall be punished diligently, whether it be by death, or other punishment, by penalty of money, or by imprisonment.

25 Then said Ezra the scribe, Blessed be the only YAHOWAH ELOHIM of my fathers, who hath put these things into the heart of the king, to glorify his house that is in Yerushalem:

26 And hath honoured me in the sight of the king, and his counsellors, and all his friends and nobles.

27 Therefore was I encouraged by the help of YAHOWAH my ELOHIM, and gathered together men of Yisra'EL to go up with me.

28 And these are the chief according to their families and several dignities, that went up with me from Babel in the reign of king Artakh'shasheth:

29 Of the sons of Pinkhas, Gershom: of the sons of Itamar, Dani'EL: of the sons of Dawid, Khamush the son of ShekanYAH:

30 Of the sons of Pharash, ZekarYAHU; and with him were counted an hundred and fifty men:

31 Of the sons of Pakhath Moab, Eliho'ainai, the son of ZerakhYAH, and with him two hundred men:

32 Of the sons of Zathu, ShekanYAH the son of Yechazi'EL, and with him three hundred men: of the sons of Adin, Obeth the son of Yahonathan, and with him two hundred and fifty men:

33 Of the sons of Ailam, YeshaYAH son of AthalYAH, and with him seventy men:

34 Of the sons of ShaphatYAH, ZebadYAH son of Mika'EL, and with him fourscore men:

35 Of the sons of Yoab, ObadYAH son of Yekhi'EL, and with him two hundred and twelve men:

36 Of the sons of BanYAH, Shelomith son of YosiphYAH, and with him an hundred and threescore men:

37 Of the sons of Bebai, ZekarYAHU son of Bebai, and with him twenty and eight men:

38 Of the sons of Azgad, Yokhanan son of Qatan, and with him an hundred and ten men:

39 Of the sons of Adoniqam the last, and these are the names of them, Eliphalet, Yu'EL, and ShemaYAH, and with them seventy men:

40 Of the sons of Bigwai, Uthai the son of ZekarYAH, and with him seventy men.

41 And these I gathered together to the river called Theras, where we pitched our tents three days: and then I surveyed them.

42 But when I had found there none of the priests and Lewy'im,

43 Then sent I unto Eliezer, and Ari'EL, and ShemaYAH,

44 And El'nathan, and Yarib, and Nathan, El'nathan, ZekarYAHU, and Meshulam, principal men and learned.

45 And I bade them that they should go unto Iddo the captain, who was in the place of the treasury:

46 And commanded them that they should speak unto Iddo, and to his brethren, and to the treasurers in that place, to send us such men as might execute the priests' office in the house of YAHOWAH our ELOHIM.

47 And by the mighty hand of our YAHOWAH our ELOHIM they brought unto us skilful men of the sons of Makhli the son of Lewi, the son of Yisra'EL, ShaeravYAH, and his sons, and his brethren, who were eighteen.

48 And KhashabYAH, and YeshaYAH, his brother, of the sons of KhananYAH, and their sons, were twenty men.

49 And of the servants of the temple whom Dawid had ordained, and the principal men for the service of the Lewy'im to wit, the servants of the temple two hundred and twenty, the catalogue of whose names were shewed.

50 And there I vowed a fast unto the young men before our YAHOWAH, to desire of him a prosperous journey both for us and them that were with us, for our children, and for the cattle:

51 For I was ashamed to ask the king footmen, and horsemen, and conduct for safeguard against our adversaries.

52 For we had said unto the king, that the power of YAHOWAH our ELOHIM should be with them that seek him, to support them in all ways.

53 And again we besought our YAHOWAH as touching these things, and found him favourable unto us.

54 Then I separated twelve of the chief of the priests, SharabYAH, and KhashabYAH, and ten men of their brethren with them:

55 And I weighed them the gold, and the silver, and the holy vessels of the house of our YAHOWAH, which the king, and his council, and the princes, and all Yisra'EL, had given.

56 And when I had weighed it, I delivered unto them six hundred and fifty talents of silver, and silver vessels of an hundred talents, and an hundred talents of gold,

57 And twenty golden vessels, and twelve vessels of brass, even of fine brass, glittering like gold.

58 And I said unto them, Both ye are holy unto YAHOWAH, and the vessels are holy, and the gold and the silver is a vow unto YAHOWAH, YAHOWAH of our fathers.

59 Watch ye, and keep them till ye deliver them to the chief of the priests and Lewy'im, and to the principal men of the families of Yisra'EL, in Yerushalem, into the chambers of the house of our ELOHIM.

60 So the priests and the Lewy'im, who had received the silver and the gold and the vessels, brought them unto Yerushalem, into the temple of YAHOWAH.

61 And from the river Theras we departed the twelfth day of the first month, and came to Yerushalem by the mighty hand of our YAHOWAH, which was with us: and from the beginning of our journey YAHOWAH delivered us from every enemy, and so we came to Yerushalem.

62 And when we had been there three days, the gold and silver that was weighed was delivered in the house of our YAHOWAH on the fourth day unto Meramoth the priest the son of UriYAH.

63 And with him was Eleazar the son of Pinkhas, and with them were Yozabad the son of Yeshua and NoadYAH the son of Binoi, Lewy'im: all was delivered them by number and weight.

64 And all the weight of them was written up the same hour.

65 Moreover they that were come out of the captivity offered sacrifice unto YAHOWAH ELOHIM of Yisra'EL, even twelve bullocks for all Yisra'EL, fourscore and sixteen rams,

66 Threescore and twelve lambs, goats for a shalom offering, twelve; all of them a sacrifice to YAHOWAH.

67 And they delivered the king's commandments unto the king's stewards' and to the governors of Aram and Kena'an; and they honoured the people and the temple of ELOHIM.

68 Now when these things were done, the rulers came unto me, and said,

69 The nation of Yisra'EL, the princes, the priests and Lewy'im, have not put away from them the strange people of the land, nor the pollutions of the Gentiles to wit, of the Kena'anim, Khittim, Perizzim, Yebusim, and the Moabim, Mitzrim, and Edomim.

70 For both they and their sons have married with their daughters, and the holy seed is mixed with the strange people of the land; and from the beginning of this matter the rulers and the great men have been partakers of this iniquity.

71 And as soon as I had heard these things, I rent my clothes, and the holy garment, and pulled off the hair from off my head and beard, and sat me down sad and very heavy.

72 So all they that were then moved at the word of YAHOWAH ELOHIM of Yisra'EL assembled unto me, whilst I mourned for the iniquity: but I sat still full of heaviness until the evening sacrifice.

73 Then rising up from the fast with my clothes and the holy garment rent, and bowing my knees, and stretching forth my hands unto YAHOWAH,

74 I said, O YAHOWAH, I am confounded and ashamed before thy face;

75 For our sins are multiplied above our heads, and our ignorances have reached up unto heaven.

76 For ever since the time of our fathers we have been and are in great sin, even unto this day.

77 And for our sins and our fathers' we with our brethren and our kings and our priests were given up unto the kings of the earth, to the sword, and to captivity, and for a prey with shame, unto this day.

78 And now in some measure hath mercy been shewed unto us from thee, O YAHOWAH, that there should be left us a root and a name in the place of thy sanctuary;

79 And to discover unto us a light in the house of YAHOWAH our ELOHIM, and to give us food in the time of our servitude.

80 Yea, when we were in bondage, we were not forsaken of our YAHOWAH; but he made us gracious before the kings of Paras, so that they gave us food;

81 Yea, and honoured the temple of our YAHOWAH, and raised up the desolate Tzion, that they have given us a sure abiding in Yehudah and Yerushalem.

82 And now, O YAHOWAH, what shall we say, having these things? for we have transgressed thy commandments, which thou gavest by the hand of thy servants the prophets, saying,

83 That the land, which ye enter into to possess as an heritage, is a land polluted with the pollutions of the strangers of the land, and they have filled it with their uncleanness.

84 Therefore now shall ye not join your daughters unto their sons, neither shall ye take their daughters unto your sons.

85 Moreover ye shall never seek to have shalom with them, that ye may be strong, and eat the good things of the land, and that ye may leave the inheritance of the land unto your children for evermore.

86 And all that is befallen is done unto us for our wicked works and great sins; for thou, O YAHOWAH, didst make our sins light,

87 And didst give unto us such a root: but we have turned back again to transgress thy Torah, and to mingle ourselves with the uncleanness of the Gentiles of the land.

88 Mightest not thou be angry with us to destroy us, till thou hadst left us neither root, seed, nor name?

89 O YAHOWAH of Yisra'EL, thou art true: for we are left a root this day.

90 Behold, now are we before thee in our iniquities, for we cannot stand any longer by reason of these things before thee.

91 And as Ezra in his prayer made his confession, weeping, and lying flat upon the ground before the temple, there gathered unto him from Yerushalem a very great multitude of men and women and children: for there was great weeping among the multitude.

92 Then ShekanYAH the son of Yekhi'EL, one of the sons of Yisra'EL, called out, and said, O Ezra, we have sinned against YAHOWAH ELOHIM, we have married strange women of the Gentiles of the land, and now is all Yisra'EL aloft.

93 Let us make an oath to YAHOWAH, that we will put away all our wives, which we have taken of the heathen, with their children,

94 Like as thou hast decreed, and as many as do obey the Torah of YAHOWAH.

95 Arise and put in execution: for to thee doth this matter appertain, and we will be with thee: do valiantly.

96 So Ezra arose, and took an oath of the chief of the priests and Lewy'im of all Yisra'EL to do after these things; and so they sware.

9 Then Ezra rising from the court of the temple went to the chamber of Yahokhanan the son of El'yashib,

2 And remained there, and did eat no meat nor drink water, mourning for the great iniquities of the multitude.

3 And there was a proclamation in all Yehudah and Yerushalem to all them that were of the captivity, that they should be gathered together at Yerushalem:

4 And that whosoever met not there within two or three days according as the elders that bare rule appointed, their cattle should be seized to the use of the temple, and himself cast out from them that were of the captivity.

5 And in three days were all they of the tribe of Yehudah and Benyamin gathered together at Yerushalem the twentieth day of the ninth month.

6 And all the multitude sat trembling in the broad court of the temple because of the present foul weather.

7 So Ezra arose up, and said unto them, Ye have transgressed the Torah in marrying strange wives, thereby to increase the sins of Yisra'EL.

8 And now by confessing give glory unto YAHOWAH ELOHIM of our fathers,

9 And do his will, and separate yourselves from the heathen of the land, and from the strange women.

10 Then cried the whole multitude, and said with a loud voice, Like as thou hast spoken, so will we do.

11 But forasmuch as the people are many, and it is foul weather, so that we cannot stand without, and this is not a work of a day or two, seeing our sin in these things is spread far:

12 Therefore let the rulers of the multitude stay, and let all them of our habitations that have strange wives come at the time appointed,

13 And with them the rulers and judges of every place, till we turn away the wrath of YAHOWAH from us for this matter.

14 Then Yahonathan the son of Asah'EL and YakhazYAH the son of Tiqwah accordingly took this matter upon them: and Meshulam and Shabtai the Lewiyi helped them.

15 And they that were of the captivity did according to all these things.

16 And Ezra the priest chose unto him the principal men of their families, all by name: and in the first day of the tenth month they sat together to examine the matter.

17 So their cause that held strange wives was brought to an end in the first day of the first month.

18 And of the priests that were come together, and had strange wives, there were found:

19 Of the sons of Yahoshua the son of Yaho-Tzadaq, and his brethren; MaasaYAH and Eliezer, and Yarib and GedalYAH.

20 And they gave their hands to put away their wives and to offer rams to make reconcilement for their errors.

21 And of the sons of Immer; Khanani, and ZebadYAH, and MaasaYAH, and ShemaYAH, and Yekhi'EL, and UzziYAH.

22 And of the sons of Pashkhur; Elioainai, MaasaYAH, Yishma'EL, and Nathan'EL, and Yozabad and Eleasah.

23 And of the Lewy'im; Yozabad, and Shimi, and QalaYAH, who was called Qelita, and PetachYAH, and Yehudah, and Eliezer.

24 Of the holy singers; El'yashib.

25 Of the porters; Shalom, and Telam and Uri.

26 Of them of Yisra'EL, of the sons of Parash; YirmeYAH, and YizziYAH, and MalkiYAH, and Meyamin, and Eleazar, and KhashabYAH, and

BenaYAH.

27 Of the sons of Ailam; MathanYAH, ZekarYA-HU, and Yekhi'EL, and Abdi, and Yeramoth, and EliYAH.

28 And of the sons of Zathu; Elioanai, El'yashib, MathanYAH, Yeramoth, and Zabad, and Aziza.

29 Of the sons of Babai; Yahokhanan, and Khanan-YAH and Zabai, and Athlai.

30 Of the sons of Bani; Meshulam, Maluk, AdaYAH, Yashub, Yishal, and Yeramoth.

31 And of the sons of Pakhath; Moab, and Adna, MaasaYAH, and BenaYAH, and MathanYAH, and Betzal'EL, Binnoi, and Menassheh.

32 And of the sons of Anan; El'yon and YishiYAH, and MalkiYAH, and ShemaYAH, and Shimon, Benyamin, Maluk, ShamarYAH:

33 And of the sons of Khashum; Matnai, and Matathah, and Zakar, Eliphalet, and Menassheh, and Shimi.

34 And of the sons of Bani; YirmeYAH, Maadai, Amram, Yu'EL, BenaYAH, and BadYAH, and Yonah, Miramoth, and El'yashib, and MathanYAH, Matnai, Yaasu, and of the sons of Shimi; Shele-mYAH, Nathan, AdaYAH, and of the sons of Zakai, Shashai, Sharai, Azar'EL, ShelemYAH, Shemar-YAH, Shalum, AmarYAH, Yoseph.

35 And of the sons of Nebo; Yay'EL, MattitYAHU, Zabad, Zebina, Yadai, Yo'EL, BenaYAH.

36 All these had taken strange wives, and they put them away with their children.

37 And the priests and Lewy'im, and they that were of Yisra'EL, dwelt in Yerushalem, and in the country, in the first day of the seventh month: so the children of Yisra'EL were in their habitations.

38 And the whole multitude came together with one accord into the broad place of the holy porch toward the east:

39 And they spake unto Ezra the priest and reader, that he would bring the Torah of Mosheh, that was given of YAHOWAH ELOHIM of Yisra'EL.

40 So Ezra the chief priest brought the Torah unto the whole multitude from man to woman, and to all the priests, to hear Torah in the first day of the seventh month.

41 And he read in the broad court before the holy porch from morning unto midday, before both men and women; and the multitude gave heed unto the Torah.

42 And Ezra the priest and reader of the Torah stood up upon a pulpit of wood, which was made for that purpose.

43 And there stood up by him MattitYAHU, Shema, AnanYAH, UriYAH, KhilqiYAH, MaasaYAH, upon the right hand:

44 And upon his left hand stood PedaYAH, Misha'EL, MalkiYAH, Khashum, and Khashbadanah, ZekarYAH, Meshulam.

45 And Ezra opened the book of the Torah before the multitude: for he sat honourably in the first place in the sight of them all.

46 And when he opened the Torah, they stood all straight up. So Ezra blessed YAHOWAH ELOHIM Most High, the ELOHIM of hosts, Almighty.

47 And all the people answered, Amen; and lifting up their hands they fell to the ground, and worshipped YAHOWAH.

48 And Yahoshua, Bani, SharabYAH, Yamin, Aqqov, Shabtai, HodYAH, MaasaYAH, and Qelita, AzarYAH, and Yozabad, and Khanan, PelaYAH, the Lewy'im, taught the Torah of YAHOWAH, making them withal to understand it.

49 Then spake the governor unto Ezra the chief priest. and reader, and to the Lewy'im that taught the multitude, even to all, saying,

50 This day is holy unto YAHOWAH; (for they all wept when they heard the Torah:)

51 Go then, and eat the fat, and drink the sweet, and send part to them that have nothing;

52 For this day is holy unto YAHOWAH: and be not sorrowful; for YAHOWAH will bring you to honour.

53 So the Lewy'im published all things to the people, saying, This day is holy to YAHOWAH; be not sorrowful.

54 Then went they their way, every one to eat and drink, and make merry, and to give part to them that had nothing, and to make great cheer;

55 Because they understood the words wherein they were instructed, and for the which they had been assembled.

THE SECOND BOOK OF
EDRAS
ALSO KNOWN AS THE FORTH BOOK OF EZRA

1 The second book of the prophet Ezra, the son of SeraYAH, the son of AzarYAH, the son of Khilqi-YAH, the son of Shalum, the sou of Tzadoq, the son of Akhitub,

2 The son of AmarYAH, the son of AzarYAH, the son of Merayoth, the son of ZerakhYAH, the son of Uzzi, the son of Buqqi, the son of Abishua, the son of Pinkhas, the son of Eleazar,

3 The son of Aharon, of the tribe of Lewi; which was captive in the land of the Medes, in the reign of Artakh'shasheth king of the Persians.

4 And the word of YAHOWAH came unto me, saying,

5 Go thy way, and shew my people their sinful deeds, and their children their wickedness which they have done against me; that they may tell their children's children:

6 Because the sins of their fathers are increased in them: for they have forgotten me, and have offered unto strange elohim.

7 Am not I even he that brought them out of the land of Mitzraim, from the house of bondage? but they have provoked me unto wrath, and despised my counsels.

8 Pull thou off then the hair of thy head, and cast all evil upon them, for they have not been obedient unto my Torah, but it is a rebellious people.

9 How long shall I forbear them, into whom I have done so much good?

10 Many kings have I destroyed for their sakes; Pharaoh with his servants and all his power have I smitten down.

11 All the nations have I destroyed before them, and in the east I have scattered the people of two provinces, even of Tzor and Tzidon, and have slain all their enemies.

12 Speak thou therefore unto them, saying, Thus saith YAHOWAH,

13 I led you through the sea and in the beginning gave you a large and safe passage; I gave you Mosheh for a leader, and Aharon for a priest.

14 I gave you light in a pillar of fire, and great wonders have I done among you; yet have ye forgotten me, saith YAHOWAH.

15 Thus saith the Almighty YAHOWAH, The quails were as a token to you; I gave you tents for your safeguard: nevertheless ye murmured there,

16 And triumphed not in my name for the destruction of your enemies, but ever to this day do ye yet murmur.

17 Where are the benefits that I have done for you? when ye were hungry and thirsty in the wilderness, did ye not cry unto me,

18 Saying, Why hast thou brought us into this wilderness to kill us? it had been better for us to have served the Mitzrim, than to die in this wilderness.

19 Then had I pity upon your mournings, and gave you manna to eat; so ye did eat angels' bread.

20 When ye were thirsty, did I not cleave the rock, and waters flowed out to your fill? for the heat I covered you with the leaves of the trees.

21 I divided among you a fruitful land, I cast out the Kena'anim, the Pherezites, and the Phelishtim, before you: what shall I yet do more for you? saith YAHOWAH.

22 Thus saith the Almighty YAHOWAH, When ye were in the wilderness, in the river of the Emorim, being athirst, and blaspheming my name,

23 I gave you not fire for your blasphemies, but cast a tree in the water, and made the river sweet.

24 What shall I do unto thee, O Ya'aqob? thou, Yehudah, wouldest not obey me: I will turn me to other nations, and unto those will I give my name, that they may keep my statutes.

25 Seeing ye have forsaken me, I will forsake you also; when ye desire me to be gracious unto you, I shall have no mercy upon you.

26 Whensoever ye shall call upon me, I will not hear you: for ye have defiled your hands with blood, and your feet are swift to commit manslaughter.

27 Ye have not as it were forsaken me, but your own selves, saith YAHOWAH.

28 Thus saith the Almighty YAHOWAH, Have I not prayed you as a father his sons, as a mother her daughters, and a nurse her young babes,

29 That ye would be my people, and I should be your ELOHIM; that ye would be my children, and I should be your father?

30 I gathered you together, as a hen gathereth her chickens under her wings: but now, what shall I do unto you? I will cast you out from my face.

31 When ye offer unto me, I will turn my face from you: for your solemn feastdays, your Renewed Months, and your circumcisions, have I forsaken.

32 I sent unto you my servants the prophets, whom ye have taken and slain, and torn their bodies in pieces, whose blood I will require of your hands, saith YAHOWAH.

33 Thus saith the Almighty YAHOWAH, Your house is desolate, I will cast you out as the wind doth stubble.

34 And your children shall not be fruitful; for they have despised my commandment, and done the thing that is an evil before me.

35 Your houses will I give to a people that shall come; which not having heard of me yet shall believe me; to whom I have shewed no signs, yet they shall do that I have commanded them.

36 They have seen no prophets, yet they shall call their sins to remembrance, and acknowledge them.

37 I take to witness the grace of the people to come, whose little ones rejoice in gladness: and though they have not seen me with bodily eyes, yet in RUAKH they believe the thing that I say.

38 And now, brother, behold what glory; and see the people that come from the east:

39 Unto whom I will give for leaders, Abraham, Yitzkhaq, and Ya'aqob, Hoshea, Amos, and Mikah, Yo'EL, ObadYAH, and Yonah,

40 Nakhum, and Khabaquq, TzephanYAH, Khagai, ZekarYAH, and Malaki, which is called also an Angel of YAHOWAH.

2 Thus saith YAHOWAH, I brought this people out of bondage, and I gave them my commandments by menservants the prophets; whom they would not hear, but despised my counsels.

2 The mother that bare them saith unto them, Go your way, ye children; for I am a widow and forsaken.

3 I brought you up with gladness; but with sorrow and heaviness have I lost you: for ye have sinned before YAHOWAH your ELOHIM, and done that thing that is evil before him.

4 But what shall I now do unto you? I am a widow and forsaken: go your way, O my children, and ask mercy of YAHOWAH.

5 As for me, O father, I call upon thee for a witness over the mother of these children, which would not keep my covenant,

6 That thou bring them to confusion, and their mother to a spoil, that there may be no offspring of them.

7 Let them be scattered abroad among the heathen, let their names be put out of the earth: for they have despised my covenant.

8 Woe be unto thee, Asshur, thou that hidest the unrighteous in thee! O thou wicked people, remember what I did unto Sedom and Amorah;

9 Whose land lieth in clods of pitch and heaps of ashes: even so also will I do unto them that hear me not, saith the Almighty YAHOWAH.

10 Thus saith YAHOWAH unto Ezra, Tell my people that I will give them the kingdom of Yerushalem, which I would have given unto Yisra'EL.

11 Their glory also will I take unto me, and give these the everlasting tabernacles, which I had prepared for them.

12 They shall have the tree of life for an ointment of sweet savour; they shall neither labour, nor be weary.

13 Go, and ye shall receive: pray for few days unto you, that they may be shortened: the kingdom is already prepared for you: watch.

14 Take heaven and earth to witness; for I have broken the evil in pieces, and created the good: for I live, saith YAHOWAH.

15 Mother, embrace thy children, and bring them up with gladness, make their feet as fast as a pillar:

for I have chosen thee, saith YAHOWAH.

16 And those that be dead will I raise up again from their places, and bring them out of the graves: for I have known my name in Yisra'EL.

17 Fear not, thou mother of the children: for I have chosen thee, saith YAHOWAH.

18 For thy help will I send my servants YeshaYAH and YirmeYAHU, after whose counsel I have sanctified and prepared for thee twelve trees laden with divers fruits,

19 And as many fountains flowing with milk and honey, and seven mighty mountains, whereupon there grow roses and lilies, whereby I will fill thy children with joy.

20 Do right to the widow, judge for the fatherless, give to the poor, defend the orphan, clothe the naked,

21 Heal the broken and the weak, laugh not a lame man to scorn, defend the maimed, and let the blind man come into the sight of my clearness.

22 Keep the old and young within thy walls.

23 Wheresoever thou findest the dead, take them and bury them, and I will give thee the first place in my resurrection.

24 Abide still, O my people, and take thy rest, for thy quietness still come.

25 Nourish thy children, O thou good nurse; stablish their feet.

26 As for the servants whom I have given thee, there shall not one of them perish; for I will require them from among thy number.

27 Be not weary: for when the day of trouble and heaviness cometh, others shall weep and be sorrowful, but thou shalt be merry and have abundance.

28 The heathen shall envy thee, but they shall be able to do nothing against thee, saith YAHOWAH.

29 My hands shall cover thee, so that thy children shall not see hell.

30 Be joyful, O thou mother, with thy children; for I will deliver thee, saith YAHOWAH.

31 Remember thy children that sleep, for I shall bring them out of the sides of the earth, and shew mercy unto them: for I am merciful, saith YAHOWAH Almighty.

32 Embrace thy children until I come and shew mercy unto them: for my wells run over, and my grace shall not fail.

33 I Ezra received a charge of YAHOWAH upon the mount Choraeb, that I should go unto Yisra'EL; but when I came unto them, they set me at nought, and despised the commandment of YAHOWAH.

34 And therefore I say unto you, O ye heathen, that hear and understand, look for your Shepherd, he shall give you everlasting rest; for he is nigh at hand, that shall come in the end of the world.

35 Be ready to the reward of the kingdom, for the everlasting light shall shine upon you for evermore.

36 Flee the shadow of this world, receive the joyfulness of your glory: I testify my Saviour openly.

37 O receive the gift that is given you, and be glad, giving thanks unto him that hath led

you to the heavenly kingdom.

38 Arise up and stand, behold the number of those that be sealed in the feast of YAHOWAH;

39 Which are departed from the shadow of the world, and have received glorious garments of YAHOWAH.

40 Take thy number, O Tzion, and shut up those of thine that are clothed in white, which have fulfilled the Torah of YAHOWAH.

41 The number of thy children, whom thou longedst for, is fulfilled: beseech the power of YAHOWAH, that thy people, which have been called from the beginning, may be hallowed.

42 I Ezra saw upon the mount Tzion a great people, whom I could not number, and they all praised YAHOWAH with songs.

43 And in the midst of them there was a young man of a high stature, taller than all the rest, and upon every one of their heads he set crowns, and was more exalted; which I marvelled at greatly.

44 So I asked the Angel, and said, Adon, what are these?

45 He answered and said unto me, These be they that have put off the mortal clothing, and put on the immortal, and have confessed the name of ELOHIM: now are they crowned, and receive palms.

46 Then said I unto the Angel, What young person is it that crowneth them, and giveth them palms in their hands?

47 So he answered and said unto me, It is the SON of ELOHIM, whom they have confessed in the world. Then began I greatly to commend them that stood so stiffly for the name of YAHOWAH.

48 Then the Angel said unto me, Go thy way, and tell my people what manner of things, and how great wonders of YAHOWAH thy ELOHIM, thou hast seen.

3 In the thirtieth year after the ruin of the city I was in Babel, and lay troubled upon my bed, and my thoughts came up over my heart:

2 For I saw the desolation of Tzion, and the wealth of them that dwelt at Babel.

3 And my ruakh was sore moved, so that I began to speak words full of fear to the Most High, and said,

4 O YAHOWAH, who bearest rule, thou spakest at the beginning, when thou didst plant the earth, and that thyself alone, and commandedst the people,

5 And gavest a body unto Adam without soul, which was the workmanship of thine hands, and didst breathe into him the breath of life, and he was made living before thee.

6 And thou leadest him into paradise, which thy right hand had planted, before ever the earth came forward.

7 And unto him thou gavest commandment to love thy way: which he transgressed, and immediately thou appointedst death in him and in his generations, of whom came nations, tribes, people, and kindreds, out of number.

8 And every people walked after their own will, and did wonderful things before thee, and despised thy commandments.

9 And again in process of time thou broughtest the flood upon those that dwelt in the world, and destroyedst them.

10 And it came to pass in every of them, that as death was to Adam, so was the flood to these.

11 Nevertheless one of them thou leftest, namely, Noakh with his household, of whom came all righteous men.

12 And it happened, that when they that dwelt upon the earth began to multiply, and had gotten them many children, and were a great people, they began again to be more ungodly than the first.

13 Now when they lived so wickedly before thee, thou didst choose thee a man from among them, whose name was Abraham.

14 Him thou lovedst, and unto him only thou shewedst thy will:

15 And madest an everlasting covenant with him, promising him that thou wouldest never forsake his seed.

16 And unto him thou gavest Yitzkhaq, and unto Yitzkhaq also thou gavest Ya'aqob and Esau. As for Ya'aqob, thou didst choose him to thee, and put by Esau: and so Ya'aqob became a great multitude.

17 And it came to pass, that when thou leadest his seed out of Mitzraim, thou broughtest them up to the mount Sinai.

18 And bowing the heavens, thou didst set fast the earth, movedst the whole world, and madest the depths to tremble, and troubledst the men of that age.

19 And thy glory went through four gates, of fire, and of earthquake, and of wind, and of cold; that thou mightest give the Torah unto the seed of Ya'aqob, and diligence unto the generation of Yisra'EL.

20 And yet tookest thou not away from them a wicked heart, that thy Torah might bring forth fruit in them.

21 For the first Adam bearing a wicked heart transgressed, and was overcome; and so be all they that are born of him.

22 Thus infirmity was made permanent; and the Torah (also) in the heart of the people with the malignity of the root; so that the good departed away, and the evil abode still.

23 So the times passed away, and the years were brought to an end: then didst thou raise thee up a servant, called Dawid:

24 Whom thou commandedst to build a city unto thy name, and to offer incense and oblations unto thee therein.

25 When this was done many years, then they that inhabited the city forsook thee,

26 And in all things did even as Adam and all his generations had done: for they also had a wicked heart:

27 And so thou gavest thy city over into the hands of thine enemies.

28 Are their deeds then any better that inhabit Babel, that they should therefore have the dominion over Tzion?

29 For when I came thither, and had seen impieties without number, then my soul saw many evildoers in this thirtieth year, so that my heart failed me.

30 For I have seen how thou sufferest them sinning, and hast spared wicked doers: and hast destroyed thy people, and hast preserved thine enemies, and hast not signified it.

31 I do not remember how this way may be left: Are they then of Babel better than they of Tzion?

32 Or is there any other people that knoweth thee beside Yisra'EL? or what generation hath so believed thy covenants as Ya'aqob?

33 And yet their reward appeareth not, and their labour hath no fruit: for I have gone here and there through the heathen, and I see that they flow in wealth, and think not upon thy commandments.

34 Weigh thou therefore our wickedness now in the balance, and their's also that dwell the world; and so shall thy name no where be found but in Yisra'EL.

35 Or when was it that they which dwell upon the earth have not sinned in thy sight? or what people have so kept thy commandments?

36 Thou shalt find that Yisra'EL by name hath kept thy precepts; but not the heathen.

4 And the Angel that was sent unto me, whose name was Uri'EL, gave me an answer,

2 And said, Thy heart hath gone to far in this world, and thinkest thou to comprehend the way of the Most High?

3 Then said I, Yea, Adoni. And he answered me, and said, I am sent to shew thee three ways, and to set forth three similitudes before thee:

4 Whereof if thou canst declare me one, I will shew thee also the way that thou desirest to see, and I shall shew thee from whence the wicked heart cometh.

5 And I said, Tell on, Adoni. Then said he unto me, Go thy way, weigh me the weight of the fire, or measure me the blast of the wind, or call me again the day that is past.

6 Then answered I and said, What man is able to do that, that thou shouldest ask such things of me?

7 And he said unto me, If I should ask thee how great dwellings are in the midst of the sea, or how many springs are in the beginning of the deep, or how many springs are above the firmament, or which are the outgoings of paradise:

8 Peradventure thou wouldest say unto me, I never went down into the deep, nor as yet into hell, neither did I ever climb up into heaven.

9 Nevertheless now have I asked thee but only of the fire and wind, and of the day wherethrough thou hast passed, and of things from which thou canst not be separated, and yet canst thou give me no answer of them.

10 He said moreover unto me, Thine own things, and such as are grown up with thee, canst thou not know;

11 How should thy vessel then be able to comprehend the way of the Highest, and, the world being now outwardly corrupted to understand the corruption that is evident in my sight?

12 Then said I unto him, It were better that we were not at all, than that we should live still in wickedness, and to suffer, and not to know wherefore.

13 He answered me, and said, I went into a forest into a plain, and the trees took counsel,

14 And said, Come, let us go and make war against the sea that it may depart away before us, and that we may make us more woods.

15 The floods of the sea also in like manner took counsel, and said, Come, let us go up and subdue the woods of the plain, that there also we may make us another country.

16 The thought of the wood was in vain, for the fire came and consumed it.

17 The thought of the floods of the sea came likewise to nought, for the sand stood up and stopped them.

18 If thou wert judge now betwixt these two, whom wouldest thou begin to justify? or whom wouldest thou condemn?

19 I answered and said, Verily it is a foolish thought that they both have devised, for the ground is given unto the wood, and the sea also hath his place to bear his floods.

20 Then answered he me, and said, Thou hast given a right judgment, but why judgest thou not thyself also?

21 For like as the ground is given unto the wood, and the sea to his floods: even so they that dwell upon the earth may understand nothing but that which is upon the earth: and he that dwelleth above the heavens may only understand the things that are above the height of the heavens.

22 Then answered I and said, I beseech thee, O Adoni, let me have understanding:

23 For it was not my mind to be curious of the high things, but of such as pass by us daily, namely, wherefore Yisra'EL is given up as a reproach to the heathen, and for what cause the people whom thou hast loved is given over unto ungodly Gentiles, and why the Torah of our forefathers is brought to nought, and the written covenants come to none effect,

24 And we pass away out of the world as grasshoppers, and our life is astonishment and fear, and we are not worthy to obtain mercy.

25 What will he then do unto his name whereby we are called? of these things have I asked.

26 Then answered he me, and said, The more thou searchest, the more thou shalt marvel; for the world hasteth fast to pass away,

27 And cannot comprehend the things that are promised to the righteous in time to come: for this world is full of unrighteousness and infirmities.

28 But as concerning the things whereof thou askest me, I will tell thee; for the evil is sown, but the destruction thereof is not yet come.

29 If therefore that which is sown be not turned upside down, and if the place where the evil is sown pass not away, then cannot it come that is sown with good.

30 For the grain of evil seed hath been sown in the heart of Adam from the beginning, and how much ungodliness hath it brought up unto this time? and how much shall it yet bring forth until the time of threshing come?

31 Ponder now by thyself, how great fruit of wickedness the grain of evil seed hath brought forth.

32 And when the ears shall be cut down, which are without number, how great a floor shall they fill?

33 Then I answered and said, How, and when shall these things come to pass? wherefore are our years few and evil?

34 And he answered me, saying, Do not thou hasten above the Most Highest: for thy haste is in vain to be above him, for thou hast much exceeded.

35 Did not the souls also of the righteous ask question of these things in their chambers, saying, How long shall I hope on this fashion? when cometh the fruit of the floor of our reward?

36 And unto these things Uri'EL the archangel gave them answer, and said, Even when the number of seeds is filled in you: for he hath weighed the world in the balance.

37 By measure hath he measured the times; and by number hath he numbered the times; and he doth not move nor stir them, until the said measure be fulfilled.

38 Then answered I and said, O YAHOWAH that bearest rule, even we all are full of impiety.

39 And for our sakes peradventure it is that the floors of the righteous are not filled, because of the sins of them that dwell upon the earth.

40 So he answered me, and said, Go thy way to a woman with child, and ask of her when she hath fulfilled her nine months, if her womb may keep the birth any longer within her.

41 Then said I, No, Adoni, that can she not. And he said unto me, In the grave the chambers of souls are like the womb of a woman:

42 For like as a woman that travaileth maketh haste to escape the necessity of the travail: even so do these places haste to deliver those things that are committed unto them.

43 From the beginning, look, what thou desirest to see, it shall be shewed thee.

44 Then answered I and said, If I have found favour in thy sight, and if it be possible, and if I be meet therefore,

45 Shew me then whether there be more to come than is past, or more past than is to come.

46 What is past I know, but what is for to come I know not.

47 And he said unto me, Stand up upon the right side, and I shall expound the similitude unto thee.

48 So I stood, and saw, and, behold, an hot burning oven passed by before me: and it happened that when the flame was gone by I looked, and, behold, the smoke remained still.

49 After this there passed by before me a watery cloud, and sent down much rain with a storm; and when the stormy rain was past, the drops remained still.

50 Then said he unto me, Consider with thyself; as the rain is more than the drops, and as the fire is greater than the smoke; but the drops and the smoke remain behind: so the quantity which is past did more exceed.

51 Then I prayed, and said, May I live, thinkest thou, until that time? or what shall happen in those days?

52 He answered me, and said, As for the tokens whereof thou askest me, I may tell thee of them in part: but as touching thy life, I am not sent to shew thee; for I do not know it.

5 Nevertheless as coming the tokens, behold, the days shall come, that they which dwell upon earth shall be taken in a great number, and the way of truth shall be hidden, and the land shall be barren of faith.

2 But iniquity shall be increased above that which now thou seest, or that thou hast heard long ago.

3 And the land, that thou seest now to have root, shalt thou see wasted suddenly.

4 But if the Most High grant thee to live, thou shalt see after the third trumpet that the sun shall suddenly shine again in the night, and the moon thrice in the day:

5 And blood shall drop out of wood, and the stone shall give his voice, and the people shall be troubled:

6 And even he shall rule, whom they look not for that dwell upon the earth, and the fowls shall take their flight away together:

7 And the Sodomitish sea shall cast out fish, and make a noise in the night, which many have not known: but they shall all hear the voice thereof.

8 There shall be a confusion also in many places, and the fire shall be oft sent out again, and the wild beasts shall change their places, and menstruous women shall bring forth Nephilim:

9 And salt waters shall be found in the sweet, and all friends shall destroy one another; then shall wit hide itself, and understanding withdraw itself into his secret chamber,

10 And shall be sought of many, and yet not be found: then shall unrighteousness and incontinency be multiplied upon earth.

11 One land also shall ask another, and say, Is righteousness that maketh a man righteous gone through thee? And it shall say, No.

12 At the same time shall men hope, but nothing obtain: they shall labour, but their ways shall not prosper.

13 To shew thee such tokens I have leave; and if thou wilt pray again, and weep as now, and fast even days, thou shalt hear yet greater things.

14 Then I awaked, and an extreme fearfulness went through all my body, and my mind was

troubled, so that it fainted.

15 So the Angel that was come to talk with me held me, comforted me, and set me up upon my feet.

16 And in the second night it came to pass, that She'alti'EL the captain of the people came unto me, saying, Where hast thou been? and why is thy countenance so heavy?

17 Knowest thou not that Yisra'EL is committed unto thee in the land of their captivity?

18 Up then, and eat bread, and forsake us not, as the shepherd that leaveth his flock in the hands of cruel wolves.

19 Then said I unto him, Go thy ways from me, and come not nigh me. And he heard what I said, and went from me.

20 And so I fasted seven days, mourning and weeping, like as Uri'EL the Angel commanded me.

21 And after seven days so it was, that the thoughts of my heart were very grievous unto me again,

22 And my soul recovered the RUAKH of understanding, and I began to talk with the Most High again,

23 And said, O YAHOWAH that bearest rule, of every wood of the earth, and of all the trees thereof, thou hast chosen thee one vine:

24 And of all lands of the whole world thou hast chosen thee one pit: and of all the flowers thereof one lily:

25 And of all the depths of the sea thou hast filled thee one river: and of all builded cities thou hast hallowed Tzion unto thyself:

26 And of all the fowls that are created thou hast named thee one dove: and of all the cattle that are made thou hast provided thee one sheep:

27 And among all the multitudes of people thou hast gotten thee one people: and unto this people, whom thou lovedst, thou gavest a Torah that is approved of all.

28 And now, O ADONAI, why hast thou given this one people over unto many? and upon the one root hast thou prepared others, and why hast thou scattered thy only one people among many?

29 And they which did gainsay thy promises, and believed not thy covenants, have trodden them down.

30 If thou didst so much hate thy people, yet shouldest thou punish them with thine own hands.

31 Now when I had spoken these words, the Angel that came to me the night afore was sent unto me,

32 And said unto me, Hear me, and I will instruct thee; hearken to the thing that I say, and I shall tell thee more.

33 And I said, Speak on, Adoni. Then said he unto me, Thou art sore troubled in mind for Yisra'EL's sake: lovest thou that people better than he that made them?

34 And I said, No, Adoni: but of very grief have I spoken: for my reins pain me every hour, while I labour to comprehend the way of the Most High, and to seek out part of his judgment.

35 And he said unto me, Thou canst not. And I said, Wherefore, Adoni? whereunto was I born then? or why was not my mother's womb then my grave, that I might not have seen the travail of Ya'aqob, and the wearisome toil of the stock of Yisra'EL?

36 And he said unto me, Number me the things that are not yet come, gather me together the dross that are scattered abroad, make me the flowers green again that are withered,

37 Open me the places that are closed, and bring me forth the winds that in them are shut up, shew me the image of a voice: and then I will declare to thee the thing that thou labourest to know.

38 And I said, O YAHOWAH that bearest rule, who may know these things, but he that hath not his dwelling with men?

39 As for me, I am unwise: how may I then speak of these things whereof thou askest me?

40 Then said he unto me, Like as thou canst do none of these things that I have spoken of, even so canst thou not find out my judgment, or in the end the love that I have promised unto my people.

41 And I said, Behold, O Adoni, yet art thou nigh unto them that be reserved till the end: and what shall they do that have been before me, or we that be now, or they that shall come after us?

42 And he said unto me, I will liken my judgment unto a ring: like as there is no slackness of the last, even so there is no swiftness of the first.

43 So I answered and said, Couldest thou not make those that have been made, and be now, and that are for to come, at once; that thou mightest shew thy judgment the sooner?

44 Then answered he me, and said, The creature may not haste above the maker; neither may the world hold them at once that shall be created therein.

45 And I said, As thou hast said unto thy servant, that thou, which givest life to all, hast given life at once to the creature that thou hast created, and the creature bare it: even so it might now also bear them that now be present at once.

46 And he said unto me, Ask the womb of a woman, and say unto her, If thou bringest forth children, why dost thou it not together, but one after another? pray her therefore to bring forth ten children at once.

47 And I said, She cannot: but must do it by distance of time.

48 Then said he unto me, Even so have I given the womb of the earth to those that be sown in it in their times.

49 For like as a young child may not bring forth the things that belong to the aged, even so have I disposed the world which I created.

50 And I asked, and said, Seeing thou hast now given me the way, I will proceed to speak before thee: for our mother, of whom thou hast told me that she is young, draweth now nigh unto age.

51 He answered me, and said, Ask a woman that beareth children, and she shall tell thee.

52 Say unto her, Wherefore are unto they whom thou hast now brought forth like those that were before, but less of stature?

53 And she shall answer thee, They that be born in the the strength of youth are of one fashion, and they that are born in the time of age, when the womb faileth, are otherwise.

54 Consider thou therefore also, how that ye are less of stature than those that were before you.

55 And so are they that come after you less than ye, as the creatures which now begin to be old, and have passed over the strength of youth.

56 Then said I, Adoni, I beseech thee, if I have found favour in thy sight, shew thy servant by whom thou visitest thy creature.

6 And he said unto me, In the beginning, when the earth was made, before the borders of the world stood, or ever the winds blew,

2 Before it thundered and lightened, or ever the foundations of paradise were laid,

3 Before the fair flowers were seen, or ever the moveable powers were established, before the innumerable multitude of angels were gathered together,

4 Or ever the heights of the air were lifted up, before the measures of the firmament were named, or ever the chimneys in Tzion were hot,

5 And ere the present years were sought out, and or ever the inventions of them that now sin were turned, before they were sealed that have gathered faith for a treasure:

6 Then did I consider these things, and they all were made through me alone, and through none other: by me also they shall be ended, and by none other.

7 Then answered I and said, What shall be the parting asunder of the times? or when shall be the end of the first, and the beginning of it that followeth?

8 And he said unto me, From Abraham unto Yitzkhaq, when Ya'aqob and Esau were born of him, Ya'aqob's hand held first the heel of Esau.

9 For Esau is the end of the world, and Ya'aqob is the beginning of it that followeth.

10 The hand of man is betwixt the heel and the hand: other question, Ezra, ask thou not.

11 I answered then and said, O YAHOWAH that bearest rule, if I have found favour in thy sight,

12 I beseech thee, shew thy servant the end of thy tokens, whereof thou shewedst me part the last night.

13 So he answered and said unto me, Stand up upon thy feet, and hear a mighty sounding voice.

14 And it shall be as it were a great motion; but the place where thou standest shall not be moved.

15 And therefore when it speaketh be not afraid: for the word is of the end, and the foundation of the earth is understood.

16 And why? because the speech of these things trembleth and is moved: for it knoweth that the end of these things must be changed.

17 And it happened, that when I had heard it I stood up upon my feet, and hearkened, and, behold, there was a voice that spake, and the sound of it was like the sound of many waters.

18 And it said, Behold, the days come, that I will begin to draw nigh, and to visit them that dwell upon the earth,

19 And will begin to make inquisition of them, what they be that have hurt unjustly with their unrighteousness, and when the affliction of Tzion shall be fulfilled;

20 And when the world, that shall begin to vanish away, shall be finished, then will I shew these tokens: the books shall be opened before the firmament, and they shall see all together:

21 And the children of a year old shall speak with their voices, the women with child shall bring forth untimely children of three or four months old, and they shall live, and be raised up.

22 And suddenly shall the sown places appear unsown, the full storehouses shall suddenly be found empty:

23 And tha trumpet shall give a sound, which when every man heareth, they shall be suddenly afraid.

24 At that time shall friends fight one against another like enemies, and the earth shall stand in fear with those that dwell therein, the springs of the fountains shall stand still, and in three hours they shall not run.

25 Whosoever remaineth from all these that I have told thee shall escape, and see my salvation, and the end of your world.

26 And the men that are received shall see it, who have not tasted death from their birth: and the heart of the inhabitants shall be changed, and turned into another meaning.

27 For evil shall be put out, and deceit shall be quenched.

28 As for faith, it shall flourish, corruption shall be overcome, and the truth, which hath been so long without fruit, shall be declared.

29 And when he talked with me, behold, I looked by little and little upon him before whom I stood.

30 And these words said he unto me; I am come to shew thee the time of the night to come.

31 If thou wilt pray yet more, and fast seven days again, I shall tell thee greater things by day than I have heard.

32 For thy voice is heard before the Most High: for the Mighty hath seen thy righteous dealing, he hath seen also thy chastity, which thou hast had ever since thy youth.

33 And therefore hath he sent me to shew thee all these things, and to say unto thee, Be of good comfort and fear not

34 And hasten not with the times that are past, to think vain things, that thou mayest not hasten from the latter times.

35 And it came to pass after this, that I wept again, and fasted seven days in like manner, that

I might fulfil the three weeks which he told me.

36 And in the eighth night was my heart vexed within me again, and I began to speak before the Most High.

37 For my ruakh was greatly set on fire, and my soul was in distress.

38 And I said, O ADONAI, thou spakest from the beginning of the creation, even the first day, and saidst thus; Let heaven and earth be made; and thy word was a perfect work.

39 And then was the RUAKH, and darkness and silence were on every side; the sound of man's voice was not yet formed.

40 Then commandedst thou a fair light to come forth of thy treasures, that thy work might appear.

41 Upon the second day thou madest the RUAKH of the firmament, and commandedst it to part asunder, and to make a division betwixt the waters, that the one part might go up, and the other remain beneath.

42 Upon the third day thou didst command that the waters should be gathered in the seventh part of the earth: six pats hast thou dried up, and kept them, to the intent that of these some being planted and tilled might serve thee.

43 For as soon as thy word went forth the work was made.

44 For immediately there was great and innumerable fruit, and many and divers pleasures for the taste, and flowers of unchangeable colour, and odours of wonderful smell: and this was done the third day.

45 Upon the fourth day thou commandedst that the sun should shine, and the moon give her light, and the stars should be in order:

46 And gavest them a charge to do service unto man, that was to be made.

47 Upon the fifth day thou saidst unto the seventh part, where the waters were gathered that it should bring forth living creatures, fowls and fishes: and so it came to pass.

48 For the dumb water and without life brought forth living things at the commandment, that all people might praise thy wondrous works.

49 Then didst thou ordain two living creatures, the one thou calledst Behemoth, and the other Leviathan;

50 And didst separate the one from the other: for the seventh part, namely, where the water was gathered together, might not hold them both.

51 Unto Behemoth thou gavest one part, which was dried up the third day, that he should dwell in the same part, wherein are a thousand hills:

52 But unto Leviathan thou gavest the seventh part, namely, the moist; and hast kept him to be devoured of whom thou wilt, and when.

53 Upon the sixth day thou gavest commandment unto the earth, that before thee it should bring forth beasts, cattle, and creeping things:

54 And after these, Adam also, whom thou madest Adon of all thy creatures: of him come we all, and the people also whom thou hast chosen.

55 All this have I spoken before thee, O ADONAI, because thou madest the world for our sakes

56 As for the other people, which also come of Adam, thou hast said that they are nothing, but be like unto spittle: and hast likened the abundance of them unto a drop that falleth from a vessel.

57 And now, O ADONAI, behold, these heathen, which have ever been reputed as nothing, have begun to be lords over us, and to devour us.

58 But we thy people, whom thou hast called thy firstborn, thy only begotten, and thy fervent lover, are given into their hands.

59 If the world now be made for our sakes, why do we not possess an inheritance with the world? how long shall this endure?

7 And when I had made an end of speaking these words, there was sent unto me the Angel which had been sent unto me the nights afore:

2 And he said unto me, Up, Ezra, and hear the words that I am come to tell thee.

3 And I said, Speak on, Adoni. Then said he unto me, The sea is set in a wide place, that it might be deep and great.

4 But put the case the entrance were narrow, and like a river;

5 Who then could go into the sea to look upon it, and to rule it? if he went not through the narrow, how could he come into the broad?

6 There is also another thing; A city is builded, and set upon a broad field, and is full of all good things:

7 The entrance thereof is narrow, and is set in a dangerous place to fall, like as if there were a fire on the right hand, and on the left a deep water:

8 And one only path between them both, even between the fire and the water, so small that there could but one man go there at once.

9 If this city now were given unto a man for an inheritance, if he never shall pass the danger set before it, how shall he receive this inheritance?

10 And I said, It is so, Adoni. Then said he unto me, Even so also is Yisra'EL's portion.

11 Because for their sakes I made the world: and when Adam transgressed my statutes, then was decreed that now is done.

12 Then were the entrances of this world made narrow, full of sorrow and travail: they are but few and evil, full of perils,: and very painful.

13 For the entrances of the elder world were wide and sure, and brought immortal fruit.

14 If then they that live labour not to enter these strait and vain things, they can never receive those that are laid up for them.

15 Now therefore why disquietest thou thyself, seeing thou art but a corruptible man? and why art thou moved, whereas thou art but mortal?

16 Why hast thou not considered in thy mind this thing that is to come, rather than that which is present?

17 Then answered I and said, O YAHOWAH that bearest rule, thou hast ordained in thy Torah, that the righteous should inherit these things, but that the ungodly should perish.

18 Nevertheless the righteous shall suffer strait things, and hope for wide: for they that have done wickedly have suffered the strait things, and yet shall not see the wide.

19 And he said unto me. There is no judge above ELOHIM, and none that hath understanding above the Highest.

20 For there be many that perish in this life, because they despise the Torah of ELOHIM that is set before them.

21 For ELOHIM hath given strait commandment to such as came, what they should do to live, even as they came, and what they should observe to avoid punishment.

22 Nevertheless they were not obedient unto him; but spake against him, and imagined vain things;

23 And deceived themselves by their wicked deeds; and said of the Most High, that he is not; and knew not his ways:

24 But his Torah have they despised, and denied his covenants; in his statutes have they not been faithful, and have not performed his works.

25 And therefore, Ezra, for the empty are empty things, and for the full are the full things.

26 Behold, the time shall come, that these tokens which I have told thee shall come to pass, and the bride shall appear, and she coming forth shall be seen, that now is withdrawn from the earth.

27 And whosoever is delivered from the foresaid evils shall see my wonders.

28 For Mine Anointed shall be revealed with those that be with him, and they that remain shall rejoice within four hundred years.

29 After these years shall The Anointed One, My Servant die, and all men that have life.

30 And the world shall be turned into the old silence seven days, like as in the former judgments: so that no man shall remain.

31 And after seven days the world, that yet awaketh not, shall be raised up, and that shall die that is corrupt

32 And the earth shall restore those that are asleep in her, and so shall the dust those that dwell in silence, and the secret places shall deliver those souls that were committed unto them.

33 And the Most High shall appear upon the seat of judgment, and misery shall pass away, and the long suffering shall have an end:

34 But judgment only shall remain, truth shall stand, and faith shall wax strong:

35 And the work shall follow, and the reward shall be shewed, and the good deeds shall be of force, and wicked deeds shall bear no rule.

*36 The pit of torment shall appear, and opposite it shall be the place of rest; and the furnace of hell shall be disclosed, and opposite it the paradise of delight.

*37 Then the Most High will say to the nations that have been raised from the dead, 'Look now, and understand whom you have denied, whom you have not served, whose commandments you have despised.

*38 Look on this side and on that; here are delight and rest, and there are fire and torments.' Thus he will speak to them on the day of judgment--

*39 A day that has no sun or moon or stars,

*40 Or cloud or thunder or lightning, or wind or water or air, or darkness or evening or morning,

*41 Or summer or spring or heat or winter or frost or cold, or hail or rain or dew,

*42 Or noon or night, or dawn or shining or brightness or light, but only the splendor of the glory of the Most High, by which all shall see what has been destined.

*43 It will last as though for a week of years.

*44 This is my judgment and its prescribed order; and to you alone I have shown these things."

*45 I answered and said, "Adoni, I said then and I say now: Blessed are those who are alive and keep your commandments!

*46 But what of those for whom I prayed? For who among the living is there that has not sinned, or who is there among mortals that has not transgressed your covenant?

*47 And now I see that the world to come will bring delight to few, but torments to many.

*48 For an evil heart has grown up in us, which has alienated us from ELOHIM, and has brought us into corruption and the ways of death, and has shown us the paths of perdition and removed us far from life-- and that not merely for a few but for almost all who have been created."

*49 He answered me and said, "Listen to me, Ezra, and I will instruct you, and will admonish you once more.

*50 For this reason the Most High has made not one world but two.

*51 Inasmuch as you have said that the righteous are not many but few, while the ungodly abound, hear the explanation for this.

*52 "If you have just a few precious stones, will you add to them lead and clay?"

*53 I said, "ADONAI, how could that be?"

*54 And he said to me, "Not only that, but ask the earth and she will tell you; defer to her, and she will declare it to you.

*55 Say to her, 'You produce gold and silver and bronze, and also iron and lead and clay;

*56 But silver is more abundant than gold, and bronze than silver, and iron than bronze, and lead than iron, and clay than lead.'

*57 Judge therefore which things are precious and desirable, those that are abundant or those that are rare?"

*58 I said, "O YAHOWAH, what is plentiful is of less worth, for what is more rare is more precious."

*59 He answered me and said, "Consider within yourself what you have thought, for the person who has what is hard to get rejoices more than the person who has what is plentiful.

*60 So also will be the judgment that I have promised; for I will rejoice over the few who shall be saved, because it is they who have made my glory to prevail now, and through them my name has now been honored.

*61 I will not grieve over the great number of

those who perish; for it is they who are now like a mist, and are similar to a flame and smoke-- they are set on fire and burn hotly, and are extinguished."

*62 I replied and said, "O earth, what have you brought forth, if the mind is made out of the dust like the other created things?

*63 For it would have been better if the dust itself had not been born, so that the mind might not have been made from it.

*64 But now the mind grows with us, and therefore we are tormented, because we perish and we know it.

*65 Let the sons of Adam lament, but let the wild animals of the field be glad; let all who have been born lament, but let the cattle and the flocks rejoice.

*66 It is much better with them than with us; for they do not look for a judgment, and they do not know of any torment or salvation promised to them after death.

*67 What does it profit us that we shall be preserved alive but cruelly tormented?

*68 For all who have been born are entangled in iniquities, and are full of sins and burdened with transgressions.

*69 And if after death we were not to come into judgment, perhaps it would have been better for us."

*70 He answered me and said, "When the Most High made the world and Adam and all who have come from him, he first prepared the judgment and the things that pertain to the judgment.

*71 But now, understand from your own words-- for you have said that the mind grows with us.

*72 For this reason, therefore, those who live on earth shall be tormented, because though they had understanding, they committed iniquity; and though they received the commandments, they did not keep them; and though they obtained the Torah, they dealt unfaithfully with what they received.

*73 What, then, will they have to say in the judgment, or how will they answer in the last times?

*74 How long the Most High has been patient with those who inhabit the world!-- and not for their sake, but because of the times that he has foreordained."

*75 I answered and said, "If I have found favor in your sight, O ADONAI, show this also to your servant: whether after death, as soon as everyone of us yields up the soul, we shall be kept in rest until those times come when you will renew the creation, or whether we shall be tormented at once?"

*76 He answered me and said, "I will show you that also, but do not include yourself with those who have shown scorn, or number yourself among those who are tormented.

*77 For you have a treasure of works stored up with the Most High, but it will not be shown to you until the last times.

*78 Now concerning death, the teaching is: When the decisive decree has gone out from the Most High that a person shall die, as the RUAKH

leaves the body to return again to him who gave it, first of all it adores the glory of the Most High.

*79 If it is one of those who have shown scorn and have not kept the way of the Most High, who have despised his Torah and hated those who fear ELOHIM--

*80 such spirits shall not enter into habitations, but shall immediately wander about in torments, always grieving and sad, in seven ways.

*81 The first way, because they have scorned the Torah of the Most High.

*82 The second way, because they cannot now make a good repentance so that they may live.

*83 The third way, they shall see the reward laid up for those who have trusted the covenants of the Most High.

*84 The fourth way, they shall consider the torment laid up for themselves in the last days.

*85 The fifth way, they shall see how the habitations of the others are guarded by angels in profound quiet.

*86 The sixth way, they shall see how some of them will cross over into torments.

*87 The seventh way, which is worse than all the ways that have been mentioned, because they shall utterly waste away in confusion and be consumed with shame, and shall wither with fear at seeing the glory of the Most High in whose presence they sinned while they were alive, and in whose presence they are to be judged in the last times.

*88 "Now this is the order of those who have kept the ways of the Most High, when they shall be separated from their mortal body.

*89 During the time that they lived in it, they laboriously served the Most High, and withstood danger every hour so that they might keep the Torah of the Lawgiver perfectly.

*90 Therefore this is the teaching concerning them:

*91 First of all, they shall see with great joy the glory of him who receives them, for they shall have rest in seven orders.

*92 The first order, because they have striven with great effort to overcome the evil thought that was formed with them, so that it might not lead them astray from life into death.

*93 The second order, because they see the perplexity in which the souls of the ungodly wander and the punishment that awaits them.

*94 The third order, they see the witness that he who formed them bears concerning them, that throughout their life they kept the Torah with which they were entrusted.

*95 The fourth order, they understand the rest that they now enjoy, being gathered into their chambers and guarded by angels in profound quiet, and the glory waiting for them in the last days.

*96 The fifth order, they rejoice that they have now escaped what is corruptible and shall inherit what is to come; and besides they see the straits and toil from which they have been delivered, and the spacious liberty that they are

*70 RESTORED VERSES OF 2 ESDRAS

to receive and enjoy in immortality.

*97 The sixth order, when it is shown them how their face is to shine like the sun, and how they are to be made like the light of the stars, being incorruptible from then on.

*98 The seventh order, which is greater than all that have been mentioned, because they shall rejoice with boldness, and shall be confident without confusion, and shall be glad without fear, for they press forward to see the face of him whom they served in life and from whom they are to receive their reward when glorified.

*99 This is the order of the souls of the righteous, as henceforth is announced; and the previously mentioned are the ways of torment that those who would not give heed shall suffer hereafter."

*100 Then I answered and said, "Will time therefore be given to the souls, after they have been separated from the bodies, to see what you have described to me?"

*101 He said to me, "They shall have freedom for seven days, so that during these seven days they may see the things of which you have been told, and afterwards they shall be gathered in their habitations."

*102 I answered and said, "If I have found favor in your sight, show further to me, your servant, whether on the day of judgment the righteous will be able to intercede for the ungodly or to entreat the Most High for them--

*103 Fathers for sons or sons for parents, brothers for brothers, relatives for their kindred, or friends for those who are most dear."

*104 He answered me and said, "Since you have found favor in my sight, I will show you this also. The day of judgment is decisive and displays to all the seal of truth. Just as now a father does not send his son, or a son his father, or a master his servant, or a friend his dearest friend, to be ill or sleep or eat or be healed in his place,

*105 So no one shall ever pray for another on that day, neither shall anyone lay a burden on another; for then all shall bear their own righteousness and unrighteousness."

106 Then said I, Abraham prayed first for the Sodomites, and Mosheh for the fathers that sinned in the wilderness:

107 And Yahoshua after him for Yisra'EL in the time of Akan:

108 And Shemu'EL and Dawid for the destruction: and Shelomoh for them that should come to the sanctuary:

109 And EliYAHU for those that received rain; and for the dead, that he might live:

110 And YechizYAHU for the people in the time of Sanchaerib: and many for many.

111 Even so now, seeing corruption is grown up, and wickedness increased, and the righteous have prayed for the ungodly: wherefore shall it not be so now also?

112 He answered me, and said, This present life is not the end where much glory doth abide; therefore have they prayed for the weak.

113 But the day of doom shall be the end of this time, and the beginning of the immortality for to come, wherein corruption is past,

114 Intemperance is at an end, infidelity is cut off, righteousness is grown, and truth is sprung up.

115 Then shall no man be able to save him that is destroyed, nor to oppress him that hath gotten the victory.

116 I answered then and said, This is my first and last saying, that it had been better not to have given the earth unto Adam: or else, when it was given him, to have restrained him from sinning.

117 For what profit is it for men now in this present time to live in heaviness, and after death to look for punishment?

118 O thou Adam, what hast thou done? for though it was thou that sinned, thou art not fallen alone, but we all that come of thee.

119 For what profit is it unto us, if there be promised us an immortal time, whereas we have done the works that bring death?

120 And that there is promised us an everlasting hope, whereas ourselves being most wicked are made vain?

121 And that there are laid up for us dwellings of health and safety, whereas we have lived wickedly?

122 And that the glory of the Most High is kept to defend them which have led a wary life, whereas we have walked in the most wicked ways of all?

123 And that there should be shewed a paradise, whose fruit endureth for ever, wherein is security and medicine, since we shall not enter into it?

124 (For we have walked in unpleasant places.)

125 And that the faces of them which have used abstinence shall shine above the stars, whereas our faces shall be blacker than darkness?

126 For while we lived and committed iniquity, we considered not that we should begin to suffer for it after death.

127 Then answered he me, and said, This is the condition of the battle, which man that is born upon the earth shall fight;

128 That, if he be overcome, he shall suffer as thou hast said: but if he get the victory, he shall receive the thing that I say.

129 For this is the life whereof Mosheh spake unto the people while he lived, saying, Choose thee life, that thou mayest live.

130 Nevertheless they believed not him, nor yet the prophets after him, no nor me which have spoken unto them,

131 That there should not be such heaviness in their destruction, as shall be joy over them that are persuaded to salvation.

132 I answered then, and said, I know, Adoni, that the Most High is called merciful, in that he hath mercy upon them which are not yet come into the world,

133 And upon those also that turn to his Torah;

134 And that he is patient, and long suffereth those that have sinned, as his creatures;

135 And that he is bountiful, for he is ready to give where it needeth;

136 And that he is of great mercy, for he multiplieth more and more mercies to them that are present, and that are past, and also to them which are to come.

137 For if he shall not multiply his mercies, the world would not continue with them that inherit therein.

138 And he pardoneth; for if he did not so of his goodness, that they which have committed iniquities might be eased of them, the ten thousandth part of men should not remain living.

139 And being judge, if he should not forgive them that are cured with his word, and put out the multitude of contentions,

140 There should be very few left peradventure in an innumerable multitude.

8 And he answered me, saying, The Most High hath made this world for many, but the world to come for few.

2 I will tell thee a similitude, Ezra; As when thou askest the earth, it shall say unto thee, that it giveth much mould whereof earthen vessels are made, but little dust that gold cometh of: even so is the course of this present world.

3 There be many created, but few shall be saved.

4 So answered I and said, Swallow then down, O my soul, understanding, and devour wisdom.

5 For thou hast agreed to give ear, and art willing to prophesy: for thou hast no longer space than only to live.

6 O Our Master, if thou suffer not thy servant, that we may pray before thee, and thou give us seed unto our heart, and culture to our understanding, that there may come fruit of it; how shall each man live that is corrupt, who beareth the place of a man?

7 For thou art alone, and we all one workmanship of thine hands, like as thou hast said.

8 For when the body is fashioned now in the mother's womb, and thou givest it members, thy creature is preserved in fire and water, and nine months doth thy workmanship endure thy creature which is created in her.

9 But that which keepeth and is kept shall both be preserved: and when the time cometh, the womb preserved delivereth up the things that grew in it.

10 For thou hast commanded out of the parts of the body, that is to say, out of the breasts, milk to be given, which is the fruit of the breasts,

11 That the thing which is fashioned may be nourished for a time, till thou disposest it to thy mercy.

12 Thou broughtest it up with thy righteousness, and nurturedst it in thy Torah, and reformedst it with thy judgment.

13 And thou shalt mortify it as thy creature, and quicken it as thy work.

14 If therefore thou shalt destroy him which with so great labour was fashioned, it is an easy thing to be ordained by thy commandment, that the thing which was made might be preserved.

15 Now therefore, I will speak; touching man in general, thou knowest best; but touching thy people, for whose sake I am sorry;

16 And for thine inheritance, for whose cause I mourn; and for Yisra'EL, for whom I am heavy; and for Ya'aqob, for whose sake I am troubled;

17 Therefore will I begin to pray before thee for myself and for them: for I see the falls of us that dwell in the land.

18 But I have heard the swiftness of the judge which is to come.

19 Therefore hear my voice, and understand my words, and I shall speak before thee. This is the beginning of the words of Ezra, before he was taken up: and I said,

20 O ADONAI, thou that dwellest in everlastingness which beholdest from above things in the heaven and in the air;

21 Whose throne is inestimable; whose glory may not be comprehended; before whom the hosts of angels stand with trembling,

22 Whose service is conversant in wind and fire; whose word is true, and sayings constant; whose commandment is strong, and ordinance fearful;

23 Whose look drieth up the depths, and indignation maketh the mountains to melt away; which the truth witnesseth:

24 O hear the prayer of thy servant, and give ear to the petition of thy creature.

25 For while I live I will speak, and so long as I have understanding I will answer.

26 O look not upon the sins of thy people; but on them which serve thee in truth.

27 Regard not the wicked inventions of the heathen, but the desire of those that keep thy testimonies in afflictions.

28 Think not upon those that have walked feignedly before thee: but remember them, which according to thy will have known thy fear.

29 Let it not be thy will to destroy them which have lived like beasts; but to look upon them that have clearly taught thy Torah.

30 Take thou no indignation at them which are deemed worse than beasts; but love them that always put their trust in thy righteousness and glory.

31 For we and our fathers do languish of such diseases: but because of us sinners thou shalt be called merciful.

32 For if thou hast a desire to have mercy upon us, thou shalt be called merciful, to us namely, that have no works of righteousness.

33 For the just, which have many good works laid up with thee, shall out of their own deeds receive reward.

34 For what is man, that thou shouldest take displeasure at him? or what is a corruptible generation, that thou shouldest be so bitter toward it?

35 For in truth them is no man among them that be born, but he hath dealt wickedly; and among the faithful there is none which hath not done amiss.

36 For in this, O ADONAI, thy righteousness and thy goodness shall be declared, if thou be merciful unto them which have not the confidence of good works.

37 Then answered he me, and said, Some things hast thou spoken aright, and according unto thy words it shall be.

38 For indeed I will not think on the disposition of them which have sinned before death, before judgment, before destruction:

39 But I will rejoice over the disposition of the righteous, and I will remember also their pilgrimage, and the salvation, and the reward, that they shall have.

40 Like as I have spoken now, so shall it come to pass.

41 For as the husbandman soweth much seed upon the ground, and planteth many trees, and yet the thing that is sown good in his season cometh not up, neither doth all that is planted take root: even so is it of them that are sown in the world; they shall not all be saved.

42 I answered then and said, If I have found grace, let me speak.

43 Like as the husbandman's seed perisheth, if it come not up, and receive not thy rain in due season; or if there come too much rain, and corrupt it:

44 Even so perisheth man also, which is formed with thy hands, and is called thine own image, because thou art like unto him, for whose sake thou hast made all things, and likened him unto the husbandman's seed.

45 Be not wroth with us but spare thy people, and have mercy upon thine own inheritance: for thou art merciful unto thy creature.

46 Then answered he me, and said, Things present are for the present, and things to cometh for such as be to come.

47 For thou comest far short that thou shouldest be able to love my creature more than I: but I have ofttimes drawn nigh unto thee, and unto it, but never to the unrighteous.

48 In this also thou art marvellous before the Most High:

49 In that thou hast humbled thyself, as it becometh thee, and hast not judged thyself worthy to be much glorified among the righteous.

50 For many great miseries shall be done to them that in the latter time shall dwell in the world, because they have walked in great pride.

51 But understand thou for thyself, and seek out the glory for such as be like thee.

52 For unto you is paradise opened, the tree of life is planted, the time to come is prepared, plenteousness is made ready, a city is builded, and rest is allowed, yea, perfect goodness and wisdom.

53 The root of evil is sealed up from you, weakness and the moth is hid from you, and corruption is fled into hell to be forgotten:

54 Sorrows are passed, and in the end is shewed the treasure of immortality.

55 And therefore ask thou no more questions concerning the multitude of them that perish.

56 For when they had taken liberty, they despised the Most High, thought scorn of his Torah, and forsook his ways.

57 Moreover they have trodden down his righteous,

58 And said in their heart, that there is no ELOHIM; yea, and that knowing they must die.

59 For as the things aforesaid shalt receive you, so thirst and pain are prepared for them: for it was not his will that men should come to nought:

60 But they which be created have defiled the name of him that made them, and were unthankful unto him which prepared life for them.

61 And therefore is my judgment now at hand.

62 These things have I not shewed unto all men, but unto thee, and a few like thee. Then answered I and said,

63 Behold, O ADONAI, now hast thou shewed me the multitude of the wonders, which thou wilt begin to do in the last times: but at what time, thou hast not shewed me.

9 He answered me then, and said, Measure thou the time diligently in itself: and when thou seest part of the signs past, which I have told thee before,

2 Then shalt thou understand, that it is the very same time, wherein the Highest will begin to visit the world which he made.

3 Therefore when there shall be seen earthquakes and uproars of the people in the world:

4 Then shalt thou well understand, that the Most High spake of those things from the days that were before thee, even from the beginning.

5 For like as all that is made in the world hath a beginning and an end, and the end is manifest:

6 Even so the times also of the Highest have plain beginnings in wonder and powerful works, and endings in effects and signs.

7 And every one that shall be saved, and shall be able to escape by his works, and by faith, whereby ye have believed,

8 Shall be preserved from the said perils, and shall see my salvation in my land, and within my borders: for I have sanctified them for me from the beginning.

9 Then shall they be in pitiful case, which now have abused my ways: and they that have cast them away despitefully shall dwell in torments.

10 For such as in their life have received benefits, and have not known me;

11 And they that have loathed my Torah, while they had yet liberty, and, when as yet place of repentance was open unto them, understood not, but despised it;

12 The same must know it after death by pain.

13 And therefore be thou not curious how the ungodly shall be punished, and when: but enquire how the righteous shall be saved, whose the world is, and for whom the world is created.

14 Then answered I and said,

15 I have said before, and now do speak, and will speak it also hereafter, that there be many more of

them which perish, than of them which shall be saved:

16 Like as a wave is greater than a drop.

17 And he answered me, saying, Like as the field is, so is also the seed; as the flowers be, such are the colours also; such as the workman is, such also is the work; and as the husbandman ls himself, so is his husbandry also: for it was the time of the world.

18 And now when I prepared the world, which was not yet made, even for them to dwell in that now live, no man spake against me.

19 For then every one obeyed: but now the manners of them which are created in this world that is made are corrupted by a perpetual seed, and by a Torah which is unsearchable rid themselves.

20 So I considered the world, and, behold, there was peril because of the devices that were come into it.

21 And I saw, and spared it greatly, and have kept me a grape of the cluster, and a plant of a great people.

22 Let the multitude perish then, which was born in vain; and let my grape be kept, and my plant; for with great labour have I made it perfect.

23 Nevertheless, if thou wilt cease yet seven days more, (but thou shalt not fast in them,

24 But go into a field of flowers, where no house is builded, and eat only the flowers of the field; taste no flesh, drink no wine, but eat flowers only;)

25 And pray unto the Highest continually, then will I come and talk with thee.

26 So I went my way into the field which is called Ardath, like as he commanded me; and there I sat among the flowers, and did eat of the herbs of the field, and the meat of the same satisfied me.

27 After seven days I sat upon the grass, and my heart was vexed within me, like as before:

28 And I opened my mouth, and began to talk before the Most High, and said,

29 O ADONAI, thou that shewest thyself unto us, thou wast shewed unto our fathers in the wilderness, in a place where no man treadeth, in a barren place, when they came out of Mitzraim.

30 And thou spakest saying, Hear me, O Yisra'EL; and mark my words, thou seed of Ya'aqob.

31 For, behold, I sow my Torah in you, and it shall bring fruit in you, and ye shall be honoured in it for ever.

32 But our fathers, which received the Torah, kept it not, and observed not thy ordinances: and though the fruit of thy Torah did not perish, neither could it, for it was thine;

33 Yet they that received it perished, because they kept not the thing that was sown in them.

34 And, lo, it ls a custom, when the ground hath received seed, or the sea a ship, or any vessel meat or drink, that, that being perished wherein it was sown or cast into,

35 That thing also which was sown, or cast therein, or received, doth perish, and remaineth not with us: but with us it hath not happened so.

36 For we that have received the Torah perish by sin, and our heart also which received it

37 Notwithstanding the Torah perisheth not, but remaineth in his force.

38 And when I spake these things in my heart, I looked back with mine eyes, and upon the right side I saw a woman, and, behold, she mourned and wept with a loud voice, and was much grieved in heart, and her clothes were rent, and she had ashes upon her head.

39 Then let I my thoughts go that I was in, and turned me unto her,

40 And said unto her, Wherefore weepest thou? why art thou so grieved in thy mind?

41 And she said unto me, Adon, let me alone, that I may bewail myself, and add unto my sorrow, for I am sore vexed in my mind, and brought very low.

42 And I said unto her, What aileth thee? tell me.

43 She said unto me, I thy servant have been barren, and had no child, though I had an husband thirty years,

44 And those thirty years I did nothing else day and night, and every hour, but make my, prayer to the Highest.

45 After thirty years ELOHIM heard me thine handmaid, looked upon my misery, considered my trouble, and gave me a son: and I was very glad of him, so was my husband also, and all my neighbours: and we gave great honour unto the Almighty.

46 And I nourished him with great travail.

47 So when he grew up, and came to the time that he should have a wife, I made a feast.

10 And it so came to pass, that when my son was entered into his wedding chamber, he fell down, and died.

2 Then we all overthrew the lights, and all my neighbours rose up to comfort me: so I took my rest unto the second day at night.

3 And it came to pass, when they had all left off to comfort me, to the end I might be quiet; then rose I up by night and fled, and came hither into this field, as thou seest.

4 And I do now purpose not to return into the city, but here to stay, and neither to eat nor drink, but continually to mourn and to fast until I die.

5 Then left I the meditations wherein I was, and spake to her in anger, saying,

6 Thou foolish woman above all other, seest thou not our mourning, and what happeneth unto us?

7 How that Tzion our mother is full of all heaviness, and much humbled, mourning very sore?

8 And now, seeing we all mourn and are sad, for we are all in heaviness, art thou grieved for one son?

9 For ask the earth, and she shall tell thee, that it is she which ought to mourn for the fall of so many that grow upon her.

10 For out of her came all at the first, and out of her shall all others come, and, behold, they walk almost all into destruction, and a multitude of them is utterly rooted out.

11 Who then should make more mourning than she, that hath lost so great a multitude; and not thou, which art sorry but for one?

12 But if thou sayest unto me, My lamentation is not like the earth's, because I have lost the fruit of my womb, which I brought forth with pains, and bare with sorrows;

13 But the earth not so: for the multitude present in it according to the course of the earth is gone, as it came:

14 Then say I unto thee, Like as thou hast brought forth with labour; even so the earth also hath given her fruit, namely, man, ever since the beginning unto him that made her.

15 Now therefore keep thy sorrow to thyself, and bear with a good courage that which hath befallen thee.

16 For if thou shalt acknowledge the determination of ELOHIM to be just, thou shalt both receive thy son in time, and shalt be commended among women.

17 Go thy way then into the city to thine husband.

18 And she said unto me, That will I not do: I will not go into the city, but here will I die.

19 So I proceeded to speak further unto her, and said,

20 Do not so, but be counselled. by me: for how many are the adversities of Tzion? be comforted in regard of the sorrow of Yerushalem.

21 For thou seest that our sanctuary is laid waste, our altar broken down, our temple destroyed;

22 Our psaltery is laid on the ground, our song is put to silence, our rejoicing is at an end, the light of our menorah is put out, the ark of our covenant is spoiled, our holy things are defiled, and the name that is called upon us is almost profaned: our children are put to shame, our priests are burnt, our Lewy'im are gone into captivity, our virgins are defiled, and our wives ravished; our righteous men carried away, our little ones destroyed, our young men are brought in bondage, and our strong men are become weak;

23 And, which is the greatest of all, the seal of Tzion hath now lost her honour; for she is delivered into the hands of them that hate us.

24 And therefore shake off thy great heaviness, and put away the multitude of sorrows, that the Mighty may be merciful unto thee again, and the Highest shall give thee rest and ease from thy labour.

25 And it came to pass while I was talking with her, behold, her face upon a sudden shined exceedingly, and her countenance glistered, so that I was afraid of her, and mused what it might be.

26 And, behold, suddenly she made a great cry very fearful: so that the earth shook at the noise of the woman.

27 And I looked, and, behold, the woman appeared unto me no more, but there was a city builded, and a large place shewed itself from the foundations: then was I afraid, and cried with a loud voice, and said,

28 Where is Uri'EL the Angel, who came unto me at the first? for he hath caused me to fall into many trances, and mine end is turned into corruption, and my prayer to rebuke.

29 And as I was speaking these words behold, he came unto me, and looked upon me.

30 And, lo, I lay as one that had been dead, and mine understanding was taken from me: and he took me by the right hand, and comforted me, and set me upon my feet, and said unto me,

31 What aileth thee? and why art thou so disquieted? and why is thine understanding troubled, and the thoughts of thine heart?

32 And I said, Because thou hast forsaken me, and yet I did according to thy words, and I went into the field, and, lo, I have seen, and yet see, that I am not able to express.

33 And he said unto me, Stand up manfully, and I will advise thee.

34 Then said I, Speak on, Adoni, in me; only forsake me not, lest I die frustrate of my hope.

35 For I have seen that I knew not, and hear that I do not know.

36 Or is my sense deceived, or my soul in a dream?

37 Now therefore I beseech thee that thou wilt shew thy servant of this vision.

38 He answered me then, and said, Hear me, and I shall inform thee, and tell thee wherefore thou art afraid: for the Highest will reveal many secret things unto thee.

39 He hath seen that thy way is right: for that thou sorrowest continually for thy people, and makest great lamentation for Tzion.

40 This therefore is the meaning of the vision which thou lately sawest:

41 Thou sawest a woman mourning, and thou begannest to comfort her:

42 But now seest thou the likeness of the woman no more, but there appeared unto thee a city builded.

43 And whereas she told thee of the death of her son, this is the solution:

44 This woman, whom thou sawest is Tzion: and whereas she said unto thee, even she whom thou seest as a city builded,

45 Whereas, I say, she said unto thee, that she hath been thirty years barren: those are the thirty years wherein there was no offering made in her.

46 But after thirty years Shelomoh builded the city and offered offerings: and then bare the barren a son.

47 And whereas she told thee that she nourished him with labour: that was the dwelling in Yerushalem.

48 But whereas she said unto thee, That my son coming into his marriage chamber happened to have a fail, and died: this was the destruction that came to Yerushalem.

49 And, behold, thou sawest her likeness, and because she mourned for her son, thou begannest to comfort her: and of these things which have chanced, these are to be opened unto thee.

50 For now the Most High seeth that thou art grieved unfeignedly, and sufferest from thy whole heart for her, so hath he shewed thee the brightness of her glory, and the comeliness of her beauty:

51 And therefore I bade thee remain in the field where no house was builded:

52 For I knew that the Highest would shew this unto thee.

53 Therefore I commanded thee to go into the field, where no foundation of any building was.

54 For in the place wherein the Highest beginneth to shew his city, there can no man's building be able to stand.

55 And therefore fear not, let not thine heart be affrighted, but go thy way in, and see the beauty and greatness of the building, as much as thine eyes be able to see:

56 And then shalt thou hear as much as thine ears may comprehend.

57 For thou art blessed above many other, and art called with the Highest; and so are but few.

58 But to morrow at night thou shalt remain here;

59 And so shall the Highest shew thee visions of the high things, which the Most High will do unto them that dwell upon the earth in the last days. So I slept that night and another, like as he commanded me.

11 Then saw I a dream, and, behold, there came up from the sea an eagle, which had twelve feathered wings, and three heads.

2 And I saw, and, behold, she spread her wings over all the earth, and all the winds of the air blew on her, and were gathered together.

3 And I beheld, and out of her feathers there grew other contrary feathers; and they became little feathers and small.

4 But her heads were at rest: the head in the midst was greater than the other, yet rested it with the residue.

5 Moreover I beheld, and, lo, the eagle flew with her feathers, and reigned upon earth, and over them that dwelt therein.

6 And I saw that all things under heaven were subject unto her, and no man spake against her, no, not one creature upon earth.

7 And I beheld, and, lo, the eagle rose upon her talons, and spake to her feathers, saying,

8 Watch not all at once: sleep every one in his own place, and watch by course:

9 But let the heads be preserved for the last.

10 And I beheld, and, lo, the voice went not out of her heads, but from the midst of her body.

11 And I numbered her contrary feathers, and, behold, there were eight of them.

12 And I looked, and, behold, on the right side there arose one feather, and reigned over all the earth;

13 And so it was, that when it reigned, the end of it came, and the place thereof appeared no more: so the next following stood up. and reigned, and had a great time;

14 And it happened, that when it reigned, the end of it came also, like as the first, so that it appeared no more.

15 Then came there a voice unto it, and said,

16 Hear thou that hast borne rule over the earth so long: this I say unto thee, before thou beginnest to appear no more,

17 There shall none after thee attain unto thy time, neither unto the half thereof.

18 Then arose the third, and reigned as the other before, and appeared no more also.

19 So went it with all the residue one after another, as that every one reigned, and then appeared no more.

20 Then I beheld, and, lo, in process of time the feathers that followed stood up upon the right side, that they might rule also; and some of them ruled, but within a while they appeared no more:

21 For some of them were set up, but ruled not.

22 After this I looked, and, behold, the twelve feathers appeared no more, nor the two little feathers:

23 And there was no more upon the eagle's body, but three heads that rested, and six little wings.

24 Then saw I also that two little feathers divided themselves from the six, and remained under the head that was upon the right side: for the four continued in their place.

25 And I beheld, and, lo, the feathers that were under the wing thought to set up themselves and to have the rule.

26 And I beheld, and, lo, there was one set up, but shortly it appeared no more.

27 And the second was sooner away than the first.

28 And I beheld, and, lo, the two that remained thought also in themselves to reign:

29 And when they so thought, behold, there awaked one of the heads that were at rest, namely, it that was in the midst; for that was greater than the two other heads.

30 And then I saw that the two other heads were joined with it.

31 And, behold, the head was turned with them that were with it, and did eat up the two feathers under the wing that would have reigned.

32 But this head put the whole earth in fear, and bare rule in it over all those that dwelt upon the earth with much oppression; and it had the governance of the world more than all the wings that had been.

33 And after this I beheld, and, lo, the head that was in the midst suddenly appeared no more, like as the wings.

34 But there remained the two heads, which also in like sort ruled upon the earth, and over those that dwelt therein.

35 And I beheld, and, lo, the head upon the right side devoured it that was upon the left side.

36 Then I head a voice, which said unto me, Look before thee, and consider the thing that thou seest.

37 And I beheld, and lo, as it were a roaring lion chased out of the wood: and I saw that he sent out

a man's voice unto the eagle, and said,

38 Hear thou, I will talk with thee, and the Highest shall say unto thee,

39 Art not thou it that remainest of the four beasts, whom I made to reign in my world, that the end of their times might come through them?

40 And the fourth came, and overcame all the beasts that were past, and had power over the world with great fearfulness, and over the whole compass of the earth with much wicked oppression; and so long time dwelt he upon the earth with deceit.

41 For the earth hast thou not judged with truth.

42 For thou hast afflicted the meek, thou hast hurt the peaceable, thou hast loved liars, and destroyed the dwellings of them that brought forth fruit, and hast cast down the walls of such as did thee no harm.

43 Therefore is thy wrongful dealing come up unto the Highest, and thy pride unto the Mighty.

44 The Highest also hath looked upon the proud times, and, behold, they are ended, and his abominations are fulfilled.

45 And therefore appear no more, thou eagle, nor thy horrible wings, nor thy wicked feathers nor thy malicious heads, nor thy hurtful claws, nor all thy vain body:

46 That all the earth may be refreshed, and may return, being delivered from thy violence, and that she may hope for the judgment and mercy of him that made her.

12 And it came to pass, whiles the lion spake these words unto the eagle, I saw,

2 And, behold, the head that remained and the four wings appeared no more, and the two went unto it and set themselves up to reign, and their kingdom was small, and fill of uproar.

3 And I saw, and, behold, they appeared no more, and the whole body of the eagle was burnt so that the earth was in great fear: then awaked I out of the trouble and trance of my mind, and from great fear, and said unto my ruakh,

4 Lo, this hast thou done unto me, in that thou searchest out the ways of the Highest.

5 Lo, yet am I weary in my mind, and very weak in my ruakh; and little strength is there in me, for the great fear wherewith I was afflicted this night.

6 Therefore will I now beseech the Highest, that he will comfort me unto the end.

7 And I said, YAHOWAH that bearest rule, if I have found grace before thy sight, and if I am justified with thee before many others, and if my prayer indeed be come up before thy face:

8 Comfort me then, and shew me thy servant the interpretation and plain difference of this fearful vision, that thou mayest perfectly comfort my soul.

9 For thou hast judged me worthy to shew me the last times.

10 And he said unto me, This is the interpretation of the vision:

11 The eagle, whom thou sawest come up from the sea, is the kingdom which was seen in the vision of thy brother Dani'EL.

12 But it was not expounded unto him, therefore now I declare it unto thee.

13 Behold, the days will come, that there shall rise up a kingdom upon earth, and it shall be feared above all the kingdoms that were before it.

14 In the same shall twelve kings reign, one after another:

15 Whereof the second shall begin to reign, and shall have more time than any of the twelve.

16 And this do the twelve wings signify, which thou sawest.

17 As for the voice which thou heardest speak, and that thou sawest not to go out from the heads but from the midst of the body thereof, this is the interpretation:

18 That after the time of that kingdom there shall arise great strivings, and it shall stand in peril of failing: nevertheless it shall not then fall, but shall be restored again to his beginning.

19 And whereas thou sawest the eight small under feathers sticking to her wings, this is the interpretation:

20 That in him there shall arise eight kings, whose times shall be but small, and their years swift.

21 And two of them shall perish, the middle time approaching: four shall be kept until their end begin to approach: but two shall be kept unto the end.

22 And whereas thou sawest three heads resting, this is the interpretation:

23 In his last days shall the Most High raise up three kingdoms, and renew many things therein, and they shall have the dominion of the earth,

24 And of those that dwell therein, with much oppression, above all those that were before them: therefore are they called the heads of the eagle.

25 For these are they that shall accomplish his wickedness, and that shall finish his last end.

26 And whereas thou sawest that the great head appeared no more, it signifieth that one of them shall die upon his bed, and yet with pain.

27 For the two that remain shall be slain with the sword.

28 For the sword of the one shall devour the other: but at the last shall he fall through the sword himself.

29 And whereas thou sawest two feathers under the wings passing over the head that is on the right side;

30 It signifieth that these are they, whom the Highest hath kept unto their end: this is the small kingdom and full of trouble, as thou sawest.

31 And the lion, whom thou sawest rising up out of the wood, and roaring, and speaking to the eagle, and rebuking her for her unrighteousness with all the words which thou hast heard;

32 This is the anointed, which the Highest hath kept for them and for their wickedness unto the end: he shall reprove them, and shall upbraid them with their cruelty.

33 For he shall set them before him alive in judgment, and shall rebuke them, and correct them.

34 For the rest of my people shall he deliver with mercy, those that have been pressed upon my borders, and he shall make them joyful until the coming of the day of judgment, whereof I have spoken unto thee from the the beginning.

35 This is the dream that thou sawest, and these are the interpretations.

36 Thou only hast been meet to know this secret of the Highest.

37 Therefore write all these things that thou hast seen in a book, and hide them:

38 And teach them to the wise of the people, whose hearts thou knowest may comprehend and keep these secrets.

39 But wait thou here thyself yet seven days more, that it may be shewed thee, whatsoever it pleaseth the Highest to declare unto thee. And with that he went his way.

40 And it came to pass, when all the people saw that the seven days were past, and I not come again into the city, they gathered them all together, from the least unto the greatest, and came unto me, and said,

41 What have we offended thee? and what evil have we done against thee, that thou forsakest us, and sittest here in this place?

42 For of all the prophets thou only art left us, as a cluster of the vintage, and as a candle in a dark place, and as a haven or ship preserved from the tempest.

43 Are not the evils which are come to us sufficient?

44 If thou shalt forsake us, how much better had it been for us, if we also had been burned in the midst of Tzion?

45 For we are not better than they that died there. And they wept with a loud voice. Then answered I them, and said,

46 Be of good comfort, O Yisra'EL; and be not heavy, thou house of Ya'aqob:

47 For the Highest hath you in remembrance, and the Mighty hath not forgotten you in temptation.

48 As for me, I have not forsaken you, neither am I departed from you: but am come into this place, to pray for the desolation of Tzion, and that I might seek mercy for the low estate of your sanctuary.

49 And now go your way home every man, and after these days will I come unto you.

50 So the people went their way into the city, like as I commanded them:

51 But I remained still in the field seven days, as the Angel commanded me; and did eat only in those days of the flowers of the field, and had my meat of the herbs

13

And it came to pass after seven days, I dreamed a dream by night:

2 And, lo, there arose a wind from the sea, that it moved all the waves thereof.

3 And I beheld, and, lo, that man waxed strong with the thousands of heaven: and when he turned his countenance to look, all the things trembled that were seen under him.

4 And whensoever the voice went out of his mouth, all they burned that heard his voice, like as the earth faileth when it feeleth the fire.

5 And after this I beheld, and, lo, there was gathered together a multitude of men, out of number, from the four winds of the heaven, to subdue the man that came out of the sea

6 But I beheld, and, lo, he had graved himself a great mountain, and flew up upon it.

7 But I would have seen the region or place whereout the hill was graven, and I could not.

8 And after this I beheld, and, lo, all they which were gathered together to subdue him were sore afraid, and yet durst fight.

9 And, lo, as he saw the violence of the multitude that came, he neither lifted up his hand, nor held sword, nor any instrument of war:

10 But only I saw that he sent out of his mouth as it had been a blast of fire, and out of his lips a flaming breath, and out of his tongue he cast out sparks and tempests.

11 And they were all mixed together; the blast of fire, the flaming breath, and the great tempest; and fell with violence upon the multitude which was prepared to fight, and burned them up every one, so that upon a sudden of an innumerable multitude nothing was to be perceived, but only dust and smell of smoke: when I saw this I was afraid.

12 Afterward saw I the same man come down from the mountain, and call unto him another peaceable Multitude.

13 And there came much people unto him, whereof some were glad, some were sorry, and some of them were bound, and other some brought of them that were offered: then was I sick through great fear, and I awaked, and said,

14 Thou hast shewed thy servant these wonders from the beginning, and hast counted me worthy that thou shouldest receive my prayer:

15 Shew me now yet the interpretation of this dream.

16 For as I conceive in mine understanding, woe unto them that shall be left in those days and much more woe unto them that are not left behind!

17 For they that were not left were in heaviness.

18 Now understand I the things that are laid up in the latter days, which shall happen unto them, and to those that are left behind.

19 Therefore are they come into great perils and many necessities, like as these dreams declare.

20 Yet is it easier for him that is in danger to come into these things, than to pass away as a cloud out of the world, and not to see the things that happen in the last days. And he answered unto me, and said,

21 The interpretation of the vision shall I shew thee, and I will open unto thee the thing that thou hast required.

22 Whereas thou hast spoken of them that are left behind, this is the interpretation:

23 He that shall endure the peril in that time hath kept himself: they that be fallen into danger are such as have works, and faith toward the Almighty.

24 Know this therefore, that they which be left behind are more blessed than they that be dead.

25 This is the meaning of the vision: Whereas thou sawest a man coming up from the midst of the sea:

26 The same is he whom the Highest hath kept a great season, which by his own self shall deliver his creature: and he shall order them that are left behind.

27 And whereas thou sawest, that out of his mouth there came as a blast of wind, and fire, and storm;

28 And that he held neither sword, nor any instrument of war, but that the rushing in of him destroyed the whole multitude that came to subdue him; this is the interpretation:

29 Behold, the days come, when the Most High will begin to deliver them that are upon the earth.

30 And he shall come to the astonishment of them that dwell on the earth.

31 And one shall undertake to fight against another, one city against another, one place against another, one people against another, and one realm against another.

32 And the time shall be when these things shall come to pass, and the signs shall happen which I shewed thee before, and then shall my Servant be declared, whom thou sawest as a man ascending.

33 And when all the people hear his voice, every man shall in their own land leave the battle they have one against another.

34 And an innumerable multitude shall be gathered together, as thou sawest them, willing to come, and to overcome him by fighting.

35 But he shall stand upon the top of the mount Tzion.

36 And Tzion shall come, and shall be shewed to all men, being prepared and builded, like as thou sawest the hill graven without hands.

37 And my Servant shall rebuke the wicked inventions of those Gentiles, which for their wicked life are fallen into the tempest;

38 And shall lay before them their evil thoughts, and the torments wherewith they shall begin to be tormented, which are like unto a flame: and he shall destroy them without labour by the Torah which is like unto me.

39 And whereas thou sawest that he gathered another peaceable multitude unto him;

40 Those are the ten tribes, which were carried away prisoners out of their own land in the time of Hoshea the king, whom Salmanasar the king of Asshur led away captive, and he carried them over the waters, and so came they into another land.

41 But they took this counsel among themselves, that they would leave the multitude of the heathen, and go forth into a further country, where never mankind dwelt,

42 That they might there keep their statutes, which they never kept in their own land.

43 And they entered into Perath by the narrow places of the river.

44 For the Most High then shewed signs for them, and held still the flood, till they were passed over.

45 For through that country there was a great way to go, namely, of a year and a half: and the same region is called Eretz-Akhereth (Arsareth).

46 Then dwelt they there until the latter time; and now when they shall begin to come,

47 The Highest shall stay the springs of the stream again, that they may go through: therefore sawest thou the multitude with shalom.

48 But those that be left behind of thy people are they that are found within my borders.

49 Now when he destroyeth the multitude of the heathen that are gathered together, he shall defend his people that remain.

50 And then shall he shew them great wonders.

51 Then said I, O YAHOWAH that bearest rule, shew me this: Wherefore have I seen the man coming up from the midst of the sea?

52 And he said unto me, Like as thou canst neither seek out nor know the things that are in the deep of the sea: even so can no man upon earth see my Son, or those that be with him, but in the day time.

53 This is the interpretation of the dream which thou sawest, and whereby thou only art here lightened.

54 For thou hast forsaken thine own way, and applied thy diligence unto my Torah, and sought it.

55 Thy life hast thou ordered in wisdom, and hast called understanding thy mother.

56 And therefore have I shewed thee the treasures of the Highest: after other three days I will speak other things unto thee, and declare unto thee mighty and wondrous things.

57 Then went I forth into the field, giving praise and thanks greatly unto the Most High because of his wonders which he did in time;

58 And because he governeth the same, and such things as fall in their seasons: and there I sat three days.

14 And it came to pass upon the third day, I sat under an oak, and, behold, there came a voice out of a bush over against me, and said, Ezra, Ezra.

2 And I said, Here am I, ADONAI And I stood up upon my feet.

3 Then said he unto me, In the bush I did manifestly reveal myself unto Mosheh, and talked with him, when my people served in Mitzraim:

4 And I sent him and led my people out of Mitzraim, and brought him up to the mount of where I held him by me a long season,

5 And told him many wondrous things, and shewed him the secrets of the times, and the end; and commanded him, saying,

6 These words shalt thou declare, and these shalt thou hide.

7 And now I say unto thee,

8 That thou lay up in thy heart the signs that I have shewed, and the dreams that thou hast seen, and the interpretations which thou hast heard:

9 For thou shalt be taken away from all, and from henceforth thou shalt remain with my Servant, and with such as be like thee, until the times be ended.

10 For the world hath lost his youth, and the times begin to wax old.

11 For the world is divided into twelve parts, and the ten parts of it are gone already, and half of a tenth part:

12 And there remaineth that which is after the half of the tenth part.

13 Now therefore set thine house in order, and reprove thy people, comfort such of them as be in trouble, and now renounce corruption,

14 Let go from thee mortal thoughts, cast away the burdens of man, put off now the weak nature,

15 And set aside the thoughts that are most heavy unto thee, and haste thee to flee from these times.

16 For yet greater evils than those which thou hast seen happen shall be done hereafter.

17 For look how much the world shall be weaker through age, so much the more shall evils increase upon them that dwell therein.

18 For the time is fled far away, and leasing is hard at hand: for now hasteth the vision to come, which thou hast seen.

19 Then answered I before thee, and said,

20 Behold, ADONAI, I will go, as thou hast commanded me, and reprove the people which are present: but they that shall be born afterward, who shall admonish them? thus the world is set in darkness, and they that dwell therein are without light.

21 For thy Torah is burnt, therefore no man knoweth the things that are done of thee, or the work that shall begin.

22 But if I have found grace before thee, send the RUAKH HA QODESH into me, and I shall write all that hath been done in the world since the beginning, which were written in thy Torah, that men may find thy path, and that they which will live in the latter days may live.

23 And he answered me, saying, Go thy way, gather the people together, and say unto them, that they seek thee not for forty days.

24 But look thou prepare thee many box trees, and take with thee SarYAH, DivriYAH, ShelemYAH, Aethan, and Uzzi'EL, these five which are ready to write swiftly;

25 And come hither, and I shall light a candle of understanding in thine heart, which shall not be put out, till the things be performed which thou shalt begin to write.

26 And when thou hast done, some things shalt thou publish, and some things shalt thou shew secretly to the wise: to morrow this hour shalt thou begin to write.

27 Then went I forth, as he commanded, and gathered all the people together, and said,

28 Hear these words, O Yisra'EL.

29 Our fathers at the beginning were strangers in Mitzraim, from whence they were delivered:

30 And received the Torah of life, which they kept not, which ye also have transgressed after them.

31 Then was the land, even the land of Tzion, parted among you by lot: but your fathers, and ye yourselves, have done unrighteousness, and have not kept the ways which the Highest commanded you.

32 And forasmuch as he is a righteous judge, he took from you in time the thing that he had given you.

33 And now are ye here, and your brethren among you.

34 Therefore if so be that ye will subdue your own understanding, and reform your hearts, ye shall be kept alive and after death ye shall obtain mercy.

35 For after death shall the judgment come, when we shall live again: and then shall the names of the righteous be manifest, and the works of the ungodly shall be declared.

36 Let no man therefore come unto me now, nor seek after me these forty days.

37 So I took the five men, as he commanded me, and we went into the field, and remained there.

38 And the next day, behold, a voice called me, saying, Ezra, open thy mouth, and drink that I give thee to drink.

39 Then opened I my mouth, and, behold, he reached me a full cup, which was full as it were with water, but the colour of it was like fire.

40 And I took it, and drank: and when I had drunk of it, my heart uttered understanding, and wisdom grew in my breast, for my ruakh strengthened my memory:

41 And my mouth was opened, and shut no more.

42 The Highest gave understanding unto the five men, and they wrote the wonderful visions of the night that were told, which they knew not: and they sat forty days, and they wrote in the day, and at night they ate bread.

43 As for me. I spake in the day, and I held not my tongue by night.

44 In forty days they wrote two hundred and four books.

45 And it came to pass, when the forty days were filled, that the Highest spake, saying, The first that thou hast written publish openly, that the worthy and unworthy may read it:

46 But keep the seventy last, that thou mayest deliver them only to such as be wise among the people:

47 For in them is the spring of understanding, the fountain of wisdom, and the stream of knowledge.

48 And I did so.

15 Behold, speak thou in the ears of my people the words of prophecy, which I will put in thy mouth, saith YAHOWAH:

2 And cause them to be written in paper: for they are faithful and true.

3 Fear not the imaginations against thee, let not the incredulity of them trouble thee, that speak against thee.

4 For all the unfaithful shall die in their unfaithfulness.

5 Behold, saith YAHOWAH, I will bring plagues upon the world; the sword, famine, death, and destruction.

6 For wickedness hath exceedingly polluted the whole earth, and their hurtful works are fulfilled.

7 Therefore saith YAHOWAH,

8 I will hold my tongue no more as touching their wickedness, which they profanely commit, neither will I suffer them in those things, in which they wickedly exercise themselves: behold, the innocent and righteous blood crieth unto me, and the souls of the just complain continually.

9 And therefore, saith YAHOWAH, I will surely avenge them, and receive unto me all the innocent blood from among them.

10 Behold, my people is led as a flock to the slaughter: I will not suffer them now to dwell in the land of Mitzraim:

11 But I will bring them with a mighty hand and a stretched out arm, and smite Mitzraim with plagues, as before, and will destroy all the land thereof.

12 Mitzraim shall mourn, and the foundation of it shall be smitten with the plague and punishment that ELOHIM shall bring upon it.

13 They that till the ground shall mourn: for their seeds shall fail through the blasting and hail, and with a fearful constellation.

14 Woe to the world and them that dwell therein!

15 For the sword and their destruction draweth nigh, and one people shall stand up and fight against another, and swords in their hands.

16 For there shall be sedition among men, and invading one another; they shall not regard their kings nor princes, and the course of their actions shall stand in their power.

17 A man shall desire to go into a city, and shall not be able.

18 For because of their pride the cities shall be troubled, the houses shall be destroyed, and men shall be afraid.

19 A man shall have no pity upon his neighbour, but shall destroy their houses with the sword, and spoil their goods, because of the lack of bread, and for great tribulation.

20 Behold, saith ELOHIM, I will call together all the kings of the earth to reverence me, which are from the rising of the sun, from the south, from the east, and Lebanon; to turn themselves one against another, and repay the things that they have done to them.

21 Like as they do yet this day unto my chosen, so will I do also, and recompense in their bosom. Thus saith YAHOWAH ELOHIM;

22 My right hand shall not spare the sinners, and my sword shall not cease over them that shed innocent blood upon the earth.

23 The fire is gone forth from his wrath, and hath consumed the foundations of the earth, and the sinners, like the straw that is kindled.

24 Woe to them that sin, and keep not my commandments! saith YAHOWAH.

25 I will not spare them: go your way, ye children, from the power, defile not my sanctuary.

26 For YAHOWAH knoweth all them that sin against him, and therefore delivereth he them unto death and destruction.

27 For now are the plagues come upon the whole earth and ye shall remain in them: for ELOHIM shall not deliver you, because ye have sinned against him.

28 Behold an horrible vision, and the appearance thereof from the east:

29 Where the nations of the dragons of Ereb shall come out with many chariots, and the multitude of them shall be carried as the wind upon earth, that all they which hear them may fear and tremble.

30 Also the Carmanians raging in wrath shall go forth as the wild boars of the wood, and with great power shall they come, and join battle with them, and shall waste a portion of the land of the Assyrians.

31 And then shall the dragons have the upper hand, remembering their nature; and if they shall turn themselves, conspiring together in great power to persecute them,

32 Then these shall be troubled bled, and keep silence through their power, and shall flee.

33 And from the land of the Assyrians shall the enemy besiege them, and consume some of them, and in their host shall be fear and dread, and strife among their kings.

34 Behold clouds from the east and from the north unto the south, and they are very horrible to look upon, full of wrath and storm.

35 They shall smite one upon another, and they shall smite down a great multitude of stars upon the earth, even their own star; and blood shall be from the sword unto the belly,

36 And dung of men unto the camel's hough.

37 And there shall be great fearfulness and trembling upon earth: and they that see the wrath shall be afraid, and trembling shall come upon them.

38 And then shall there come great storms from the south, and from the north, and another part from the west.

39 And strong winds shall arise from the east, and shall open it; and the cloud which he raised up in wrath, and the star stirred to cause fear toward the east and west wind, shall be destroyed.

40 The great and mighty clouds shall be puffed up full of wrath, and the star, that they may make all the earth afraid, and them that dwell therein; and they shall pour out over every high and eminent place an horrible star,

41 Fire, and hail, and flying swords, and many waters, that all fields may be full, and all rivers, with the abundance of great waters.

42 And they shall break down the cities and walls, mountains and hills, trees of the wood, and grass of the meadows, and their corn.

43 And they shall go stedfastly unto Babel, and make her afraid.

44 They shall come to her, and besiege her, the star and all wrath shall they pour out upon her: then shall the dust and smoke go up unto the heaven, and all they that be about her shall bewail her.

45 And they that remain under her shall do service unto them that have put her in fear.

46 And thou, Asia, that art partaker of the hope of Babel, and art the glory of her person:

47 Woe be unto thee, thou wretch, because thou hast made thyself like unto her; and hast decked thy daughters in whoredom, that they might please and glory in thy lovers, which have always desired to commit whoredom with thee.

48 Thou hast followed her that is hated in all her works and inventions: therefore saith ELOHIM,

49 I will send plagues upon thee; widowhood, poverty, famine, sword, and pestilence, to waste thy houses with destruction and death.

50 And the glory of thy Power shall be dried up as a flower, the heat shall arise that is sent over thee.

51 Thou shalt be weakened as a poor woman with stripes, and as one chastised with wounds, so that the mighty and lovers shall not be able to receive thee.

52 Would I with jealousy have so proceeded against thee, saith YAHOWAH,

53 If thou hadst not always slain my chosen, exalting the stroke of thine hands, and saying over their dead, when thou wast drunken,

54 Set forth the beauty of thy countenance?

55 The reward of thy whoredom shall be in thy bosom, therefore shalt thou receive recompence.

56 Like as thou hast done unto my chosen, saith YAHOWAH, even so shall ELOHIM do unto thee, and shall deliver thee into mischief

57 Thy children shall die of hunger, and thou shalt fall through the sword: thy cities shall be broken down, and all thine shall perish with the sword in the field.

58 They that be in the mountains shall die of hunger, and eat their own flesh, and drink their own blood, for very hunger of bread, and thirst of water.

59 Thou as unhappy shalt come through the sea, and receive plagues again.

60 And in the passage they shall rush on the idle city, and shall destroy some portion of thy land, and consume part of thy glory, and shall return to Babel that was destroyed.

61 And thou shalt be cast down by them as stubble, and they shall be unto thee as fire;

62 And shall consume thee, and thy cities, thy land, and thy mountains; all thy woods and thy fruitful trees shall they burn up with fire.

63 Thy children shall they carry away captive, and, look, what thou hast, they shall spoil it, and mar the beauty of thy face.

16 Woe be unto thee, Babel, and Asia! woe be unto thee, Mitzraim and Aram!

2 Gird up yourselves with cloths of sack and hair, bewail your children, and be sorry; for your destruction is at hand.

3 A sword is sent upon you, and who may turn it back?

4 A fire is sent among you, and who may quench it?

5 Plagues are sent unto you, and what is he that may drive them away?

6 May any man drive away an hungry lion in the wood? or may any one quench the fire in stubble, when it hath begun to burn?

7 May one turn again the arrow that is shot of a strong archer?

8 The mighty YAHOWAH sendeth the plagues and who is he that can drive them away?

9 A fire shall go forth from his wrath, and who is he that may quench it?

10 He shall cast lightnings, and who shall not fear? he shall thunder, and who shall not be afraid?

11 YAHOWAH shall threaten, and who shall not be utterly beaten to powder at his presence?

12 The earth quaketh, and the foundations thereof; the sea ariseth up with waves from the deep, and the waves of it are troubled, and the fishes thereof also, before YAHOWAH, and before the glory of his power:

13 For strong is his right hand that bendeth the bow, his arrows that he shooteth are sharp, and shall not miss, when they begin to be shot into the ends of the world.

14 Behold, the plagues are sent, and shall not return again, until they come upon the earth.

15 The fire is kindled, and shall not be put out, till it consume the foundation of the earth.

16 Like as an arrow which is shot of a mighty archer returneth not backward: even so the plagues that shall be sent upon earth shall not return again.

17 Woe is me! woe is me! who will deliver me in those days?

18 The beginning of sorrows and great mournings; the beginning of famine and great death; the beginning of wars, and the powers shall stand in fear; the beginning of evils! what shall I do when these evils shall come?

19 Behold, famine and plague, tribulation and anguish, are sent as scourges for amendment.

20 But for all these things they shall not turn from their wickedness, nor be always mindful of the scourges.

21 Behold, victuals shall be so good cheap upon earth, that they shall think themselves to be in good case, and even then shall evils grow upon earth, sword, famine, and great confusion.

22 For many of them that dwell upon earth shall perish of famine; and the other, that escape the hunger, shall the sword destroy.

23 And the dead shall be cast out as dung, and there shall be no man to comfort them: for the earth shall be wasted, and the cities shall be cast down.

24 There shall be no man left to till the earth, and to sow it

25 The trees shall give fruit, and who shall gather them?

26 The grapes shall ripen, and who shall tread them? for all places shall be desolate of men:

27 So that one man shall desire to see another, and to hear his voice.

28 For of a city there shall be ten left, and two of the field, which shall hide themselves in the thick groves, and in the clefts of the rocks.

29 As in an orchard of Olives upon every tree there are left three or four olives;

30 Or as when a vineyard is gathered, there are left some clusters of them that diligently seek through the vineyard:

31 Even so in those days there shall be three or four left by them that search their houses with the sword.

32 And the earth shall be laid waste, and the fields thereof shall wax old, and her ways and all her paths shall grow full of thorns, because no man shall travel therethrough.

33 The virgins shall mourn, having no bridegrooms; the women shall mourn, having no husbands; their daughters shall mourn, having no helpers.

34 In the wars shall their bridegrooms be destroyed, and their husbands shall perish of famine.

35 Hear now these things and understand them, ye servants of YAHOWAH.

36 Behold, the word of YAHOWAH, receive it: believe not the elohim of whom YAHOWAH spake.

37 Behold, the plagues draw nigh, and are not slack.

38 As when a woman with child in the ninth month bringeth forth her son, with two or three hours of her birth great pains compass her womb, which pains, when the child cometh forth, they slack not a moment:

39 Even so shall not the plagues be slack to come upon the earth, and the world shall mourn, and sorrows shall come upon it on every side.

40 O my people, hear my word: make you ready to thy battle, and in those evils be even as pilgrims upon the earth.

41 He that selleth, let him be as he that fleeth away: and he that buyeth, as one that will lose:

42 He that occupieth merchandise, as he that hath no profit by it: and he that buildeth, as he that shall not dwell therein:

43 He that soweth, as if he should not reap: so also he that planteth the vineyard, as he that shall not gather the grapes:

44 They that marry, as they that shall get no children; and they that marry not, as the widowers.

45 And therefore they that labour labour in vain:

46 For strangers shall reap their fruits, and spoil their goods, overthrow their houses, and take their children captives, for in captivity and famine shall they get children.

47 And they that occupy their merchandise with robbery, the more they deck their cities, their houses, their possessions, and their own persons:

48 The more will I be angry with them for their sin, saith YAHOWAH.

49 Like as a whore envieth a right honest and virtuous woman:

50 So shall righteousness hate iniquity, when she decketh herself, and shall accuse her to her face, when he cometh that shall defend him that diligently searcheth out every sin upon earth.

51 And therefore be ye not like thereunto, nor to the works thereof.

52 For yet a little, and iniquity shall be taken away out of the earth, and righteousness shall reign among you.

53 Let not the sinner say that he hath not sinned: for ELOHIM shall burn coals of fire upon his head, which saith before YAHOWAH ELOHIM and his glory, I have not sinned.

54 Behold, YAHOWAH knoweth all the works of men, their imaginations, their thoughts, and their hearts:

55 Which spake but the word, Let the earth be made; and it was made: Let the heaven be made; and it was created.

56 In his word were the stars made, and he knoweth the number of them.

57 He searcheth the deep, and the treasures thereof; he hath measured the sea, and what it containeth.

58 He hath shut the sea in the midst of the waters, and with his word hath he hanged the earth upon the waters.

59 He spreadeth out the heavens like a vault; upon the waters hath he founded it.

60 In the desert hath he made springs of water, and pools upon the tops of the mountains, that the floods might pour down from the high rocks to water the earth.

61 He made man, and put his heart in the midst of the body, and gave him breath, life, and understanding.

62 Yea and the RUAKH of Almighty ELOHIM, which made all things, and searcheth out all hidden things in the secrets of the earth,

63 Surely he knoweth your inventions, and what ye think in your hearts, even them that sin, and would hide their sin.

64 Therefore hath YAHOWAH exactly searched out all your works, and he will put you all to shame.

65 And when your sins are brought forth, ye shall be ashamed before men, and your own sins shall be your accusers in that day.

66 What will ye do? or how will ye hide your sins before ELOHIM and his angels?

67 Behold, ELOHIM himself is the judge, fear him: leave off from your sins, and forget your iniquities, to meddle no more with them for ever: so shall ELOHIM lead you forth, and deliver you from all trouble.

68 For, behold, the burning wrath of a great multitude is kindled over you, and they shall take away certain of you, and feed you, being idle, with things offered unto idols.

69 And they that consent unto them shall be had in derision and in reproach, and trodden under foot.

70 For there shall be in every place, and in the next cities, a great insurrection upon those that fear YAHOWAH.

71 They shall be like mad men, sparing none, but still spoiling and destroying those that fear YAHOWAH.

72 For they shall waste and take away their goods, and cast them out of their houses.

73 Then shall they be known, who are my chosen; and they shall be tried as the gold in the fire.

74 Hear, O ye my beloved, saith YAHOWAH: behold, the days of trouble are at hand, but I will deliver you from the same.

75 Be ye not afraid neither doubt; for ELOHIM is your guide,

76 And the guide of them who keep my commandments and precepts, saith YAHOWAH ELOHIM: let not your sins weigh you down, and let not your iniquities lift up themselves.

77 Woe be unto them that are bound with their sins, and covered with their iniquities like as a field is covered over with bushes, and the path thereof covered with thorns, that no man may travel through!

78 It is left undressed, and is cast into the fire to be consumed therewith.

THE BOOK OF
TOBIT

1 The book of the words of TobiYAH, son of Tobi'EL, the son of Anani'EL, the son of Adu'EL, the son of Gaba'EL, of the seed of Asa'EL, of the tribe of Naphtali;

2 Who in the time of Enemessar king of the Assyrians was led captive out of Thisbe, which is at the right hand of that city, which is called properly Naphtali in Galilah (Galilee) above Asher.

3 I TobiYAH have walked all the days of my life in the ways of truth and justice, and I did many almsdeeds to my brethren, and my nation, who came with me to Ninweh, into the land of the Assyrians.

4 And when I was in mine own country, in the land of Yisra'EL being but young, all the tribe of Naphtali my father fell from the house of Yerushalem, which was chosen out of all the tribes of Yisra'EL, that all the tribes should sacrifice there, where the temple of the habitation of the Most High was consecrated and built for all ages.

5 Now all the tribes which together revolted, and the house of my father Naphtali, sacrificed unto the heifer Baal.

6 But I alone went often to Yerushalem at the feasts, as it was ordained unto all the people of Yisra'EL by an everlasting decree, having the firstfruits and tenths of increase, with that which was first shorn; and them gave I at the altar to the priests the children of Aharon.

7 The first tenth part of all increase I gave to the sons of Aharon, who ministered at Yerushalem: another tenth part I sold away, and went, and spent it every year at Yerushalem:

8 And the third I gave unto them to whom it was meet, as Deborah my father's mother had commanded me, because I was left an orphan by my father.

9 Furthermore, when I was come to the age of a man, I married Khannah of mine own kindred, and of her I begat TobiYAH.

10 And when we were carried away captives to Ninweh, all my brethren and those that were of my kindred did eat of the bread of the Gentiles.

11 But I kept myself from eating;

12 Because I remembered ELOHIM with all my heart.

13 And the Most High gave me grace and favour before Enemessar, so that I was his purveyor.

14 And I went into Madai, and left in trust with Gaba'EL, the brother of GabriYAH, at Rages a city of Madai ten talents of silver.

15 Now when Enemessar was dead, Sanchaerib his son reigned in his stead; whose estate was troubled, that I could not go into Madai.

16 And in the time of Enemessar I gave many alms to my brethren, and gave my bread to the hungry,

17 And my clothes to the naked: and if I saw any of my nation dead, or cast about the walls of Ninweh, I buried him.

18 And if the king Sanchaerib had slain any, when he was come, and fled from Yehudah, I buried them privily; for in his wrath he killed many; but the bodies were not found, when they were sought for of the king.

19 And when one of the Ninevites went and complained of me to the king, that I buried them, and hid myself; understanding that I was sought for to be put to death, I withdrew myself for fear.

20 Then all my goods were forcibly taken away, neither was there any thing left me, beside my wife Khannah and my son TobiYAH.

21 And there passed not five and fifty days, before two of his sons killed him, and they fled into the mountains of Ararath; and Esar-Khaddon his son reigned in his stead; who appointed over his father's accounts, and over all his affairs, Akhiakharus my brother Ana'EL's son.

22 And Akhiakharus intreating for me, I returned to Ninweh. Now Akhiakharus was cupbearer, and keeper of the signet, and steward, and overseer of the accounts: and Esar-Khaddon appointed him next unto him: and he was my brother's son.

2 Now when I was come home again, and my wife Khannah was restored unto me, with my son TobiYAH, in the feast of Shebuot, which is the holy feast of the seven weeks, there was a good dinner prepared me, in the which I sat down to eat.

2 And when I saw abundance of meat, I said to my son, Go and bring what poor man soever thou shalt find out of our brethren, who is mindful of YAHOWAH; and, lo, I tarry for thee.

3 But he came again, and said, Father, one of our nation is strangled, and is cast out in the marketplace.

4 Then before I had tasted of any meat, I started up, and took him up into a room until the going down of the sun.

5 Then I returned, and washed myself, and ate my meat in heaviness,

6 Remembering that prophecy of Amos, as he said, Your feasts shall be turned into mourning, and all your mirth into lamentation.

7 Therefore I wept: and after the going down of the sun I went and made a grave, and buried him.

8 But my neighbours mocked me, and said, This man is not yet afraid to be put to death for this matter: who fled away; and yet, lo, he burieth the dead again.

9 The same night also I returned from the burial, and slept by the wall of my courtyard, being polluted and my face was uncovered:

10 And I knew not that there were sparrows in the wall, and mine eyes being open, the sparrows mut-

ed warm dung into mine eyes, and a whiteness came in mine eyes: and I went to the physicians, but they helped me not: moreover Akhiakharus did nourish me, until I went into Elymais.

11 And my wife Khannah did take women's works to do.

12 And when she had sent them home to the owners, they paid her wages, and gave her also besides a kid.

13 And when it was in my house, and began to cry, I said unto her, From whence is this kid? is it not stolen? render it to the owners; for it is not lawful to eat any thing that is stolen.

14 But she replied upon me, It was given for a gift more than the wages. Howbeit I did not believe her, but bade her render it to the owners: and I was abashed at her. But she replied upon me, Where are thine alms and thy righteous deeds? behold, thou and all thy works are known.

3 Then I being grieved did weep, and in my sorrow prayed, saying,

2 O YAHOWAH, thou art just, and all thy works and all thy ways are mercy and truth, and thou judgest truly and justly for ever.

3 Remember me, and look on me, punish me not for my sins and ignorances, and the sins of mg fathers, who have sinned before thee:

4 For they obeyed not thy commandments: wherefore thou hast delivered us for a spoil, and unto captivity, and unto death, and for a proverb of reproach to all the heathen among whom we are dispersed.

5 And now thy judgments are many and true: deal with me according to my sins and my fathers': because we have not kept thy commandments, neither have walked in truth before thee.

6 Now therefore deal with me as seemeth best unto thee, and command my ruakh to be taken from me, that I may be dissolved, and become earth: for it is profitable for me to die rather than to live, because I have heard false reproaches, and have much sorrow: command therefore that I may now be delivered out of this distress, and go into the everlasting place: turn not thy face away from me.

7 It came to pass the same day, that in Ecbatane a city of Madai Sara the daughter of Ragu'EL was also reproached by her father's maids;

8 Because that she had been married to seven husbands, whom Ashmedai the evil ruakh had killed, before they had lain with her. Dost thou not know, said they, that thou hast strangled thine husbands? thou hast had already seven husbands, neither wast thou named after any of them.

9 Wherefore dost thou beat us for them? if they be dead, go thy ways after them, let us never see of thee either son or daughter.

10 Whe she heard these things, she was very sorrowful, so that she thought to have strangled herself; and she said, I am the only daughter of my father, and if I do this, it shall be a reproach unto

him, and I shall bring his old age with sorrow unto the grave.

11 Then she prayed toward the window, and said, Blessed art thou, O YAHOWAH my ELOHIM, and thine holy and glorious name is blessed and honourable for ever: let all thy works praise thee for ever.

12 And now, O YAHOWAH, I set I mine eyes and my face toward thee,

13 And say, Take me out of the earth, that I may hear no more the reproach.

14 Thou knowest, YAHOWAH, that I am pure from all sin with man,

15 And that I never polluted my name, nor the name of my father, in the land of my captivity: I am the only daughter of my father, neither hath he any child to be his heir, neither any near kinsman, nor any son of his alive, to whom I may keep myself for a wife: my seven husbands are already dead; and why should I live? but if it please not thee that I should die, command some regard to be had of me, and pity taken of me, that I hear no more reproach.

16 So the prayers of them both were heard before the majesty of the great ELOHIM.

17 And Rapha'EL was sent to heal them both, that is, to scale away the whiteness of TobiYAH's eyes, and to give Sara the daughter of Ragu'EL for a wife to TobiYAH the son of TobiYAH; and to bind Ashmedai the evil ruakh; because she belonged to TobiYAH by right of inheritance. The selfsame time came TobiYAH home, and entered into his house, and Sara the daughter of Ragu'EL came down from her upper chamber.

4 In that day TobiYAH remembered the money which he had committed to Gaba'EL in Rages of Madai,

2 And said with himself, I have wished for death; wherefore do I not call for my son TobiYAH that I may signify to him of the money before I die?

3 And when he had called him, he said, My son, when I am dead, bury me; and despise not thy mother, but honour her all the days of thy life, and do that which shall please her, and grieve her not.

4 Remember, my son, that she saw many dangers for thee, when thou wast in her womb: and when she is dead, bury her by me in one grave.

5 My son, be mindful of YAHOWAH our ELOHIM all thy days, and let not thy will be set to sin, or to transgress his commandments: do uprightly all thy life long, and follow not the ways of unrighteousness.

6 For if thou deal truly, thy doings shall prosperously succeed to thee, and to all them that live justly.

7 Give alms of thy substance; and when thou givest alms, let not thine eye be envious, neither turn thy face from any poor, and the face of ELOHIM shall not be turned away from thee.

8 If thou hast abundance give alms accordingly: if thou have but a little, be not afraid to give according to that little:

9 For thou layest up a good treasure for thyself against the day of necessity.

10 Because that alms do deliver from death, and suffereth not to come into darkness.

11 For alms is a good gift unto all that give it in the sight of the Most High.

12 Beware of all whoredom, my son, and chiefly take a wife of the seed of thy fathers, and take not a strange woman to wife, which is not of thy father's tribe: for we are the children of the prophets, Noakh, Abraham, Yitzkhaq, and Ya'aqob: remember, my son, that our fathers from the beginning, even that they all married wives of their own kindred, and were blessed in their children, and their seed shall inherit the land.

13 Now therefore, my son, love thy brethren, and despise not in thy heart thy brethren, the sons and daughters of thy people, in not taking a wife of them: for in pride is destruction and much trouble, and in lewdness is decay and great want: for lewdness is the mother of famine.

14 Let not the wages of any man, which hath wrought for thee, tarry with thee, but give him it out of hand: for if thou serve ELOHIM, he will also repay thee: be circumspect my son, in all things thou doest, and be wise in all thy conversation.

15 Do that to no man which thou hatest: drink not wine to make thee drunken: neither let drunkenness go with thee in thy journey.

16 Give of thy bread to the hungry, and of thy garments to them that are naked; and according to thine abundance give alms: and let not thine eye be envious, when thou givest alms.

17 Pour out thy bread on the burial of the just, but give nothing to the wicked.

18 Ask counsel of all that are wise, and despise not any counsel that is profitable.

19 Bless YAHOWAH thy ELOHIM alway, and desire of him that thy ways may be directed, and that all thy paths and counsels may prosper: for every nation hath not counsel; but YAHOWAH himself giveth all good things, and he humbleth whom he will, as he will; now therefore, my son, remember my commandments, neither let them be put out of thy mind.

20 And now I signify this to they that I committed ten talents to Gaba'EL the son of GabriYAH at Rages in Madai.

21 And fear not, my son, that we are made poor: for thou hast much wealth, if thou fear ELOHIM, and depart from all sin, and do that which is pleasing in his sight.

5 TobiYAH then answered and said, Father, I will do all things which thou hast commanded me:

2 But how can I receive the money, seeing I know him not?

3 Then he gave him the handwriting, and said unto him, Seek thee a man which may go with thee, whiles I yet live, and I will give him wages: and go and receive the money.

4 Therefore when he went to seek a man, he found Rapha'EL that was an Angel.

5 But he knew not; and he said unto him, Canst thou go with me to Rages? and knowest thou those places well?

6 To whom the Angel said, I will go with thee, and I know the way well: for I have lodged with our brother Gaba'EL.

7 Then TobiYAH said unto him, Tarry for me, till I tell my father.

8 Then he said unto him, Go and tarry not. So he went in and said to his father, Behold, I have found one which will go with me. Then he said, Call him unto me, that I may know of what tribe he is, and whether he be a trusty man to go with thee.

9 So he called him, and he came in, and they saluted one another.

10 Then TobiYAH said unto him, Brother, shew me of what tribe and family thou art.

11 To whom he said, Dost thou seek for a tribe or family, or an hired man to go with thy son? Then TobiYAH said unto him, I would know, brother, thy kindred and name.

12 Then he said, I am AzarYAH, the son of KhananYAH the great, and of thy brethren.

13 Then TobiYAH said, Thou art welcome, brother; be not now angry with me, because I have enquired to know thy tribe and thy family; for thou art my brother, of an honest and good stock: for I know KhananYAH and Jonathas, sons of that great ShemaYAH, as we went together to Yerushalem to worship, and offered the firstborn, and the tenths of the fruits; and they were not seduced with the error of our brethren: my brother, thou art of a good stock.

14 But tell me, what wages shall I give thee? wilt thou a drachm a day, and things necessary, as to mine own son?

15 Yea, moreover, if ye return safe, I will add something to thy wages.

16 So they were well pleased. Then said he to TobiYAH, Prepare thyself for the journey, and ELOHIM send you a good journey. And when his son had prepared all things for the journey, his father said, Go thou with this man, and ELOHIM, which dwelleth in heaven, prosper your journey, and the Angel of ELOHIM keep you company. So they went forth both, and the young man's dog with them.

17 But Khannah his mother wept, and said to TobiYAH, Why hast thou sent away our son? is he not the staff of our hand, in going in and out before us?

18 Be not greedy to add money to money: but let it be as refuse in respect of our child.

19 For that which YAHOWAH hath given us to live with doth suffice us.

20 Then said TobiYAH to her, Take no care, my sister; he shall return in safety, and thine eyes shall see him.

21 For the good Angel will keep him company, and his journey shall be prosperous, and he shall return safe.

22 Then she made an end of weeping.

6 And as they went on their journey, they came in the evening to the river Tigris, and they lodged there.

2 And when the young man went down to wash himself, a fish leaped out of the river, and would have devoured him.

3 Then the Angel said unto him, Take the fish. And the young man laid hold of the fish, and drew it to land.

4 To whom the Angel said, Open the fish, and take the heart and the liver and the gall, and put them up safely.

5 So the young man did as the Angel commanded him; and when they had roasted the fish, they did eat it: then they both went on their way, till they drew near to Ecbatane.

6 Then the young man said to the Angel, Brother AzarYAH, to what use is the heart and the liver and the gal of the fish?

7 And he said unto him, Touching the heart and the liver, if a devil or an evil ruakh trouble any, we must make a smoke thereof before the man or the woman, and the party shall be no more vexed.

8 As for the gall, it is good to anoint a man that hath whiteness in his eyes, and he shall be healed.

9 And when they were come near to Rages,

10 The Angel said to the young man, Brother, to day we shall lodge with Ragu'EL, who is thy cousin; he also hath one only daughter, named Sara; I will speak for her, that she may be given thee for a wife.

11 For to thee doth the right of her appertain, seeing thou only art of her kindred.

12 And the maid is fair and wise: now therefore hear me, and I will speak to her father; and when we return from Rages we will celebrate the marriage: for I know that Ragu'EL cannot marry her to another according to the Torah of Mosheh, but he shall be guilty of death, because the right of inheritance doth rather appertain to thee than to any other.

13 Then the young man answered the Angel, I have heard, brother AzarYAH that this maid hath been given to seven men, who all died in the marriage chamber.

14 And now I am the only son of my father, and I am afraid, lest if I go in unto her, I die, as the other before: for a wicked ruakh loveth her, which hurteth no body, but those which come unto her; wherefore I also fear lest I die, and bring my father's and my mother's life because of me to the grave with sorrow: for they have no other son to bury them.

15 Then the Angel said unto him, Dost thou not remember the precepts which thy father gave thee, that thou shouldest marry a wife of thine own kindred? wherefore hear me, O my brother; for she shall be given thee to wife; and make thou no reckoning of the evil ruakh; for this same night shall she be given thee in marriage.

16 And when thou shalt come into the marriage chamber, thou shalt take the ashes of perfume, and shalt lay upon them some of the heart and liver of the fish, and shalt make a smoke with it:

17 And the devil shall smell it, and flee away, and never come again any more: but when thou shalt come to her, rise up both of you, and pray to ELOHIM which is merciful, who will have pity on you, and save you: fear not, for she is appointed unto thee from the beginning; and thou shalt preserve her, and she shall go with thee. Moreover I suppose that she shall bear thee children. Now when TobiYAH had heard these things, he loved her, and his heart was effectually joined to her.

7 And when they were come to Ecbatane, they came to the house of Ragu'EL, and Sara met them: and after they had saluted one another, she brought them into the house.

2 Then said Ragu'EL to Edna his wife, How like is this young man to TobiYAH my cousin!

3 And Ragu'EL asked them, From whence are ye, brethren? To whom they said, We are of the sons of Nephthalim, which are captives in Ninweh.

4 Then he said to them, Do ye know TobiYAH our kinsman? And they said, We know him. Then said he, Is he in good health?

5 And they said, He is both alive, and in good health: and TobiYAH said, He is my father.

6 Then Ragu'EL leaped up, and kissed him, and wept,

7 And blessed him, and said unto him, Thou art the son of an honest and good man. But when he had heard that TobiYAH was blind, he was sorrowful, and wept.

8 And likewise Edna his wife and Sara his daughter wept. Moreover they entertained them cheerfully; and after that they had killed a ram of the flock, they set store of meat on the table. Then said TobiYAH to Rapha'EL, Brother AzarYAH, speak of those things of which thou didst talk in the way, and let this business be dispatched.

9 So he communicated the matter with Ragu'EL: and Ragu'EL said to TobiYAH, Eat and drink, and make merry:

10 For it is meet that thou shouldest marry my daughter: nevertheless I will declare unto thee the truth.

11 I have given my daughter in marriage te seven men, who died that night they came in unto her: nevertheless for the present be merry. But TobiYAH said, I will eat nothing here, till we agree and swear one to another.

12 Ragu'EL said, Then take her from henceforth according to the manner, for thou art her cousin, and she is thine, and the merciful ELOHIM give you good success in all things.

13 Then he called his daughter Sara, and she came to her father, and he took her by the hand, and gave her to be wife to TobiYAH, saying, Behold, take her after the Torah of Mosheh, and lead her away to thy father. And he blessed them;

14 And called Edna his wife, and took paper, and did write an instrument of covenants, and sealed it.

15 Then they began to eat.

16 After Ragu'EL called his wife Edna, and said unto her, Sister, prepare another chamber, and bring her in thither.

17 Which when she had done as he had bidden her, she brought her thither: and she wept, and she received the tears of her daughter, and said unto her,

18 Be of good comfort, my daughter; YAHOWAH of heaven and earth give thee joy for this thy sorrow: be of good comfort, my daughter.

8 And when they had supped, they brought Tobi-YAH in unto her.

2 And as he went, he remembered the words of Rapha'EL, and took the ashes of the perfumes, and put the heart and the liver of the fish thereupon, and made a smoke therewith.

3 The which smell when the evil ruakh had smelled, he fled into the utmost parts of Mitzraim, and the Angel bound him.

4 And after that they were both shut in together, TobiYAH rose out of the bed, and said, Sister, arise, and let us pray that ELOHIM would have pity on us.

5 Then began TobiYAH to say, Blessed art thou, O ELOHIM of our fathers, and blessed is thy holy and glorious name for ever; let the heavens bless thee, and all thy creatures.

6 Thou madest Adam, and gavest him Khawah his wife for an helper and stay: of them came mankind: thou hast said, It is not good that man should be alone; let us make unto him an aid like unto himself.

7 And now, O YAHOWAH, I take not this my sister for lush but uprightly: therefore mercifully ordain that we may become aged together.

8 And she said with him, Amen.

9 So they slept both that night. And Ragu'EL arose, and went and made a grave,

10 Saying, I fear lest he also be dead.

11 But when Ragu'EL was come into his house,

12 He said unto his wife Edna. Send one of the maids, and let her see whether he be alive: if he be not, that we may bury him, and no man know it.

13 So the maid opened the door, and went in, and found them both asleep,

14 And came forth, and told them that he was alive.

15 Then Ragu'EL praised ELOHIM, and said, O ELOHIM, thou art worthy to be praised with all pure and holy praise; therefore let thy saints praise thee with all thy creatures; and let all thine angels and thine elect praise thee for ever.

16 Thou art to be praised, for thou hast made me joyful; and that is not come to me which I suspected; but thou hast dealt with us according to thy great mercy.

17 Thou art to be praised because thou hast had mercy of two that were the only begotten children of their fathers: grant them mercy, O YAHOWAH, and finish their life in health with joy and mercy.

18 Then Ragu'EL bade his servants to fill the grave.

19 And he kept the wedding feast fourteen days.

20 For before the days of the marriage were finished, Ragu'EL had said unto him by an oath, that he should not depart till the fourteen days of the marriage were expired;

21 And then he should take the half of his goods, and go in safety to his father; and should have the rest when I and my wife be dead.

9 Then TobiYAH called Rapha'EL, and said unto him,

2 Brother AzarYAH, take with thee a servant, and two camels, and go to Rages of Madai to Gaba'EL, and bring me the money, and bring him to the wedding.

3 For Ragu'EL hath sworn that I shall not depart.

4 But my father counteth the days; and if I tarry long, he will be very sorry.

5 So Rapha'EL went out, and lodged with Gaba'EL, and gave him the handwriting: who brought forth bags which were sealed up, and gave them to him.

6 And early in the morning they went forth both together, and came to the wedding: and TobiYAH blessed his wife.

10 Now TobiYAH his father counted every day: and when the days of the journey were expired, and they came not,

2 Then TobiYAH said, Are they detained? or is Gaba'EL dead, and there is no man to give him the money?

3 Therefore he was very sorry.

4 Then his wife said unto him, My son is dead, seeing he stayeth long; and she began to wail him, and said,

5 Now I care for nothing, my son, since I have let thee go, the light of mine eyes.

6 To whom TobiYAH said, Hold thy shalom, take no care, for he is safe.

7 But she said, Hold thy shalom, and deceive me not; my son is dead. And she went out every day into the way which they went, and did eat no meat on the daytime, and ceased not whole nights to bewail her son TobiYAH, until the fourteen days of the wedding were expired, which Ragu'EL had sworn that he should spend there. Then TobiYAH said to Ragu'EL, Let me go, for my father and my mother look no more to see me.

8 But his father in law said unto him, Tarry with me, and I will send to thy father, and they shall declare unto him how things go with thee.

9 But TobiYAH said, No; but let me go to my father.

10 Then Ragu'EL arose, and gave him Sara his wife, and half his goods, servants, and cattle, and money:

11 And he blessed them, and sent them away, saying, The ELOHIM of heaven give you a prosperous journey, my children.

12 And he said to his daughter, Honour thy father and thy mother in law, which are now thy parents,

that I may hear good report of thee. And he kissed her. Edna also said to TobiYAH, YAHOWAH of heaven restore thee, my dear brother, and grant that I may see thy children of my daughter Sara before I die, that I may rejoice before YAHOWAH: behold, I commit my daughter unto thee of special trust; where are do not entreat her evil.

11 After these things TobiYAH went his way, praising ELOHIM that he had given him a prosperous journey, and blessed Ragu'EL and Edna his wife, and went on his way till they drew near unto Ninweh.

2 Then Rapha'EL said to TobiYAH, Thou knowest, brother, how thou didst leave thy father:

3 Let us haste before thy wife, and prepare the house.

4 And take in thine hand the gall of the fish. So they went their way, and the dog went after them.

5 Now Khannah sat looking about toward the way for her son.

6 And when she espied him coming, she said to his father, Behold, thy son cometh, and the man that went with him.

7 Then said Rapha'EL, I know, TobiYAH, that thy father will open his eyes.

8 Therefore anoint thou his eyes with the gall, and being pricked therewith, he shall rub, and the whiteness shall fall away, and he shall see thee.

9 Then Khannah ran forth, and fell upon the neck of her son, and said unto him, Seeing I have seen thee, my son, from henceforth I am content to die. And they wept both.

10 TobiYAH also went forth toward the door, and stumbled: but his son ran unto him,

11 And took hold of his father: and he strake of the gall on his fathers' eyes, saying, Be of good hope, my father.

12 And when his eyes began to smart, he rubbed them;

13 And the whiteness pilled away from the corners of his eyes: and when he saw his son, he fell upon his neck.

14 And he wept, and said, Blessed art thou, O ELOHIM, and blessed is thy name for ever; and blessed are all thine holy angels:

15 For thou hast scourged, and hast taken pity on me: for, behold, I see my son TobiYAH. And his son went in rejoicing, and told his father the great things that had happened to him in Madai.

16 Then TobiYAH went out to meet his daughter in law at the gate of Ninweh, rejoicing and praising ELOHIM: and they which saw him go marvelled, because he had received his sight.

17 But TobiYAH gave thanks before them, because ELOHIM had mercy on him. And when he came near to Sara his daughter in law, he blessed her, saying, Thou art welcome, daughter: ELOHIM be blessed, which hath brought thee unto us, and blessed be thy father and thy mother. And there was joy among all his brethren which were at Ninweh.

18 And Akhiakharus, and Nasbas his brother's son, came:

19 And TobiYAH' wedding was kept seven days with great joy.

12 Then TobiYAH called his son TobiYAH, and said unto him, My son, see that the man have his wages, which went with thee, and thou must give him more.

2 And TobiYAH said unto him, O father, it is no harm to me to give him half of those things which I have brought:

3 For he hath brought me again to thee in safety, and made whole my wife, and brought me the money, and likewise healed thee.

4 Then the old man said, It is due unto him.

5 So he called the Angel, and he said unto him, Take half of all that ye have brought and go away in safety.

6 Then he took them both apart, and said unto them, Bless ELOHIM, praise him, and magnify him, and praise him for the things which he hath done unto you in the sight of all that live. It is good to praise ELOHIM, and exalt his name, and honourably to shew forth the works of ELOHIM; therefore be not slack to praise him.

7 It is good to keep close the secret of a king, but it is honourable to reveal the works of ELOHIM. Do that which is good, and no evil shall touch you.

8 Prayer is good with fasting and alms and righteousness. A little with righteousness is better than much with unrighteousness. It is better to give alms than to lay up gold:

9 For alms doth deliver from death, and shall purge away all sin. Those that exercise alms and righteousness shall be filled with life:

10 But they that sin are enemies to their own life.

11 Surely I will keep close nothing from you. For I said, It was good to keep close the secret of a king, but that it was honourable to reveal the works of ELOHIM.

12 Now therefore, when thou didst pray, and Sara thy daughter in law, I did bring the remembrance of your prayers before the Holy One: and when thou didst bury the dead, I was with thee likewise.

13 And when thou didst not delay to rise up, and leave thy dinner, to go and cover the dead, thy good deed was not hid from me: but I was with thee.

14 And now ELOHIM hath sent me to heal thee and Sara thy daughter in law.

15 I am Rapha'EL, one of the seven holy angels, which present the prayers of the saints, and which go in and out before the glory of the Holy One.

16 Then they were both troubled, and fell upon their faces: for they feared.

17 But he said unto them, Fear not, for it shall go well with you; praise ELOHIM therefore.

18 For not of any favour of mine, but by the will of our ELOHIM I came; wherefore praise him for ever.

19 All these days I did appear unto you; but I did neither eat nor drink, but ye did see a vision.

20 Now therefore give ELOHIM thanks: for I go up to him that sent me; but write all things which are done in a book.

21 And when they arose, they saw him no more.

22 Then they confessed the great and wonderful works of ELOHIM, and how the Angel of YAHOWAH had appeared unto them.

13 Then TobiYAH wrote a prayer of rejoicing, and said, Blessed be ELOHIM that liveth for ever, and blessed be his kingdom.

2 For he doth scourge, and hath mercy: he leadeth down to hell, and bringeth up again: neither is there any that can avoid his hand.

3 Confess him before the Gentiles, ye children of Yisra'EL: for he hath scattered us among them.

4 There declare his greatness, and extol him before all the living: for he is our YAHOWAH, and he is the ELOHIM our Father for ever.

5 And he will scourge us for our iniquities, and will have mercy again, and will gather us out of all nations, among whom he hath scattered us.

6 If ye turn to him with your whole heart, and with your whole mind, and deal uprightly before him, then will he turn unto you, and will not hide his face from you. Therefore see what he will do with you, and confess him with your whole mouth, and praise YAHOWAH of might, and extol the everlasting King. In the land of my captivity do I praise him, and declare his might and majesty to a sinful nation. O ye sinners, turn and do justice before him: who can tell if he will accept you, and have mercy on you?

7 I will extol my ELOHIM, and my soul shall praise the King of heaven, and shall rejoice in his greatness.

8 Let all men speak, and let all praise him for his righteousness.

9 O Yerushalem, the holy city, he will scourge thee for thy children's works, and will have mercy again on the sons of the righteous.

10 Give praise to YAHOWAH, for he is good: and praise the everlasting King, that his tabernacle may be builded in thee again with joy, and let him make joyful there in thee those that are captives, and love in thee for ever those that are miserable.

11 Many nations shall come from far to the name of YAHOWAH ELOHIM with gifts in their hands, even gifts to the King of heaven; all generations shall praise thee with great joy.

12 Cursed are all they which hate thee, and blessed shall all be which love thee for ever.

13 Rejoice and be glad for the children of the just: for they shall be gathered together, and shall bless YAHOWAH of the just.

14 O blessed are they which love thee, for they shall rejoice in thy shalom: blessed are they which have been sorrowful for all thy scourges; for they shall rejoice for thee, when they have seen all thy glory, and shall be glad for ever.

15 Let my soul bless ELOHIM the great King.

16 For Yerushalem shall be built up with sapphires and emeralds, and precious stone: thy walls and towers and battlements with pure gold.

17 And the streets of Yerushalem shall be paved with beryl and carbuncle and stones of Ophir.

18 And all her streets shall say, Alleluia; and they shall praise him, saying, Blessed be ELOHIM, which hath extolled it for ever.

14 So TobiYAH made an end of praising ELOHIM.

2 And he was eight and fifty years old when he lost his sight, which was restored to him after eight years: and he gave alms, and he increased in the fear of YAHOWAH ELOHIM, and praised him.

3 And when he was very aged he called his son, and the sons of his son, and said to him, My son, take thy children; for, behold, I am aged, and am ready to depart out of this life.

4 Go into Madai my son, for I surely believe those things which Yonah the prophet spake of Ninweh, that it shall be overthrown; and that for a time shalom shall rather be in Madai; and that our brethren shall lie scattered in the earth from that good land: and Yerushalem shall be desolate, and the house of ELOHIM in it shall be burned, and shall be desolate for a time;

5 And that again ELOHIM will have mercy on them, and bring them again into the land, where they shall build a temple, but not like to the first, until the time of that age be fulfilled; and afterward they shall return from all places of their captivity, and build up Yerushalem gloriously, and the house of ELOHIM shall be built in it for ever with a glorious building, as the prophets have spoken thereof.

6 And all nations shall turn, and fear YAHOWAH ELOHIM truly, and shall bury their idols.

7 So shall all nations praise YAHOWAH, and his people shall confess ELOHIM, and YAHOWAH shall exalt his people; and all those which love YAHOWAH ELOHIM in truth and justice shall rejoice, shewing mercy to our brethren.

8 And now, my son, depart out of Ninweh, because that those things which the prophet Yonah spake shall surely come to pass.

9 But keep thou the Torah and the commandments, and shew thyself merciful and just, that it may go well with thee.

10 And bury me decently, and thy mother with me; but tarry no longer at Ninweh. Remember, my son, how Haman handled Akhiakharus that brought him up, how out of light he brought him into darkness, and how he rewarded him again: yet Akhiakharus was saved, but the other had his reward: for he went down into darkness. Menassheh gave alms, and escaped the snares of death which they had set for him: but Haman fell into the snare, and perished.

11 Wherefore now, my son, consider what alms doeth, and how righteousness doth deliver. When he had said these things, he gave up the ghost in the bed, being an hundred and

TOBIT

eight and fifty years old; and he buried him honourably.

12 And when Khannah his mother was dead, he buried her with his father. But TobiYAH departed with his wife and children to Ecbatane to Ragu'EL his father in law,

13 Where he became old with honour, and he buried his father and mother in law honoura-bly, and he inherited their substance, and his father TobiYAH's.

14 And he died at Ecbatane in Madai, being an hundred and seven and twenty years old.

15 But before he died he heard of the destruction of Ninweh, which was taken by Nebukad'netzar and Assuerus: and before his death he rejoiced over Ninweh.

THE BOOK OF
JUDITH

1 In the twelfth year of the reign of Nebukad'netzar, who reigned in Ninweh, the great city; in the days of Arphaxad, which reigned over the Medes in Ecbatane,

2 And built in Ecbatane walls round about of stones hewn three cubits broad and six cubits long, and made the height of the wall seventy cubits, and the breadth thereof fifty cubits:

3 And set the towers thereof upon the gates of it an hundred cubits high, and the breadth thereof in the foundation threescore cubits:

4 And he made the gates thereof, even gates that were raised to the height of seventy cubits, and the breadth of them was forty cubits, for the going forth of his mighty armies, and for the setting in array of his footmen:

5 Even in those days king Nebukad'netzar made war with king Arphaxad in the great plain, which is the plain in the borders of Ragau.

6 And there came unto him all they that dwelt in the hill country, and all that dwelt by Euphrates, and Tigris and Hydaspes, and the plain of Aryok the king of the Elymeans, and very many nations of the sons of Chelod, assembled themselves to the battle.

7 Then Nebukad'netzar king of the Assyrians sent unto all that dwelt in Persia, and to all that dwelt westward, and to those that dwelt in Cilicia, and Dameseq, and Lebanon, and Antilibanus, and to all that dwelt upon the sea coast,

8 And to those among the nations that were of Karmel, and Gil'ad, and the higher Galilah, and the great plain of Yizre'EL,

9 And to all that were in Shomron and the cities thereof, and beyond Yarden unto Yerushalem, and Betane, and Kelus, and Qadesh, and the river of Mitzraim, and Takhpenes, and Raamses, and all the land of Goshen,

10 Until ye come beyond Tanis and Memphis, and to all the inhabitants of Mitzraim, until ye come to the borders of Ethiopia.

11 But all the inhabitants of the land made light of the commandment of Nebukad'netzar king of the Assyrians, neither went they with him to the battle; for they were not afraid of him: yea, he was before them as one man, and they sent away his ambassadors from them without effect, and with disgrace.

12 Therefore Nebukad'netzar was very angry with all this country, and sware by his throne and kingdom, that he would surely be avenged upon all those coasts of Cilicia, and Dameseq, and Aram, and that he would slay with the sword all the inhabitants of the land of Moab, and the children of Ammon, and all Yehudah, and all that were in Mitzraim, till ye come to the borders of the two seas.

13 Then he marched in battle array with his power against king Arphaxad in the seventeenth year, and he prevailed in his battle: for he overthrew all the power of Arphaxad, and all his horsemen, and all his chariots,

14 And became Adon of his cities, and came unto Ecbatane, and took the towers, and spoiled the streets thereof, and turned the beauty thereof into shame.

15 He took also Arphaxad in the mountains of Ragau, and smote him through with his darts, and destroyed him utterly that day.

16 So he returned afterward to Ninweh, both he and all his company of sundry nations being a very great multitude of men of war, and there he took his ease, and banqueted, both he and his army, an hundred and twenty days.

2 And in the eighteenth year, the two and twentieth day of the first month, there was talk in the house of Nebukad'netzar king of the Assyrians that he should, as he said, avenge himself on all the earth.

2 So he called unto him all his officers, and all his nobles, and communicated with them his secret counsel, and concluded the afflicting of the whole earth out of his own mouth.

3 Then they decreed to destroy all flesh, that did not obey the commandment of his mouth.

4 And when he had ended his counsel, Nebukad'netzar king of the Assyrians called Holofernes the chief captain of his army, which was next unto him, and said unto him.

5 Thus saith the great king, the Adon of the whole earth, Behold, thou shalt go forth from my presence, and take with thee men that trust in their own strength, of footmen an hundred and twenty thousand; and the number of horses with their riders twelve thousand.

6 And thou shalt go against all the west country, because they disobeyed my commandment.

7 And thou shalt declare unto that they prepare for me earth and water: for I will go forth in my wrath against them and will cover the whole face of the earth with the feet of mine army, and I will give them for a spoil unto them:

8 So that their slain shall fill their valleys and brooks and the river shall be filled with their dead, till it overflow:

9 And I will lead them captives to the utmost parts of all the earth.

10 Thou therefore shalt go forth. and take beforehand for me all their coasts: and if they will yield themselves unto thee, thou shalt reserve them for me till the day of their punishment.

11 But concerning them that rebel, let not thine eye spare them; but put them to the slaughter, and spoil them wheresoever thou goest.

JUDITH

12 For as I live, and by the power of my kingdom, whatsoever I have spoken, that will I do by mine hand.

13 And take thou heed that thou transgress none of the commandments of thy Adon, but accomplish them fully, as I have commanded thee, and defer not to do them.

14 Then Holofernes went forth from the presence of his Adon, and called ail the governors and captains, and the officers of the army of Asshur;

15 And he mustered the chosen men for the battle, as his Adon had commanded him, unto an hundred and twenty thousand, and twelve thousand archers on horseback;

16 And he ranged them, as a great army is ordered for the war.

17 And he took camels and asses for their carriages, a very great number; and sheep and oxen and goats without number for their provision:

18 And plenty of victual for every man of the army, and very much gold and silver out of the king's house.

19 Then he went forth and all his power to go before king Nebukad'netzar in the voyage, and to cover all the face of the earth westward with their chariots, and horsemen, and their chosen footmen.

20 A great number also sundry countries came with them like locusts, and like the sand of the earth: for the multitude was without number.

21 And they went forth of Ninweh three days' journey toward the plain of Bectileth, and pitched from Bectileth near the mountain which is at the left hand of the upper Cilicia.

22 Then he took all his army, his footmen, and horsemen and chariots, and went from thence into the hill country;

23 And destroyed Phud and Lud, and spoiled all the children of Rasses, and the children of Yisra'EL, which were toward the wilderness at the south of the land of the Kelianim.

24 Then he went over Euphrates, and went through Mesopotamia, and destroyed all the high cities that were upon the river Arbonai, till ye come to the sea.

25 And he took the borders of Cilicia, and killed all that resisted him, and came to the borders of Japheth, which were toward the south, over against Arabia.

26 He compassed also all the children of Madian, and burned up their tabernacles, and spoiled their sheepcotes.

27 Then he went down into the plain of Dameseq in the time of wheat harvest, and burnt up all their fields, and destroyed their flocks and herds, also he spoiled their cities, and utterly wasted their countries, and smote all their young men with the edge of the sword.

28 Therefore the fear and dread of him fell upon all the inhabitants of the sea coasts, which were in Sidon and Tyre, and them that dwelt in Sur and Ocina, and all that dwelt in Yemna'an; and they that dwelt in Ashdod and Ashqelon feared him greatly.

3 So they sent ambassadors unto him to treat of shalom, saying,

2 Behold, we the servants of Nebukad'netzar the great king lie before thee; use us as shall be good in thy sight.

3 Behold, our houses, and all our places, and all our fields of wheat, and flocks, and herds, and all the lodges of our tents lie before thy face; use them as it pleaseth thee.

4 Behold, even our cities and the inhabitants thereof are thy servants; come and deal with them as seemeth good unto thee.

5 So the men came to Holofernes, and declared unto him after this manner.

6 Then came he down toward the sea coast, both he and his army, and set garrisons in the high cities, and took out of them chosen men for aid.

7 So they and all the country round about received them with garlands, with dances, and with timbrels.

8 Yet he did cast down their frontiers, and cut down their groves: for he had decreed to destroy all the elohim of the land, that all nations should worship Nebukad'netzar only, and that all tongues and tribes should call upon him as elohim.

9 Also he came over against Yizre'EL near unto Yehudah, over against the great strait of Yehudah.

10 And he pitched between Geba and Scythopolis, and there he tarried a whole month, that he might gather together all the carriages of his army.

4 Now the children of Yisra'EL, that dwelt in Yehudah, heard all that Holofernes the chief captain of Nebukad'netzar king of the Assyrians had done to the nations, and after what manner he had spoiled all their temples, and brought them to nought.

2 Therefore they were exceedingly afraid of him, and were troubled for Yerushalem, and for the temple of YAHOWAH their ELOHIM:

3 For they were newly returned from the captivity, and all the people of Yehudah were lately gathered together: and the vessels, and the altar, and the house, were sanctified after the profanation.

4 Therefore they sent into all the coasts of Shomron, and the villages and to Beth-Khoron, and Belmen, and Yerikho, and to Khoba, and Esora, and to the valley of Salem:

5 And possessed themselves beforehand of all the tops of the high mountains, and fortified the villages that were in them, and laid up victuals for the provision of war: for their fields were of late reaped.

6 Also Yaho'yaqim the high priest, which was in those days in Yerushalem, wrote to them that dwelt in Beth-Ulyah, and Betomestham, which is over against Yizre'EL toward the open country, near to Dothaim,

7 Charging them to keep the passages of the hill country: for by them there was an entrance into

Yehudah, and it was easy to stop them that would come up, because the passage was straight, for two men at the most.

8 And the children of Yisra'EL did as Yaho'yaqim the high priest had commanded them, with the ancients of all the people of Yisra'EL, which dwelt at Yerushalem.

9 Then every man of Yisra'EL cried to ELOHIM with great fervency, and with great vehemency did they humble their souls:

10 Both they, and their wives and their children, and their cattle, and every stranger and hireling, and their servants bought with money, put sack-cloth upon their loins.

11 Thus every man and women, and the little children, and the inhabitants of Yerushalem, fell before the temple, and cast ashes upon their heads, and spread out their sackcloth before the face of YAHOWAH: also they put sackcloth about the altar,

12 And cried to the ELOHIM of Yisra'EL all with one consent earnestly, that he would not give their children for a prey, and their wives for a spoil, and the cities of their inheritance to destruction, and the sanctuary to profanation and reproach, and for the Gentiles to rejoice at.

13 So ELOHIM heard their prayers, and looked upon their afflictions: for the people fasted many days in all Yehudah and Yerushalem before the sanctuary of YAHOWAH Almighty.

14 And Yaho'yaqim the high priest, and all the priests that stood before YAHOWAH, and they which ministered unto YAHOWAH, had their loins girt with sackcloth, and offered the daily burnt offerings, with the vows and free gifts of the people,

15 And had ashes on their mitres, and cried unto YAHOWAH with all their power, that he would look upon all the house of Yisra'EL graciously.

5 Then was it declared to Holofernes, the chief captain of the army of Asshur, that the children of Yisra'EL had prepared for war, and had shut up the passages of the hill country, and had fortified all the tops of the high hills and had laid impediments in the champaign countries:

2 Wherewith he was very angry, and called all the princes of Moab, and the captains of Ammon, and all the governors of the sea coast,

3 And he said unto them, Tell me now, ye sons of Kena'an, who this people is, that dwelleth in the hill country, and what are the cities that they inhabit, and what is the multitude of their army, and wherein is their power and strength, and what king is set over them, or captain of their army;

4 And why have they determined not to come and meet me, more than all the inhabitants of the west.

5 Then said Akhior, the captain of all the sons of Ammon, Let Adoni now hear a word from the mouth of thy servant, and I will declare unto thee the truth concerning this people, which dwelleth near thee, and inhabiteth the hill countries: and there shall no lie come out of the mouth of thy servant.

6 This people are descended of the Chaldeans:

7 And they sojourned heretofore in Mesopotamia, because they would not follow the elohim of their fathers, which were in the land of Chaldea.

8 For they left the way of their ancestors, and worshipped the ELOHIM of heaven, the ELOHIM whom they knew: so they cast them out from the face of their elohim, and they fled into Mesopotamia, and sojourned there many days.

9 Then their ELOHIM commanded them to depart from the place where they sojourned, and to go into the land of Kena'an: where they dwelt, and were increased with gold and silver, and with very much cattle.

10 But when a famine covered all the land of Kena'an, they went down into Mitzraim, and sojourned there, while they were nourished, and became there a great multitude, so that one could not number their nation.

11 Therefore the king of Mitzraim rose up against them, and dealt subtilly with them, and brought them low with labouring in brick, and made them slaves.

12 Then they cried unto their ELOHIM, and he smote all the land of Mitzraim with incurable plagues: so the Mitzrim cast them out of their sight.

13 And ELOHIM dried the Red sea before them,

14 And brought them to Mount Sinai, and Qadesh-Barne, and cast forth all that dwelt in the wilderness.

15 So they dwelt in the land of the Emorim, and they destroyed by their strength all them of Esebon, and passing over Yarden they possessed all the hill country.

16 And they cast forth before them the Kena'anim, the Perizzim, the Yebusim, and the Shikmim, and all the Girgashim, and they dwelt in that country many days.

17 And whilst they sinned not before their ELOHIM, they prospered, because the ELOHIM that hateth iniquity was with them.

18 But when they departed from the way which he appointed them, they were destroyed in many battles very sore, and were led captives into a land that was not their's, and the temple of their ELOHIM was cast to the ground, and their cities were taken by the enemies.

19 But now are they returned to their ELOHIM, and are come up from the places where they were scattered, and have possessed Yerushalem, where their sanctuary is, and are seated in the hill country; for it was desolate.

20 Now therefore, Adoni and governor, if there be any error against this people, and they sin against their ELOHIM, let us consider that this shall be their ruin, and let us go up, and we shall overcome them.

21 But if there be no iniquity in their nation, let Adoni now pass by, lest their YAHOWAH defend them, and their ELOHIM be for them, and we become a reproach before all the world.

22 And when Akhior had finished these sayings, all the people standing round about the tent murmured, and the chief men of Holofernes, and all that dwelt by the sea side, and in Moab, spake that he should kill him.

23 For, say they, we will not be afraid of the face of the children of Yisra'EL: for, lo, it is a people that have no strength nor power for a strong battle

24 Now therefore, Adon Holofernes, we will go up, and they shall be a prey to be devoured of all thine army.

6 And when the tumult of men that were about the council was ceased, Holofernes the chief captain of the army of Asshur said unto Akhior and all the Moabim before all the company of other nations,

2 And who art thou, Akhior, and the hirelings of Ephraim, that thou hast prophesied against us as to day, and hast said, that we should not make war with the people of Yisra'EL, because their ELOHIM will defend them? and who is ELOHIM but Nebukad'netzar?

3 He will send his power, and will destroy them from the face of the earth, and their ELOHIM shall not deliver them: but we his servants will destroy them as one man; for they are not able to sustain the power of our horses.

4 For with them we will tread them under foot, and their mountains shall be drunken with their blood, and their fields shall be filled with their dead bodies, and their footsteps shall not be able to stand before us, for they shall utterly perish, saith king Nebukad'netzar, Adon of all the earth: for he said, None of my words shall be in vain.

5 And thou, Akhior, an hireling of Ammon, which hast spoken these words in the day of thine iniquity, shalt see my face no more from this day, until I take vengeance of this nation that came out of Mitzraim.

6 And then shall the sword of mine army, and the multitude of them that serve me, pass through thy sides, and thou shalt fall among their slain, when I return.

7 Now therefore my servants shall bring thee back into the hill country, and shall set thee in one of the cities of the passages:

8 And thou shalt not perish, till thou be destroyed with them.

9 And if thou persuade thyself in thy mind that they shall be taken, let not thy countenance fall: I have spoken it, and none of my words shall be in vain.

10 Then Holofernes commanded his servants, that waited in his tent, to take Akhior, and bring him to Beth-Ulyah, and deliver him into the hands of the children of Yisra'EL.

11 So his servants took him, and brought him out of the camp into the plain, and they went from the midst of the plain into the hill country, and came unto the fountains that were under Beth-Ulyah.

12 And when the men of the city saw them, they took up their weapons, and went out of the city to the top of the hill: and every man that used a sling kept them from coming up by casting of stones against them.

13 Nevertheless having gotten privily under the hill, they bound Akhior, and cast him down, and left him at the foot of the hill, and returned to their Adon.

14 But the children of Yisra'EL descended from their city, and came unto him, and loosed him, and brought him to Beth-Ulyah, and presented him to the governors of the city:

15 Which were in those days UzziYAH the son of Mikah, of the tribe of Shimon, and Chabris the son of Gotoni'EL, and Charmis the son of Malki'EL.

16 And they called together all the ancients of the city, and all their youth ran together, and their women, to the assembly, and they set Akhior in the midst of all their people. Then UzziYAH asked him of that which was done.

17 And he answered and declared unto them the words of the council of Holofernes, and all the words that he had spoken in the midst of the princes of Asshur, and whatsoever Holofernes had spoken proudly against the house of Yisra'EL.

18 Then the people fell down and worshipped ELOHIM, and cried unto ELOHIM. saying,

19 O YAHOWAH ELOHIM of heaven, behold their pride, and pity the low estate of our nation, and look upon the face of those that are sanctified unto thee this day.

20 Then they comforted Akhior, and praised him greatly.

21 And UzziYAH took him out of the assembly unto his house, and made a feast to the elders; and they called on the ELOHIM of Yisra'EL all that night for help.

7 The next day Holofernes commanded all his army, and all his people which were come to take his part, that they should remove their camp against Beth-Ulyah, to take aforehand the ascents of the hill country, and to make war against the children of Yisra'EL.

2 Then their strong men removed their camps in that day, and the army of the men of war was an hundred and seventy thousand footmen, and twelve thousand horsemen, beside the baggage, and other men that were afoot among them, a very great multitude.

3 And they camped in the valley near unto Beth-Ulyah, by the fountain, and they spread themselves in breadth over Dothaim even to Belmaim, and in length from Beth-Ulyah unto Cynamon, which is over against Yizre'EL.

4 Now the children of Yisra'EL, when they saw the multitude of them, were greatly troubled and said every one to his neighbour, Now will these men lick up the face of the earth; for neither the high mountains, nor the valleys, nor

the hills, are able to bear their weight.

5 Then every man took up his weapons of war, and when they had kindled fires upon their towers, they remained and watched all that night.

6 But in the second day Holofernes brought forth all his horsemen in the sight of the children of Yisra'EL which were in Beth-Ulyah,

7 And viewed the passages up to the city, and came to the fountains of their waters, and took them, and set garrisons of men of war over them, and he himself removed toward his people.

8 Then came unto him all the chief of the children of Esau, and all the governors of the people of Moab, and the captains of the sea coast, and said,

9 Let our Adon now hear a word, that there be not an overthrow in thine army.

10 For this people of the children of Yisra'EL do not trust in their spears, but in the height of the mountains wherein they dwell, because it is not easy to come up to the tops of their mountains.

11 Now therefore, Adoni, fight not against them in battle array, and there shall not so much as one man of their people perish.

12 Remain in thy camp, and keep all the men of thine army, and let thy servants get into their hands the fountain of water, which issueth forth of the foot of the mountain:

13 For all the inhabitants of Beth-Ulyah have their water thence; so shall thirst kill them, and they shall give up their city, and we and our people shall go up to the tops of the mountains that are near, and will camp upon them, to watch that none go out of the city.

14 So they and their wives and their children shall be consumed with fire, and before the sword come against them, they shall be overthrown in the streets where they dwell.

15 Thus shalt thou render them an evil reward; because they rebelled, and met not thy person peaceably.

16 And these words pleased Holofernes and all his servants, and he appointed to do as they had spoken.

17 So the camp of the children of Ammon departed, and with them five thousand of the Assyrians, and they pitched in the valley, and took the waters, and the fountains of the waters of the children of Yisra'EL.

18 Then the children of Esau went up with the children of Ammon, and camped in the hill country over against Dothaim: and they sent some of them toward the south, and toward the east over against Ekrebel, which is near unto Kusi, that is upon the brook Mochmur; and the rest of the army of the Assyrians camped in the plain, and covered the face of the whole land; and their tents and carriages were pitched to a very great multitude.

19 Then the children of Yisra'EL cried unto YAHOWAH their ELOHIM, because their heart failed, for all their enemies had compassed them round about, and there was no way to escape out from among them.

20 Thus all the company of Asshur remained about them, both their footmen, chariots, and horsemen, four and thirty days, so that all their vessels of water failed all the inhibitants of Beth-Ulyah.

21 And the cisterns were emptied, and they had not water to drink their fill for one day; for they gave them drink by measure.

22 Therefore their young children were out of heart, and their women and young men fainted for thirst, and fell down in the streets of the city, and by the passages of the gates, and there was no longer any strength in them.

23 Then all the people assembled to UzziYAH, and to the chief of the city, both young men, and women, and children, and cried with a loud voice, and said before all the elders,

24 ELOHIM be judge between us and you: for ye have done us great injury, in that ye have not required shalom of the children of Asshur.

25 For now we have no helper: but ELOHIM hath sold us into their hands, that we should be thrown down before them with thirst and great destruction.

26 Now therefore call them unto you, and deliver the whole city for a spoil to the people of Holofernes, and to all his army.

27 For it is better for us to be made a spoil unto them, than to die for thirst: for we will be his servants, that our souls may live, and not see the death of our infants before our eyes, nor our wives nor our children to die.

28 We take to witness against you the heaven and the earth, and our ELOHIM and YAHOWAH of our fathers, which punisheth us according to our sins and the sins of our fathers, that he do not according as we have said this day.

29 Then there was great weeping with one consent in the midst of the assembly; and they cried unto YAHOWAH ELOHIM with a loud voice.

30 Then said UzziYAH to them, Brethren, be of good courage, let us yet endure five days, in the which space YAHOWAH our ELOHIM may turn his mercy toward us; for he will not forsake us utterly.

31 And if these days pass, and there come no help unto us, I will do according to your word.

32 And he dispersed the people, every one to their own charge; and they went unto the walls and towers of their city, and sent the women and children into their houses: and they were very low brought in the city.

8 Now at that time Yehudiyth heard thereof, which was the daughter of Merari, the son of Ox, the son of Yoseph, the son of Ozel, the son of Elcia, the son of KhananYAH, the son of Gid'on, the son of Raphaim, the son of Akhitub, the son of Elihu, the son of Eliab, the son of Nathan'EL, the son of Sama'EL, the son of Salasadal, the son of Yisra'EL.

2 And Menassheh was her husband, of her tribe and kindred, who died in the barley harvest.

3 For as he stood overseeing them that bound sheaves in the field, the heat came upon his head, and he fell on his bed, and died in the city of Beth-Ulyah: and they buried him with his fathers in the field between Dothaim and Balamo.

4 So Yehudiyth was a widow in her house three years and four months.

5 And she made her a tent upon the top of her house, and put on sackcloth upon her loins and ware her widow's apparel.

6 And she fasted all the days of her widowhood, save the eves of the sabbaths, and the sabbaths, and the eves of the Renewed Months, and the Renewed Months and the feasts and solemn days of the house of Yisra'EL.

7 She was also of a goodly countenance, and very beautiful to behold: and her husband Menassheh had left her gold, and silver, and menservants and maidservants, and cattle, and lands; and she remained upon them.

8 And there was none that gave her an ill word; ar she feared ELOHIM greatly.

9 Now when she heard the evil words of the people against the governor, that they fainted for lack of water; for Yehudiyth had heard all the words that UzziYAH had spoken unto them, and that he had sworn to deliver the city unto the Assyrians after five days;

10 Then she sent her waitingwoman, that had the government of all things that she had, to call UzziYAH and Chabris and Charmis, the ancients of the city.

11 And they came unto her, and she said unto them, Hear me now, O ye governors of the inhabitants of Beth-Ulyah: for your words that ye have spoken before the people this day are not right, touching this oath which ye made and pronounced between ELOHIM and you, and have promised to deliver the city to our enemies, unless within these days YAHOWAH turn to help you.

12 And now who are ye that have tempted ELOHIM this day, and stand instead of ELOHIM among the children of men?

13 And now try YAHOWAH Almighty, but ye shall never know any thing.

14 For ye cannot find the depth of the heart of man, neither can ye perceive the things that he thinketh: then how can ye search out ELOHIM, that hath made all these things, and know his mind, or comprehend his purpose? Nay, my brethren, provoke not YAHOWAH our ELOHIM to anger.

15 For if he will not help us within these five days, he hath power to defend us when he will, even every day, or to destroy us before our enemies.

16 Do not bind the counsels of YAHOWAH our ELOHIM: for ELOHIM is not as man, that he may be threatened; neither is he as the son of man, that he should be wavering.

17 Therefore let us wait for salvation of him, and call upon him to help us, and he will hear our voice, if it please him.

18 For there arose none in our age, neither is there any now in these days neither tribe, nor family, nor people, nor city among us, which worship elohim made with hands, as hath been aforetime.

19 For the which cause our fathers were given to the sword, and for a spoil, and had a great fall before our enemies.

20 But we know none other elohim, therefore we trust that he will not dispise us, nor any of our nation.

21 For if we be taken so, all Yehudah shall lie waste, and our sanctuary shall be spoiled; and he will require the profanation thereof at our mouth.

22 And the slaughter of our brethren, and the captivity of the country, and the desolation of our inheritance, will he turn upon our heads among the Gentiles, wheresoever we shall be in bondage; and we shall be an offence and a reproach to all them that possess us.

23 For our servitude shall not be directed to favour: but YAHOWAH our ELOHIM shall turn it to dishonour.

24 Now therefore, O brethren, let us shew an example to our brethren, because their hearts depend upon us, and the sanctuary, and the house, and the altar, rest upon us.

25 Moreover let us give thanks to YAHOWAH our ELOHIM, which trieth us, even as he did our fathers.

26 Remember what things he did to Abraham, and how he tried Yitzkhaq, and what happened to Ya'aqob in Mesopotamia of Aram, when he kept the sheep of Laban his mother's brother.

27 For he hath not tried us in the fire, as he did them, for the examination of their hearts, neither hath he taken vengeance on us: but YAHOWAH doth scourge them that come near unto him, to admonish them.

28 Then said UzziYAH to her, All that thou hast spoken hast thou spoken with a good heart, and there is none that may gainsay thy words.

29 For this is not the first day wherein thy wisdom is manifested; but from the beginning of thy days all the people have known thy understanding, because the disposition of thine heart is good.

30 But the people were very thirsty, and compelled us to do unto them as we have spoken, and to bring an oath upon ourselves, which we will not break.

31 Therefore now pray thou for us, because thou art a godly woman, and YAHOWAH will send us rain to fill our cisterns, and we shall faint no more.

32 Then said Yehudiyth unto them, Hear me, and I will do a thing, which shall go throughout all generations to the children of our nation.

33 Ye shall stand this night in the gate, and I will go forth with my waitingwoman: and within the days that ye have promised to deliver the city to our enemies YAHOWAH will visit Yisra'EL by mine hand.

34 But enquire not ye of mine act: for I will not declare it unto you, till the things be finished that I do.

35 Then said UzziYAH and the princes unto her, Go in shalom, and YAHOWAH ELOHIM be before thee, to take vengeance on our enemies.

36 So they returned from the tent, and went to their wards.

9 Yehudiyth fell upon her face, and put ashes upon her head, and uncovered the sackcloth wherewith she was clothed; and about the time that the incense of that evening was offered in Yerushalem in the house of YAHOWAH Yehudiyth cried with a loud voice, and said,

2 O YAHOWAH ELOHIM of my father Shimon, to whom thou gavest a sword to take vengeance of the strangers, who loosened the girdle of a maid to defile her, and discovered the thigh to her shame, and polluted her virginity to her reproach; for thou saidst, It shall not be so; and yet they did so:

3 Wherefore thou gavest their rulers to be slain, so that they dyed their bed in blood, being deceived, and smotest the servants with their lords, and the lords upon their thrones;

4 And hast given their wives for a prey, and their daughters to be captives, and all their spoils to be divided among thy dear children; which were moved with thy zeal, and abhorred the pollution of their blood, and called upon thee for aid: O ELOHIM, O my ELOHIM, hear me also a widow.

5 For thou hast wrought not only those things, but also the things which fell out before, and which ensued after; thou hast thought upon the things which are now, and which are to come.

6 Yea, what things thou didst determine were ready at hand, and said, Lo, we are here: for all thy ways are prepared, and thy judgments are in thy foreknowledge.

7 For, behold, the Assyrians are multiplied in their power; they are exalted with horse and man; they glory in the strength of their footmen; they trust in shield, and spear, and bow, and sling; and know not that thou art YAHOWAH that breakest the battles: YAHOWAH is thy name.

8 Throw down their strength in thy power, and bring down their force in thy wrath: for they have purposed to defile thy sanctuary, and to pollute the tabernacle where thy glorious name resteth and to cast down with sword the horn of thy altar.

9 Behold their pride, and send thy wrath upon their heads: give into mine hand, which am a widow, the power that I have conceived.

10 Smite by the deceit of my lips the servant with the prince, and the prince with the servant: break down their stateliness by the hand of a woman.

11 For thy power standeth not in multitude nor thy might in strong men: for thou art a ELOHIM of the afflicted, an helper of the oppressed, an upholder of the weak, a protector of the forlorn, a saviour of them that are without hope.

12 I pray thee, I pray thee, O ELOHIM of my father, and ELOHIM of the inheritance of Yisra'EL, YAHOWAH of the heavens and earth, Creator of the waters, king of every creature, hear thou my prayer:

13 And make my speech and deceit to be their wound and stripe, who have purposed cruel things against thy covenant, and thy hallowed house, and against the top of Tzion, and against the house of the possession of thy children.

14 And make every nation and tribe to acknowledge that thou art the ELOHIM of all power and might, and that there is none other that protecteth the people of Yisra'EL but thou.

10 Now after that she had ceased to cry unto the ELOHIM of Yisra'EL, and bad made an end of all these words.

2 She rose where she had fallen down, and called her maid, and went down into the house in the which she abode in the sabbath days, and in her feast days,

3 And pulled off the sackcloth which she had on, and put off the garments of her widowhood, and washed her body all over with water, and anointed herself with precious ointment, and braided the hair of her head, and put on a tire upon it, and put on her garments of gladness, wherewith she was clad during the life of Menassheh her husband.

4 And she took sandals upon her feet, and put about her her bracelets, and her chains, and her rings, and her earrings, and all her ornaments, and decked herself bravely, to allure the eyes of all men that should see her.

5 Then she gave her maid a bottle of wine, and a cruse of oil, and filled a bag with parched corn, and lumps of figs, and with fine bread; so she folded all these things together, and laid them upon her.

6 Thus they went forth to the gate of the city of Beth-Ulyah, and found standing there UzziYAH and the ancients of the city, Chabris and Charmis.

7 And when they saw her, that her countenance was altered, and her apparel was changed, they wondered at her beauty very greatly, and said unto her.

8 The ELOHIM, the ELOHIM of our fathers give thee favour, and accomplish thine enterprizes to the glory of the children of Yisra'EL, and to the exaltation of Yerushalem. Then they worshipped ELOHIM.

9 And she said unto them, Command the gates of the city to be opened unto me, that I may go forth to accomplish the things whereof ye have spoken with me. So they commanded the young men to open unto her, as she had spoken.

10 And when they had done so, Yehudiyth went out, she, and her maid with her; and the men of the city looked after her, until she was gone down the mountain, and till she had passed the valley, and could see her no more.

11 Thus they went straight forth in the valley: and the first watch of the Assyrians met her,

12 And took her, and asked her, Of what people art thou? and whence comest thou? and whither goest thou? And she said, I am a woman of the

JUDITH

Hebrews, and am fled from them: for they shall be given you to be consumed:

13 And I am coming before Holofernes the chief captain of your army, to declare words of truth; and I will shew him a way, whereby he shall go, and win all the hill country, without losing the body or life of any one of his men.

14 Now when the men heard her words, and beheld her countenance, they wondered greatly at her beauty, and said unto her,

15 Thou hast saved thy life, in that thou hast hasted to come down to the presence of our Adon: now therefore come to his tent, and some of us shall conduct thee, until they have delivered thee to his hands.

16 And when thou standest before him, be not afraid in thine heart, but shew unto him according to thy word; and he will entreat thee well.

17 Then they chose out of them an hundred men to accompany her and her maid; and they brought her to the tent of Holofernes.

18 Then was there a concourse throughout all the camp: for her coming was noised among the tents; and they came about her, as she stood without the tent of Holofernes, till they told him of her.

19 And they wondered at her beauty, and admired the children of Yisra'EL because of her, and every one said to his neighbour, Who would despise this people, that have among them such women? surely it is not good that one man of them be left who being let go might deceive the whole earth.

20 And they that lay near Holofernes went out, and all his servants and they brought her into the tent.

21 Now Holofernes rested upon his bed under a canopy, which was woven with purple, and gold, and emeralds, and precious stones.

22 So they shewed him of her; and he came out before his tent with silver lamps going before him.

23 And when Yehudiyth was come before him and his servants they all marvelled at the beauty of her countenance; and she fell down upon her face, and did reverence unto him: and his servants took her up.

11 Then said Holofernes unto her, Woman, be of good comfort, fear not in thine heart: for I never hurt any that was willing to serve Nebukad'netzar, the king of all the earth.

2 Now therefore, if thy people that dwelleth in the mountains had not set light by me, I would not have lifted up my spear against them: but they have done these things to themselves.

3 But now tell me wherefore thou art fled from them, and art come unto us: for thou art come for safeguard; be of good comfort, thou shalt live this night, and hereafter:

4 For none shall hurt thee, but entreat thee well, as they do the servants of king Nebukad'netzar Adoni.

5 Then Yehudiyth said unto him, Receive the words of thy servant, and suffer thine handmaid to speak in thy presence, and I will declare no lie to Adoni this night.

6 And if thou wilt follow the words of thine handmaid, ELOHIM will bring the thing perfectly to pass by thee; and Adoni shall not fail of his purposes.

7 As Nebukad'netzar king of all the earth liveth, and as his power liveth, who hath sent thee for the upholding of every living thing: for not only men shall serve him by thee, but also the beasts of the field, and the cattle, and the fowls of the air, shall live by thy power under Nebukad'netzar and all his house.

8 For we have heard of thy wisdom and thy policies, and it is reported in all the earth, that thou only art excellent in all the kingdom, and mighty in knowledge, and wonderful in feats of war.

9 Now as concerning the matter, which Akhior did speak in thy council, we have heard his words; for the men of Beth-Ulyah saved him, and he declared unto them all that he had spoken unto thee.

10 Therefore, O Adon and governor, respect not his word; but lay it up in thine heart, for it is true: for our nation shall not be punished, neither can sword prevail against them, except they sin against their ELOHIM.

11 And now, that Adoni be not defeated and frustrate of his purpose, even death is now fallen upon them, and their sin hath overtaken them, wherewith they will provoke their ELOHIM to anger whensoever they shall do that which is not fit to be done:

12 For their victuals fail them, and all their water is scant, and they have determined to lay hands upon their cattle, and purposed to consume all those things, that ELOHIM hath forbidden them to eat by his Torah:

13 And are resolved to spend the firstfruits of the the tenths of wine and oil, which they had sanctified, and reserved for the priests that serve in Yerushalem before the face of our ELOHIM; the which things it is not lawful for any of the people so much as to touch with their hands.

14 For they have sent some to Yerushalem, because they also that dwell there have done the like, to bring them a licence from the senate.

15 Now when they shall bring them word, they will forthwith do it, and they shall be given to thee to be destroyed the same day.

16 Wherefore I thine handmaid, knowing all this, am fled from their presence; and ELOHIM hath sent me to work things with thee, whereat all the earth shall be astonished, and whosoever shall hear it.

17 For thy servant is religious, and serveth the ELOHIM of heaven day and night: now therefore Adoni, I will remain with thee, and thy servant will go out by night into the valley, and I will pray unto ELOHIM, and he will tell me when they have committed their sins:

18 And I will come and shew it unto thee: then thou shalt go forth with all thine army, and there shall be none of them that shall resist thee.

19 And I will lead thee through the midst of Ye-hudah, until thou come before Yerushalem; and I will set thy throne in the midst thereof; and thou shalt drive them as sheep that have no shepherd, and a dog shall not so much as open his mouth at thee: for these things were told me according to my foreknowledge, and they were declared unto me, and I am sent to tell thee.

20 Then her words pleased Holofernes and all his servants; and they marvelled at her wisdom, and said,

21 There is not such a woman from one end of the earth to the other, both for beauty of face, and wisdom of words.

22 Likewise Holofernes said unto her. ELOHIM hath done well to send thee before the people, that strength might be in our hands and destruction upon them that lightly regard Adoni.

23 And now thou art both beautiful in thy countenance, and witty in thy words: surely if thou do as thou hast spoken thy ELOHIM shall   be my ELOHIM, and thou shalt dwell in the house of king Nebukad'netzar, and shalt be renowned through the whole earth.

12 Then he commanded to bring her in where his plate was set; and bade that they should prepare for her of his own meats, and that she should drink of his own wine.

2 And Yehudiyth said, I will not eat thereof, lest there be an offence: but provision shall be made for me of the things that I have brought.

3 Then Holofernes said unto her, If thy provision should fail, how should we give thee the like? for there be none with us of thy nation.

4 Then said Yehudiyth unto him As thy soul liveth, Adoni, thine handmaid shall not spend those things that I have, before YAHOWAH work by mine hand the things that he hath determined.

5 Then the servants of Holofernes brought her into the tent, and she slept till midnight, and she arose when it was toward the morning watch,

6 And sent to Holofernes, saving, Let Adoni now command that thine handmaid may go forth unto prayer.

7 Then Holofernes commanded his guard that they should not stay her: thus she abode in the camp three days, and went out in the night into the valley of Beth-Ulyah, and washed herself in a fountain of water by the camp.

8 And when she came out, she besought YAHOWAH ELOHIM of Yisra'EL to direct her way to the raising up of the children of her people.

9 So she came in clean, and remained in the tent, until she did eat her meat at evening.

10 And in the fourth day Holofernes made a feast to his own servants only, and called none of the officers to the banquet.

11 Then said he to Bagoas the eunuch, who had charge over all that he had, Go now, and persuade this Hebrew woman which is with thee, that she come unto us, and eat and drink with us.

12 For, lo, it will be a shame for our person, if we shall let such a woman go, not having had her company; for if we draw her not unto us, she will laugh us to scorn.

13 Then went Bagoas from the presence of Holofernes, and came to her, and he said, Let not this fair damsel fear to come to Adoni, and to be honoured in his presence, and drink wine, and be merry with us and be made this day as one of the daughters of the Assyrians, which serve in the house of Nebukad'netzar.

14 Then said Yehudiyth unto him, Who am I now, that I should gainsay Adoni? surely whatsoever pleaseth him I will do speedily, and it shall be my joy unto the day of my death.

15 So she arose, and decked herself with her apparel and all her woman's attire, and her maid went and laid soft skins on the ground for her over against Holofernes, which she had received of Bagoas far her daily use, that she might sit and eat upon them.

16 Now when Yehudiyth came in and sat down, Holofernes his heart was ravished with her, and his mind was moved, and he desired greatly her company; for he waited a time to deceive her, from the day that he had seen her.

17 Then said Holofernes unto her, Drink now, and be merry with us.

18 So Yehudiyth said, I will drink now, Adoni, because my life is magnified in me this day more than all the days since I was born.

19 Then she took and ate and drank before him what her maid had prepared.

20 And Holofernes took great delight in her, and drank more wine than he had drunk at any time in one day since he was born.

13 Now when the evening was come, his servants made haste to depart, and Bagoas shut his tent without, and dismissed the waiters from the presence of his Adon; and they went to their beds: for they were all weary, because the feast had been long.

2 And Yehudiyth was left along in the tent, and Holofernes lying along upon his bed: for he was filled with wine.

3 Now Yehudiyth had commanded her maid to stand without her bedchamber, and to wait for her. coming forth, as she did daily: for she said she would go forth to her prayers, and she spake to Bagoas according to the same purpose.

4 So all went forth and none was left in the bedchamber, neither little nor great. Then Yehudiyth, standing by his bed, said in her heart, O YAHOWAH ELOHIM of all power, look at this present upon the works of mine hands for the exaltation of Yerushalem.

5 For now is the time to help thine inheritance, and to execute thine enterprizes to the destruction of the enemies which are risen against us.

6 Then she came to the pillar of the bed, which was at Holofernes' head, and took down his fauchion from thence,

JUDITH

7 And approached to his bed, and took hold of the hair of his head, and said, Strengthen me, O YAHOWAH ELOHIM of Yisra'EL, this day.

8 And she smote twice upon his neck with all her might, and she took away his head from him.

9 And tumbled his body down from the bed, and pulled down the canopy from the pillars; and anon after she went forth, and gave Holofernes his head to her maid;

10 And she put it in her bag of meat: so they twain went together according to their custom unto prayer: and when they passed the camp, they compassed the valley, and went up the mountain of Beth-Ulyah, and came to the gates thereof.

11 Then said Yehudiyth afar off, to the watchmen at the gate, Open, open now the gate: ELOHIM, even our ELOHIM, is with us, to shew his power yet in Yerushalem, and his forces against the enemy, as he hath even done this day.

12 Now when the men of her city heard her voice, they made haste to go down to the gate of their city, and they called the elders of the city.

13 And then they ran all together, both small and great, for it was strange unto them that she was come: so they opened the gate, and received them, and made a fire for a light, and stood round about them.

14 Then she said to them with a loud voice, Praise, praise ELOHIM, praise ELOHIM, I say, for he hath not taken away his mercy from the house of Yisra'EL, but hath destroyed our enemies by mine hands this night.

15 So she took the head out of the bag, and shewed it, and said unto them, behold the head of Holofernes, the chief captain of the army of Asshur, and behold the canopy, wherein he did lie in his drunkenness; and YAHOWAH hath smitten him by the hand of a woman.

16 As YAHOWAH liveth, who hath kept me in my way that I went, my countenance hath deceived him to his destruction, and yet hath he not committed sin with me, to defile and shame me.

17 Then all the people were wonderfully astonished, and bowed themselves and worshipped ELOHIM, and said with one accord, Blessed be thou, O our ELOHIM, which hast this day brought to nought the enemies of thy people.

18 Then said UzziYAH unto her, O daughter, blessed art thou of the Most High ELOHIM above all the women upon the earth; and blessed be YAHOWAH ELOHIM, which hath created the heavens and the earth, which hath directed thee to the cutting off of the head of the chief of our enemies.

19 For this thy confidence shall not depart from the heart of men, which remember the power of ELOHIM for ever.

20 And ELOHIM turn these things to thee for a perpetual praise, to visit thee in good things because thou hast not spared thy life for the affliction of our nation, but hast revenged our ruin, walking a straight way before our ELOHIM. And all the people said; So be it, so be it.

14 Then said Yehudiyth unto them, Hear me now, my brethren, and take this head, and hang it upon the highest place of your walls.

2 And so soon as the morning shall appear, and the sun shall come forth upon the earth, take ye every one his weapons, and go forth every valiant man out of the city, and set ye a captain over them, as though ye would go down into the field toward the watch of the Assyrians; but go not down.

3 Then they shall take their armour, and shall go into their camp, and raise up the captains of the army of Asshur, and shall run to the tent of Holofernes, but shall not find him: then fear shall fall upon them, and they shall flee before your face.

4 So ye, and all that inhabit the coast of Yisra'EL, shall pursue them, and overthrow them as they go.

5 But before ye do these things, call me Akhior the Ammonite, that he may see and know him that despised the house of Yisra'EL, and that sent him to us as it were to his death.

6 Then they called Akhior out of the house of UzziYAH; and when he was come, and saw the head of Holofernes in a man's hand in the assembly of the people, he fell down on his face, and his ruakh failed.

7 But when they had recovered him, he fell at Yehudiyth's feet, and reverenced her, and said, Blessed art thou in all the tabernacles of Yehudah, and in all nations, which hearing thy name shall be astonished.

8 Now therefore tell me all the things that thou hast done in these days. Then Yehudiyth declared unto him in the midst of the people all that she had done, from the day that she went forth until that hour she spake unto them.

9 And when she had left off speaking, the people shouted with a loud voice, and made a joyful noise in their city.

10 And when Akhior had seen all that the ELOHIM of Yisra'EL had done, he believed in ELOHIM greatly, and circumcised the flesh of his foreskin, and was joined unto the house of Yisra'EL unto this day.

11 And as soon as the morning arose, they hanged the head of Holofernes upon the wall, and every man took his weapons, and they went forth by bands unto the straits of the mountain.

12 But when the Assyrians saw them, they sent to their leaders, which came to their captains and tribunes, and to every one of their rulers.

13 So they came to Holofernes' tent, and said to him that had the charge of all his things, Waken now our Adon: for the slaves have been bold to come down against us to battle, that they may be utterly destroyed.

14 Then went in Bagoas, and knocked at the door of the tent; for he thought that he had slept with Yehudiyth.

15 But because none answered, he opened it, and went into the bedchamber, and found him cast upon the floor dead, and his head was taken from him.

16 Therefore he cried with a loud voice, with weeping, and sighing, and a mighty cry, and rent his garments.

17 After he went into the tent where Yehudiyth lodged: and when he found her not, he leaped out to the people, and cried,

18 These slaves have dealt treacherously; one woman of the Hebrews hath brought shame upon the house of king Nebukad'netzar: for, behold, Holofernes lieth upon the ground without a head.

19 When the captains of the Assyrians' army heard these words, they rent their coats and their minds were wonderfully troubled, and there was a cry and a very great noise throughout the camp.

15 And when they that were in the tents heard, they were astonished at the thing that was done.

2 And fear and trembling fell upon them, so that there was no man that durst abide in the sight of his neighbour, but rushing out all together, they fled into every way of the plain, and of the hill country.

3 They also that had camped in the mountains round about Beth-Ulyah fled away. Then the children of Yisra'EL, every one that was a warrior among them, rushed out upon them.

4 Then sent UzziYAH to Betomastaim, and to Bebai, and Khobai, and Qolah and to all the coasts of Yisra'EL, such as should tell the things that were done, and that all should rush forth upon their enemies to destroy them.

5 Now when the children of Yisra'EL heard it, they all fell upon them with one consent, and slew them unto Khobai: likewise also they that came from Yerushalem, and from all the hill country, (for men had told them what things were done in the camp of their enemies) and they that were in Gil'ad, and in Galilah, chased them with a great slaughter, until they were past Dameseq and the borders thereof.

6 And the residue that dwelt at Beth-Ulyah, fell upon the camp of Asshur, and spoiled them, and were greatly enriched.

7 And the children of Yisra'EL that returned from the slaughter had that which remained; and the villages and the cities, that were in the mountains and in the plain, gat many spoils: for the multitude was very great.

8 Then Yaho'yaqim the high priest, and the ancients of the children of Yisra'EL that dwelt in Yerushalem, came to behold the good things that ELOHIM had shewed to Yisra'EL, and to see Yehudiyth, and to salute her.

9 And when they came unto her, they blessed her with one accord, and said unto her, Thou art the exaltation of Yerushalem, thou art the great glory of Yisra'EL, thou art the great rejoicing of our nation:

10 Thou hast done all these things by thine hand: thou hast done much good to Yisra'EL, and ELOHIM is pleased therewith: blessed be thou of the Almighty YAHOWAH for evermore. And all the people said, So be it.

11 And the people spoiled the camp the space of thirty days: and they gave unto Yehudiyth Holofernes his tent, and all his plate, and beds, and vessels, and all his stuff: and she took it and laid it on her mule; and made ready her carts, and laid them thereon.

12 Then all the women of Yisra'EL ran together to see her, and blessed her, and made a dance among them for her: and she took branches in her hand, and gave also to the women that were with her.

13 And they put a garland of olive upon her and her maid that was with her, and she went before all the people in the dance, leading all the women: and all the men of Yisra'EL followed in their armour with garlands, and with songs in their mouths.

16 Then Yehudiyth began to sing this thanksgiving in all Yisra'EL, and all the people sang after her this song of praise.

2 And Yehudiyth said, Begin unto my ELOHIM with timbrels, sing unto my YAHOWAH with cymbals: tune unto him a new psalm: exalt him, and call upon his name.

3 For ELOHIM breaketh the battles: for among the camps in the midst of the people he hath delivered me out of the hands of them that persecuted me.

4 Asshur came out of the mountains from the north, he came with ten thousands of his army, the multitude whereof stopped the torrents, and their horsemen have covered the hills.

5 He bragged that he would burn up my borders, and kill my young men with the sword, and dash the sucking children against the ground, and make mine infants as a prey, and my virgins as a spoil.

6 But the Almighty YAHOWAH hath disappointed them by the hand of a woman.

7 For the mighty one did not fall by the young men, neither did the sons of the Titans smite him, nor high giants set upon him: but Yehudiyth the daughter of Merari weakened him with the beauty of her countenance.

8 For she put off the garment of her widowhood for the exaltation of those that were oppressed in Yisra'EL, and anointed her face with ointment, and bound her hair in a tire, and took a linen garment to deceive him.

9 Her sandals ravished his eyes, her beauty took his mind prisoner, and the fauchion passed through his neck.

10 The Persians quaked at her boldness, and the Medes were daunted at her hardiness.

11 Then my afflicted shouted for joy, and my weak ones cried aloud; but they were astonished: these lifted up their voices, but they were overthrown.

12 The sons of the damsels have pierced them through, and wounded them as fugatives' children: they perished by the battle of YAHOWAH.

13 I will sing unto YAHOWAH a new song: O YAHOWAH, thou art great and glorious, wonderful in strength, and invincible.

14 Let all creatures serve thee: for thou spakest, and they were made, thou didst send forth thy RUAKH, and it created them, and there is

JUDITH

none that can resist thy voice.

15 For the mountains shall be moved from their foundations with the waters, the rocks shall melt as wax at thy presence: yet thou art merciful to them that fear thee.

16 For all sacrifice is too little for a sweet savour unto thee, and all the fat is not sufficient for thy burnt offering: but he that feareth YAHOWAH is great at all times.

17 Woe to the nations that rise up against my kindred! YAHOWAH Almighty will take vengeance of them in the day of judgment, in putting fire and worms in their flesh; and they shall feel them, and weep for ever.

18 Now as soon as they entered into Yerushalem, they worshipped YAHOWAH; and as soon as the people were purified, they offered their burnt offerings, and their free offerings, and their gifts.

19 Yehudiyth also dedicated all the stuff of Holofernes, which the people had given her, and gave the canopy, which she had taken out of his bedchamber, for a gift unto YAHOWAH.

20 So the people continued feasting in Yerushalem before the sanctuary for the space of three months and Yehudiyth remained with them.

21 After this time every one returned to his own inheritance, and Yehudiyth went to Beth-Ulyah, and remained in her own possession, and was in her time honourable in all the country.

22 And many desired her, but none knew her all the days of her life, after that Menassheh her husband was dead, and was gathered to his people.

23 But she increased more and more in honour, and waxed old in her husband's house, being an hundred and five years old, and made her maid free; so she died in Beth-Ulyah: and they buried her in the cave of her husband Menassheh.

24 And the house of Yisra'EL lamented her seven days: and before she died, she did distribute her goods to all them that were nearest of kindred to Menassheh her husband, and to them that were the nearest of her kindred.

25 And there was none that made the children of Yisra'EL any more afraid in the days of Yehudiyth, nor a long time after her death.

THE REST OF THE BOOK OF
ESTHER

The Rest of the Chapters of the Book of Esther

104 Then Mordekai said, ELOHIM hath done these things.

5 For I remember a dream which I saw concerning these matters, and nothing thereof hath failed.

6 A little fountain became a river, and there was light, and the sun, and much water: this river is Esther, whom the king married, and made queen:

7 And the two dragons are I and Haman.

8 And the heathen were those that were assembled to destroy the name of the Yehudim:

9 And my nation is this Yisra'EL, which cried to ELOHIM, and were saved: for YAHOWAH hath saved his people, and YAHOWAH hath delivered us from all those evils, and ELOHIM hath wrought signs and great wonders, which have not been done among the Gentiles.

10 Therefore hath he made two lots, one for the people of ELOHIM, and another for all the Gentiles.

11 And these two lots came at the hour, and time, and day of judgment, before ELOHIM among all nations.

12 So ELOHIM remembered his people, and justified his inheritance.

13 Therefore those days shall be unto them in the month Adar, the fourteenth and fifteenth day of the same month, with an assembly, and joy, and with gladness before ELOHIM, according to the generations for ever among his people.

11 In the fourth year of the reign of Ptolemeus and Qlio'patrah, Dozitios, who said he was a priest and Lewy'im, and Ptolemeus his son, brought this epistle of Phurim, which they said was the same, and that Lizimakos the son of Ptolemeus, that was in Yerushalem, had interpreted it.

2 In the second year of the reign of Artakh'shasheth the great, in the first day of the month Nisan, Mordekai the son of Yair, the son of Shimi, the son of Qish, of the tribe of Benyamin, had a dream;

3 Who was a Yehudi, and dwelt in the city of Susa, a great man, being a servitor in the king's court.

4 He was also one of the captives, which Nebukad'netzar the king of Babel carried from Yerushalem with YekonYAH king of Yehudah; and this was his dream:

5 Behold a noise of a tumult, with thunder, and earthquakes, and uproar in the land:

6 And, behold, two great dragons came forth ready to fight, and their cry was great.

7 And at their cry all nations were prepared to battle, that they might fight against the righteous people.

8 And lo a day of darkness and obscurity, tribulation and anguish, affliction and great uproar, upon earth.

9 And the whole righteous nation was troubled, fearing their own evils, and were ready to perish.

10 Then they cried unto ELOHIM, and upon their cry, as it were from a little fountain, was made a great flood, even much water.

11 The light and the sun rose up, and the lowly were exalted, and devoured the glorious.

12 Now when Mordekai, who had seen this dream, and what ELOHIM had determined to do, was awake, he bare this dream in mind, and until night by all means was desirous to know it.

12 And Mordekai took his rest in the court with Bigtan and Teresh, the two eunuchs of the king, and keepers of the palace.

2 And he heard their devices, and searched out their purposes, and learned that they were about to lay hands upon Artakh'shasheth the king; and so he certified the king of them.

3 Then the king examined the two eunuchs, and after that they had confessed it, they were strangled.

4 And the king made a record of these things, and Mordekai also wrote thereof.

5 So the king commanded, Mordekai to serve in the court, and for this he rewarded him.

6 Howbeit Haman the son of Hamedatha the Agagim, who was in great honour with the king, sought to molest Mordekai and his people because of the two eunuchs of the king.

13 The copy of the letters was this: The great king Artakh'shasheth writeth these things to the princes and governours that are under him from Hodu unto Kush in an hundred and seven and twenty provinces.

2 After that I became Adon over many nations and had dominion over the whole world, not lifted up with presumption of my authority, but carrying myself always with equity and mildness, I purposed to settle my subjects continually in a quiet life, and making my kingdom peaceable, and open for passage to the utmost coasts, to renew shalom, which is desired of all men.

3 Now when I asked my counsellors how this might be brought to pass, Haman, that excelled in wisdom among us, and was approved for his constant good will and steadfast fidelity, and had the honour of the second place in the kingdom,

4 Declared unto us, that in all nations throughout the world there was scattered a certain malicious people, that had Torah contrary to all nations, and continually despised the commandments of kings, so as the uniting of our kingdoms, honourably intended by us cannot go forward.

5 Seeing then we understand that this people alone is continually in opposition unto all men,

differing in the strange manner of their Torah, and evil affected to our state, working all the mischief they can that our kingdom may not be firmly established:

6 Therefore have we commanded, that all they that are signified in writing unto you by Haman, who is ordained over the affairs, and is next unto us, shall all, with their wives and children, be utterly destroyed by the sword of their enemies, without all mercy and pity, the fourteenth day of the twelfth month Adar of this present year:

7 That they, who of old and now also are malicious, may in one day with violence go into the grave, and so ever hereafter cause our affairs to be well settled, and without trouble.

8 Then Mordekai thought upon all the works of YAHOWAH, and made his prayer unto him,

9 Saying, O YAHOWAH, YAHOWAH, the King Almighty: for the whole world is in thy power, and if thou hast appointed to save Yisra'EL, there is no man that can gainsay thee:

10 For thou hast made heaven and earth, and all the wondrous things under the heaven.

11 Thou art YAHOWAH of all things, and and there is no man that can resist thee, which art YAHOWAH.

12 Thou knowest all things, and thou knowest, YAHOWAH, that it was neither in contempt nor pride, nor for any desire of glory, that I did not bow down to proud Haman.

13 For I could have been content with good will for the salvation of Yisra'EL to kiss the soles of his feet.

14 But I did this, that I might not prefer the glory of man above the glory of ELOHIM: neither will I worship any but thee, O ELOHIM, neither will I do it in pride.

15 And now, O YAHOWAH ELOHIM and King, spare thy people: for their eyes are upon us to bring us to nought; yea, they desire to destroy the inheritance, that hath been thine from the beginning.

16 Despise not the portion, which thou hast delivered out of Mitzraim for thine own self.

17 Hear my prayer, and be merciful unto thine inheritance: turn our sorrow into joy, that we may live, O YAHOWAH, and praise thy name: and destroy not the mouths of them that praise thee, O YAHOWAH.

18 All Yisra'EL in like manner cried most earnestly unto YAHOWAH, because their death was before their eyes.

14 Queen Esther also, being in fear of death, resorted unto YAHOWAH:

2 And laid away her glorious apparel, and put on the garments of anguish and mourning: and instead of precious ointments, she covered her head with ashes and dung, and she humbled her body greatly, and all the places of her joy she filled with her torn hair.

3 And she prayed unto YAHOWAH ELOHIM of Yisra'EL, saying, O my YAHOWAH, thou only art our King: help me, desolate woman, which have no helper but thee:

4 For my danger is in mine hand.

5 From my youth up I have heard in the tribe of my family that thou, O YAHOWAH, tookest Yisra'EL from among all people, and our fathers from all their predecessors, for a perpetual inheritance, and thou hast performed whatsoever thou didst promise them.

6 And now we have sinned before thee: therefore hast thou given us into the hands of our enemies,

7 Because we worshipped their elohim: O YAHOWAH, thou art righteous.

8 Nevertheless it satisfieth them not, that we are in bitter captivity: but they have stricken hands with their idols,

9 That they will abolish the thing that thou with thy mouth hast ordained, and destroy thine inheritance, and stop the mouth of them that praise thee, and quench the glory of thy house, and of thine altar,

10 And open the mouths of the heathen to set forth the praises of the idols, and to magnify a fleshly king for ever.

11 O YAHOWAH, give not thy sceptre unto them that be nothing, and let them not laugh at our fall; but turn their device upon themselves, and make him an example, that hath begun this against us.

12 Remember, O YAHOWAH, make thyself known in time of our affliction, and give me boldness, O King of the nations, and YAHOWAH of all power.

13 Give me eloquent speech in my mouth before the lion: turn his heart to hate him that fighteth against us, that there may be an end of him, and of all that are likeminded to him:

14 But deliver us with thine hand, and help me that am desolate, and which have no other help but thee.

15 Thou knowest all things, O YAHOWAH; thou knowest that I hate the glory of the unrighteous, and abhor the bed of the uncircumcised, and of all the heathen.

16 Thou knowest my necessity: for I abhor the sign of my high estate, which is upon mine head in the days wherein I shew myself, and that I abhor it as a menstruous rag, and that I wear it not when I am private by myself.

17 And that thine handmaid hath not eaten at Haman's table, and that I have not greatly esteemed the king's feast, nor drunk the wine of the drink offerings.

18 Neither had thine handmaid any joy since the day that I was brought hither to this present, but in thee, O YAHOWAH ELOHIM of Abraham.

19 O thou mighty ELOHIM above all, hear the voice of the forlorn and deliver us out of the hands of the mischievous, and deliver me out of my fear.

15 And upon the third day, when she had ended her prayers, she laid away her mourning garments, and put on her glorious apparel.

2 And being gloriously adorned, after she had called upon ELOHIM, who is the beholder and saviour of all things, she took two maids with her:

3 And upon the one she leaned, as carrying herself daintily;

4 And the other followed, bearing up her train.

5 And she was ruddy through the perfection of her beauty, and her countenance was cheerful and very amiable: but her heart was in anguish for fear.

6 Then having passed through all the doors, she stood before the king, who sat upon his royal throne, and was clothed with all his robes of majesty, all glittering with gold and precious stones; and he was very dreadful.

7 Then lifting up his countenance that shone with majesty, he looked very fiercely upon her: and the queen fell down, and was pale, and fainted, and bowed herself upon the head of the maid that went before her.

8 Then ELOHIM changed the ruakh of the king into mildness, who in a fear leaped from his throne, and took her in his arms, till she came to herself again, and comforted her with loving words and said unto her,

9 Esther, what is the matter? I am thy brother, be of good cheer:

10 Thou shalt not die, though our our commandment be general: come near.

11 And so be held up his golden sceptre, and laid it upon her neck,

12 And embraced her, and said, Speak unto me.

13 Then said she unto him, I saw thee, Adoni, as an Angel of ELOHIM, and my heart was troubled for fear of thy majesty.

14 For wonderful art thou, Adon, and thy countenance is full of grace.

15 And as she was speaking, she fell down for faintness.

16 Then the king was troubled, and all his servants comforted her.

16 The great king Artakh'shasheth unto the princes and governors of an hundred and seven and twenty provinces from Hodu unto Kush, and unto all our faithful subjects, greeting.

2 Many, the more often they are honoured with the great bounty of their gracious princes, the more proud they are waxen,

3 And endeavour to hurt not our subjects only, but not being able to bear abundance, do take in hand to practise also against those that do them good:

4 And take not only thankfulness away from among men, but also lifted up with the glorious words of lewd persons, that were never good, they think to escape the justice of ELOHIM, that seeth all things and hateth evil.

5 Oftentimes also fair speech of those, that are put in trust to manage their friends' affairs, hath caused many that are in authority to be partakers of innocent blood, and hath enwrapped them in remediless calamities:

6 Beguiling with the falsehood and deceit of their lewd disposition the innocency and goodness of princes.

7 Now ye may see this, as we have declared, not so much by ancient histories, as ye may, if ye search what hath been wickedly done of late through the pestilent behaviour of them that are unworthily placed in authority.

8 And we must take care for the time to come, that our kingdom may be quiet and peaceable for all men,

9 Both by changing our purposes, and always judging things that are evident with more equal proceeding.

10 For Haman, a Macedonian, the son of Amadatha, being indeed a stranger from the Persian blood, and far distant from our goodness, and as a stranger received of us,

11 Had so far forth obtained the favour that we shew toward every nation, as that he was called our father, and was continually honoured of all the next person unto the king.

12 But he, not bearing his great dignity, went about to deprive us of our kingdom and life:

13 Having by manifold and cunning deceits sought of us the destruction, as well of Mordekai, who saved our life, and continually procured our good, as also of blameless Esther, partaker of our kingdom, with their whole nation.

14 For by these means he thought, finding us destitute of friends to have translated the kingdom of the Persians to the Macedonians.

15 But we find that the Yehudim, whom this wicked wretch hath delivered to utter destruction, are no evildoers, but live by most just Torah:

16 And that they be children of the Most High and most mighty, living ELOHIM, who hath ordered the kingdom both unto us and to our progenitors in the most excellent manner.

17 Wherefore ye shall do well not to put in execution the letters sent unto you by Haman the son of Amadatha.

18 For he that was the worker of these things, is hanged at the gates of Susa with all his family: ELOHIM, who ruleth all things, speedily rendering vengeance to him according to his deserts.

19 Therefore ye shall publish the copy of this letter in all places, that the Yehudim may freely live after their own Torah.

20 And ye shall aid them, that even the same day, being the thirteenth day of the twelfth month Adar, they may be avenged on them, who in the time of their affliction shall set upon them.

21 For Almighty ELOHIM hath turned to joy unto them the day, wherein the chosen people should have perished.

22 Ye shall therefore among your solemn feasts keep it an high day with all feasting:

23 That both now and hereafter there may be safety to us and the well affected Persians; but to those which do conspire against us a memorial of destruction.

24 Therefore every city and country whatsoever,

which shall not do according to these things, shall be destroyed without mercy with fire and sword, and shall be made not only unpassable for men, but also most hateful to wild beasts and fowls for ever.

THE WISDOM OF
SOLOMON
ALSO KNOWN AS THE BOOK OF WISDOM

1 Love righteousness, ye that be judges of the earth: think of ELOHIM with a good (heart,) and in simplicity of heart seek him.

2 For he will be found of them that tempt him not; and sheweth himself unto such as do not distrust him.

3 For froward thoughts separate from ELOHIM: and his power, when it is tried, reproveth the unwise.

4 For into a malicious soul wisdom shall not enter; nor dwell in the body that is subject unto sin.

5 For the RUAKH HA QODESH of discipline will flee deceit, and remove from thoughts that are without understanding, and will not abide when unrighteousness cometh in.

6 For wisdom is a loving RUAKH; and will not acquit a blasphemer of his words: for ELOHIM is witness of his reins, and a true beholder of his heart, and a hearer of his tongue.

7 For the Spirit of YAHOWAH filleth the world: and that which containeth all things hath knowledge of the voice.

8 Therefore he that speaketh unrighteous things cannot be hid: neither shall vengeance, when it punisheth, pass by him.

9 For inquisition shall be made into the counsels of the ungodly: and the sound of his words shall come unto ELOHIM for the manifestation of his wicked deeds.

10 For the ear of jealousy heareth all things: and the noise of murmurings is not hid.

11 Therefore beware of murmuring, which is unprofitable; and refrain your tongue from backbiting: for there is no word so secret, that shall go for nought: and the mouth that belieth slayeth the soul.

12 Seek not death in the error of your life: and pull not upon yourselves destruction with the works of your hands.

13 For ELOHIM made not death: neither hath he pleasure in the destruction of the living.

14 For he created all things, that they might have their being: and the generations of the world were healthful; and there is no poison of destruction in them, nor the kingdom of death upon the earth:

15 (For righteousness is immortal:)

16 But ungodly men with their works and words called it to them: for when they thought to have it their friend, they consumed to nought, and made a covenant with it, because they are worthy to take part with it.

2 For the ungodly said, reasoning with themselves, but not aright, Our life is short and tedious, and in the death of a man there is no remedy: neither was there any man known to have returned from the grave.

2 For we are born at all adventure: and we shall be hereafter as though we had never been: for the breath in our nostrils is as smoke, and a little spark in the moving of our heart:

3 Which being extinguished, our body shall be turned into ashes, and our ruakh shall vanish as the soft air,

4 And our name shall be forgotten in time, and no man shall have our works in remembrance, and our life shall pass away as the trace of a cloud, and shall be dispersed as a mist, that is driven away with the beams of the sun, and overcome with the heat thereof.

5 For our time is a very shadow that passeth away; and after our end there is no returning: for it is fast sealed, so that no man cometh again.

6 Come on therefore, let us enjoy the good things that are present: and let us speedily use the creatures like as in youth.

7 Let us fill ourselves with costly wine and ointments: and let no flower of the spring pass by us:

8 Let us crown ourselves with rosebuds, before they be withered:

9 Let none of us go without his part of our voluptuousness: let us leave tokens of our joyfulness in every place: for this is our portion, and our lot is this.

10 Let us oppress the poor righteous man, let us not spare the widow, nor reverence the ancient gray hairs of the aged.

11 Let our strength be the Torah of justice: for that which is feeble is found to be nothing worth.

12 Therefore let us lie in wait for the righteous; because he is not for our turn, and he is clean contrary to our doings: he upbraideth us with our offending the Torah, and objecteth to our infamy the transgressions of our education.

13 He professeth to have the knowledge of ELOHIM: and he calleth himself the child of YAHOWAH.

14 He was made to reprove our thoughts.

15 He is grievous unto us even to behold: for his life is not like other men's, his ways are of another fashion.

16 We are esteemed of him as counterfeits: he abstaineth from our ways as from filthiness: he pronounceth the end of the just to be blessed, and maketh his boast that YAHOWAH is his father.

17 Let us see if his words be true: and let us prove what shall happen in the end of him.

18 For if the just man be the son of ELOHIM, he will help him, and deliver him from the hand of his enemies.

19 Let us examine him with despitefulness and torture, that we may know his meekness, and prove his patience.

20 Let us condemn him with a shameful death: for by his own saying he shall be respected.

21 Such things they did imagine, and were deceived: for their own wickedness hath blinded them.

22 As for the mysteries of ELOHIM, they kn ew them not: neither hoped they for the wages of righteousness, nor discerned a reward for blameless souls.

23 For ELOHIM created man to be immortal, and made him to be an image of his own eternity.

24 Nevertheless through envy of the devil came death into the world: and they that do hold of his side do find it.

3 But the souls of the righteous are in the hand of ELOHIM, and there shall no torment touch them.

2 In the sight of the unwise they seemed to die: and their departure is taken for misery,

3 And their going from us to be utter destruction: but they are in shalom.

4 For though they be punished in the sight of men, yet is their hope full of immortality.

5 And having been a little chastised, they shall be greatly rewarded: for ELOHIM proved them, and found them worthy for himself.

6 As gold in the furnace hath he tried them, and received them as a burnt offering.

7 And in the time of their visitation they shall shine, and run to and fro like sparks among the stubble.

8 They shall judge the heathen, and have dominion over the people, and their YAHOWAH shall reign for ever.

9 They that put their trust in him shall understand the truth: and such as be faithful in love shall abide with him: for grace and mercy is to his saints, and he hath care for his elect.

10 But the ungodly shall be punished according to their own imaginations, which have neglected the righteous, and forsaken YAHOWAH.

11 For whoso despiseth wisdom and nurture, he is miserable, and their hope is vain, their labours unfruitful, and their works unprofitable:

12 Their wives are foolish, and their children wicked:

13 Their offspring is cursed. Wherefore blessed is the barren that is undefiled, which hath not known the sinful bed: she shall have fruit in the visitation of souls.

14 And blessed is the eunuch, which with his hands hath wrought no iniquity, nor imagined wicked things against ELOHIM: for unto him shall be given the special gift of faith, and an inheritance in the temple of YAHOWAH more acceptable to his mind.

15 For glorious is the fruit of good labours: and the root of wisdom shall never fall away.

16 As for the children of adulterers, they shall not come to their perfection, and the seed of an unrighteous bed shall be rooted out.

17 For though they live long, yet shall they be nothing regarded: and their last age shall be without honour.

18 Or, if they die quickly, they have no hope, neither comfort in the day of trial.

19 For horrible is the end of the unrighteous generation.

4 Better it is to have no children, and to have virtue: for the memorial thereof is immortal: because it is known with ELOHIM, and with men.

2 When it is present, men take example at it; and when it is gone, they desire it: it weareth a crown, and triumpheth for ever, having gotten the victory, striving for undefiled rewards.

3 But the multiplying brood of the ungodly shall not thrive, nor take deep rooting from bastard slips, nor lay any fast foundation.

4 For though they flourish in branches for a time; yet standing not last, they shall be shaken with the wind, and through the force of winds they shall be rooted out.

5 The imperfect branches shall be broken off, their fruit unprofitable, not ripe to eat, yea, meet for nothing.

6 For children begotten of unlawful beds are witnesses of wickedness against their parents in their trial.

7 But though the righteous be prevented with death, yet shall he be in rest.

8 For honourable age is not that which standeth in length of time, nor that is measured by number of years.

9 But wisdom is the gray hair unto men, and an unspotted life is old age.

10 He pleased YAHOWAH, and was beloved of him: so that living among sinners he was translated.

11 Yea speedily was he taken away, lest that wickedness should alter his understanding, or deceit beguile his soul.

12 For the bewitching of naughtiness doth obscure things that are honest; and the wandering of concupiscence doth undermine the simple mind.

13 He, being made perfect in a short time, fulfilled a long time:

14 For his soul pleased ELOHIM: therefore hasted he to take him away from among the wicked.

15 This the people saw, and understood it not, neither laid they up this in their minds, That his grace and mercy is with his saints, and that he hath respect unto his chosen.

16 Thus the righteous that is dead shall condemn the ungodly which are living; and youth that is soon perfected the many years and old age of the unrighteous.

17 For they shall see the end of the wise, and shall not understand what is in his counsel hath decreed of him, and to what end YAHOWAH hath set him in safety.

18 They shall see him, and despise him; but YAHOWAH shall laugh them to scorn: and they shall hereafter be a vile carcase, and a reproach among the dead for evermore.

19 For he shall rend them, and cast them down headlong, that they shall be speechless; and he shall shake them from the foundation; and they

shall be utterly laid waste, and be in sorrow; and their memorial shall perish.

20 And when they cast up the accounts of their sins, they shall come with fear: and their own iniquities shall convince them to their face.

5 Then shall the righteous man stand in great boldness before the face of such as have afflicted him, and made no account of his labours.

2 When they see it, they shall be troubled with terrible fear, and shall be amazed at the strangeness of his salvation, so far beyond all that they looked for.

3 And they repenting and groaning for anguish of ruakh shall say within themselves, This was he, whom we had sometimes in derision, and a proverb of reproach:

4 We fools accounted his life madness, and his end to be without honour:

5 How is he numbered among the children of ELOHIM, and his lot is among the saints!

6 Therefore have we erred from the way of truth, and the light of righteousness hath not shined unto us, and the sun of righteousness rose not upon us.

7 We wearied ourselves in the way of wickedness and destruction: yea, we have gone through deserts, where there lay no way: but as for the way of YAHOWAH, we have not known it.

8 What hath pride profited us? or what good hath riches with our vaunting brought us?

9 All those things are passed away like a shadow, and as a post that hasted by;

10 And as a ship that passeth over the waves of the water, which when it is gone by, the trace thereof cannot be found, neither the pathway of the keel in the waves;

11 Or as when a bird hath flown through the air, there is no token of her way to be found, but the light air being beaten with the stroke of her wings and parted with the violent noise and motion of them, is passed through, and therein afterwards no sign where she went is to be found;

12 Or like as when an arrow is shot at a mark, it parteth the air, which immediately cometh together again, so that a man cannot know where it went through:

13 Even so we in like manner, as soon as we were born, began to draw to our end, and had no sign of virtue to shew; but were consumed in our own wickedness.

14 For the hope of the Godly is like dust that is blown away with the wind; like a thin froth that is driven away with the storm; like as the smoke which is dispersed here and there with a tempest, and passeth away as the remembrance of a guest that tarrieth but a day.

15 But the righteous live for evermore; their reward also is with YAHOWAH, and the care of them is with the Most High.

16 Therefore shall they receive a glorious kingdom, and a beautiful crown from YAHOWAH'S hand: for with his right hand shall he cover them,

and with his arm shall he protect them.

17 He shall take to him his jealousy for complete armour, and make the creature his weapon for the revenge of his enemies.

18 He shall put on righteousness as a breastplate, and true judgment instead of an helmet.

19 He shall take holiness for an invincible shield.

20 His severe wrath shall he sharpen for a sword, and the world shall fight with him against the unwise.

21 Then shall the right aiming thunderbolts go abroad; and from the clouds, as from a well drawn bow, shall they fly to the mark.

22 And hailstones full of wrath shall be cast as out of a stone bow, and the water of the sea shall rage against them, and the floods shall cruelly drown them.

23 Yea, a mighty wind shall stand up against them, and like a storm shall blow them away: thus iniquity shall lay waste the whole earth, and ill dealing shall overthrow the thrones of the mighty.

6 Hear therefore, O ye kings, and understand; learn, ye that be judges of the ends of the earth.

2 Give ear, ye that rule the people, and glory in the multitude of heathen.

3 For power is given you of YAHOWAH, and sovereignty from the Highest, who shall try your works, and search out your counsels.

4 Because, being ministers of his kingdom, ye have not judged aright, nor kept the Torah, nor walked after the counsel of ELOHIM;

5 Horribly and speedily shall he come upon you: for a sharp judgment shall be to them that be in high places.

6 For mercy will soon pardon the meanest: but mighty men shall be mightily tormented.

7 For he which is ADON of all the Worlds shall fear no man's person, neither shall he stand in awe of any man's greatness: for he hath made the small and great, and careth for all alike.

8 But a sore trial shall come upon the mighty.

9 Unto you therefore, O kings, do I speak, that ye may learn wisdom, and not fall away.

10 For they that keep holiness holily shall be judged holy: and they that have learned such things shall find what to answer.

11 Wherefore set your affection upon my words; desire them, and ye shall be instructed.

12 Wisdom is glorious, and never fadeth away: yea, she is easily seen of them that love her, and found of such as seek her.

13 She preventeth them that desire her, in making herself first known unto them.

14 Whoso seeketh her early shall have no great travail: for he shall find her sitting at his doors.

15 To think therefore upon her is perfection of wisdom: and whoso watcheth for her shall quickly be without care.

16 For she goeth about seeking such as are worthy of her, sheweth herself favourably unto them in the ways, and meeteth them in every thought.

17 For the very true beginning of her is the desire of discipline; and the care of discipline is love;

18 And love is the keeping of her Torah; and the giving heed unto her Torah is the assurance of incorruption;

19 And incorruption maketh us near unto YAHOWAH:

20 Therefore the desire of wisdom bringeth to a kingdom.

21 If your delight be then in thrones and sceptres, O ye kings of the people, honour wisdom, that ye may reign for evermore.

22 As for wisdom, what she is, and how she came up, I will tell you, and will not hide mysteries from you: but will seek her out from the beginning of her nativity, and bring the knowledge of her into light, and will not pass over the truth.

23 Neither will I go with consuming envy; for such a man shall have no fellowship with wisdom.

24 But the multitude of the wise is the welfare of the world: and a wise king is the upholding of the people.

25 Receive therefore instruction through my words, and it shall do you good.

7 I myself also am a mortal man, like to all, and the offspring of him that was first made of the earth,

2 And in my mother's womb was fashioned to be flesh in the time of ten months, being compacted in blood, of the seed of man, and the pleasure that came with sleep.

3 And when I was born, I drew in the common air, and fell upon the earth, which is of like nature, and the first voice which I uttered was crying, as all others do.

4 I was nursed in swaddling clothes, and that with cares.

5 For there is no king that had any other beginning of birth.

6 For all men have one entrance into life, and the like going out.

7 Wherefore I prayed, and understanding was given me: I called upon him, and the RUAKH of Wisdom came to me.

8 I preferred her before sceptres and thrones, and esteemed riches nothing in comparison of her.

9 Neither compared I unto her any precious stone, because all gold in respect of her is as a little sand, and silver shall be counted as clay before her.

10 I loved her above health and beauty, and chose to have her instead of light: for the light that cometh from her never goeth out.

11 All good things together came to me with her, and innumerable riches in her hands.

12 And I rejoiced in them all, because wisdom goeth before them: and I knew not that she was the mother of them.

13 I learned diligently, and do communicate her liberally: I do not hide her riches.

14 For she is a treasure unto men that never faileth: which they that use become the friends of YAHOWAH, being commended for the gifts that come from learning.

15 YAHOWAH hath granted me to speak as I would, and to conceive as is meet for the things that are given me: because it is he that leadeth unto wisdom, and directeth the wise.

16 For in his hand are both we and our words; all wisdom also, and knowledge of workmanship.

17 For he hath given me certain knowledge of the things that are, namely, to know how the world was made, and the operation of the elements:

18 The beginning, ending, and midst of the times: the alterations of the turning of the sun, and the change of seasons:

19 The circuits of years, and the positions of stars:

20 The natures of living creatures, and the furies of wild beasts: the violence of winds, and the reasonings of men: the diversities of plants and the virtues of roots:

21 And all such things as are either secret or manifest, them I know.

22 For wisdom, which is the worker of all things, taught me: for in her is an understanding RUAKH holy, one only, manifold, subtil, lively, clear, undefiled, plain, not subject to hurt, loving the thing that is good quick, which cannot be letted, ready to do good,

23 Kind to man, steadfast, sure, free from care, having all power, overseeing all things, and going through all understanding, pure, and most subtil, spirits.

24 For wisdom is more moving than any motion: she passeth and goeth through all things by reason of her pureness.

25 For she is the breath of the power of ELOHIM, and a pure influence flowing from the glory of the Almighty: therefore can no defiled thing fall into her.

26 For she is the brightness of the everlasting light, the unspotted mirror of the power of ELOHIM, and the image of his goodness.

27 And being but one, she can do all things: and remaining in herself, she maketh all things new: and in all ages entering into holy souls, she maketh them friends of ELOHIM, and prophets.

28 For ELOHIM loveth none but him that dwelleth with wisdom.

29 For she is more beautiful than the sun, and above all the order of stars: being compared with the light, she is found before it.

30 For after this cometh night: but vice shall not prevail against wisdom.

8 Wisdom reacheth from one end to another mightily: and sweetly doth she order all things.

2 I loved her, and sought her out from my youth, I desired to make her my spouse, and I was a lover of her beauty.

3 In that she is conversant with YAHOWAH, she magnifieth her nobility: yea, ADON of all things himself loved her.

4 For she is privy to the mysteries of the knowledge of ELOHIM, and a lover of his works.

5 If riches be a possession to be desired in this life; what is richer than wisdom, that worketh all things?

6 And if prudence work; who of all that are is a more cunning workman than she?

7 And if a man love righteousness her labours are virtues: for she teacheth temperance and prudence, justice and fortitude: which are such things, as en can have nothing more profitable in their life.

8 If a man desire much experience, she knoweth things of old, and conjectureth aright what is to come: she knoweth the subtilties of speeches, and can expound dark sentences: she foreseeth signs and wonders, and the events of seasons and times.

9 Therefore I purposed to take her to me to live with me, knowing that she would be a counsellor of good things, and a comfort in cares and grief.

10 For her sake I shall have estimation among the multitude, and honour with the elders, though I be young.

11 I shall be found of a quick conceit in judgment, and shall be admired in the sight of great men.

12 When I hold my tongue, they shall bide my leisure, and when I speak, they shall give good ear unto me: if I talk much, they shall lay their hands upon their mouth.

13 Moreover by the means of her I shall obtain immortality, and leave behind me an everlasting memorial to them that come after me.

14 I shall set the people in order, and the Gentiles shall be subject unto me.

15 Horrible tyrants shall be afraid, when they do but hear of me; I shall be found good among the multitude, and valiant in war.

16 After I am come into mine house, I will repose myself with her: for her conversation hath no bitterness; and to live with her hath no sorrow, but mirth and joy.

17 Now when I considered these things in myself, and pondered them in my heart, how that to be allied unto wisdom is immortality;

18 And great pleasure it is to have her friendship; and in the works of her hands are infinite riches; and in the exercise of conference with her, prudence; and in talking with her, a good report; I went about seeking how to take her to me.

19 For I was a witty child, and had a good RUAKH.

20 Yea rather, being good, I came into a body undefiled.

21 Nevertheless, when I perceived that I could not otherwise obtain her, except ELOHIM gave her me; and that was a point of wisdom also to know whose gift she was; I prayed unto YAHOWAH, and besought him, and with my whole heart I said,

9 O ELOHIM of my fathers, and ADON of mercy, who hast made all things with thy word,

2 And ordained man through thy wisdom, that he should have dominion over the creatures which thou hast made,

3 And order the world according to equity and righteousness, and execute judgment with an upright heart:

4 Give me wisdom, that sitteth by thy throne; and reject me not from among thy children:

5 For I thy servant and son of thine handmaid am a feeble person, and of a short time, and too young for the understanding of judgment and Torah.

6 For though a man be never so perfect among the children of men, yet if thy wisdom be not with him, he shall be nothing regarded.

7 Thou hast chosen me to be a king of thy people, and a judge of thy sons and daughters:

8 Thou hast commanded me to build a temple upon thy holy mount, and an altar in the city wherein thou dwellest, a resemblance of the holy tabernacle, which thou hast prepared from the beginning.

9 And wisdom was with thee: which knoweth thy works, and was present when thou madest the world, and knew what was acceptable in thy sight, and right in thy commandments.

10 O send her out of thy holy heavens, and from the throne of thy glory, that being present she may labour with me, that I may know what is pleasing unto thee.

11 For she knoweth and understandeth all things, and she shall lead me soberly in my doings, and preserve me in her power.

12 So shall my works be acceptable, and then shall I judge thy people righteously, and be worthy to sit in my father's seat.

13 For what man is he that can know the counsel of ELOHIM? or who can think what the will of YAHOWAH is?

14 For the thoughts of mortal men are miserable, and our devices are but uncertain.

15 For the corruptible body presseth down the soul, and the earthy tabernacle weigheth down the mind that museth upon many things.

16 And hardly do we guess aright at things that are upon earth, and with labour do we find the things that are before us: but the things that are in heaven who hath searched out?

17 And thy counsel who hath known, except thou give wisdom, and send thy RUAKH HA QODESH from above?

18 For so the ways of them which lived on the earth were reformed, and men were taught the things that are pleasing unto thee, and were saved through wisdom.

10 She preserved the first formed father of the world, that was created alone, and brought him out of his fall,

2 And gave him power to rule all things.

3 But when the unrighteous went away from her in his anger, he perished also in the fury wherewith he murdered his brother.

4 For whose cause the earth being drowned with the flood, wisdom again preserved it, and directed the course of the righteous in a piece of wood of small value.

5 Moreover, the Gentiles in their wicked conspiracy being confounded, she found out the righteous, and preserved him blameless unto YAHOWAH, and kept him strong against his tender compassion toward his son.

6 When the ungodly perished, she delivered the righteous man, who fled from the fire which fell down upon the five cities.

7 Of whose wickedness even to this day the waste land that smoketh is a testimony, and plants bearing fruit that never come to ripeness: and a standing pillar of salt is a monument of an unbelieving soul.

8 For regarding not wisdom, they gat not only this hurt, that they knew not the things which were good; but also left behind them to the world a memorial of their foolishness: so that in the things wherein they offended they could not so much as be hid.

9 Rut wisdom delivered from pain those that attended upon her.

10 When the righteous fled from his brother's wrath she guided him in right paths, shewed him the kingdom of YAHOWAH, and gave him knowledge of holy things, made him rich in his travels, and multiplied the fruit of his labours.

11 In the covetousness of such as oppressed him she stood by him, and made him rich.

12 She defended him from his enemies, and kept him safe from those that lay in wait, and in a sore conflict she gave him the victory; that he might know that goodness is stronger than all.

13 When the righteous was sold, she forsook him not, but delivered him from sin: she went down with him into the pit,

14 And left him not in bonds, till she brought him the sceptre of the kingdom, and power against those that oppressed him: as for them that had accused him, she shewed them to be liars, and gave him perpetual glory.

15 She delivered the righteous people and blameless seed from the nation that oppressed them.

16 She entered into the soul of the servant of YAHOWAH, and withstood dreadful kings in wonders and signs;

17 Rendered to the righteous a reward of their labours, guided them in a marvellous way, and was unto them for a cover by day, and a light of stars in the night season;

18 Brought them through the Red sea, and led them through much water:

19 But she drowned their enemies, and cast them up out of the bottom of the deep.

20 Therefore the righteous spoiled the ungodly, and praised thy holy name, O YAHOWAH, and magnified with one accord thine hand, that fought for them.

21 For wisdom opened the mouth of the dumb, and made the tongues of them that cannot speak eloquent.

11 She prospered their works in the hand of the holy prophet.

2 They went through the wilderness that was not inhabited, and pitched tents in places where there lay no way.

3 They stood against their enemies, and were avenged of their adversaries.

4 When they were thirsty, they called upon thee, and water was given them out of the flinty rock, and their thirst was quenched out of the hard stone.

5 For by what things their enemies were punished, by the same they in their need were benefited.

6 For instead of of a perpetual running river troubled with foul blood,

7 For a manifest reproof of that commandment, whereby the infants were slain, thou gavest unto them abundance of water by a means which they hoped not for:

8 Declaring by that thirst then how thou hadst punished their adversaries.

9 For when they were tried albeit but in mercy chastised, they knew how the ungodly were judged in wrath and tormented, thirsting in another manner than the just.

10 For these thou didst admonish and try, as a father: but the other, as a severe king, thou didst condemn and punish.

11 Whether they were absent or present, they were vexed alike.

12 For a double grief came upon them, and a groaning for the remembrance of things past.

13 For when they heard by their own punishments the other to be benefited, they had some feeling of YAHOWAH.

14 For whom they respected with scorn, when he was long before thrown out at the casting forth of the infants, him in the end, when they saw what came to pass, they admired.

15 But for the foolish devices of their wickedness, wherewith being deceived they worshipped serpents void of reason, and vile beasts, thou didst send a multitude of unreasonable beasts upon them for vengeance;

16 That they might know, that wherewithal a man sinneth, by the same also shall he be punished.

17 For thy Almighty hand, that made the world of matter without form, wanted not means to send among them a multitude of bears or fierce lions,

18 Or unknown wild beasts, full of rage, newly created, breathing out either a fiery vapour, or filthy scents of scattered smoke, or shooting horrible sparkles out of their eyes:

19 Whereof not only the harm might dispatch them at once, but also the terrible sight utterly destroy them.

20 Yea, and without these might they have fallen down with one blast, being persecuted of vengeance, and scattered abroad through the breath of thy power: but thou hast ordered all things in measure and number and weight.

21 For thou canst shew thy great strength at all times when thou wilt; and who may withstand the power of thine arm?

22 For the whole world before thee is as a little grain of the balance, yea, as a drop of the morning dew that falleth down upon the earth.

23 But thou hast mercy upon all; for thou canst do all things, and winkest at the sins of men, because

they should amend.

24 For thou lovest all the things that are, and abhorrest nothing which thou hast made: for never wouldest thou have made any thing, if thou hadst hated it.

25 And how could any thing have endured, if it had not been thy will? or been preserved, if not called by thee?

26 But thou sparest all: for they are thine, O ADON, thou lover of souls.

12 For thine incorruptible RUAKH is in all things.
2 Therefore chastenest thou them by little and little that offend, and warnest them by putting them in remembrance wherein they have offended, that leaving their wickedness they may believe on thee, O YAHOWAH.

3 For it was thy will to destroy by the hands of our fathers both those old inhabitants of thy holy land,

4 Whom thou hatedst for doing most odious works of witchcrafts, and wicked sacrifices;

5 And also those merciless murderers of children, and devourers of man's flesh, and the feasts of blood,

6 With their priests out of the midst of their idolatrous crew, and the parents, that killed with their own hands souls destitute of help:

7 That the land, which thou esteemedst above all other, might receive a worthy colony of ELOHIM'S children.

8 Nevertheless even those thou sparedst as men, and didst send wasps, forerunners of thine host, to destroy them by little and little.

9 Not that thou wast unable to bring the ungodly under the hand of the righteous in battle, or to destroy them at once with cruel beasts, or with one rough word:

10 But executing thy judgments upon them by little and little, thou gavest them place of repentance, not being ignorant that they were a naughty generation, and that their malice was bred in them, and that their cogitation would never be changed.

11 For it was a cursed seed from the beginning; neither didst thou for fear of any man give them pardon for those things wherein they sinned.

12 For who shall say, What hast thou done? or who shall withstand thy judgment? or who shall accuse thee for the nations that perish, whom thou made? or who shall come to stand against thee, to be revenged for the unrighteous men?

13 For neither is there any ELOHIM but thou that careth for all, to whom thou mightest shew that thy judgment is not unright.

14 Neither shall king or tyrant be able to set his face against thee for any whom thou hast punished.

15 Forsomuch then as thou art righteous thyself, thou orderest all things righteously: thinking it not agreeable with thy power to condemn him that hath not deserved to be punished.

16 For thy power is the beginning of righteousness, and because thy domain is over all, it maketh thee to be gracious unto all.

17 For when men will not believe that thou art of a full power, thou shewest thy strength, and among them that know it thou makest their boldness manifest.

18 But thou, mastering thy power, judgest with equity, and orderest us with great favour: for thou mayest use power when thou wilt.

19 But by such works hast thou taught thy people that the just man should be merciful, and hast made thy children to be of a good hope that thou givest repentance for sins.

20 For if thou didst punish the enemies of thy children, and the condemned to death, with such deliberation, giving them time and place, whereby they might be delivered from their malice:

21 With how great circumspection didst thou judge thine own sons, unto whose fathers thou hast sworn, and made covenants of good promises?

22 Therefore, whereas thou dost chasten us, thou scourgest our enemies a thousand times more, to the intent that, when we judge, we should carefully think of thy goodness, and when we ourselves are judged, we should look for mercy.

23 Wherefore, whereas men have lived dissolutely and unrighteously, thou hast tormented them with their own abominations.

24 For they went astray very far in the ways of error, and held them for elohim, which even among the beasts of their enemies were despised, being deceived, as children of no understanding.

25 Therefore unto them, as to children without the use of reason, thou didst send a judgment to mock them.

26 But they that would not be reformed by that correction, wherein he dallied with them, shall feel a judgment worthy of ELOHIM.

27 For, look, for what things they grudged, when they were punished, that is, for them whom they thought to be elohim; [now] being punished in them, when they saw it, they acknowledged him to be the true ELOHIM, whom before they denied to know: and therefore came extreme damnation upon them.

13 Surely vain are all men by nature, who are ignorant of ELOHIM, and could not out of the good things that are seen know him that is: neither by considering the works did they acknowledge the workmaster;

2 But deemed either fire, or wind, or the swift air, or the circle of the stars, or the violent water, or the lights of heaven, to be the elohim which govern the world.

3 With whose beauty if they being delighted took them to be elohim; let them know how much better the Creator of them is: for the first author of beauty hath created them.

4 But if they were astonished at their power and virtue, let them understand by them, how much mightier he is that made them.

5 For by the greatness and beauty of the creatures proportionably the maker of them is seen.

6 But yet for this they are the less to be blamed: for they peradventure err, seeking ELOHIM, and desirous to find him.

7 For being conversant in his works they search him diligently, and believe their sight: because the things are beautiful that are seen.

8 Howbeit neither are they to be pardoned.

9 For if they were able to know so much, that they could aim at the world; how did they not sooner find out the ADON and Creator thereof?

10 But miserable are they, and in dead things is their hope, who call them elohim, which are the works of men's hands, gold and silver, to shew art in, and resemblances of beasts, or a stone good for nothing, the work of an ancient hand.

11 Now a carpenter that felleth timber, after he hath sawn down a tree meet for the purpose, and taken off all the bark skilfully round about, and hath wrought it handsomely, and made a vessel thereof fit for the service of man's life;

12 And after spending the refuse of his work to dress his meat, hath filled himself;

13 And taking the very refuse among those which served to no use, being a crooked piece of wood, and full of knots, hath carved it diligently, when he had nothing else to do, and formed it by the skill of his understanding, and fashioned it to the image of a man;

14 Or made it like some vile beast, laying it over with vermilion, and with paint colouring it red, and covering every spot therein;

15 And when he had made a convenient room for it, set it in a wall, and made it fast with iron:

16 For he provided for it that it might not fall, knowing that it was unable to help itself; for it is an image, and hath need of help:

17 Then maketh he prayer for his goods, for his wife and children, and is not ashamed to speak to that which hath no life.

18 For health he calleth upon that which is weak: for life prayeth to that which is dead; for aid humbly beseecheth that which hath least means to help: and for a good journey he asketh of that which cannot set a foot forward:

19 And for gaining and getting, and for good success of his hands, asketh ability to do of him, that is most unable to do any thing.

14 Again, one preparing himself to sail, and about to pass through the raging waves, calleth upon a piece of wood more rotten than the vessel that carrieth him.

2 For verily desire of gain devised that, and the workman built it by his skill.

3 But thy providence, O Father, governeth it: for thou hast made a way in the sea, and a safe path in the waves;

4 Shewing that thou canst save from all danger: yea, though a man went to sea without art.

5 Nevertheless thou wouldest not that the works of thy wisdom should be idle, and therefore do men commit their lives to a small piece of wood, and passing the rough sea in a weak vessel are saved.

6 For in the old time also, when the proud giants perished, the hope of the world governed by thy hand escaped in a weak vessel, and left to all ages a seed of generation.

7 For blessed is the wood whereby righteousness cometh.

8 But that which is made with hands is cursed, as well it, as he that made it: he, because he made it; and it, because, being corruptible, it was called elohim.

9 For the ungodly and his ungodliness are both alike hateful unto YAHOWAH.

10 For that which is made shall be punished together with him that made it.

11 Therefore even upon the idols of the Gentiles shall there be a visitation: because in the creature of ELOHIM they are become an abomination, and stumblingblocks to the souls of men, and a snare to the feet of the unwise.

12 For the devising of idols was the beginning of spiritual fornication, and the invention of them the corruption of life.

13 For neither were they from the beginning, neither shall they be for ever.

14 For by the vain glory of men they entered into the world, and therefore shall they come shortly to an end.

15 For a father afflicted with untimely mourning, when he hath made an image of his child soon taken away, now honoured him as an elohim, which was then a dead man, and delivered to those that were under him ceremonies and sacrifices.

16 Thus in process of time an ungodly custom grown strong was kept as a Torah, and graven images were worshipped by the commandments of kings.

17 Whom men could not honour in presence, because they dwelt far off, they took the counterfeit of his visage from far, and made an express image of a king whom they honoured, to the end that by this their forwardness they might flatter him that was absent, as if he were present.

18 Also the singular diligence of the artificer did help to set forward the ignorant to more superstition.

19 For he, peradventure willing to please one in authority, forced all his skill to make the resemblance of the best fashion.

20 And so the multitude, allured by the grace of the work, took him now for a elohim, which a little before was but honoured.

21 And this was an occasion to deceive the world: for men, serving either calamity or tyranny, did ascribe unto stones and stocks the incommunicable name.

22 Moreover this was not enough for them, that they erred in the knowledge of ELOHIM; but whereas they lived in the great war of ignorance, those so great plagues called they shalom.

23 For whilst they slew their children in sacrifices, or used secret ceremonies, or made revellings of strange rites;

24 They kept neither lives nor marriages any longer undefiled: but either one slew another traiterously, or grieved him by adultery.

25 So that there reigned in all men without exception blood, manslaughter, theft, and dissimulation, corruption, unfaithfulness, tumults, perjury,

26 Disquieting of good men, forgetfulness of good turns, defiling of souls, changing of kind, disorder in marriages, adultery, and shameless uncleanness.

27 For the worshipping of idols not to be named is the beginning, the cause, and the end, of all evil.

28 For either they are mad when they be merry, or prophesy lies, or live unjustly, or else lightly forswear themselves.

29 For insomuch as their trust is in idols, which have no life; though they swear falsely, yet they look not to be hurt.

30 Howbeit for both causes shall they be justly punished: both because they thought not well of YAHOWAH, giving heed unto idols, and also unjustly swore in deceit, despising holiness.

31 For it is not the power of them by whom they swear: but it is the just vengeance of sinners, that punisheth always the offence of the ungodly.

15 But thou, O ELOHIM, art gracious and true, longsuffering, and in mercy ordering all things,

2 For if we sin, we are thine, knowing thy power: but we will not sin, knowing that we are counted thine.

3 For to know thee is perfect righteousness: yea, to know thy power is the root of immortality.

4 For neither did the mischievous invention of men deceive us, nor an image spotted with divers colours, the painter's fruitless labour;

5 The sight whereof enticeth fools to lust after it, and so they desire the form of a dead image, that hath no breath.

6 Both they that make them, they that desire them, and they that worship them, are lovers of evil things, and are worthy to have such things to trust upon.

7 For the potter, tempering soft earth, fashioneth every vessel with much labour for our service: yea, of the same clay he maketh both the vessels that serve for clean uses, and likewise also all such as serve to the contrary: but what is the use of either sort, the potter himself is the judge.

8 And employing his labours lewdly, he maketh a vain elohim of the same clay, even he which a little before was made of earth himself, and within a little while after returneth to the same, out when his life which was lent him shall be demanded.

9 Notwithstanding his care is, not that he shall have much labour, nor that his life is short: but striveth to excel goldsmiths and silversmiths, and endeavoureth to do like the workers in brass, and counteth it his glory to make counterfeit things.

10 His heart is ashes, his hope is more vile than earth, and his life of less value than clay:

11 Forasmuch as he knew not his Maker, and him that inspired into him an active soul, and breathed in a living RUAKH.

12 But they counted our life a pastime, and our time here a market for gain: for, say they, we must be getting every way, though it be by evil means.

13 For this man, that of earthly matter maketh brittle vessels and graven images, knoweth himself to offend above all others.

14 And all the enemies of thy people, that hold them in subjection, are most foolish, and are more miserable than very babes.

15 For they counted all the idols of the heathen to be elohim: which neither have the use of eyes to see, nor noses to draw breath, nor ears to hear, nor fingers of hands to handle; and as for their feet, they are slow to go.

16 For man made them, and he that borrowed his own RUAKH fashioned them: but no man can make a elohim like unto himself.

17 For being mortal, he worketh a dead thing with wicked hands: for he himself is better than the things which he worshippeth: whereas he lived once, but they never.

18 Yea, they worshipped those beasts also that are most hateful: for being compared together, some are worse than others.

19 Neither are they beautiful, so much as to be desired in respect of beasts: but they went without the praise of YAHOWAH and his blessing.

16 Therefore by the like were they punished worthily, and by the multitude of beasts tormented.

2 Instead of which punishment, dealing graciously with thine own people, thou preparedst for them meat of a strange taste, even quails to stir up their appetite:

3 To the end that they, desiring food, might for the ugly sight of the beasts sent among them lothe even that, which they must needs desire; but these, suffering penury for a short space, might be made partakers of a strange taste.

4 For it was requisite, that upon them exercising tyranny should come penury, which they could not avoid: but to these it should only be shewed how their enemies were tormented.

5 For when the horrible fierceness of beasts came upon these, and they perished with the stings of crooked serpents, thy wrath endured not for ever:

6 But they were troubled for a small season, that they might be admonished, having a sign of salvation, to put them in remembrance of the commandment of thy Torah.

7 For he that turned himself toward it was not saved by the thing that he saw, but by thee, that art the Saviour of all.

8 And in this thou madest thine enemies confess, that it is thou who deliverest from all evil:

9 For them the bitings of grasshoppers and flies killed, neither was there found any remedy for their life: for they were worthy to be punished by such.

10 But thy sons not the very teeth of venomous dragons overcame: for thy mercy was ever by them, and healed them.

11 For they were pricked, that they should remember thy words; and were quickly saved, that not falling into deep forgetfulness, they might be continually mindful of thy goodness.

12 For it was neither herb, nor mollifying plaister, that restored them to health: but thy word, O YAHOWAH, which healeth all things.

13 For thou hast power of life and death: thou leadest to the gates of hell, and bringest up again.

14 A man indeed killeth through his malice: and the RUAKH, when it is gone forth, returneth not; neither the soul received up cometh again.

15 But it is not possible to escape thine hand.

16 For the ungodly, that denied to know thee, were scourged by the strength of thine arm: with strange rains, hails, and showers, were they persecuted, that they could not avoid, and through fire were they consumed.

17 For, which is most to be wondered at, the fire had more force in the water, that quencheth all things: for the world fighteth for the righteous.

18 For sometime the flame was mitigated, that it might not burn up the beasts that were sent against the ungodly; but themselves might see and perceive that they were persecuted with the judgment of YAHOWAH.

19 And at another time it burneth even in the midst of water above the power of fire, that it might destroy the fruits of an unjust land.

20 Instead whereof thou feddest thine own people with angels' food, and didst send them from heaven bread prepared without their labour, able to content every man's delight, and agreeing to every taste.

21 For thy sustenance declared thy sweetness unto thy children, and serving to the appetite of the eater, tempered itself to every man's liking.

22 But snow and ice endured the fire, and melted not, that they might know that fire burning in the hail, and sparkling in the rain, did destroy the fruits of the enemies.

23 But this again did even forget his own strength, that the righteous might be nourished.

24 For the creature that serveth thee, who art the Maker increaseth his strength against the unrighteous for their punishment, and abateth his strength for the benefit of such as put their trust in thee.

25 Therefore even then was it altered into all fashions, and was obedient to thy grace, that nourisheth all things, according to the desire of them that had need:

26 That thy children, O YAHOWAH, whom thou lovest, might know, that it is not the growing of fruits that nourisheth man: but that it is thy word, which preserveth them that put their trust in thee.

27 For that which was not destroyed of the fire, being warmed with a little sunbeam, soon melted away:

28 That it might be known, that we must prevent the sun to give thee thanks, and at the dayspring pray unto thee.

29 For the hope of the unthankful shall melt away as the winter's hoar frost, and shall run away as unprofitable water.

17 For great are thy judgments, and cannot be expressed: therefore unnurtured souls have erred.

2 For when unrighteous men thought to oppress the holy nation; they being shut up in their houses, the prisoners of darkness, and fettered with the bonds of a long night, lay [there] exiled from the eternal providence.

3 For while they supposed to lie hid in their secret sins, they were scattered under a dark veil of forgetfulness, being horribly astonished, and troubled with [strange] apparitions.

4 For neither might the corner that held them keep them from fear: but noises [as of waters] falling down sounded about them, and sad visions appeared unto them with heavy countenances.

5 No power of the fire might give them light: neither could the bright flames of the stars endure to lighten that horrible night.

6 Only there appeared unto them a fire kindled of itself, very dreadful: for being much terrified, they thought the things which they saw to be worse than the sight they saw not.

7 As for the illusions of art magick, they were put down, and their vaunting in wisdom was reproved with disgrace.

8 For they, that promised to drive away terrors and troubles from a sick soul, were sick themselves of fear, worthy to be laughed at.

9 For though no terrible thing did fear them; yet being scared with beasts that passed by, and hissing of serpents,

10 They died for fear, denying that they saw the air, which could of no side be avoided.

11 For wickedness, condemned by her own witness, is very timorous, and being pressed with conscience, always forecasteth grievous things.

12 For fear is nothing else but a betraying of the succours which reason offereth.

13 And the expectation from within, being less, counteth the ignorance more than the cause which bringeth the torment.

14 But they sleeping the same sleep that night, which was indeed intolerable, and which came upon them out of the bottoms of inevitable hell,

15 Were partly vexed with monstrous apparitions, and partly fainted, their heart failing them: for a sudden fear, and not looked for, came upon them.

16 So then whosoever there fell down was straitly kept, shut up in a prison without iron bars,

17 For whether he were husbandman, or shepherd, or a labourer in the field, he was overtaken, and endured that necessity, which could not be avoided: for they were all bound with one chain of darkness.

18 Whether it were a whistling wind, or a melodious noise of birds among the spreading branches, or a pleasing fall of water running violently,

19 Or a terrible sound of stones cast down, or a running that could not be seen of skipping beasts, or a roaring voice of most savage wild beasts, or a rebounding echo from the hollow mountains; these things made them to swoon for fear.

20 For the whole world shined with clear light, and none were hindered in their labour:

21 Over them only was spread an heavy night, an image of that darkness which should afterward receive them: but yet were they unto themselves more grievous than the darkness.

18 Nevertheless thy saints had a very great light, whose voice they hearing, and not seeing their shape, because they also had not suffered the same things, they counted them happy.

2 But for that they did not hurt them now, of whom they had been wronged before, they thanked them, and besought them pardon for that they had been enemies.

3 Instead whereof thou gavest them a burning pillar of fire, both to be a guide of the unknown journey, and an harmless sun to entertain them honourably.

4 For they were worthy to be deprived of light and imprisoned in darkness, who had kept thy sons shut up, by whom the uncorrupt light of the Torah was to be given unto the world.

5 And when they had determined to slay the babes of the saints, one child being cast forth, and saved, to reprove them, thou tookest away the multitude of their children, and destroyedst them altogether in a mighty water.

6 Of that night were our fathers certified afore, that assuredly knowing unto what oaths they had given credence, they might afterwards be of good cheer.

7 So of thy people was accepted both the salvation of the righteous, and destruction of the enemies.

8 For wherewith thou didst punish our adversaries, by the same thou didst glorify us, whom thou hadst called.

9 For the righteous children of good men did sacrifice secretly, and with one consent made a holy Torah, that the saints should be like partakers of the same good and evil, the fathers now singing out the songs of praise.

10 But on the other side there sounded an ill according cry of the enemies, and a lamentable noise was carried abroad for children that were bewailed.

11 The master and the servant were punished after one manner; and like as the king, so suffered the common person.

12 So they all together had innumerable dead with one kind of death; neither were the living sufficient to bury them: for in one moment the noblest offspring of them was destroyed.

13 For whereas they would not believe any thing by reason of the enchantments; upon the destruction of the firstborn, they acknowledged this people to be the sons of ELOHIM.

14 For while all things were in quiet silence, and that night was in the midst of her swift course,

15 Thine Almighty word leaped down from heaven out of thy royal throne, as a fierce man of war into the midst of a land of destruction,

16 And brought thine unfeigned commandment as a sharp sword, and standing up filled all things with death; and it touched the heaven, but it stood upon the earth.

17 Then suddenly visions of horrible dreams troubled them sore, and terrors came upon them unlooked for.

18 And one thrown here, and another there, half dead, shewed the cause of his death.

19 For the dreams that troubled them did foreshew this, lest they should perish, and not know why they were afflicted.

20 Yea, the tasting of death touched the righteous also, and there was a destruction of the multitude in the wilderness: but the wrath endured not long.

21 For then the blameless man made haste, and stood forth to defend them; and bringing the shield of his proper ministry, even prayer, and the propitiation of incense, set himself against the wrath, and so brought the calamity to an end, declaring that he was thy servant.

22 So he overcame the destroyer, not with strength of body, nor force of arms, but with a word subdued him that punished, alleging the oaths and covenants made with the fathers.

23 For when the dead were now fallen down by heaps one upon another, standing between, he stayed the wrath, and parted the way to the living.

24 For in the long garment was the whole world, and in the four rows of the stones was the glory of the fathers graven, and thy Majesty upon the daidem of his head.

25 Unto these the destroyer gave place, and was afraid of them: for it was enough that they only tasted of the wrath.

19 As for the ungodly, wrath came upon them without mercy unto the end: for he knew before what they would do;

2 How that having given them leave to depart, and sent them hastily away, they would repent and pursue them.

3 For whilst they were yet mourning and making lamentation at the graves of the dead, they added another foolish device, and pursued them as fugitives, whom they had intreated to be gone.

4 For the destiny, whereof they were worthy, drew them unto this end, and made them forget the things that had already happened, that they might fulfil the punishment which was wanting to their torments:

5 And that thy people might pass a wonderful way: but they might find a strange death.

6 For the whole creature in his proper kind was fashioned again anew, serving the peculiar commandments that were given unto them, that thy children might be kept without hurt:

7 As namely, a cloud shadowing the camp; and where water stood before, dry land appeared; and out of the Red sea a way without impediment; and out of the violent stream a green field:

8 Wherethrough all the people went that were defended with thy hand, seeing thy marvellous strange wonders.

9 For they went at large like horses, and leaped like lambs, praising thee, O YAHOWAH, who hadst delivered them.

10 For they were yet mindful of the things that were done while they sojourned in the strange land, how the ground brought forth flies instead of cattle, and how the river cast up a multitude of frogs instead of fishes.

11 But afterwards they saw a new generation of fowls, when, being led with their appetite, they asked delicate meats.

12 For quails came up unto them from the sea for their contentment.

13 And punishments came upon the sinners not without former signs by the force of thunders: for they suffered justly according to their own wickedness, insomuch as they used a more hard and hateful behaviour toward strangers.

14 For the Sodomites did not receive those, whom they knew not when they came: but these
brought friends into bondage, that had well deserved of them.

15 And not only so, but peradventure some respect shall be had of those, because they used strangers not friendly:

16 But these very grievously afflicted them, whom they had received with feastings, and were already made partakers of the same Torah with them.

17 Therefore even with blindness were these stricken, as those were at the doors of the righteous man: when, being compassed about with horrible great darkness, every one sought the passage of his own doors.

18 For the elements were changed in themselves by a kind of harmony, like as in a psaltery notes change the name of the tune, and yet are always sounds; which may well be perceived by the sight of the things that have been done.

19 For earthly things were turned into watery, and the things, that before swam in the water, now went upon the ground.

20 The fire had power in the water, forgetting his own virtue: and the water forgat his own quenching nature.

21 On the other side, the flames wasted not the flesh of the corruptible living things, though they walked therein; neither melted they the icy kind of heavenly meat that was of nature apt to melt.

22 For in all things, O YAHOWAH, thou didst magnify thy people, and glorify them, neither didst thou lightly regard them: but didst assist them in every time and place.

THE BOOK OF
ECCLESIASTICUS
ALSO CALLED THE WISDOM OF YAHOSHUA THE SON OF SIRACH

A PROLOGUE MADE BY AN UNCERTAIN AUTHOR

This Yahoshua was the son of Sirach, and grandchild to Yahoshua of the same name with him: this man therefore lived in the latter times, after the people had been led away captive, and called home a again, and almost after all the prophets. Now his grandfather Yahoshua, as he himself witnesseth, was a man of great diligence and wisdom among the Hebrews, who did not only gather the grave and short sentences of wise men, that had been before him, but himself also uttered some of his own, full of much understanding and wisdom. When as therefore the first Yahoshua died, leaving this book almost perfected, Sirach his son receiving it after him left it to his own son Yahoshua, who, having gotten it into his hands, compiled it all orderly into one volume, and called it Wisdom, intituling it both by his own name, his father's name, and his grandfather's; alluring the hearer by the very name of Wisdom to have a greater love to the study of this book. It containeth therefore wise sayings, dark sentences, and parables, and certain particular ancient godly stories of men that pleased ELOHIM; also his prayer and song; moreover, what benefits ELOHIM had vouchsafed his people, and what plagues he had heaped upon their enemies. This Yahoshua did imitate Shelomoh, and was no less famous for wisdom and learning, both being indeed a man of great learning, and so reputed also.

THE PROLOGUE OF THE WISDOM OF YAHOSHUA THE SON OF SIRACH

Whereas many and great things have been delivered unto us by the Torah and the prophets, and by others that have followed their steps, for the which things Yisra'EL ought to be commended for learning and wisdom; and whereof not only the readers must needs become skilful themselves, but also they that desire to learn be able to profit them which are without, both by speaking and writing: my grandfather Yahoshua, when he had much given himself to the reading of the Torah, and the prophets, and other books of our fathers, and had gotten therein good judgment, was drawn on also himself to write something pertaining to learning and wisdom; to the intent that those which are desirous to learn, and are addicted to these things, might profit much more in living according to the Torah. Wherefore let me intreat you to read it with favour and attention, and to pardon us, wherein we may seem to come short of some words, which we have laboured to interpret. FOR THE SAME THINGS UTTERED IN HEBREW, AND TRANSLATED INTO ANOTHER TONGUE, HAVE NOT THE SAME FORCE IN THEM: and not only these things, but the TORAH itself, and the PROPHETS, and THE REST OF THE BOOKS, HAVE NO SMALL DIFFERENCE, WHEN THEY ARE SPOKEN IN THEIR OWN LANGUAGE. For in the eight and thirtieth year coming into Mitzraim, when Euergetes was king, and continuing there some time, I found a book of no small learning: therefore I thought it most necessary for me to bestow some diligence and travail to interpret it; using great watchfulness and skill in that space to bring the book to an end, and set it forth for them also, which in a strange country are willing to learn, being prepared before in manners to live after the Torah.

1 All wisdom cometh from YAHOWAH, and is with him for ever.

2 Who can number the sand of the sea, and the drops of rain, and the days of eternity?

3 Who can find out the height of heaven, and the breadth of the earth, and the deep, and wisdom?

4 Wisdom hath been created before all things, and the understanding of prudence from everlasting.

5 The word of ELOHIM Most High is the fountain of wisdom; and her ways are everlasting commandments.

6 To whom hath the root of wisdom been revealed? or who hath known her wise counsels?

7 [Unto whom hath the knowledge of wisdom been made manifest? and who hath understood her great experience?]

8 There is one wise and greatly to be feared, YAHOWAH sitting upon his throne.

9 He created her, and saw her, and numbered her, and poured her out upon all his works.

10 She is with all flesh according to his gift, and he hath given her to them that love him.

11 The fear of YAHOWAH is honour, and glory, and gladness, and a crown of rejoicing.

12 The fear of YAHOWAH maketh a merry heart, and giveth joy, and gladness, and a long life.

13 Whoso feareth YAHOWAH, it shall go well with him at the last, and he shall find favour in the day of his death.

14 To fear YAHOWAH is the beginning of wisdom: and it was created with the faithful in the womb.

15 She hath built an everlasting foundation with men, and she shall continue with their seed.

16 To fear YAHOWAH is fulness of wisdom, and filleth men with her fruits.

17 She filleth all their house with things desirable, and the garners with her increase.

18 The fear of YAHOWAH is a crown of wisdom, making shalom and perfect health to flourish; both which are the gifts of ELOHIM: and it enlargeth their rejoicing that love him.

19 Wisdom raineth down skill and knowledge of understanding, and exalteth them to honour that hold her fast.

20 The root of wisdom is to fear YAHOWAH, and the branches thereof are long life.

21 The fear of YAHOWAH driveth away sins: and where it is present, it turneth away wrath.

22 A furious man cannot be justified; for the sway of his fury shall be his destruction.

23 A patient man will tear for a time, and afterward joy shall spring up unto him.

24 He will hide his words for a time, and the lips of many shall declare his wisdom.

25 The parables of knowledge are in the treasures of wisdom: but godliness is an abomination to a sinner.

26 If thou desire wisdom, keep the commandments, and YAHOWAH shall give her unto thee.

27 For the fear of YAHOWAH is wisdom and instruction: and faith and meekness are his delight.

28 Distrust not the fear of YAHOWAH when thou art poor: and come not unto him with a double heart.

29 Be not an hypocrite in the sight of men, and take good heed what thou speakest.

30 Exalt not thyself, lest thou fall, and bring dishonour upon thy soul, and so ELOHIM discover thy secrets, and cast thee down in the midst of the congregation, because thou camest not in truth to the fear of YAHOWAH, but thy heart is full of deceit.

2 My son, if thou come to serve YAHOWAH, prepare thy soul for temptation.

2 Set thy heart aright, and constantly endure, and make not haste in time of trouble.

3 Cleave unto him, and depart not away, that thou mayest be increased at thy last end.

4 Whatsoever is brought upon thee take cheerfully, and be patient when thou art changed to a low estate.

5 For gold is tried in the fire, and acceptable men in the furnace of adversity.

6 Believe in him, and he will help thee; order thy way aright, and trust in him.

7 Ye that fear YAHOWAH, wait for his mercy; and go not aside, lest ye fall.

8 Ye that fear YAHOWAH, believe him; and your reward shall not fail.

9 Ye that fear YAHOWAH, hope for good, and for everlasting joy and mercy.

10 Look at the generations of old, and see; did ever any trust in YAHOWAH, and was confounded? or did any abide in his fear, and was forsaken? or whom did he ever despise, that called upon him?

11 For YAHOWAH is full of compassion and mercy, longsuffering, and very pitiful, and forgiveth sins, and saveth in time of affliction.

12 Woe be to fearful hearts, and faint hands, and the sinner that goeth two ways!

13 Woe unto him that is fainthearted! for he believeth not; therefore shall he not be defended.

14 Woe unto you that have lost patience! and what will ye do when YAHOWAH shall visit you?

15 They that fear YAHOWAH will not disobey his Word; and they that love him will keep his ways.

16 They that fear YAHOWAH will seek that which is well, pleasing unto him; and they that love him shall be filled with the Torah.

17 They that fear YAHOWAH will prepare their hearts, and humble their souls in his sight,

18 Saying, We will fall into the hands of YAHOWAH, and not into the hands of men: for as his majesty is, so is his mercy.

3 Hear me your father, O children, and do thereafter, that ye may be safe.

2 For YAHOWAH hath given the father honour over the children, and hath confirmed the authority of the mother over the sons.

3 Whoso honoureth his father maketh an atonement for his sins:

4 And he that honoureth his mother is as one that layeth up treasure.

5 Whoso honoureth his father shall have joy of his own children; and when he maketh his prayer, he shall be heard.

6 He that honoureth his father shall have a long life; and he that is obedient unto YAHOWAH shall be a comfort to his mother.

7 He that feareth YAHOWAH will honour his father, and will do service unto his parents, as to his masters.

8 Honour thy father and mother both in word and deed, that a blessing may come upon thee from them.

9 For the blessing of the father establisheth the houses of children; but the curse of the mother rooteth out foundations.

10 Glory not in the dishonour of thy father; for thy father's dishonour is no glory unto thee.

11 For the glory of a man is from the honour of his father; and a mother in dishonour is a reproach to the children.

12 My son, help thy father in his age, and grieve him not as long as he liveth.

13 And if his understanding fail, have patience with him; and despise him not when thou art in thy full strength.

14 For the relieving of thy father shall not be forgotten: and instead of sins it shall be added to build thee up.

15 In the day of thine affliction it shall be remembered; thy sins also shall melt away, as the ice in the fair warm weather.

16 He that forsaketh his father is as a blasphemer; and he that angereth his mother is cursed: of ELOHIM.

17 My son, go on with thy business in meekness; so shalt thou be beloved of him that is approved.

18 The greater thou art, the more humble thyself, and thou shalt find favour before YAHOWAH.

19 Many are in high place, and of renown: but mysteries are revealed unto the meek.

20 For the power of YAHOWAH is great, and he is honoured of the lowly.

21 Seek not out things that are too hard for thee, neither search the things that are above thy strength.

22 But what is commanded thee, think thereupon with reverence, for it is not needful for thee to see with thine eyes the things that are in secret.

23 Be not curious in unnecessary matters: for more things are shewed unto thee than men understand.

24 For many are deceived by their own vain opinion; and an evil suspicion hath overthrown their judgment.

25 Without eyes thou shalt want light: profess not the knowledge therefore that thou hast not.

26 A stubborn heart shall fare evil at the last; and he that loveth danger shall perish therein.

27 An obstinate heart shall be laden with sorrows; and the wicked man shall heap sin upon sin.

28 In the punishment of the proud there is no remedy; for the plant of wickedness hath taken root in him.

29 The heart of the prudent will understand a parable; and an attentive ear is the desire of a wise man.

30 Water will quench a flaming fire; and alms maketh an atonement for sins.

31 And he that requiteth good turns is mindful of that which may come hereafter; and when he falleth, he shall find a stay.

4 My son, defraud not the poor of his living, and make not the needy eyes to wait long.

2 Make not an hungry soul sorrowful; neither provoke a man in his distress.

3 Add not more trouble to an heart that is vexed; and defer not to give to him that is in need.

4 Reject not the supplication of the afflicted; neither turn away thy face from a poor man.

5 Turn not away thine eye from the needy, and give him none occasion to curse thee:

6 For if he curse thee in the bitterness of his soul, his prayer shall be heard of him that made him.

7 Get thyself the love of the congregation, and bow thy head to a great man.

8 Let it not grieve thee to bow down thine ear to the poor, and give him a friendly answer with meekness.

9 Deliver him that suffereth wrong from the hand of the oppressor; and be not fainthearted when thou sittest in judgment.

10 Be as a father unto the fatherless, and instead of an husband unto their mother: so shalt thou be as the son of the Most High, and he shall love thee more than thy mother doth.

11 Wisdom exalteth her children, and layeth hold of them that seek her.

12 He that loveth her loveth life; and they that seek to her early shall be filled with joy.

13 He that holdeth her fast shall inherit glory; and wheresoever she entereth, YAHOWAH will bless.

14 They that serve her shall minister to the Holy One: and them that love her YAHOWAH doth love.

15 Whoso giveth ear unto her shall judge the heathen: and he that attendeth unto her shall dwell securely.

16 If a man commit himself unto her, he shall inherit her; and his generation shall hold her in possession.

17 For at the first she will walk with him by crooked ways, and bring fear and dread upon him, and torment him with her discipline, until she may trust his soul, and try him by her Torah.

18 Then will she return the straight way unto him, and comfort him, and shew him her secrets.

19 But if he go wrong, she will forsake him, and give him over to his own ruin.

20 Observe the opportunity, and beware of evil; and be not ashamed when it concerneth thy soul.

21 For there is a shame that bringeth sin; and there is a shame which is glory and grace.

22 Accept no person against thy soul, and let not the reverence of any man cause thee to fall.

23 And refrain not to speak, when there is occasion to do good, and hide not thy wisdom in her beauty.

24 For by speech wisdom shall be known: and learning by the word of the tongue.

25 In no wise speak against the truth; but be abashed of the error of thine ignorance.

26 Be not ashamed to confess thy sins; and force not the course of the river.

27 Make not thyself an underling to a foolish man; neither accept the person of the mighty.

28 Strive for the truth unto death, and YAHOWAH shall fight for thee.

29 Be not hasty in thy tongue, and in thy deeds slack and remiss.

30 Be not as a lion in thy house, nor frantick among thy servants.

31 Let not thine hand be stretched out to receive, and shut when thou shouldest repay.

5 Set thy heart upon thy goods; and say not, I have enough for my life.

2 Follow not thine own mind and thy strength, to walk in the ways of thy heart:

3 And say not, Who shall controul me for my works? for YAHOWAH will surely revenge thy pride.

4 Say not, I have sinned, and what harm hath happened unto me? for YAHOWAH is longsuffering, he will in no wise let thee go.

5 Concerning propitiation, be not without fear to add sin unto sin:

6 And say not His mercy is great; he will be pacified for the multitude of my sins: for mercy and wrath come from him, and his indignation resteth upon sinners.

7 Make no tarrying to turn to YAHOWAH, and put not off from day to day: for suddenly shall the wrath of YAHOWAH come forth, and in thy security thou shalt be destroyed, and perish in the day of vengeance.

8 Set not thine heart upon goods unjustly gotten, for they shall not profit thee in the day of calamity.
9 Winnow not with every wind, and go not into every way: for so doth the sinner that hath a double tongue.
10 Be stedfast in thy understanding; and let thy word be the same.
11 Be swift to hear; and let thy life be sincere; and with patience give answer.
12 If thou hast understanding, answer thy neighbour; if not, lay thy hand upon thy mouth.
13 Honour and shame is in talk: and the tongue of man is his fall.
14 Be not called a whisperer, and lie not in wait with thy tongue: for a foul shame is upon the thief, and an evil condemnation upon the double tongue.
15 Be not ignorant of any thing in a great matter or a small.

6 Instead of a friend become not an enemy; for [thereby] thou shalt inherit an ill name, shame, and reproach: even so shall a sinner that hath a double tongue.
2 Extol not thyself in the counsel of thine own heart; that thy soul be not torn in pieces as a bull [straying alone.]
3 Thou shalt eat up thy leaves, and lose thy fruit, and leave thyself as a dry tree.
4 A wicked soul shall destroy him that hath it, and shall make him to be laughed to scorn of his enemies.
5 Sweet language will multiply friends: and a fair-speaking tongue will increase kind greetings.
6 Be in shalom with many: nevertheless have but one counsellor of a thousand.
7 If thou wouldest get a friend, prove him first and be not hasty to credit him.
8 For some man is a friend for his own occasion, and will not abide in the day of thy trouble.
9 And there is a friend, who being turned to enmity, and strife will discover thy reproach.
10 Again, some friend is a companion at the table, and will not continue in the day of thy affliction.
11 But in thy prosperity he will be as thyself, and will be bold over thy servants.
12 If thou be brought low, he will be against thee, and will hide himself from thy face.
13 Separate thyself from thine enemies, and take heed of thy friends.
14 A faithfull friend is a strong defence: and he that hath found such an one hath found a treasure.
15 Nothing doth countervail a faithful friend, and his excellency is invaluable.
16 A faithful friend is the medicine of life; and they that fear YAHOWAH shall find him.
17 Whoso feareth YAHOWAH shall direct his friendship aright: for as he is, so shall his neighbour be also.
18 My son, gather instruction from thy youth up: so shalt thou find wisdom till thine old age.

19 Come unto her as one that ploweth and soweth, and wait for her good fruits: for thou shalt not toil much in labouring about her, but thou shalt eat of her fruits right soon.
20 She is very unpleasant to the unlearned: he that is without understanding will not remain with her.
21 She will lie upon him as a mighty stone of trial; and he will cast her from him ere it be long.
22 For wisdom is according to her name, and she is not manifest unto many.
23 Give ear, my son, receive my advice, and refuse not my counsel,
24 And put thy feet into her fetters, and thy neck into her chain.
25 Bow down thy shoulder, and bear her, and be not grieved with her bonds.
26 Come unto her with thy whole heart, and keep her ways with all thy power.
27 Search, and seek, and she shall be made known unto thee: and when thou hast got hold of her, let her not go.
28 For at the last thou shalt find her rest, and that shall be turned to thy joy.
29 Then shall her fetters be a strong defence for thee, and her chains a robe of glory.
30 For there is a golden ornament upon her, and her bands are purple lace.
31 Thou shalt put her on as a robe of honour, and shalt put her about thee as a crown of joy.
32 My son, if thou wilt, thou shalt be taught: and if thou wilt apply thy mind, thou shalt be prudent.
33 If thou love to hear, thou shalt receive understanding: and if thou bow thine ear, thou shalt be wise,
34 Stand in the multitude of the elders; and cleave unto him that is wise.
35 Be willing to hear every godly discourse; and let not the parables of understanding escape thee.
36 And if thou seest a man of understanding, get thee betimes unto him, and let thy foot wear the steps of his door.
37 Let thy mind be upon the ordinances of YAHOWAH and meditate continually in his commandments: he shall establish thine heart, and give thee wisdom at thine owns desire.

7 Do no evil, so shall no harm come unto thee.
2 Depart from the unjust, and iniquity shall turn away from thee.
3 My son, sow not upon the furrows of unrighteousness, and thou shalt not reap them sevenfold.
4 Seek not of YAHOWAH preeminence, neither of the king the seat of honour.
5 justify not thyself before YAHOWAH; and boast not of thy wisdom before the king.
6 Seek not to be judge, being not able to take away iniquity; lest at any time thou fear the person of the mighty, an stumblingblock in the way of thy uprightness.
7 Offend not against the multitude of a city, and then thou shalt not cast thyself down among the people.

8 Bind not one sin upon another; for in one thou shalt not be unpunished.

9 Say not, ELOHIM will look upon the multitude of my oblations, and when I offer to the Most High ELOHIM, he will accept it.

10 Be not fainthearted when thou makest thy prayer, and neglect not to give alms.

11 Laugh no man to scorn in the bitterness of his soul: for there is one which humbleth and exalteth.

12 Devise not a lie against thy brother; neither do the like to thy friend.

13 Use not to make any manner of lie: for the custom thereof is not good.

14 Use not many words in a multitude of elders, and make not much babbling when thou prayest.

15 Hate not laborious work, neither husbandry, which the Most High hath ordained.

16 Number not thyself among the multitude of sinners, but remember that wrath will not tarry long.

17 Humble thyself greatly: for the vengeance of the ungodly is fire and worms.

18 Change not a friend for any good by no means; neither a faithful brother for the gold of Ophir.

19 Forego not a wise and good woman: for her grace is above gold.

20 Whereas thy servant worketh truly, entreat him not evil. nor the hireling that bestoweth himself wholly for thee.

21 Let thy soul love a good servant, and defraud him not of liberty.

22 Hast thou cattle? have an eye to them: and if they be for thy profit, keep them with thee.

23 Hast thou children? instruct them, and bow down their neck from their youth.

24 Hast thou daughters? have a care of their body, and shew not thyself cheerful toward them.

25 Marry thy daughter, and so shalt thou have performed a weighty matter: but give her to a man of understanding.

26 Hast thou a wife after thy mind? forsake her not: but give not thyself over to a light woman.

27 Honour thy father with thy whole heart, and forget not the sorrows of thy mother.

28 Remember that thou wast begotten of them; and how canst thou recompense them the things that they have done for thee?

29 Fear YAHOWAH with all thy soul, and reverence his priests.

30 Love him that made thee with all thy strength, and forsake not his ministers.

31 Fear YAHOWAH, and honor the priest; and give him his portion, as it is commanded thee; the firstfruits, and the trespass offering, and the gift of the shoulders, and the sacrifice of sanctification, and the firstfruits of the holy things.

32 And stretch thine hand unto the poor, that thy blessing may be perfected.

33 A gift hath grace in the sight of every man living; and for the dead detain it not.

34 Fail not to be with them that weep, and mourn with them that mourn.

35 Be not slow to visit the sick: for that shall make thee to be beloved.

36 Whatsoever thou takest in hand, remember the end, and thou shalt never do amiss.

8 Strive not with a mighty man' lest thou fall into his hands.

2 Be not at variance with a rich man, lest he overweigh thee: for gold hath destroyed many, and perverted the hearts of kings.

3 Strive not with a man that is full of tongue, and heap not wood upon his fire.

4 Jest not with a rude man, lest thy ancestors be disgraced.

5 Reproach not a man that turneth from sin, but remember that we are all worthy of punishment.

6 Dishonour not a man in his old age: for even some of us wax old.

7 Rejoice not over thy greatest enemy being dead, but remember that we die all.

8 Despise not the discourse of the wise, but acquaint thyself with their proverbs: for of them thou shalt learn instruction, and how to serve great men with ease.

9 Miss not the discourse of the elders: for they also learned of their fathers, and of them thou shalt learn understanding, and to give answer as need requireth.

10 Kindle not the coals of a sinner, lest thou be burnt with the flame of his fire.

11 Rise not up [in anger] at the presence of an injurious person, lest he lie in wait to entrap thee in thy words

12 Lend not unto him that is mightier than thyself; for if thou lendest him, count it but lost.

13 Be not surety above thy power: for if thou be surety, take care to pay it.

14 Go not to Torah with a judge; for they will judge for him according to his honour.

15 Travel not by the way with a bold fellow, lest he become grievous unto thee: for he will do according to his own will, and thou shalt perish with him through his folly.

16 Strive not with an angry man, and go not with him into a solitary place: for blood is as nothing in his sight, and where there is no help, he will overthrow thee.

17 Consult not with a fool; for he cannot keep counsel.

18 Do no secret thing before a stranger; for thou knowest not what he will bring forth.

19 Open not thine heart to every man, lest he requite thee with a shrewd turn.

9 Be not jealous over the wife of thy bosom, and teach her not an evil lesson against thyself.

2 Give not thy soul unto a woman to set her foot upon thy substance.

3 Meet not with an harlot, lest thou fall into her snares.

4 Use not much the company of a woman that is a singer, lest thou be taken with her attempts.

5 Gaze not on a maid, that thou fall not by those things that are precious in her.

6 Give not thy soul unto harlots, that thou lose not thine inheritance.

7 Look not round about thee in the streets of the city, neither wander thou in the solitary place thereof.

8 Turn away thine eye from a beautiful woman, and look not upon another's beauty; for many have been deceived by the beauty of a woman; for herewith love is kindled as a fire.

9 Sit not at all with another man's wife, nor sit down with her in thine arms, and spend not thy money with her at the wine; lest thine heart incline unto her, and so through thy desire thou fall into destruction.

10 Forsake not an old friend; for the new is not comparable to him: a new friend is as new wine; when it is old, thou shalt drink it with pleasure.

11 Envy not the glory of a sinner: for thou knowest not what shall be his end.

12 Delight not in the thing that the ungodly have pleasure in; but remember they shall not go unpunished unto their grave.

13 Keep thee far from the man that hath power to kill; so shalt thou not doubt the fear of death: and if thou come unto him, make no fault, lest he take away thy life presently: remember that thou goest in the midst of snares, and that thou walkest upon the battlements of the city.

14 As near as thou canst, guess at thy neighbour, and consult with the wise.

15 Let thy talk be with the wise, and all thy communication in the Torah of the Most High.

16 And let just men eat and drink with thee; and let thy glorying be in the fear of YAHOWAH.

17 For the hand of the artificer the work shall be commended: and the wise ruler of the people for his speech.

18 A man of an ill tongue is dangerous in his city; and he that is rash in his talk shall be hated.

10 A wise judge will instruct his people; and the government of a prudent man is well ordered.

2 As the judge of the people is himself, so are his officers; and what manner of man the ruler of the city is, such are all they that dwell therein.

3 An unwise king destroyeth his people; but through the prudence of them which are in authority the city shall be inhabited.

4 The power of the earth is in the hand of YAHOWAH, and in due time he will set over it one that is profitable.

5 In the hand of ELOHIM is the prosperity of man: and upon the person of the scribe shall he lay his honour.

6 Bear not hatred to thy neighbour for every wrong; and do nothing at all by injurious practices.

7 Pride is hateful before ELOHIM and man: and by both doth one commit iniquity.

8 Because of unrighteous dealings, injuries, and riches got by deceit, the kingdom is translated from one people to another.

9 Why is earth and ashes proud? There is not a more wicked thing than a covetous man: for such an one setteth his own soul to sale; because while he liveth he casteth away his bowels.

10 The physician cutteth off a long disease; and he that is to day a king to morrow shall die.

11 For when a man is dead, he shall inherit creeping things, beasts, and worms.

12 The beginning of pride is when one departeth from ELOHIM, and his heart is turned away from his Maker.

13 For pride is the beginning of sin, and he that hath it shall pour out abomination: and therefore YAHOWAH brought upon them strange calamities, and overthrew them utterly.

14 YAHOWAH hath cast down the thrones of proud princes, and set up the meek in their stead.

15 YAHOWAH hath plucked up the roots of the proud heathen, and planted the lowly in their place.

16 YAHOWAH overthrew countries of the heathen, and destroyed them to the foundations of the earth.

17 He took some of them away, and destroyed them, and hath made their memorial to cease from the earth.

18 Pride was not made for men, nor furious anger for them that are born of a woman.

19 They that fear YAHOWAH are a sure seed, and they that love him an honourable plant: they that regard not the Torah are a dishonourable seed; they that transgress the commandments are a deceivable seed.

20 Among brethren he that is chief is honorable; so are they that fear YAHOWAH in his eyes.

21 The fear of YAHOWAH goeth before the obtaining of authority: but roughness and pride is the losing thereof.

22 Whether he be rich, noble, or poor, their glory is the fear of YAHOWAH.

23 It is not meet to despise the poor man that hath understanding; neither is it convenient to magnify a sinful man.

24 Great men, and judges, and potentates, shall be honoured; yet is there none of them greater than he that feareth YAHOWAH.

25 Unto the servant that is wise shall they that are free do service: and he that hath knowledge will not grudge when he is reformed.

26 Be not overwise in doing thy business; and boast not thyself in the time of thy distress.

27 Better is he that laboureth, and aboundeth in all things, than he that boasteth himself, and wanteth bread.

28 My son, glorify thy soul in meekness, and give it honour according to the dignity thereof.

29 Who will justify him that sinneth against his own soul? and who will honour him that dishonoureth his own life?

30 The poor man is honoured for his skill, and the rich man is honoured for his riches.

31 He that is honoured in poverty, how much more in riches? and he that is dishonourable in riches, how much more in poverty?

11 Wisdom lifteth up the head of him that is of low degree, and maketh him to sit among great men.

2 Commend not a man for his beauty; neither abhor a man for his outward appearance.

3 The bee is little among such as fly; but her fruit is the chief of sweet things.

4 Boast not of thy clothing and raiment, and exalt not thyself in the day of honour: for the works of YAHOWAH are wonderful, and his works among men are hidden.

5 Many kings have sat down upon the ground; and one that was never thought of hath worn the crown.

6 Many mighty men have been greatly disgraced; and the honourable delivered into other men's hands.

7 Blame not before thou hast examined the truth: understand first, and then rebuke.

8 Answer not before thou hast heard the cause: neither interrupt men in the midst of their talk.

9 Strive not in a matter that concerneth thee not; and sit not in judgment with sinners.

10 My son, meddle not with many matters: for if thou meddle much, thou shalt not be innocent; and if thou follow after, thou shalt not obtain, neither shalt thou escape by fleeing.

11 There is one that laboureth, and taketh pains, and maketh haste, and is so much the more behind.

12 Again, there is another that is slow, and hath need of help, wanting ability, and full of poverty; yet the eye of YAHOWAH looked upon him for good, and set him up from his low estate,

13 And lifted up his head from misery; so that many that saw it marvelled at him.

14 Prosperity and adversity, life and death, poverty and riches, come of YAHOWAH.

15 Wisdom, knowledge, and understanding of the Torah, are of YAHOWAH: love, and the way of good works, are from him.

16 Error and darkness had their beginning together with sinners: and evil shall wax old with them that glory therein.

17 The gift of YAHOWAH remaineth with the godly, and his favour bringeth prosperity for ever.

18 There is that waxeth rich by his wariness and pinching, and this is the portion of his reward:

19 Whereas he saith, I have found rest, and now will eat continually of my goods; and yet he knoweth not what time shall come upon him, and that he must leave those things to others, and die.

20 Be stedfast in thy covenant, and be conversant therein, and wax old in thy work.

21 Marvel not at the works of sinners; but trust in YAHOWAH, and abide in thy labour: for it is an easy thing in the sight of YAHOWAH on the sudden to make a poor man rich.

22 The blessing of YAHOWAH is in the reward of the godly, and suddenly he maketh his blessing flourish.

23 Say not, What profit is there of my service? and what good things shall I have hereafter?

24 Again, say not, I have enough, and possess many things, and what evil shall I have hereafter?

25 In the day of prosperity there is a forgetfulness of affliction: and in the day of affliction there is no more remembrance of prosperity.

26 For it is an easy thing unto YAHOWAH in the day of death to reward a man according to his ways.

27 The affliction of an hour maketh a man forget pleasure: and in his end his deeds shall be discovered.

28 Judge none blessed before his death: for a man shall be known in his children.

29 Bring not every man into thine house: for the deceitful man hath many trains.

30 Like as a partridge taken [and kept] in a cage, so is the heart of the proud; and like as a spy, watcheth he for thy fall:

31 For he lieth in wait, and turneth good into evil, and in things worthy praise will lay blame upon thee.

32 Of a spark of fire a heap of coals is kindled: and a sinful man layeth wait for blood.

33 Take heed of a mischievous man, for he worketh wickedness; lest he bring upon thee a perpetual blot.

34 Receive a stranger into thine house, and he will disturb thee, and turn thee out of thine own.

12 When thou wilt do good know to whom thou doest it; so shalt thou be thanked for thy benefits.

2 Do good to the godly man, and thou shalt find a recompence; and if not from him, yet from the Most High.

3 There can no good come to him that is always occupied in evil, nor to him that giveth no alms.

4 Give to the godly man, and help not a sinner.

5 Do well unto him that is lowly, but give not to the ungodly: hold back thy bread, and give it not unto him, lest he overmaster thee thereby: for [else] thou shalt receive twice as much evil for all the good thou shalt have done unto him.

6 For the Most High hateth sinners, and will repay vengeance unto the ungodly, and keepeth them against the mighty day of their punishment.

7 Give unto the good, and help not the sinner.

8 A friend cannot be known in prosperity: and an enemy cannot be hidden in adversity.

9 In the prosperity of a man enemies will be grieved: but in his adversity even a friend will depart.

10 Never trust thine enemy: for like as iron rusteth, so is his wickedness.

11 Though he humble himself, and go crouching, yet take good heed and beware of him, and thou shalt be unto him as if thou hadst wiped a lookingglass, and thou shalt know

that his rust hath not been altogether wiped away.

12 Set him not by thee, lest, when he hath overthrown thee, he stand up in thy place; neither let him sit at thy right hand, lest he seek to take thy seat, and thou at the last remember my words, and be pricked therewith.

13 Who will pity a charmer that is bitten with a serpent, or any such as come nigh wild beasts?

14 So one that goeth to a sinner, and is defiled with him in his sins, who will pity?

15 For a while he will abide with thee, but if thou begin to fall, he will not tarry.

16 An enemy speaketh sweetly with his lips, but in his heart he imagineth how to throw thee into a pit: he will weep with his eyes, but if he find opportunity, he will not be satisfied with blood.

17 If adversity come upon thee, thou shalt find him there first; and though he pretend to help thee, yet shall he undermine thee.

18 He will shake his head, and clap his hands, and whisper much, and change his countenance.

13 He that toucheth pitch shall be defiled therewith; and he that hath fellowship with a proud man shall be like unto him.

2 Burden not thyself above thy power while thou livest; and have no fellowship with one that is mightier and richer than thyself: for how agree the kettle and the earthen pot together? for if the one be smitten against the other, it shall be broken.

3 The rich man hath done wrong, and yet he threateneth withal: the poor is wronged, and he must intreat also.

4 If thou be for his profit, he will use thee: but if thou have nothing, he will forsake thee.

5 If thou have any thing, he will live with thee: yea, he will make thee bare, and will not be sorry for it.

6 If he have need of thee, he will deceive thee, and smile upon thee, and put thee in hope; he will speak thee fair, and say, What wantest thou?

7 And he will shame thee by his meats, until he have drawn thee dry twice or thrice, and at the last he will laugh thee to scorn afterward, when he seeth thee, he will forsake thee, and shake his head at thee.

8 Beware that thou be not deceived and brought down in thy jollity.

9 If thou be invited of a mighty man, withdraw thyself, and so much the more will he invite thee.

10 Press thou not upon him, lest thou be put back; stand not far off, lest thou be forgotten.

11 Affect not to be made equal unto him in talk, and believe not his many words: for with much communication will he tempt thee, and smiling upon thee will get out thy secrets:

12 But cruelly he will lay up thy words, and will not spare to do thee hurt, and to put thee in prison.

13 Observe, and take good heed, for thou walkest in peril of thy overthrowing: when thou hearest these things, awake in thy sleep.

14 Love YAHOWAH all thy life, and call upon him for thy salvation.

15 Every beast loveth his like, and every man loveth his neighbor.

16 All flesh consorteth according to kind, and a man will cleave to his like.

17 What fellowship hath the wolf with the lamb? so the sinner with the godly.

18 What agreement is there between the hyena and a dog? and what shalom between the rich and the poor?

19 As the wild ass is the lion's prey in the wilderness: so the rich eat up the poor.

20 As the proud hate humility: so doth the rich abhor the poor.

21 A rich man beginning to fall is held up of his friends: but a poor man being down is thrust away by his friends.

22 When a rich man is fallen, he hath many helpers: he speaketh things not to be spoken, and yet men justify him: the poor man slipped, and yet they rebuked him too; he spake wisely, and could have no place.

23 When a rich man speaketh, every man holdeth his tongue, and, look, what he saith, they extol it to the clouds: but if the poor man speak, they say, What fellow is this? and if he stumble, they will help to overthrow him.

24 Riches are good unto him that hath no sin, and poverty is evil in the mouth of the ungodly.

25 The heart of a man changeth his countenance, whether it be for good or evil: and a merry heart maketh a cheerful countenance.

26 A cheerful countenance is a token of a heart that is in prosperity; and the finding out of parables is a wearisome labour of the mind.

14 Blessed is the man that hath not slipped with his mouth, and is not pricked with the multitude of sins.

2 Blessed is he whose conscience hath not condemned him, and who is not fallen from his hope in YAHOWAH.

3 Riches are not comely for a niggard: and what should an envious man do with money?

4 He that gathereth by defrauding his own soul gathereth for others, that shall spend his goods riotously.

5 He that is evil to himself, to whom will he be good? he shall not take pleasure in his goods.

6 There is none worse than he that envieth himself; and this is a recompence of his wickedness.

7 And if he doeth good, he doeth it unwillingly; and at the last he will declare his wickedness.

8 The envious man hath a wicked eye; he turneth away his face, and despiseth men.

9 A covetous man's eye is not satisfied with his portion; and the iniquity of the wicked drieth up his soul.

10 A wicked eye envieth [his] bread, and he is a niggard at his table.

11 My son, according to thy ability do good to thyself, and give YAHOWAH his due offering.

12 Remember that death will not be long in coming, and that the covenant of the grave is not shewed unto thee.

13 Do good unto thy friend before thou die, and according to thy ability stretch out thy hand and give to him.

14 Defraud not thyself of the good day, and let not the part of a good desire overpass thee.

15 Shalt thou not leave thy travails unto another? and thy labours to be divided by lot?

16 Give, and take, and sanctify thy soul; for there is no seeking of dainties in the grave.

17 All flesh waxeth old as a garment: for the covenant from the beginning is, Thou shalt die the death.

18 As of the green leaves on a thick tree, some fall, and some grow; so is the generation of flesh and blood, one cometh to an end, and another is born.

19 Every work rotteth and consumeth away, and the worker thereof shall go withal.

20 Blessed is the man that doth meditate good things in wisdom, and that reasoneth of holy things by his understanding.

21 He that considereth her ways in his heart shall also have understanding in her secrets.

22 Go after her as one that traceth, and lie in wait in her ways.

23 He that prieth in at her windows shall also hearken at her doors.

24 He that doth lodge near her house shall also fasten a pin in her walls.

25 He shall pitch his tent nigh unto her, and shall lodge in a lodging where good things are.

26 He shall set his children under her shelter, and shall lodge under her branches.

27 By her he shall be covered from heat, and in her glory shall he dwell.

15 He that feareth YAHOWAH will do good, and he that hath the knowledge of the Torah shall obtain her.

2 And as a mother shall she meet him, and receive him as a wife married of a virgin.

3 With the bread of understanding shall she feed him, and give him the water of wisdom to drink.

4 He shall be stayed upon her, and shall not be moved; and shall rely upon her, and shall not be confounded.

5 She shall exalt him above his neighbours, and in the midst of the congregation shall she open his mouth.

6 He shall find joy and a crown of gladness, and she shall cause him to inherit an everlasting name.

7 But foolish men shall not attain unto her, and sinners shall not see her.

8 For she is far from pride, and men that are liars cannot remember her.

9 Praise is not seemly in the mouth of a sinner, for it was not sent him of YAHOWAH.

10 For praise shall be uttered in wisdom, and YAHOWAH will prosper it.

11 Say not thou, It is through YAHOWAH that I fell away: for thou oughtest not to do the things that he hateth.

12 Say not thou, He hath caused me to err: for he hath no need of the sinful man.

13 YAHOWAH hateth all abomination; and they that fear ELOHIM love it not.

14 He himself made man from the beginning, and left him in the hand of his counsel;

15 If thou wilt, to keep the commandments, and to perform acceptable faithfulness.

16 He hath set fire and water before thee: stretch forth thy hand unto whether thou wilt.

17 Before man is life and death; and whether him liketh shall be given him.

18 For the wisdom of YAHOWAH is great, and he is mighty in power, and beholdeth all things:

19 And his eyes are upon them that fear him, and he knoweth every work of man.

20 He hath commanded no man to do wickedly, neither hath he given any man licence to sin.

16 Desire not a multitude of unprofitable children, neither delight in ungodly sons.

2 Though they multiply, rejoice not in them, except the fear of YAHOWAH be with them.

3 Trust not thou in their life, neither respect their multitude: for one that is just is better than a thousand; and better it is to die without children, than to have them that are ungodly.

4 For by one that hath understanding shall the city be replenished: but the kindred of the wicked shall speedily become desolate.

5 Many such things have I seen with mine eyes, and mine ear hath heard greater things than these.

6 In the congregation of the ungodly shall a fire be kindled; and in a rebellious nation wrath is set on fire.

7 He was not pacified toward the old giants, who fell away in the strength of their foolishness.

8 Neither spared he the place where Lot sojourned, but abhorred them for their pride.

9 He pitied not the people of perdition, who were taken away in their sins:

10 Nor the six hundred thousand footmen, who were gathered together in the hardness of their hearts.

11 And if there be one stiffnecked among the people, it is marvel if he escape unpunished: for mercy and wrath are with him; he is mighty to forgive, and to pour out displeasure.

12 As his mercy is great, so is his correction also: he judgeth a man according to his works

13 The sinner shall not escape with his spoils: and the patience of the godly shall not be frustrate.

14 Make way for every work of mercy: for every man shall find according to his works.

15 YAHOWAH hardened Pharaoh, that he should not know him, that his powerful works might be known to the world.

16 His mercy is manifest to every creature; and he hath separated his light from the darkness with an adamant.

17 Say not thou, I will hide myself from YAHOWAH: shall any remember me from above? I shall not be remembered among so many people: for what is my soul among such an infinite number of creatures?

18 Behold, the heaven, and the heaven of heavens, the deep, and the earth, and all that therein is, shall be moved when he shall visit.

19 The mountains also and foundations of the earth be shaken with trembling, when YAHOWAH looketh upon them.

20 No heart can think upon these things worthily: and who is able to conceive his ways?

21 It is a tempest which no man can see: for the most part of his works are hid.

22 Who can declare the works of his justice? or who can endure them? for his covenant is afar off, and the trial of all things is in the end.

23 He that wanteth understanding will think upon vain things: and a foolish man erring imagineth follies.

24 My son, hearken unto me, and learn knowledge, and mark my words with thy heart.

25 I will shew forth doctrine in weight, and declare his knowledge exactly.

26 The works of YAHOWAH are done in judgment from the beginning: and from the time he made them he disposed the parts thereof.

27 He garnished his works for ever, and in his hand are the chief of them unto all generations: they neither labour, nor are weary, nor cease from their works.

28 None of them hindereth another, and they shall never disobey his word.

29 After this YAHOWAH looked upon the earth, and filled it with his blessings.

30 With all manner of living things hath he covered the face thereof; and they shall return into it again.

17 YAHOWAH created man of the earth, and turned him into it again.

2 He gave them few days, and a short time, and power also over the things therein.

3 He endued them with strength by themselves, and made them according to his image,

4 And put the fear of man upon all flesh, and gave him dominion over beasts and fowls.

5 They received the use of the five operations of YAHOWAH, and in the sixth place he imparted them understanding, and in the seventh speech, an interpreter of the cogitations thereof.]

6 Counsel, and a tongue, and eyes, ears, and a heart, gave he them to understand.

7 Withal he filled them with the knowledge of understanding, and shewed them good and evil.

8 He set his eye upon their hearts, that he might shew them the greatness of his works.

9 He gave them to glory in his marvellous acts for ever, that they might declare his works with understanding.

10 And the elect shall praise his holy name.

11 Beside this he gave them knowledge, and the Torah of life for an heritage.

12 He made an everlasting covenant with them, and shewed them his judgments.

13 Their eyes saw the majesty of his glory, and their ears heard his glorious voice.

14 And he said unto them, Beware of all unrighteousness; and he gave every man commandment concerning his neighbour.

15 Their ways are ever before him, and shall not be hid from his eyes.

16 Every man from his youth is given to evil; neither could they make to themselves fleshy hearts for stony.

17 For in the division of the nations of the whole earth he set a ruler over every people; but Yisra'EL is YAHOWAH'S portion:

18 Whom, being his firstborn, he nourisheth with discipline, and giving him the light of his love doth not forsake him.

19 Therefore all their works are as the sun before him, and his eyes are continually upon their ways.

20 None of their unrighteous deeds are hid from him, but all their sins are before YAHOWAH

21 But YAHOWAH being gracious and knowing his workmanship, neither left nor forsook them, but spared them.

22 The alms of a man is as a signet with him, and he will keep the good deeds of man as the apple of the eye, and give repentance to his sons and daughters.

23 Afterwards he will rise up and reward them, and render their recompence upon their heads.

24 But unto them that repent, he granted them return, and comforted those that failed in patience.

25 Return unto YAHOWAH, and forsake thy sins, make thy prayer before his face, and offend less.

26 Turn again to the Most High, and turn away from iniquity: for he will lead thee out of darkness into the light of health, and hate thou abomination vehemently.

27 Who shall praise the Most High in the grave, instead of them which live and give thanks?

28 Thanksgiving perisheth from the dead, as from one that is not: the living and sound in heart shall praise YAHOWAH.

29 How great is the lovingkindness of YAHOWAH our ELOHIM, and his compassion unto such as turn unto him in holiness!

30 For all things cannot be in men, because the son of man is not immortal.

31 What is brighter than the sun? yet the light thereof faileth; and flesh and blood will imagine evil.

32 He vieweth the power of the height of heaven; and all men are but earth and ashes.

18 He that liveth for ever Hath created all things in general.

2 YAHOWAH only is righteous, and there is none other but he,

3 Who governeth the world with the palm of his hand, and all things obey his will: for he is the King of all, by his power dividing holy things among them from profane.

4 To whom hath he given power to declare his works? and who shall find out his noble acts?

5 Who shall number the strength of his majesty? and who shall also tell out his mercies?

6 As for the wondrous works of YAHOWAH, there may nothing be taken from them, neither may any thing be put unto them, neither can the ground of them be found out.

7 When a man hath done, then he beginneth; and when he leaveth off, then he shall be doubtful.

8 What is man, and whereto serveth he? what is his good, and what is his evil?

9 The number of a man's days at the most are an hundred years.

10 As a drop of water unto the sea, and a gravelstone in comparison of the sand; so are a thousand years to the days of eternity.

11 Therefore is ELOHIM patient with them, and poureth forth his mercy upon them.

12 He saw and perceived their end to be evil; therefore he multiplied his compassion.

13 The mercy of man is toward his neighbour; but the mercy of YAHOWAH is upon all flesh: he reproveth, and nurtureth, and teacheth and bringeth again, as a shepherd his flock.

14 He hath mercy on them that receive discipline, and that diligently seek after his judgments.

15 My son, blemish not thy good deeds, neither use uncomfortable words when thou givest any thing.

16 Shall not the dew asswage the heat? so is a word better than a gift.

17 Lo, is not a word better than a gift? but both are with a gracious man.

18 A fool will upbraid churlishly, and a gift of the envious consumeth the eyes.

19 Learn before thou speak, and use physick or ever thou be sick.

20 Before judgment examine thyself, and in the day of visitation thou shalt find mercy.

21 Humble thyself before thou be sick, and in the time of sins shew repentance.

22 Let nothing hinder thee to pay thy vow in due time, and defer not until death to be justified.

23 Before thou prayest, prepare thyself; and be not as one that tempteth YAHOWAH.

24 Think upon the wrath that shall be at the end, and the time of vengeance, when he shall turn away his face.

25 When thou hast enough, remember the time of hunger: and when thou art rich, think upon poverty and need.

26 From the morning until the evening the time is changed, and all things are soon done before YAHOWAH.

27 A wise man will fear in every thing, and in the day of sinning he will beware of offence: but a fool will not observe time.

28 Every man of understanding knoweth wisdom, and will give praise unto him that found her.

29 They that were of understanding in sayings became also wise themselves, and poured forth exquisite parables.

30 Go not after thy lusts, but refrain thyself from thine appetites.

31 If thou givest thy soul the desires that please her, she will make thee a laughingstock to thine enemies that malign thee.

32 Take not pleasure in much good cheer, neither be tied to the expence thereof.

33 Be not made a beggar by banqueting upon borrowing, when thou hast nothing in thy purse: for thou shalt lie in wait for thine own life, and be talked on.

19 A labouring man that A is given to drunkenness shall not be rich: and he that contemneth small things shall fall by little and little.

2 Wine and women will make men of understanding to fall away: and he that cleaveth to harlots will become impudent.

3 Moths and worms shall have him to heritage, and a bold man shall be taken away.

4 He that is hasty to give credit is lightminded; and he that sinneth shall offend against his own soul.

5 Whoso taketh pleasure in wickedness shall be condemned: but he that resisteth pleasures crowneth his life.

6 He that can rule his tongue shall live without strife; and he that hateth babbling shall have less evil.

7 Rehearse not unto another that which is told unto thee, and thou shalt fare never the worse.

8 Whether it be to friend or foe, talk not of other men's lives; and if thou canst without offence, reveal them not.

9 For he heard and observed thee, and when time cometh he will hate thee.

10 If thou hast heard a word, let it die with thee; and be bold, it will not burst thee.

11 A fool travaileth with a word, as a woman in labour of a child.

12 As an arrow that sticketh in a man's thigh, so is a word within a fool's belly.

13 Admonish a friend, it may be he hath not done it: and if he have done it, that he do it no more.

14 Admonish thy friend, it may be he hath not said it: and if he have, that he speak it not again.

15 Admonish a friend: for many times it is a slander, and believe not every tale.

16 There is one that slippeth in his speech, but not from his heart; and who is he that hath not offended with his tongue?

17 Admonish thy neighbour before thou threaten him; and not being angry, give place to the Torah of the Most High.

18 The fear of YAHOWAH is the first step to be accepted [of him,] and wisdom obtaineth his love.

19 The knowledge of the commandments of YAHOWAH is the doctrine of life: and they that do

things that please him shall receive the fruit of the tree of immortality.

20 The fear of YAHOWAH is all wisdom; and in all wisdom is the performance of the Torah, and the knowledge of his omnipotency.

21 If a servant say to his master, I will not do as it pleaseth thee; though afterward he do it, he angereth him that nourisheth him.

22 The knowledge of wickedness is not wisdom, neither at any time the counsel of sinners prudence.

23 There is a wickedness, and the same an abomination; and there is a fool wanting in wisdom.

24 He that hath small understanding, and feareth ELOHIM, is better than one that hath much wisdom, and transgresseth the Torah of the Most High.

25 There is an exquisite subtilty, and the same is unjust; and there is one that turneth aside to make judgment appear; and there is a wise man that justifieth in judgment.

26 There is a wicked man that hangeth down his head sadly; but inwardly he is full of deceit,

27 Casting down his countenance, and making as if he heard not: where he is not known, he will do thee a mischief before thou be aware.

28 And if for want of power he be hindered from sinning, yet when he findeth opportunity he will do evil.

29 A man may be known by his look, and one that hath understanding by his countenance, when thou meetest him.

30 A man's attire, and excessive laughter, and gait, shew what he is.

20 There is a reproof that is not comely: again, some man holdeth his tongue, and he is wise.

2 It is much better to reprove, than to be angry secretly: and he that confesseth his fault shall be preserved from hurt.

3 How good is it, when thou art reproved, to shew repentance! for so shalt thou escape wilful sin.

4 As is the lust of an eunuch to deflower a virgin; so is he that executeth judgment with violence.

5 There is one that keepeth silence, and is found wise: and another by much babbling becometh hateful.

6 Some man holdeth his tongue, because he hath not to answer: and some keepeth silence, knowing his time.

7 A wise man will hold his tongue till he see opportunity: but a babbler and a fool will regard no time.

8 He that useth many words shall be abhorred; and he that taketh to himself authority therein shall be hated.

9 There is a sinner that hath good success in evil things; and there is a gain that turneth to loss.

10 There is a gift that shall not profit thee; and there is a gift whose recompence is double.

11 There is an abasement because of glory; and there is that lifteth up his head from a low estate.

12 There is that buyeth much for a little, and repayeth it sevenfold.

13 A wise man by his words maketh him beloved: but the graces of fools shall be poured out.

14 The gift of a fool shall do thee no good when thou hast it; neither yet of the envious for his necessity: for he looketh to receive many things for one.

15 He giveth little, and upbraideth much; he openeth his mouth like a crier; to day he lendeth, and to morrow will he ask it again: such an one is to be hated of ELOHIM and man.

16 The fool saith, I have no friends, I have no thank for all my good deeds, and they that eat my bread speak evil of me.

17 How oft, and of how many shall he be laughed to scorn! for he knoweth not aright what it is to have; and it is all one unto him as if he had it not.

18 To slip upon a pavement is better than to slip with the tongue: so the fall of the wicked shall come speedily.

19 An unseasonable tale will always be in the mouth of the unwise.

20 A wise sentence shall be rejected when it cometh out of a fool's mouth; for he will not speak it in due season.

21 There is that is hindered from sinning through want: and when he taketh rest, he shall not be troubled.

22 There is that destroyeth his own soul through bashfulness, and by accepting of persons overthroweth himself.

23 There is that for bashfulness promiseth to his friend, and maketh him his enemy for nothing.

24 A lie is a foul blot in a man, yet it is continually in the mouth of the untaught.

25 A thief is better than a man that is accustomed to lie: but they both shall have destruction to heritage.

26 The disposition of a liar is dishonourable, and his shame is ever with him.

27 A wise man shall promote himself to honour with his words: and he that hath understanding will please great men.

28 He that tilleth his land shall increase his heap: and he that pleaseth great men shall get pardon for iniquity.

29 Presents and gifts blind the eyes of the wise, and stop up his mouth that he cannot reprove.

30 Wisdom that is hid, and treasure that is hoarded up, what profit is in them both?

31 Better is he that hideth his folly than a man that hideth his wisdom.

32 Necessary patience in seeking ing YAHOWAH is better than he that leadeth his life without a guide.

21 My son, hast thou sinned? do so no more, but ask pardon for thy former sins.

2 Flee from sin as from the face of a serpent: for if thou comest too near it, it will bite thee: the teeth thereof are as the teeth of a lion, slaying the souls of men.

3 All iniquity is as a two edged sword, the wounds whereof cannot be healed.

4 To terrify and do wrong will waste riches: thus the house of proud men shall be made desolate.

5 A prayer out of a poor man's mouth reacheth to the ears of ELOHIM, and his judgment cometh speedily.

6 He that hateth to be reproved is in the way of sinners: but he that feareth YAHOWAH will repent from his heart.

7 An eloquent man is known far and near; but a man of understanding knoweth when he slippeth.

8 He that buildeth his house with other men's money is like one that gathereth himself stones for the tomb of his burial.

9 The congregation of the wicked is like tow wrapped together: and the end of them is a flame of fire to destroy them.

10 The way of sinners is made plain with stones, but at the end thereof is the pit of hell.

11 He that keepeth the Torah of YAHOWAH getteth the understanding thereof: and the perfection of the fear of YAHOWAH is wisdom.

12 He that is not wise will not be taught: but there is a wisdom which multiplieth bitterness.

13 The knowledge of a wise man shall abound like a flood: and his counsel is like a pure fountain of life.

14 The inner parts of a fool are like a broken vessel, and he will hold no knowledge as long as he liveth.

15 If a skilful man hear a wise word, he will commend it, and add unto it: but as soon as one of no understanding heareth it, it displeaseth him, and he casteth it behind his back.

16 The talking of a fool is like a burden in the way: but grace shall be found in the lips of the wise.

17 They enquire at the mouth of the wise man in the congregation, and they shall ponder his words in their heart.

18 As is a house that is destroyed, so is wisdom to a fool: and the knowledge of the unwise is as talk without sense.

19 Doctrine unto fools is as fetters on the feet, and like manacles on the right hand.

20 A fool lifteth up his voice with laughter; but a wise man doth scarce smile a little.

21 Learning is unto a wise man as an ornament of gold, and like a bracelet upon his right arm.

22 A foolish man's foot is soon in his [neighbour's] house: but a man of experience is ashamed of him.

23 A fool will peep in at the door into the house: but he that is well nurtured will stand without.

24 It is the rudeness of a man to hearken at the door: but a wise man will be grieved with the disgrace.

25 The lips of talkers will be telling such things as pertain not unto them: but the words of such as have understanding are weighed in the balance.

26 The heart of fools is in their mouth: but the mouth of the wise is in their heart.

27 When the ungodly curseth Satan, he curseth his own soul.

28 A whisperer defileth his own soul, and is hated wheresoever he dwelleth.

22 A slothful man is compared to a filthy stone, and every one will hiss him out to his disgrace.

2 A slothful man is compared to the filth of a dunghill: every man that takes it up will shake his hand.

3 An evilnurtured man is the dishonour of his father that begat him: and a [foolish] daughter is born to his loss.

4 A wise daughter shall bring an inheritance to her husband: but she that liveth dishonestly is her father's heaviness.

5 She that is bold dishonoureth both her father and her husband, but they both shall despise her.

6 A tale out of season [is as] musick in mourning: but stripes and correction of wisdom are never out of time.

7 Whoso teacheth a fool is as one that glueth a potsherd together, and as he that waketh one from a sound sleep.

8 He that telleth a tale to a fool speaketh to one in a slumber: when he hath told his tale, he will say, What is the matter?

9 If children live honestly, and have wherewithal, they shall cover the baseness of their parents.

10 But children, being haughty, through disdain and want of nurture do stain the nobility of their kindred.

11 Weep for the dead, for he hath lost the light: and weep for the fool, for he wanteth understanding: make little weeping for the dead, for he is at rest: but the life of the fool is worse than death.

12 Seven days do men mourn for him that is dead; but for a fool and an ungodly man all the days of his life.

13 Talk not much with a fool, and go not to him that hath no understanding: beware of him, lest thou have trouble, and thou shalt never be defiled with his fooleries: depart from him, and thou shalt find rest, and never be disquieted with madness.

14 What is heavier than lead? and what is the name thereof, but a fool?

15 Sand, and salt, and a mass of iron, is easier to bear, than a man without understanding.

16 As timber girt and bound together in a building cannot be loosed with shaking: so the heart that is stablished by advised counsel shall fear at no time.

17 A heart settled upon a thought of understanding is as a fair plaistering on the wall of a gallery.

18 Pales set on an high place will never stand against the wind: so a fearful heart in the imagination of a fool cannot stand against any fear.

19 He that pricketh the eye will make tears to fall: and he that pricketh the heart maketh it to shew her knowledge.

20 Whoso casteth a stone at the birds frayeth them away: and he that upbraideth his friend breaketh friendship.

21 Though thou drewest a sword at thy friend, yet despair not: for there may be a returning [to favour.]

22 If thou hast opened thy mouth against thy friend, fear not; for there may be a reconciliation: except for upbraiding, or pride, or disclosing of secrets, or a treacherous wound: for for these things every friend will depart.

23 Be faithful to thy neighbour in his poverty, that thou mayest rejoice in his prosperity: abide stedfast unto him in the time of his trouble, that thou mayest be heir with him in his heritage: for a mean estate is not always to be contemned: nor the rich that is foolish to be had in admiration.

24 As the vapour and smoke of a furnace goeth before the fire; so reviling before blood.

25 I will not be ashamed to defend a friend; neither will I hide myself from him.

26 And if any evil happen unto me by him, every one that heareth it will beware of him.

27 Who shall set a watch before my mouth, and a seal of wisdom upon my lips, that I fall not suddenly by them, and that my tongue destroy me not?

23 O YAHOWAH, Father and Governor of all my whole life, leave me not to their counsels, and let me not fall by them.

2 Who will set scourges over my thoughts, and the discipline of wisdom over mine heart? that they spare me not for mine ignorances, and it pass not by my sins:

3 Lest mine ignorances increase, and my sins abound to my destruction, and I fall before mine adversaries, and mine enemy rejoice over me, whose hope is far from thy mercy.

4 O YAHOWAH, Father and ELOHIM of my life, give me not a proud look, but turn away from thy servants always a haughty mind.

5 Turn away from me vain hopes and concupiscence, and thou shalt hold him up that is desirous always to serve thee.

6 Let not the greediness of the belly nor lust of the flesh take hold of me; and give not over me thy servant into an impudent mind.

7 Hear, O ye children, the discipline of the mouth: he that keepeth it shall never be taken in his lips.

8 The sinner shall be left in his foolishness: both the evil speaker and the proud shall fall thereby.

9 Accustom not thy mouth to swearing; neither use thyself to the naming of the Holy One.

10 For as a servant that is continually beaten shall not be without a blue mark: so he that sweareth and nameth ELOHIM continually shall not be faultless.

11 A man that useth much swearing shall be filled with iniquity, and the plague shall never depart from his house: if he shall offend, his sin shall be upon him: and if he acknowledge not his sin, he maketh a double offence: and if he swear in vain, he shall not be innocent, but his house shall be full of calamities.

12 There is a word that is clothed about with death: ELOHIM grant that it be not found in the heritage of Ya'aqob; for all such things shall be far from the godly, and they shall not wallow in their sins.

13 Use not thy mouth to intemperate swearing, for therein is the word of sin.

14 Remember thy father and thy mother, when thou sittest among great men. Be not forgetful before them, and so thou by thy custom become a fool, and wish that thou hadst not been born, and curse they day of thy nativity.

15 The man that is accustomed to opprobrious words will never be reformed all the days of his life.

16 Two sorts of men multiply sin, and the third will bring wrath: a hot mind is as a burning fire, it will never be quenched till it be consumed: a fornicator in the body of his flesh will never cease till he hath kindled a fire.

17 All bread is sweet to a whoremonger, he will not leave off till he die.

18 A man that breaketh wedlock, saying thus in his heart, Who seeth me? I am compassed about with darkness, the walls cover me, and no body seeth me; what need I to fear? the Most High will not remember my sins:

19 Such a man only feareth the eyes of men, and knoweth not that the eyes of YAHOWAH are ten thousand times brighter than the sun, beholding all the ways of men, and considering the most secret parts.

20 He knew all things ere ever they were created; so also after they were perfected he looked upon them all.

21 This man shall be punished in the streets of the city, and where he suspecteth not he shall be taken.

22 Thus shall it go also with the wife that leaveth her husband, and bringeth in an heir by another.

23 For first, she hath disobeyed the Torah of the Most High; and secondly, she hath trespassed against her own husband; and thirdly, she hath played the whore in adultery, and brought children by another man.

24 She shall be brought out into the congregation, and inquisition shall be made of her children.

25 Her children shall not take root, and her branches shall bring forth no fruit.

26 She shall leave her memory to be cursed, and her reproach shall not be blotted out.

27 And they that remain shall know that there is nothing better than the fear of YAHOWAH, and that there is nothing sweeter than to take heed unto the commandments of YAHOWAH.

28 It is great glory to follow YAHOWAH, and to be received of him is long life.

24 Wisdom shall praise herself, and shall glory in the midst of her people.

2 In the congregation of the Most High shall she open her mouth, and triumph before his power.

3 I came out of the mouth of the Most High, and covered the earth as a cloud.

4 I dwelt in high places, and my throne is in a cloudy pillar.

5 I alone compassed the circuit of heaven, and walked in the bottom of the deep.

6 In the waves of the sea and in all the earth, and in every people and nation, I got a possession.

7 With all these I sought rest: and in whose inheritance shall I abide?

8 So the Creator of all things gave me a commandment, and he that made me caused my tabernacle to rest, and said, Let thy dwelling be in Ya'aqob, and thine inheritance in Yisra'EL.

9 He created me from the beginning before the world, and I shall never fail.

10 In the holy tabernacle I served before him; and so was I established in Tzion.

11 Likewise in the beloved city he gave me rest, and in Yerushalem was my power.

12 And I took root in an honourable people, even in the portion of YAHOWAH'S inheritance.

13 I was exalted like a cedar in Lebanon, and as a cypress tree upon the mountains of Khermon.

14 I was exalted like a palm tree in En-gaddi, and as a rose plant in Yerikho, as a fair olive tree in a pleasant field, and grew up as a plane tree by the water.

15 I gave a sweet smell like cinnamon and aspalathus, and I yielded a pleasant odour like the best myrrh, as galbanum, and onyx, and sweet storax, and as the fume of frankincense in the tabernacle.

16 As the turpentine tree I stretched out my branches, and my branches are the branches of honour and grace.

17 As the vine brought I forth pleasant savour, and my flowers are the fruit of honour and riches.

18 I am the mother of fair love, and fear, and knowledge, and holy hope: I therefore, being eternal, am given to all my children which are named of him.

19 Come unto me, all ye that be desirous of me, and fill yourselves with my fruits.

20 For my memorial is sweeter than honey, and mine inheritance than the honeycomb.

21 They that eat me shall yet be hungry, and they that drink me shall yet be thirsty.

22 He that obeyeth me shall never be confounded, and they that work by me shall not do amiss.

23 All these things are the book of the covenant of the Most High ELOHIM, even the Torah which Mosheh commanded for an heritage unto the congregations of Ya'aqob.

24 Faint not to be strong in YAHOWAH; that he may confirm you, cleave unto him: for YAHOWAH Almighty is ELOHIM alone, and beside him there is no other Saviour.

25 He filleth all things with his wisdom, as Phison and as Tigris in the time of the new fruits.

26 He maketh the understanding to abound like Perath, and as Yarden in the time of the harvest.

27 He maketh the doctrine of knowledge appear as the light, and as Geon in the time of vintage.

28 The first man knew her not perfectly: no more shall the last find her out.

29 For her thoughts are more than the sea, and her counsels profounder than the great deep.

30 I also came out as a brook from a river, and as a conduit into a garden.

31 I said, I will water my best garden, and will water abundantly my garden bed: and, lo, my brook became a river, and my river became a sea.

32 I will yet make doctrine to shine as the morning, and will send forth her light afar off.

33 I will yet pour out doctrine as prophecy, and leave it to all ages for ever.

34 Behold that I have not laboured for myself only, but for all them that seek wisdom.

25 In three things I was beautified, and stood up beautiful both before ELOHIM and men: the unity of brethren, the love of neighbours, a man and a wife that agree together.

2 Three sorts of men my soul hateth, and I am greatly offended at their life: a poor man that is proud, a rich man that is a liar, and an old adulterer that doateth.

3 If thou hast gathered nothing in thy youth, how canst thou find any thing in thine age?

4 O how comely a thing is judgment for gray hairs, and for ancient men to know counsel!

5 O how comely is the wisdom of old men, and understanding and counsel to men of honour.

6 Much experience is the crown of old men, and the fear of ELOHIM is their glory.

7 There be nine things which I have judged in mine heart to be happy, and the tenth I will utter with my tongue: A man that hath joy of his children; and he that liveth to see the fall of his enemy:

8 Well is him that dwelleth with a wife of understanding, and that hath not slipped with his tongue, and that hath not served a man more unworthy than himself:

9 Well is him that hath found prudence, and he that speaketh in the ears of them that will hear:

10 O how great is he that findeth wisdom! yet is there none above him that feareth YAHOWAH.

11 But the love of YAHOWAH passeth all things for illumination: he that holdeth it, whereto shall he be likened?

12 The fear of YAHOWAH is the beginning of his love: and faith is the beginning of cleaving unto him.

13 [Give me] any plague, but the plague of the heart: and any wickedness, but the wickedness of a woman:

14 And any affliction, but the affliction from them that hate me: and any revenge, but the revenge of enemies.

15 There is no head above the head of a serpent; and there is no wrath above the wrath of an enemy.

16 I had rather dwell with a lion and a dragon, than to keep house with a wicked woman.

17 The wickedness of a woman changeth her face, and darkeneth her countenance like sackcloth.

18 Her husband shall sit among his neighbours; and when he heareth it shall sigh bitterly.

19 All wickedness is but little to the wickedness of a woman: let the portion of a sinner fall upon her.

20 As the climbing up a sandy way is to the feet of the aged, so is a wife full of words to a quiet man.

21 Stumble not at the beauty of a woman, and desire her not for pleasure.

22 A woman, if she maintain her husband, is full of anger, impudence, and much reproach.

23 A wicked woman abateth the courage, maketh an heavy countenance and a wounded heart: a woman that will not comfort her husband in distress maketh weak hands and feeble knees.

24 Of the woman came the beginning of sin, and through her we all die.

25 Give the water no passage; neither a wicked woman liberty to gad abroad.

26 If she go not as thou wouldest have her, cut her off from thy flesh, and give her a bill of divorce, and let her go.

26 Blessed is the man that hath a virtuous wife, for the number of his days shall be double.

2 A virtuous woman rejoiceth her husband, and he shall fulfil the years of his life in shalom.

3 A good wife is a good portion, which shall be given in the portion of them that fear YAHOWAH.

4 Whether a man be rich or poor, if he have a good heart toward YAHOWAH, he shall at all times rejoice with a cheerful countenance.

5 There be three things that mine heart feareth; and for the fourth I was sore afraid: the slander of a city, the gathering together of an unruly multitude, and a false accusation: all these are worse than death.

6 But a grief of heart and sorrow is a woman that is jealous over another woman, and a scourge of the tongue which communicateth with all.

7 An evil wife is a yoke shaken to and fro: he that hath hold of her is as though he held a scorpion.

8 A drunken woman and a gadder abroad causeth great anger, and she will not cover her own shame.

9 The whoredom of a woman may be known in her haughty looks and eyelids.

10 If thy daughter be shameless, keep her in straitly, lest she abuse herself through overmuch liberty.

11 Watch over an impudent eye: and marvel not if she trespass against thee.

12 She will open her mouth, as a thirsty traveller when he hath found a fountain, and drink of every water near her: by every hedge will she sit down, and open her quiver against every arrow.

13 The grace of a wife delighteth her husband, and her discretion will fatten his bones.

14 A silent and loving woman is a gift of YAHOWAH; and there is nothing so much worth as a mind well instructed.

15 A shamefaced and faithful woman is a double grace, and her continent mind cannot be valued.

16 As the sun when it ariseth in the high heaven; so is the beauty of a good wife in the ordering of her house.

17 As the clear light is upon the holy menorah; so is the beauty of the face in ripe age.

18 As the golden pillars are upon the sockets of silver; so are the fair feet with a constant heart.

19 My son, keep the flower of thine age sound; and give not thy strength to strangers.

20 When thou hast gotten a fruitful possession through all the field, sow it with thine own seed, trusting in the goodness of thy stock.

21 So thy race which thou leavest shall be magnified, having the confidence of their good descent.

22 An harlot shall be accounted as spittle; but a married woman is a tower against death to her husband.

23 A wicked woman is given as a portion to a wicked man: but a godly woman is given to him that feareth YAHOWAH.

24 A dishonest woman contemneth shame: but an honest woman will reverence her husband.

25 A shameless woman shall be counted as a dog; but she that is shamefaced will fear YAHOWAH.

26 A woman that honoureth her husband shall be judged wise of all; but she that dishonoureth him in her pride shall be counted ungodly of all.

27 A loud crying woman and a scold shall be sought out to drive away the enemies.

28 There be two things that grieve my heart; and the third maketh me angry: a man of war that suffereth poverty; and men of understanding that are not set by; and one that returneth from righteousness to sin; YAHOWAH prepareth such an one for the sword.

29 A merchant shall hardly keep himself from doing wrong; and an huckster shall not be freed from sin.

27 Many have sinned for a small matter; and he that seeketh for abundance will turn his eyes away.

2 As a nail sticketh fast between the joinings of the stones; so doth sin stick close between buying and selling.

3 Unless a man hold himself diligently in the fear of YAHOWAH, his house shall soon be overthrown.

4 As when one sifteth with a sieve, the refuse remaineth; so the filth of man in his talk.

5 The furnace proveth the potter's vessels; so the trial of man is in his reasoning.

6 The fruit declareth if the tree have been dressed; so is the utterance of a conceit in the heart of man.

7 Praise no man before thou hearest him speak; for this is the trial of men.

8 If thou followest righteousness, thou shalt obtain her, and put her on, as a glorious long robe.

9 The birds will resort unto their like; so will truth return unto them that practise in her.

10 As the lion lieth in wait for the prey; so sin for them that work iniquity.

11 The discourse of a godly man is always with wisdom; but a fool changeth as the moon.

12 If thou be among the indiscreet, observe the time; but be continually among men of understanding.

13 The discourse of fools is irksome, and their sport is the wantonness of sin.

14 The talk of him that sweareth much maketh the hair stand upright; and their brawls make one stop his ears.

15 The strife of the proud is bloodshedding, and their revilings are grievous to the ear.

16 Whoso discovereth secrets loseth his credit; and shall never find friend to his mind.

17 Love thy friend, and be faithful unto him: but if thou betrayest his secrets, follow no more after him.

18 For as a man hath destroyed his enemy; so hast thou lost the love of thy neighbor.

19 As one that letteth a bird go out of his hand, so hast thou let thy neighbour go, and shalt not get him again

20 Follow after him no more, for he is too far off; he is as a roe escaped out of the snare.

21 As for a wound, it may be bound up; and after reviling there may be reconcilement: but he that betrayeth secrets is without hope.

22 He that winketh with the eyes worketh evil: and he that knoweth him will depart from him.

23 When thou art present, he will speak sweetly, and will admire thy words: but at the last he will writhe his mouth, and slander thy sayings.

24 I have hated many things, but nothing like him; for YAHOWAH will hate him.

25 Whoso casteth a stone on high casteth it on his own head; and a deceitful stroke shall make wounds.

26 Whoso diggeth a pit shall fall therein: and he that setteth a trap shall be taken therein.

27 He that worketh mischief, it shall fall upon him, and he shall not know whence it cometh.

28 Mockery and reproach are from the proud; but vengeance, as a lion, shall lie in wait for them.

29 They that rejoice at the fall of the righteous shall be taken in the snare; and anguish shall consume them before they die.

30 Malice and wrath, even these are abominations; and the sinful man shall have them both.

28

He that revengeth shall find vengeance from YAHOWAH, and he will surely keep his sins [in remembrance.]

2 Forgive thy neighbour the hurt that he hath done unto thee, so shall thy sins also be forgiven when thou prayest.

3 One man beareth hatred against another, and doth he seek pardon from YAHOWAH?

4 He sheweth no mercy to a man, which is like himself: and doth he ask forgiveness of his own sins?

5 If he that is but flesh nourish hatred, who will intreat for pardon of his sins?

6 Remember thy end, and let enmity cease; [remember] corruption and death, and abide in the commandments.

7 Remember the commandments, and bear no malice to thy neighbour: [remember] the covenant of the Highest, and wink at ignorance.

8 Abstain from strife, and thou shalt diminish thy sins: for a furious man will kindle strife,

9 A sinful man disquieteth friends, and maketh debate among them that be at shalom.

10 As the matter of the fire is, so it burneth: and as a man's strength is, so is his wrath; and according to his riches his anger riseth; and the stronger they are which contend, the more they will be inflamed.

11 An hasty contention kindleth a fire: and an hasty fighting sheddeth blood.

12 If thou blow the spark, it shall burn: if thou spit upon it, it shall be quenched: and both these come out of thy mouth.

13 Curse the whisperer and doubletongued: for such have destroyed many that were at shalom.

14 A backbiting tongue hath disquieted many, and driven them from nation to nation: strong cities hath it pulled down, and overthrown the houses of great men.

15 A backbiting tongue hath cast out virtuous women, and deprived them of their labours.

16 Whoso hearkeneth unto it shall never find rest, and never dwell quietly.

17 The stroke of the whip maketh marks in the flesh: but the stroke of the tongue breaketh the bones.

18 Many have fallen by the edge of the sword: but not so many as have fallen by the tongue.

19 Well is he that is defended through the venom thereof; who hath not drawn the yoke thereof, nor hath been bound in her bands.

20 For the yoke thereof is a yoke of iron, and the bands thereof are bands of brass.

21 The death thereof is an evil death, the grave were better than it.

22 It shall not have rule over them that fear ELOHIM, neither shall they be burned with the flame thereof.

23 Such as forsake YAHOWAH shall fall into it; and it shall burn in them, and not be quenched; it shall be sent upon them as a lion, and devour them as a leopard.

24 Look that thou hedge thy possession about with thorns, and bind up thy silver and gold,

25 And weigh thy words in a balance, and make a door and bar for thy mouth.

26 Beware thou slide not by it, lest thou fall before him that lieth in wait.

29

He that is merciful will lend unto his neighbour; and he that strengtheneth his hand keepeth the commandments.

2 Lend to thy neighbour in time of his need, and pay thou thy neighbour again in due season.

3 Keep thy word, and deal faithfully with him, and thou shalt always find the thing that is necessary for thee.

4 Many, when a thing was lent them, reckoned it to be found, and put them to trouble that helped them.

5 Till he hath received, he will kiss a man's hand; and for his neighbour's money he will speak submissly: but when he should repay, he will prolong the time, and return words of grief, and complain of the time.

6 If he prevail, he shall hardly receive the half, and he will count as if he had found it: if not, he hath deprived him of his money, and he hath gotten him an enemy without cause: he payeth him with cursings and railings; and for honour he will pay him disgrace.

7 Many therefore have refused to lend for other men's ill dealing, fearing to be defrauded.

8 Yet have thou patience with a man in poor estate, and delay not to shew him mercy.

9 Help the poor for the commandment's sake, and turn him not away because of his poverty.

10 Lose thy money for thy brother and thy friend, and let it not rust under a stone to be lost.

11 Lay up thy treasure according to the commandments of the Most High, and it shall bring thee more profit than gold.

12 Shut up alms in thy storehouses: and it shall deliver thee from all affliction.

13 It shall fight for thee against thine enemies better than a mighty shield and strong spear.

14 An honest man is surety for his neighbour: but he that is impudent will forsake him.

15 Forget not the friendship of thy surety, for he hath given his life for thee.

16 A sinner will overthrow the good estate of his surety:

17 And he that is of an unthankful mind will leave him [in danger] that delivered him.

18 Suretiship hath undone many of good estate, and shaken them as a wave of the sea: mighty men hath it driven from their houses, so that they wandered among strange nations.

19 A wicked man transgressing the commandments of YAHOWAH shall fall into suretiship: and he that undertaketh and followeth other men's business for gain shall fall into suits.

20 Help thy neighbour according to thy power, and beware that thou thyself fall not into the same.

21 The chief thing for life is water, and bread, and clothing, and an house to cover shame.

22 Better is the life of a poor man in a mean cottage, than delicate fare in another man's house.

23 Be it little or much, hold thee contented, that thou hear not the reproach of thy house.

24 For it is a miserable life to go from house to house: for where thou art a stranger, thou darest not open thy mouth.

25 Thou shalt entertain, and feast, and have no thanks: moreover thou shalt hear bitter words:

26 Come, thou stranger, and furnish a table, and feed me of that thou hast ready.

27 Give place, thou stranger, to an honourable man; my brother cometh to be lodged, and I have need of mine house.

28 These things are grievous to a man of understanding; the upbraiding of houseroom, and reproaching of the lender.

30 He that loveth his son causeth him oft to feel the rod, that he may have joy of him in the end.

2 He that chastiseth his son shall have joy in him, and shall rejoice of him among his acquaintance.

3 He that teacheth his son grieveth the enemy: and before his friends he shall rejoice of him.

4 Though his father die, yet he is as though he were not dead: for he hath left one behind him that is like himself.

5 While he lived, he saw and rejoiced in him: and when he died, he was not sorrowful.

6 He left behind him an avenger against his enemies, and one that shall requite kindness to his friends.

7 He that maketh too much of his son shall bind up his wounds; and his bowels will be troubled at every cry.

8 An horse not broken becometh headstrong: and a child left to himself will be wilful.

9 Cocker thy child, and he shall make thee afraid: play with him, and he will bring thee to heaviness.

10 Laugh not with him, lest thou have sorrow with him, and lest thou gnash thy teeth in the end.

11 Give him no liberty in his youth, and wink not at his follies.

12 Bow down his neck while he is young, and beat him on the sides while he is a child, lest he wax stubborn, and be disobedient unto thee, and so bring sorrow to thine heart.

13 Chastise thy son, and hold him to labour, lest his lewd behaviour be an offence unto thee.

14 Better is the poor, being sound and strong of constitution, than a rich man that is afflicted in his body.

15 Health and good estate of body are above all gold, and a strong body above infinite wealth.

16 There is no riches above a sound body, and no joy above the joy of the heart.

17 Death is better than a bitter life or continual sickness.

18 Delicates poured upon a mouth shut up are as messes of meat set upon a grave.

19 What good doeth the offering unto an idol? for neither can it eat nor smell: so is he that is persecuted of YAHOWAH.

20 He seeth with his eyes and groaneth, as an eunuch that embraceth a virgin and sigheth.

21 Give not over thy mind to heaviness, and afflict not thyself in thine own counsel.

22 The gladness of the heart is the life of man, and the joyfulness of a man prolongeth his days.

23 Love thine own soul, and comfort thy heart, remove sorrow far from thee: for sorrow hath killed many, and there is no profit therein.

24 Envy and wrath shorten the life, and carefulness bringeth age before the time.

25 A cheerful and good heart will have a care of his meat and diet.

31 Watching for riches consumeth the flesh, and the care thereof driveth away sleep.

2 Watching care will not let a man slumber, as a sore disease breaketh sleep,

3 The rich hath great labour in gathering riches together; and when he resteth, he is filled with his delicates.

4 The poor laboureth in his poor estate; and when he leaveth off, he is still needy.

5 He that loveth gold shall not be justified, and he that followeth corruption shall have enough thereof.

6 Gold hath been the ruin of many, and their destruction was present.

7 It is a stumblingblock unto them that sacrifice unto it, and every fool shall be taken therewith.

8 Blessed is the rich that is found without blemish, and hath not gone after gold.

9 Who is he? and we will call him blessed: for wonderful things hath he done among his people.

10 Who hath been tried thereby, and found perfect? then let him glory. Who might offend, and hath not offended? or done evil, and hath not done it?

11 His goods shall be established, and the congregation shall declare his alms.

12 If thou sit at a bountiful table, be not greedy upon it, and say not, There is much meat on it.

13 Remember that a wicked eye is an evil thing: and what is created more wicked than an eye? therefore it weepeth upon every occasion.

14 Stretch not thine hand whithersoever it looketh, and thrust it not with him into the dish.

15 Judge not thy neighbour by thyself: and be discreet in every point.

16 Eat as it becometh a man, those things which are set before thee; and devour not, lest thou be hated.

17 Leave off first for manners' sake; and be not unsatiable, lest thou offend.

18 When thou sittest among many, reach not thine hand out first of all.

19 A very little is sufficient for a man well nurtured, and he fetcheth not his wind short upon his bed.

20 Sound sleep cometh of moderate eating: he riseth early, and his wits are with him: but the pain of watching, and choler, and pangs of the belly, are with an unsatiable man.

21 And if thou hast been forced to eat, arise, go forth, vomit, and thou shalt have rest.

22 My son, hear me, and despise me not, and at the last thou shalt find as I told thee: in all thy works be quick, so shall there no sickness come unto thee.

23 Whoso is liberal of his meat, men shall speak well of him; and the report of his good housekeeping will be believed.

24 But against him that is a niggard of his meat the whole city shall murmur; and the testimonies of his niggardness shall not be doubted of.

25 Shew not thy valiantness in wine; for wine hath destroyed many.

26 The furnace proveth the edge by dipping: so doth wine the hearts of the proud by drunkeness.

27 Wine is as good as life to a man, if it be drunk moderately: what life is then to a man that is without wine? for it was made to make men glad.

28 Wine measurably drunk and in season bringeth gladness of the heart, and cheerfulness of the mind:

29 But wine drunken with excess maketh bitterness of the mind, with brawling and quarrelling.

30 Drunkenness increaseth the rage of a fool till he offend: it diminisheth strength, and maketh wounds.

31 Rebuke not thy neighbour at the wine, and despise him not in his mirth: give him no despiteful words, and press not upon him with urging him [to drink.]

32 If thou be made the master [of a feast,] lift not thyself up, but be among them as one of the rest; take diligent care for them, and so sit down.

2 And when thou hast done all thy office, take thy place, that thou mayest be merry with them, and receive a crown for thy well ordering of the feast.

3 Speak, thou that art the elder, for it becometh thee, but with sound judgment; and hinder not musick.

4 Pour not out words where there is a musician, and shew not forth wisdom out of time.

5 A concert of musick in a banquet of wine is as a signet of carbuncle set in gold.

6 As a signet of an emerald set in a work of gold, so is the melody of musick with pleasant wine.

7 Speak, young man, if there be need of thee: and yet scarcely when thou art twice asked.

8 Let thy speech be short, comprehending much in few words; be as one that knoweth and yet holdeth his tongue.

9 If thou be among great men, make not thyself equal with them; and when ancient men are in place, use not many words.

10 Before the thunder goeth lightning; and before a shamefaced man shall go favour.

11 Rise up betimes, and be not the last; but get thee home without delay.

12 There take thy pastime, and do what thou wilt: but sin not by proud speech.

13 And for these things bless him that made thee, and hath replenished thee with his good things.

14 Whoso feareth YAHOWAH will receive his discipline; and they that seek him early shall find favour.

15 He that seeketh the Torah shall be filled therewith: but the hypocrite will be offended thereat.

16 They that fear YAHOWAH shall find judgment, and shall kindle justice as a light.

17 A sinful man will not be reproved, but findeth an excuse according to his will.

18 A man of counsel will be considerate; but a strange and proud man is not daunted with fear, even when of himself he hath done without counsel.

19 Do nothing without advice; and when thou hast once done, repent not.

20 Go not in a way wherein thou mayest fall, and stumble not among the stones.

21 Be not confident in a plain way.

22 And beware of thine own children.

23 In every good work trust thy own soul; for this is the keeping of the commandments.

24 He that believeth in YAHOWAH taketh heed to the commandment; and he that trusteth in him shall fare never the worse.

33 There shall no evil happen unto him that feareth YAHOWAH; but in temptation even again he will deliver him.

2 A wise man hateth not the Torah; but he that is an hypocrite therein is as a ship in a storm.

3 A man of understanding trusteth in the Torah; and the Torah is faithful unto him, as an oracle.

4 Prepare what to say, and so thou shalt be heard: and bind up instruction, and then make answer.

5 The heart of the foolish is like a cartwheel; and his thoughts are like a rolling axletree.

6 A stallion horse is as a mocking friend, he neigheth under every one that sitteth upon him.

7 Why doth one day excel another, when as all the light of every day in the year is of the sun?

8 By the knowledge of YAHOWAH they were distinguished: and he altered seasons and feasts.

9 Some of them hath he made high days, and hallowed them, and some of them hath he made ordinary days.

10 And all men are from the ground, and Adam was created of earth:

11 In much knowledge YAHOWAH hath divided them, and made their ways diverse.

12 Some of them hath he blessed and exalted and some of them he sanctified, and set near himself: but some of them hath he cursed and brought low, and turned out of their places.

13 As the clay is in the potter's hand, to fashion it at his pleasure: so man is in the hand of him that made him, to render to them as liketh him best.

14 Good is set against evil, and life against death: so is the godly against the sinner, and the sinner against the godly.

15 So look upon all the works of the Most High; and there are two and two, one against another.

16 I awaked up last of all, as one that gathereth after the grapegatherers: by the blessing of YAHOWAH I profited, and tred my winepress like a gatherer of grapes.

17 Consider that I laboured not for myself only, but for all them that seek learning.

18 Hear me, O ye great men of the people, and hearken with your ears, ye rulers of the congregation.

19 Give not thy son and wife, thy brother and friend, power over thee while thou livest, and give not thy goods to another: lest it repent thee, and thou intreat for the same again.

20 As long as thou livest and hast breath in thee, give not thyself over to any.

21 For better it is that thy children should seek to thee, than that thou shouldest stand to their courtesy.

22 In all thy works keep to thyself the preeminence; leave not a stain in thine honour.

23 At the time when thou shalt end thy days, and finish thy life, distribute thine inheritance.

24 Fodder, a wand, and burdens, are for the ass; and bread, correction, and work, for a servant. .

25 If thou set thy servant to labour, thou shalt find rest: but if thou let him go idle, he shall seek liberty.

26 A yoke and a collar do bow the neck: so are tortures and torments for an evil servant.

27 Send him to labour, that he be not idle; for idleness teacheth much evil.

28 Set him to work, as is fit for him: if he be not obedient, put on more heavy fetters.

29 But be not excessive toward any; and without discretion do nothing.

30 If thou have a servant, let him be unto thee as thyself, because thou hast bought him with a price.

31 If thou have a servant, entreat him as a brother: for thou hast need of him, as of thine own soul: if thou entreat him evil, and he run from thee, which way wilt thou go to seek him?

34 The hopes of a man void of understanding are vain and false: and dreams lift up fools.

2 Whoso regardeth dreams is like him that catcheth at a shadow, and followeth after the wind.

3 The vision of dreams is the resemblance of one thing to another, even as the likeness of a face to a face.

4 Of an unclean thing what can be cleansed? and from that thing which is false what truth can come?

5 Divinations, and soothsayings, and dreams, are vain: and the heart fancieth, as a woman's heart in travail.

6 If they be not sent from the Most High in thy visitation, set not thy heart upon them.

7 For dreams have deceived many, and they have failed that put their trust in them.

8 The Torah shall be found perfect without lies: and wisdom is perfection to a faithful mouth.

9 A man that hath travelled knoweth many things; and he that hath much experience will declare wisdom.

10 He that hath no experience knoweth little: but he that hath travelled is full of prudence.

11 When I travelled, I saw many things; and I understand more than I can express.

12 I was ofttimes in danger of death: yet I was delivered because of these things.

13 The ruakh of those that fear YAHOWAH shall live; for their hope is in him that saveth them.

14 Whoso feareth YAHOWAH shall not fear nor be afraid; for he is his hope.

15 Blessed is the soul of him that feareth YAHOWAH: to whom doth he look? and

who is his strength?

16 For the eyes of YAHOWAH are upon them that love him, he is their mighty protection and strong stay, a defence from heat, and a cover from the sun at noon, a preservation from stumbling, and an help from falling.

17 He raiseth up the soul, and lighteneth the eyes: he giveth health, life, and blessing.

18 He that sacrificeth of a thing wrongfully gotten, his offering is ridiculous; and the gifts of unjust men are not accepted.

19 The Most High is not pleased with the offerings of the wicked; neither is he pacified for sin by the multitude of sacrifices.

20 Whoso bringeth an offering of the goods of the poor doeth as one that killeth the son before his father's eyes.

21 The bread of the needy is their life: he that defraudeth him thereof is a man of blood.

22 He that taketh away his neighbour's living slayeth him; and he that defraudeth the labourer of his hire is a bloodshedder.

23 When one buildeth, and another pulleth down, what profit have they then but labour?

24 When one prayeth, and another curseth, whose voice will YAHOWAH hear?

25 He that washeth himself after the touching of a dead body, if he touch it again, what availeth his washing?

26 So is it with a man that fasteth for his sins, and goeth again, and doeth the same: who will hear his prayer? or what doth his humbling profit him?

35 He that keepeth the Torah bringeth offerings enough: he that taketh heed to the commandment offereth a shalom offering.

2 He that requiteth a goodturn offereth fine flour; and he that giveth alms sacrificeth praise.

3 To depart from wickedness is a thing pleasing to YAHOWAH; and to forsake unrighteousness is a propitiation.

4 Thou shalt not appear empty before YAHOWAH.

5 For all these things [are to be done] because of the commandment.

6 The offering of the righteous maketh the altar fat, and the sweet savour thereof is before the Most High.

7 The sacrifice of a just man is acceptable. and the memorial thereof shall never be forgotten.

8 Give YAHOWAH his honour with a good eye, and diminish not the firstfruits of thine hands.

9 In all thy gifts shew a cheerful countenance, and dedicate thy tithes with gladness.

10 Give unto the Most High according as he hath enriched thee; and as thou hast gotten, give with a cheerful eye.

11 For YAHOWAH recompenseth, and will give thee seven times as much.

12 Do not think to corrupt with gifts; for such he will not receive: and trust not to unrighteous sacrifices; for YAHOWAH is judge, and with him is no respect of persons.

13 He will not accept any person against a poor man, but will hear the prayer of the oppressed.

14 He will not despise the supplication of the fatherless; nor the widow, when she poureth out her complaint.

15 Do not the tears run down the widow's cheeks? and is not her cry against him that causeth them to fall?

16 He that serveth YAHOWAH shall be accepted with favour, and his prayer shall reach unto the clouds.

17 The prayer of the humble pierceth the clouds: and till it come nigh, he will not be comforted; and will not depart, till the Most High shall behold to judge righteously, and execute judgment.

18 For YAHOWAH will not be slack, neither will the Mighty be patient toward them, till he have smitten in sunder the loins of the unmerciful, and repayed vengeance to the heathen; till he have taken away the multitude of the proud, and broken the sceptre of the unrighteous;

19 Till he have rendered to every man according to his deeds, and to the works of men according to their devices; till he have judged the cause of his people, and made them to rejoice in his mercy.

20 Mercy is seasonable in the time of affliction, as clouds of rain in the time of drought.

36 Have mercy upon us, O YAHOWAH ELOHIM of all, and behold us:

2 And send thy fear upon all the nations that seek not after thee.

3 Lift up thy hand against the strange nations, and let them see thy power.

4 As thou wast sanctified in us before them: so be thou magnified among them before us.

5 And let them know thee, as we have known thee, that there is no ELOHIM but only thou, O ELOHIM.

6 Shew new signs, and make other strange wonders: glorify thy hand and thy right arm, that they may set forth thy wondrous works.

7 Raise up indignation, and pour out wrath: take away the adversary, and destroy the enemy.

8 Sake the time short, remember the covenant, and let them declare thy wonderful works.

9 Let him that escapeth be consumed by the rage of the fire; and let them perish that oppress the people.

10 Smite in sunder the heads of the rulers of the heathen, that say, There is none other but we.

11 Gather all the tribes of Ya'aqob together, and inherit thou them, as from the beginning.

12 O YAHOWAH, have mercy upon the people that is called by thy name, and upon Yisra'EL, whom thou hast named thy firstborn.

13 O be merciful unto Yerushalem, thy holy city, the place of thy rest.

14 Fill Tzion with thine unspeakable oracles, and thy people with thy glory:

15 Give testimony unto those that thou hast possessed from the beginning, and raise up prophets that have been in thy name.

BEN SIRA (SIRACH)

16 Reward them that wait for thee, and let thy prophets be found faithful.

17 O YAHOWAH, hear the prayer of thy servants, according to the blessing of Aharon over thy people, that all they which dwell upon the earth may know that thou art YAHOWAH, the eternal ELOHIM.

18 The belly devoureth all meats, yet is one meat better than another.

19 As the palate tasteth divers kinds of venison: so doth an heart of understanding false speeches.

20 A froward heart causeth heaviness: but a man of experience will recompense him.

21 A woman will receive every man, yet is one daughter better than another.

22 The beauty of a woman cheereth the countenance, and a man loveth nothing better.

23 If there be kindness, meekness, and comfort, in her tongue, then is not her husband like other men.

24 He that getteth a wife beginneth a possession, a help like unto himself, and a pillar of rest.

25 Where no hedge is, there the possession is spoiled: and he that hath no wife will wander up and down mourning.

26 Who will trust a thief well appointed, that skippeth from city to city? so [who will believe] a man that hath no house, and lodgeth wheresoever the night taketh him?

37

Every friend saith, I am his friend also: but there is a friend, which is only a friend in name.

2 Is it not a grief unto death, when a companion and friend is turned to an enemy?

3 O wicked imagination, whence camest thou in to cover the earth with deceit?

4 There is a companion, which rejoiceth in the prosperity of a friend, but in the time of trouble will be against him.

5 There is a companion, which helpeth his friend for the belly, and taketh up the buckler against the enemy.

6 Forget not thy friend in thy mind, and be not unmindful of him in thy riches.

7 Every counsellor extolleth counsel; but there is some that counselleth for himself.

8 Beware of a counsellor, and know before what need he hath; for he will counsel for himself; lest he cast the lot upon thee,

9 And say unto thee, Thy way is good: and afterward he stand on the other side, to see what shall befall thee.

10 Consult not with one that suspecteth thee: and hide thy counsel from such as envy thee.

11 Neither consult with a woman touching her of whom she is jealous; neither with a coward in matters of war; nor with a merchant concerning exchange; nor with a buyer of selling; nor with an envious man of thankfulness; nor with an unmerciful man touching kindness; nor with the slothful for any work; nor with an hireling for a year of finishing work; nor with an idle servant of much business: hearken not unto these in any matter of counsel.

12 But be continually with a godly man, whom thou knowest to keep the commandments of YAHOWAH, whose, mind is according to thy mind, and will sorrow with thee, if thou shalt miscarry.

13 And let the counsel of thine own heart stand: for there is no man more faithful unto thee than it.

14 For a man's mind is sometime wont to tell him more than seven watchmen, that sit above in an high tower.

15 And above all this pray to the Most High, that he will direct thy way in truth.

16 Let reason go before every enterprize, and counsel before every action.

17 The countenance is a sign of changing of the heart.

18 Four manner of things appear: good and evil, life and death: but the tongue ruleth over them continually.

19 There is one that is wise and teacheth many, and yet is unprofitable to himself.

20 There is one that sheweth wisdom in words, and is hated: he shall be destitute of all food.

21 For grace is not given, him from YAHOWAH, because he is deprived of all wisdom.

22 Another is wise to himself; and the fruits of understanding are commendable in his mouth.

23 A wise man instructeth his people; and the fruits of his understanding fail not.

24 A wise man shall be filled with blessing; and all they that see him shall count him happy.

25 The days of the life of man may be numbered: but the days of Yisra'EL are innumerable.

26 A wise man shall inherit glory among his people, and his name shall be perpetual.

27 My son, prove thy soul in thy life, and see what is evil for it, and give not that unto it.

28 For all things are not profitable for all men, neither hath every soul pleasure in every thing.

29 Be not unsatiable in any dainty thing, nor too greedy upon meats:

30 For excess of meats bringeth sickness, and surfeiting will turn into choler.

31 By surfeiting have many perished; but he that taketh heed prolongeth his life.

38

Honour a physician with the honour due unto him for the uses which ye may have of him: for YAHOWAH hath created him.

2 For of the Most High cometh healing, and he shall receive honour of the king.

3 The skill of the physician shall lift up his head: and in the sight of great men he shall be in admiration.

4 YAHOWAH hath created medicines out of the earth; and he that is wise will not abhor them.

5 Was not the water made sweet with wood, that the virtue thereof might be known?

6 And he hath given men skill, that he might be honoured in his marvellous works.

ECCLESIASTICUS

7 With such doth he heal [men,] and taketh away their pains.

8 Of such doth the apothecary make a confection; and of his works there is no end; and from him is shalom over all the earth,

9 My son, in thy sickness be not negligent: but pray unto YAHOWAH, and he will make thee whole.

10 Leave off from sin, and order thine hands aright, and cleanse thy heart from all wickedness.

11 Give a sweet savour, and a memorial of fine flour; and make a fat offering, as not being.

12 Then give place to the physician, for YAHOWAH hath created him: let him not go from thee, for thou hast need of him.

13 There is a time when in their hands there is good success.

14 For they shall also pray unto YAHOWAH, that he would prosper that, which they give for ease and remedy to prolong life.

15 He that sinneth before his Maker, let him fall into the hand of the physician.

16 My son, let tears fall down over the dead, and begin to lament, as if thou hadst suffered great harm thyself; and then cover his body according to the custom, and neglect not his burial.

17 Weep bitterly, and make great moan, and use lamentation, as he is worthy, and that a day or two, lest thou be evil spoken of: and then comfort thyself for thy heaviness.

18 For of heaviness cometh death, and the heaviness of the heart breaketh strength.

19 In affliction also sorrow remaineth: and the life of the poor is the curse of the heart.

20 Take no heaviness to heart: drive it away, and member the last end.

21 Forget it not, for there is no turning again: thou shalt not do him good, but hurt thyself.

22 Remember my judgment: for thine also shall be so; yesterday for me, and to day for thee.

23 When the dead is at rest, let his remembrance rest; and be comforted for him, when his Spirit is departed from him.

24 The wisdom of a learned man cometh by opportunity of leisure: and he that hath little business shall become wise.

25 How can he get wisdom that holdeth the plough, and that glorieth in the goad, that driveth oxen, and is occupied in their labours, and whose talk is of bullocks?

26 He giveth his mind to make furrows; and is diligent to give the kine fodder.

27 So every carpenter and workmaster, that laboureth night and day: and they that cut and grave seals, and are diligent to make great variety, and give themselves to counterfeit imagery, and watch to finish a work:

28 The smith also sitting by the anvil, and considering the iron work, the vapour of the fire wasteth his flesh, and he fighteth with the heat of the furnace: the noise of the hammer and the anvil is ever in his ears, and his eyes look still upon the pattern of the thing that he maketh; he setteth his mind to finish his work, and watcheth to polish it perfectly:

29 So doth the potter sitting at his work, and turning the wheel about with his feet, who is alway carefully set at his work, and maketh all his work by number;

30 He fashioneth the clay with his arm, and boweth down his strength before his feet; he applieth himself to lead it over; and he is diligent to make clean the furnace.

31 All these trust to their hands: and every one is wise in his work.

32 Without these cannot a city be inhabited: and they shall not dwell where they will, nor go up and down:

33 They shall not be sought for in publick counsel, nor sit high in the congregation: they shall not sit on the judges' seat, nor understand the sentence of judgment: they cannot declare justice and judgment; and they shall not be found where parables are spoken.

34 But they will maintain the state of the world, and [all] their desire is in the work of their craft.

39 But he that giveth his mind to the Torah of the Most High, and is occupied in the meditation thereof, will seek out the wisdom of all the ancient, and be occupied in prophecies.

2 He will keep the sayings of the renowned men: and where subtil parables are, he will be there also.

3 He will seek out the secrets of grave sentences, and be conversant in dark parables.

4 He shall serve among great men, and appear before princes: he will travel through strange countries; for he hath tried the good and the evil among men.

5 He will give his heart to resort early to YAHOWAH that made him, and will pray before the Most High, and will open his mouth in prayer, and make supplication for his sins.

6 When the great YAHOWAH will, he shall be filled with the RUAKH of understanding: he shall pour out wise sentences, and give thanks unto YAHOWAH in his prayer.

7 He shall direct his counsel and knowledge, and in his secrets shall he meditate.

8 He shall shew forth that which he hath learned, and shall glory in the Torah of the covenant of YAHOWAH.

9 Many shall commend his understanding; and so long as the world endureth, it shall not be blotted out; his memorial shall not depart away, and his name shall live from generation to generation.

10 Nations shall shew forth his wisdom, and the congregation shall declare his praise.

11 If he die, he shall leave a greater name than a thousand: and if he live, he shall increase it.

12 Yet have I more to say, which I have thought upon; for I am filled as the moon at the full.

13 Hearken unto me, ye holy children, and bud forth as a rose growing by the brook of the field:

14 And give ye a sweet savour as frankincense, and flourish as a lily, send forth a smell, and sing a song

of praise, bless YAHOWAH in all his works.

15 Magnify his name, and shew forth his praise with the songs of your lips, and with harps, and in praising him ye shall say after this manner:

16 All the works of YAHOWAH are exceeding good, and whatsoever he commandeth shall be accomplished in due season.

17 And none may say, What is this? wherefore is that? for at time convenient they shall all be sought out: at his commandment the waters stood as an heap, and at the words of his mouth the receptacles of waters.

18 At his commandment is done whatsoever pleaseth him; and none can hinder, when he will save.

19 The works of all flesh are before him, and nothing can be hid from his eyes.

20 He seeth from everlasting to everlasting; and there is nothing wonderful before him.

21 A man need not to say, What is this? wherefore is that? for he hath made all things for their uses.

22 His blessing covered the dry land as a river, and watered it as a flood.

23 As he hath turned the waters into saltness: so shall the heathen inherit his wrath.

24 As his ways are plain unto the holy; so are they stumblingblocks unto the wicked.

25 For the good are good things created from the beginning: so evil things for sinners.

26 The principal things for the whole use of man's life are water, fire, iron, and salt, flour of wheat, honey, milk, and the blood of the grape, and oil, and clothing.

27 All these things are for good to the godly: so to the sinners they are turned into evil.

28 There be spirits that are created for vengeance, which in their fury lay on sore strokes; in the time of destruction they pour out their force, and appease the wrath of him that made them.

29 Fire, and hail, and famine, and death, all these were created for vengeance;

30 Teeth of wild beasts, and scorpions, serpents, and the sword punishing the wicked to destruction.

31 They shall rejoice in his commandment, and they shall be ready upon earth, when need is; and when their time is come, they shall not transgress his word.

32 Therefore from the beginning I was resolved, and thought upon these things, and have left them in writing.

33 All the works of YAHOWAH are good: and he will give every needful thing in due season.

34 So that a man cannot say, This is worse than that: for in time they shall all be well approved.

35 And therefore praise ye YAHOWAH with the whole heart and mouth, and bless the name of YAHOWAH.

40 Great travail is created for every man, and an heavy yoke is upon the sons of Adam, from the day that they go out of their mother's womb, till the day that they return to the mother of all things.

2 Their imagination of things to come, and the day of death, [trouble] their thoughts, and [cause] fear of heart;

3 From him that sitteth on a throne of glory, unto him that is humbled in earth and ashes;

4 From him that weareth purple and a crown, unto him that is clothed with a linen frock.

5 Wrath, and envy, trouble, and unquietness, fear of death, and anger, and strife, and in the time of rest upon his bed his night sleep, do change his knowledge.

6 A little or nothing is his rest, and afterward he is in his sleep, as in a day of keeping watch, troubled in the vision of his heart, as if he were escaped out of a battle.

7 When all is safe, he awaketh, and marvelleth that the fear was nothing.

8 [Such things happen] unto all flesh, both man and beast, and that is sevenfold more upon sinners.

9 Death, and bloodshed, strife, and sword, calamities, famine, tribulation, and the scourge;

10 These things are created for the wicked, and for their sakes came the flood.

11 All things that are of the earth shall turn to the earth again: and that which is of the waters doth return into the sea.

12 All bribery and injustice shall be blotted out: but true dealing shall endure for ever.

13 The goods of the unjust shall be dried up like a river, and shall vanish with noise, like a great thunder in rain.

14 While he openeth his hand he shall rejoice: so shall transgressors come to nought.

15 The children of the ungodly shall not bring forth many branches: but are as unclean roots upon a hard rock.

16 The weed growing upon every water and bank of a river shall be pulled up before all grass.

17 Bountifulness is as a most fruitful garden, and mercifulness endureth for ever.

18 To labour, and to be content with that a man hath, is a sweet life: but he that findeth a treasure is above them both.

19 Children and the building of a city continue a man's name: but a blameless wife is counted above them both.

20 Wine and musick rejoice the heart: but the love of wisdom is above them both.

21 The pipe and the psaltery make sweet melody: but a pleasant tongue is above them both.

22 Thine eye desireth favour and beauty: but more than both corn while it is green.

23 A friend and companion never meet amiss: but above both is a wife with her husband.

24 Brethren and help are against time of trouble: but alms shall deliver more than them both.

25 Gold and silver make the foot stand sure: but counsel is esteemed above them both.

26 Riches and strength lift up the heart: but the fear of YAHOWAH is above them both: there is no want in the fear of YAHOWAH, and it needeth not to seek help.

27 The fear of YAHOWAH is a fruitful garden, and covereth him above all glory.

28 My son, lead not a beggar's life; for better it is to die than to beg.

29 The life of him that dependeth on another man's table is not to be counted for a life; for he polluteth himself with other men's meat: but a wise man well nurtured will beware thereof.

30 Begging is sweet in the mouth of the shameless: but in his belly there shall burn a fire.

41 O death, how bitter is the remembrance of thee to a man that liveth at rest in his possessions, unto the man that hath nothing to vex him, and that hath prosperity in all things: yea, unto him that is yet able to receive meat!

2 O death, acceptable is thy sentence unto the needy, and unto him whose strength faileth, that is now in the last age, and is vexed with all things, and to him that despaireth, and hath lost patience!

3 Fear not the sentence of death, remember them that have been before thee, and that come after; for this is the sentence of YAHOWAH over all flesh.

4 And why art thou against the pleasure of the Most High? there is no inquisition in the grave, whether thou have lived ten, or an hundred, or a thousand years.

5 The children of sinners are abominable children, and they that are conversant in the dwelling of the ungodly.

6 The inheritance of sinners' children shall perish, and their posterity shall have a perpetual reproach.

7 The children will complain of an ungodly father, because they shall be reproached for his sake.

8 Woe be unto you, ungodly men, which have forsaken the Torah of the Most High ELOHIM! for if ye increase, it shall be to your destruction:

9 And if ye be born, ye shall be born to a curse: and if ye die, a curse shall be your portion.

10 All that are of the earth shall turn to earth again: so the ungodly shall go from a curse to destruction.

11 The mourning of men is about their bodies: but an ill name of sinners shall be blotted out.

12 Have regard to thy name; for that shall continue with thee above a thousand great treasures of gold.

13 A good life hath but few days: but a good name endureth for ever.

14 My children, keep discipline in shalom: for wisdom that is hid, and a treasure that is not seen, what profit is in them both?

15 A man that hideth his foolishness is better than a man that hideth his wisdom.

16 Therefore be shamefaced according to my word: for it is not good to retain all shamefacedness; neither is it altogether approved in every thing.

17 Be ashamed of whoredom before father and mother: and of a lie before a prince and a mighty man;

18 Of an offence before a judge and ruler; of iniquity before a congregation and people; of unjust dealing before thy partner and friend;

19 And of theft in regard of the place where thou sojournest, and in regard of the truth of ELOHIM and his covenant; and to lean with thine elbow upon the meat; and of scorning to give and take;

20 And of silence before them that salute thee; and to look upon an harlot;

21 And to turn away thy face from thy kinsman; or to take away a portion or a gift; or to gaze upon another man's wife.

22 Or to be overbusy with his maid, and come not near her bed; or of upbraiding speeches before friends; and after thou hast given, upbraid not;

23 Or of iterating and speaking again that which thou hast heard; and of revealing of secrets.

24 So shalt thou be truly shamefaced and find favour before all men.

42 Of these things be not thou ashamed, and accept no person to sin thereby:

2 Of the Torah of the Most High, and his covenant; and of judgment to justify the ungodly;

3 Of reckoning with thy partners and travellers; or of the gift of the heritage of friends;

4 Of exactness of balance and weights; or of getting much or little;

5 And of merchants' indifferent selling; of much correction of children; and to make the side of an evil servant to bleed.

6 Sure keeping is good, where an evil wife is; and shut up, where many hands are.

7 Deliver all things in number and weight; and put all in writing that thou givest out, or receivest in.

8 Be not ashamed to inform the unwise and foolish, and the extreme aged that contendeth with those that are young: thus shalt thou be truly learned, and approved of all men living.

9 The father waketh for the daughter, when no man knoweth; and the care for her taketh away sleep: when she is young, lest she pass away the flower of her age; and being married, lest she should be hated:

10 In her virginity, lest she should be defiled and gotten with child in her father's house; and having an husband, lest she should misbehave herself; and when she is married, lest she should be barren.

11 Keep a sure watch over a shameless daughter, lest she make thee a laughingstock to thine enemies, and a byword in the city, and a reproach among the people, and make thee ashamed before the multitude.

12 Behold not every body's beauty, and sit not in the midst of women.

13 For from garments cometh a moth, and from women wickedness.

14 Better is the churlishness of a man than a courteous woman, a woman, I say, which bringeth shame and reproach.

15 I will now remember the works of YAHOWAH, and declare the things that I have seen: In the words of YAHOWAH are his works.

16 The sun that giveth light looketh upon all things, and the work thereof is full of the glory of YAHOWAH.

17 YAHOWAH hath not given power to the saints to declare all his marvellous works, which the Almighty YAHOWAH firmly settled, that whatsoever is might be established for his glory.

18 He seeketh out the deep, and the heart, and considereth their crafty devices: for YAHOWAH knoweth all that may be known, and he beholdeth the signs of the world.

19 He declareth the things that are past, and for to come, and revealeth the steps of hidden things.

20 No thought escapeth him, neither any word is hidden from him.

21 He hath garnished the excellent works of his wisdom, and he is from everlasting to everlasting: unto him may nothing be added, neither can he be diminished, and he hath no need of any counsellor.

22 Oh how desirable are all his works! and that a man may see even to a spark.

23 All these things live and remain for ever for all uses, and they are all obedient.

24 All things are double one against another: and he hath made nothing imperfect.

25 One thing establisheth the good or another: and who shall be filled with beholding his glory?

43 The pride of the height, the clear firmament, the beauty of heaven, with his glorious shew;

2 The sun when it appeareth, declaring at his rising a marvellous instrument, the work of the Most High:

3 At noon it parcheth the country, and who can abide the burning heat thereof?

4 A man blowing a furnace is in works of heat, but the sun burneth the mountains three times more; breathing out fiery vapours, and sending forth bright beams, it dimmeth the eyes.

5 Great is YAHOWAH that made it; and at his commandment runneth hastily.

6 He made the moon also to serve in her season for a declaration of times, and a sign of the world.

7 From the moon is the sign of feasts, a light that decreaseth in her perfection.

8 The month is called after her name, increasing wonderfully in her changing, being an instrument of the armies above, shining in the firmament of heaven;

9 The beauty of heaven, the glory of the stars, an ornament giving light in the highest places of YAHOWAH.

10 At the commandment of the Holy One they will stand in their order, and never faint in their watches.

11 Look upon the rainbow, and praise him that made it; very beautiful it is in the brightness thereof.

12 It compasseth the heaven about with a glorious circle, and the hands of the Most High have bended it.

13 By his commandment he maketh the snow to fall aplace, and sendeth swiftly the lightnings of his judgment.

14 Through this the treasures are opened: and clouds fly forth as fowls.

15 By his great power he maketh the clouds firm, and the hailstones are broken small.

16 At his sight the mountains are shaken, and at his will the south wind bloweth.

17 The noise of the thunder maketh the earth to tremble: so doth the northern storm and the whirlwind: as birds flying he scattereth the snow, and the falling down thereof is as the lighting of grasshoppers:

18 The eye marvelleth at the beauty of the whiteness thereof, and the heart is astonished at the raining of it.

19 The hoarfrost also as salt he poureth on the earth, and being congealed, it lieth on the top of sharp stakes.

20 When the cold north wind bloweth, and the water is congealed into ice, it abideth upon every gathering together of water, and clotheth the water as with a breastplate.

21 It devoureth the mountains, and burneth the wilderness, and consumeth the grass as fire.

22 A present remedy of all is a mist coming speedily, a dew coming after heat refresheth.

23 By his counsel he appeaseth the deep, and planteth islands therein.

24 They that sail on the sea tell of the danger thereof; and when we hear it with our ears, we marvel thereat.

25 For therein be strange and wondrous works, variety of all kinds of beasts and whales created.

26 By him the end of them hath prosperous success, and by his word all things consist.

27 We may speak much, and yet come short: wherefore in sum, he is all.

28 How shall we be able to magnify him? for he is great above all his works.

29 YAHOWAH is terrible and very great, and marvellous is his power.

30 When ye glorify YAHOWAH, exalt him as much as ye can; for even yet will he far exceed: and when ye exalt him, put forth all your strength, and be not weary; for ye can never go far enough.

31 Who hath seen him, that he might tell us? and who can magnify him as he is?

32 There are yet hid greater things than these be, for we have seen but a few of his works.

33 For YAHOWAH hath made all things; and to the godly hath he given wisdom.

44 Let us now praise famous men, and our fathers that begat us.

2 YAHOWAH hath wrought great glory by them through his great power from the beginning.

3 Such as did bear rule in their kingdoms, men renowned for their power, giving counsel by their understanding, and declaring prophecies:

4 Leaders of the people by their counsels, and by their knowledge of learning meet for the people, wise and eloquent are their instructions:

5 Such as found out musical tunes, and recited verses in writing:

6 Rich men furnished with ability, living peaceably in their habitations:

7 All these were honoured in their generations, and were the glory of their times.

8 There be of them, that have left a name behind them, that their praises might be reported.

9 And some there be, which have no memorial; who are perished, as though they had never been; and are become as though they had never been born; and their children after them.

10 But these were merciful men, whose righteousness hath not been forgotten.

11 With their seed shall continually remain a good inheritance, and their children are within the covenant.

12 Their seed standeth fast, and their children for their sakes.

13 Their seed shall remain for ever, and their glory shall not be blotted out.

14 Their bodies are buried in shalom; but their name liveth for evermore.

15 The people will tell of their wisdom, and the congregation will shew forth their praise.

16 Enoch pleased YAHOWAH, and was translated, being an example of repentance to all generations.

17 Noakh was found perfect and righteous; in the time of wrath he was taken in exchange [for the world;] therefore was he left as a remnant unto the earth, when the flood came.

18 An everlasting covenant was made with him, that all flesh should perish no more by the flood.

19 Abraham was a great father of many people: in glory was there none like unto him;

20 Who kept the Torah of the Most High, and was in covenant with him: he established the covenant in his flesh; and when he was proved, he was found faithful.

21 Therefore he assured him by an oath, that he would bless the nations in his seed, and that he would multiply him as the dust of the earth, and exalt his seed as the stars, and cause them to inherit from sea to sea, and from the river unto the utmost part of the land.

22 With Yitzkhaq did he establish likewise [for Abraham his father's sake] the blessing of all men, and the covenant, And made it rest upon the head of Ya'aqob. He acknowledged him in his blessing, and gave him an heritage, and divided his portions; among the twelve tribes did he part them.

45 And he brought out of him a merciful man, which found favour in the sight of all flesh, even Mosheh, beloved of ELOHIM and men, whose memorial is blessed.

2 He made him like to the glorious saints, and magnified him, so that his enemies stood in fear of him.

3 By his words he caused the wonders to cease, and he made him glorious in the sight of kings, and gave him a commandment for his people, and shewed him part of his glory.

4 He sanctified him in his faithfuless and meekness, and chose him out of all men.

5 He made him to hear his voice, and brought him into the dark cloud, and gave him commandments before his face, even the Torah of life and knowledge, that he might teach Ya'aqob his covenants, and Yisra'EL his judgments.

6 He exalted Aharon, an holy man like unto him, even his brother, of the tribe of Lewi.

7 An everlasting covenant he made with him and gave him the priesthood among the people; he beautified him with comely ornaments, and clothed him with a robe of glory.

8 He put upon him perfect glory; and strengthened him with rich garments, with breeches, with a long robe, and the ephod.

9 And he compassed him with pomegranates, and with many golden bells round about, that as he went there might be a sound, and a noise made that might be heard in the temple, for a memorial to the children of his people;

10 With an holy garment, with gold, and blue silk, and purple, the work of the embroiderer, with a breastplate of judgment, and with Urim and Thummim;

11 With twisted scarlet, the work of the cunning workman, with precious stones graven like seals, and set in gold, the work of the jeweller, with a writing engraved for a memorial, after the number of the tribes of Yisra'EL.

12 He set a crown of gold upon the mitre, wherein was engraved Holiness, an ornament of honour, a costly work, the desires of the eyes, goodly and beautiful.

13 Before him there were none such, neither did ever any stranger put them on, but only his children and his children's children perpetually.

14 Their sacrifices shall be wholly consumed every day twice continually.

15 Mosheh consecrated him, and anointed him with holy oil: this was appointed unto him by an everlasting covenant, and to his seed, so long as the heavens should remain, that they should minister unto him, and execute the office of the priesthood, and bless the people in his name.

16 He chose him out of all men living to offer sacrifices to YAHOWAH, incense, and a sweet savour, for a memorial, to make reconciliation for his people.

17 He gave unto him his commandments, and authority in the statutes of judgments, that he should teach Ya'aqob the testimonies, and inform Yisra'EL in his Torah.

18 Strangers conspired together against him, and maligned him in the wilderness, even the men that were of Dathan's and Abiron's side, and the congregation of Core, with fury and wrath.

19 This YAHOWAH saw, and it displeased him, and in his wrathful indignation were they consumed: he did wonders upon them, to consume them with the fiery flame.

20 But he made Aharon more honourable, and gave him an heritage, and divided unto him the firstfruits of the increase; especially he prepared bread in abundance:

21 For they eat of the sacrifices of YAHOWAH, which he gave unto him and his seed.

22 Howbeit in the land of the people he had no inheritance, neither had he any portion among the people: for YAHOWAH himself is his portion and inheritance.

23 The third in glory is Pinkhas the son of Eleazar, because he had zeal in the fear of YAHOWAH, and stood up with good courage of heart: when the people were turned back, and made reconciliation for Yisra'EL.

24 Therefore was there a covenant of shalom made with him, that he should be the chief of the sanctuary and of his people, and that he and his posterity should have the dignity of the priesthood for ever:

25 According to the covenant made with Dawid son of Jesse, of the tribe of Yehudah, that the inheritance of the king should be to his posterity alone: so the inheritance of Aharon should also be unto his seed.

26 ELOHIM give you wisdom in your heart to judge his people in righteousness, that their good things be not abolished, and that their glory may endure for ever.

46 Yahoshua the son a Nun was valiant in the wars, and was the successor of Mosheh in prophecies, who according to his name was made great for the saving of the elect of ELOHIM, and taking vengeance of the enemies that rose up against them, that he might set Yisra'EL in their inheritance.

2 How great glory gat he, when he did lift up his hands, and stretched out his sword against the cities!

3 Who before him so stood to it? for YAHOWAH himself brought his enemies unto him.

4 Did not the sun go back by his means? and was not one day as long as two?

5 He called upon the Most High YAHOWAH, when the enemies pressed upon him on every side; and the great YAHOWAH heard him.

6 And with hailstones of mighty power he made the battle to fall violently upon the heathen, and in the descent [of Beth-Khoron] he destroyed them that resisted, that the heathen might know all their strength, because he fought in the sight of YAHOWAH, and he followed the Mighty One.

7 In the time of Mosheh also he did a work of mercy, he and Kalaeb the son of Yephuneh, in that they withstood the congregation, and withheld the people from sin, and appeased the wicked murmuring.

8 And of six hundred thousand people on foot, they two were preserved to bring them in to the heritage, even unto the land that floweth with milk and honey.

9 YAHOWAH gave strength also unto Kalaeb, which remained with him unto his old age: so that he entered upon the high places of the land, and his seed obtained it for an heritage:

10 That all the children of Yisra'EL might see that it is good to follow YAHOWAH.

11 And concerning the judges, every one by name, whose heart went not a whoring, nor departed from YAHOWAH, let their memory be blessed.

12 Let their bones flourish out of their place, and let the name of them that were honoured be continued upon their children.

13 Shemu'EL, the prophet of YAHOWAH, beloved of YAHOWAH his ELOHIM, established a kingdom, and anointed princes over his people.

14 By the Torah of YAHOWAH he judged the congregation, and YAHOWAH had respect unto Ya'aqob.

15 By his faithfulness he was found a true prophet, and by his word he was known to be faithful in vision.

16 He called upon the mighty YAHOWAH, when his enemies pressed upon him on every side, when he offered the sucking lamb.

17 And YAHOWAH thundered from heaven, and with a great noise made his voice to be heard.

18 And he destroyed the rulers of the Tyrians, and all the princes cf the Phelishtim.

19 And before his long sleep he made protestations in the sight of YAHOWAH and his anointed, I have not taken any man's goods, so much as a shoe: and no man did accuse him.

20 And after his death he prophesied, and shewed the king his end, and lifted up his voice from the earth in prophecy, to blot out the wickedness of the people.

47 And after him rose up Nathan to prophesy in the time of Dawid.

2 As is the fat taken away from the shalom offering, so was Dawid chosen out of the children of Yisra'EL.

3 He played with lions as with kids, and with bears as with lambs.

4 Slew he not a giant, when he was yet but young? and did he not take away reproach from the people, when he lifted up his hand with the stone in the sling, and beat down the boasting of Goliath?

5 For he called upon the Most High YAHOWAH; and he gave him strength in his right hand to slay that mighty warrior, and set up the horn of his people.

6 So the people honoured him with ten thousands, and praised him in the blessings of YAHOWAH, in that he gave him a crown of glory.

7 For he destroyed the enemies on every side, and brought to nought the Phelishtim his adversaries,

and brake their horn in sunder unto this day.

8 In all his works he praised the Holy One Most High with words of glory; with his whole heart he sung songs, and loved him that made him.

9 He set singers also before the altar, that by their voices they might make sweet melody, and daily sing praises in their songs.

10 He beautified their feasts, and set in order the solemn times until the end, that they might praise his holy name, and that the temple might sound from morning.

11 YAHOWAH took away his sins, and exalted his horn for ever: he gave him a covenant of kings, and a throne of glory in Yisra'EL.

12 After him rose up a wise son, and for his sake he dwelt at large.

13 Shelomoh reigned in a peaceable time, and was honoured; for ELOHIM made all quiet round about him, that he might build an house in his name, and prepare his sanctuary for ever.

14 How wise wast thou in thy youth and, as a flood, filled with understanding!

15 Thy soul covered the whole earth, and thou filledst it with dark parables.

16 Thy name went far unto the islands; and for thy shalom thou wast beloved.

17 The countries marvelled at thee for thy songs, and proverbs, and parables, and interpretations.

18 By the name of YAHOWAH ELOHIM, which is called YAHOWAH ELOHIM of Yisra'EL, thou didst gather gold as tin and didst multiply silver as lead.

19 Thou didst bow thy loins unto women, and by thy body thou wast brought into subjection.

20 Thou didst stain thy honour, and pollute thy seed: so that thou broughtest wrath upon thy children, and wast grieved for thy folly.

21 So the kingdom was divided, and out of Ephraim ruled a rebellious kingdom.

22 But YAHOWAH will never leave off his mercy, neither shall any of his works perish, neither will he abolish the posterity of his elect, and the seed of him that loveth him he will not take away: wherefore he gave a remnant unto Ya'aqob, and out of him a root unto Dawid.

23 Thus rested Shelomoh with his fathers, and of his seed he left behind him Roboam, even the foolishness of the people, and one that had no understanding, who turned away the people through his counsel. There was also Jeroboam the son of Nebat, who caused Yisra'EL to sin, and shewed Ephraim the way of sin:

24 And their sins were multiplied exceedingly, that they were driven out of the land.

25 For they sought out all wickedness, till the vengeance came upon them.

48
Then stood up EliYAHU the prophet as fire, and his word burned like a lamp.

2 He brought a sore famine upon them, and by his zeal he diminished their number.

3 By the word of YAHOWAH he shut up the heaven, and also three times brought down fire.

4 O EliYAHU, how wast thou honoured in thy wondrous deeds! and who may glory like unto thee!

5 Who didst raise up a dead man from death, and his soul from the place of the dead, by the word of the Most High:

6 Who broughtest kings to destruction, and honorable men from their bed:

7 Who heardest the rebuke of YAHOWAH in Sinai , and in Khoreb the judgment of vengeance:

8 Who annointedst kings to take revenge, and prophets to succeed after him:

9 Who was taken up in a whirlwind of fire, and in a chariot of fiery horses:

10 Who wast ordained for reproofs in their times, to pacify the wrath of YAHOWAH'S judgment, before it brake forth into fury, and to turn the heart of the father unto the son, and to restore the tribes of Ya'aqob.

11 Blessed are they that saw thee, and slept in love; for we shall surely live.

12 EliYAHU it was, who was covered with a whirlwind: and Elisha was filled with his RUAKH: whilst he lived, he was not moved with the presence of any prince, neither could any bring him into subjection.

13 No word could overcome him; and after his death his body prophesied.

14 He did wonders in his life, and at his death were his works marvellous.

15 For all this the people repented not, neither departed they from their sins, till they were spoiled and carried out of their land, and were scattered through all the earth: yet there remained a small people, and a ruler in the house of Dawid:

16 Of whom some did that which was pleasing to ELOHIM, and some multiplied sins.

17 Ezekias fortified his city, and brought in water into the midst thereof: he digged the hard rock with iron, and made wells for waters.

18 In his time Sanchaerib came up, and sent Rabsaces, and lifted up his hand against Tzion, and boasted proudly.

19 Then trembled their hearts and hands, and they were in pain, as women in travail.

20 But they called upon YAHOWAH which is merciful, and stretched out their hands toward him: and immediately the Holy One heard them out of heaven, and delivered them by the ministry of YeshaYAH.

21 He smote the host of the Assyrians, and his Angel destroyed them.

22 For Ezekias had done the thing that pleased YAHOWAH, and was strong in the ways of Dawid his father, as YeshaYAH the prophet, who was great and faithful in his vision, had commanded him.

23 In his time the sun went backward, and he lengthened the king's life.

24 He saw by an excellent RUAKH what should come to pass at the last, and he comforted them that mourned in Tzion.

25 He shewed what should come to pass for ever, and secret things or ever they came.

49 The remembrance of YoshiYAH is like the composition of the perfume that is made by the art of the apothecary: it is sweet as honey in all mouths, and as musick at a banquet of wine.

2 He behaved himself uprightly in the conversion of the people, and took away the abominations of iniquity.

3 He directed his heart unto YAHOWAH, and in the time of the ungodly he established the worship of ELOHIM.

4 All, except Dawid and Ezekias and YoshiYAH, were defective: for they forsook the Torah of the Most High, even the kings of Yehudah failed.

5 Therefore he gave their power unto others, and their glory to a strange nation.

6 They burnt the chosen city of the sanctuary, and made the streets desolate, according to the prophecy of YirmeYAH.

7 For they entreated him evil, who nevertheless was a prophet, sanctified in his mother's womb, that he might root out, and afflict, and destroy; and that he might build up also, and plant.

8 It was Ezekiel who saw the glorious vision, which was shewed him upon the chariot of the Kerbim.

9 For he made mention of the enemies under the figure of the rain, and directed them that went right.

10 And of the twelve prophets let the memorial be blessed, and let their bones flourish again out of their place: for they comforted Ya'aqob, and delivered them by assured hope.

11 How shall we magnify Zerubabel? even he was as a signet on the right hand:

12 So was Yahoshua the son of Yaho-Tzadaq: who in their time builded the house, and set up an holy temple to YAHOWAH, which was prepared for everlasting glory.

13 And among the elect was NekhemYAH, whose renown is great, who raised up for us the walls that were fallen, and set up the gates and the bars, and raised up our ruins again.

14 But upon the earth was no man created like Enoch; for he was taken from the earth.

15 Neither was there a young man born like Yoseph, a governor of his brethren, a stay of the people, whose bones were regarded of YAHOWAH.

16 Sem and Seth were in great honour among men, and so was Adam above every living thing in creation.

50 Shimon the high priest, the son of Khonaiw, who in his life repaired the house again, and in his days fortified the temple:

2 And by him was built from the foundation the double height, the high fortress of the wall about the temple:

3 In his days the cistern to receive water, being in compass as the sea, was covered with plates of brass:

4 He took care of the temple that it should not fall, and fortified the city against besieging:

5 How was he honoured in the midst of the people in his coming out of the sanctuary!

6 He was as the morning star in the midst of a cloud, and as the moon at the full:

7 As the sun shining upon the temple of the Most High, and as the rainbow giving light in the bright clouds:

8 And as the flower of roses in the spring of the year, as lilies by the rivers of waters, and as the branches of the frankincense tree in the time of summer:

9 As fire and incense in the censer, and as a vessel of beaten gold set with all manner of precious stones:

10 And as a fair olive tree budding forth fruit, and as a cypress tree which groweth up to the clouds.

11 When he put on the robe of honour, and was clothed with the perfection of glory, when he went up to the holy altar, he made the garment of holiness honourable.

12 When he took the portions out of the priests' hands, he himself stood by the hearth of the altar, compassed about, as a young cedar in Lebanon; and as palm trees compassed they him round about.

13 So were all the sons of Aharon in their glory, and the oblations of YAHOWAH in their hands, before all the congregation of Yisra'EL.

14 And finishing the service at the altar, that he might adorn the offering of the Most High Almighty,

15 He stretched out his hand to the cup, and poured of the blood of the grape, he poured out at the foot of the altar a sweetsmelling savour unto the Most High King of all.

16 Then shouted the sons of Aharon, and sounded the silver trumpets, and made a great noise to be heard, for a remembrance before the Most High.

17 Then all the people together hasted, and fell down to the earth upon their faces to worship their YAHOWAH ELOHIM Almighty, the Most High.

18 The singers also sang praises with their voices, with great variety of sounds was there made sweet melody.

19 And the people besought YAHOWAH, the Most High, by prayer before him that is merciful, till the solemnity of YAHOWAH was ended, and they had finished his service.

20 Then he went down, and lifted up his hands over the whole congregation of the children of Yisra'EL, to give the blessing of YAHOWAH with his lips, and to rejoice in his name.

21 And they bowed themselves down to worship the second time, that they might receive a blessing from the Most High.

22 Now therefore bless ye the ELOHIM of all, which only doeth wondrous things every where, which exalteth our days from the womb, and dealeth with us according to his mercy.

23 He grant us joyfulness of heart, and that shalom may be in our days in Yisra'EL for ever:

24 That he would confirm his mercy with us, and deliver us at his time!

25 There be two manner of Gentiles which my heart abhorreth, and the third is no nation:

26 They that sit upon the mountain of Shomron, and they that dwell among the Phelishtim, and that foolish people that dwell in Shekem.

27 Yahoshua the son of Sirach of Yerushalem hath written in this book the instruction of understanding and knowledge, who out of his heart poured forth wisdom.

28 Blessed is he that shall be exercised in these things; and he that layeth them up in his heart shall become wise.

29 For if he do them, he shall be strong to all things: for the light of YAHOWAH leadeth him, who giveth wisdom to the godly. Blessed be the name of YAHOWAH for ever. Amen, Amen.

A PRAYER OF YAHOSHUA THE SON OF SIRACH.

51 I will thank thee, O YAHOWAH and King, and praise thee, O ELOHIM my Saviour: I do give praise unto thy name:

2 For thou art my defender and helper, and has preserved my body from destruction, and from the snare of the slanderous tongue, and from the lips that forge lies, and has been mine helper against mine adversaries:

3 And hast delivered me, according to the multitude of they mercies and greatness of thy name, from the teeth of them that were ready to devour me, and out of the hands of such as sought after my life, and from the manifold afflictions which I had;

4 From the choking of fire on every side, and from the midst of the fire which I kindled not;

5 From the depth of the belly of hell, from an unclean tongue, and from lying words.

6 By an accusation to the king from an unrighteous tongue my soul drew near even unto death, my life was near to the hell beneath.

7 They compassed me on every side, and there was no man to help me: I looked for the succour of men, but there was none.

8 Then thought I upon thy mercy, O YAHOWAH, and upon thy acts of old, how thou deliverest such as wait for thee, and savest them out of the hands of the enemies.

9 Then lifted I up my supplications from the earth, and prayed for deliverance from death.

10 I called upon YAHOWAH, the Father of my YAHOWAH, that he would not leave me in the days of my trouble, and in the time of the proud, when there was no help.

11 I will praise thy name continually, and will sing praises with thanksgiving; and so my prayer was heard:

12 For thou savedst me from destruction, and deliveredst me from the evil time: therefore will I give thanks, and praise thee, and bless they name, O YAHOWAH.

13 When I was yet young, or ever I went abroad, I desired wisdom openly in my prayer.

14 I prayed for her before the temple, and will seek her out even to the end.

15 Even from the flower till the grape was ripe hath my heart delighted in her: my foot went the right way, from my youth up sought I after her.

16 I bowed down mine ear a little, and received her, and gat much learning.

17 I profited therein, therefore will I ascribe glory unto him that giveth me wisdom.

18 For I purposed to do after her, and earnestly I followed that which is good; so shall I not be confounded.

19 My soul hath wrestled with her, and in my doings I was exact: I stretched forth my hands to the heaven above, and bewailed my ignorances of her.

20 I directed my soul unto her, and I found her in pureness: I have had my heart joined with her from the beginning, therefore shall I not be foresaken.

21 My heart was troubled in seeking her: therefore have I gotten a good possession.

22 YAHOWAH hath given me a tongue for my reward, and I will praise him therewith.

23 Draw near unto me, ye unlearned, and dwell in the house of learning.

24 Wherefore are ye slow, and what say ye to these things, seeing your souls are very thirsty?

25 I opened my mouth, and said, Buy her for yourselves without money.

26 Put your neck under the yoke, and let your soul receive instruction: she is hard at hand to find.

27 Behold with your eyes, how that I have but little labour, and have gotten unto me much rest.

28 Get learning with a great sum of money, and get much gold by her.

29 Let your soul rejoice in his mercy, and be not ashamed of his praise.

30 Work your work betimes, and in his time he will give you your reward.

BEN SIRA (SIRACH)

THE BOOK OF
BARUCH

1 And these are the words of the book, which Baruk the son of NeriYAHU, the son of Macha'saeYAHU, the son of TzidqiYAHU, the son of ChasadYAHU, the son of KhilqiYAHU, wrote in Babel,

2 In the fifth year, and in the seventh day of the month, what time as the Chaldeans took Yerushalem, and burnt it with fire.

3 And Baruk did read the words of this book in the hearing of YekonYAH the son of Yaho'yaqim king of Yehudah, and in the ears of all the people that came to hear the book,

4 And in the hearing of the nobles, and of the king's sons, and in the hearing of the elders, and of all the people, from the lowest unto the highest, even of all them that dwelt at Babel by the river Siaha.

5 Whereupon they wept, fasted, and prayed before YAHOWAH.

6 They made also a collection of money according to every man's power:

7 And they sent it to Yerushalem unto Yaho'yaqim the high priest, the son of KhilqiYAHU, son of Shalum, and to the priests, and to all the people which were found with him at Yerushalem,

8 At the same time when he received the vessels of the house of YAHOWAH, that were carried out of the temple, to return them into the land of Yehudah, the tenth day of the month Siywan, namely, silver vessels, which TzidqiYAHU the son of YoshiYAH king of Yehudah had made,

9 After that Nebukad'netzar king of Babel had carried away YekonYAH, and the princes, and the captives, and the mighty men, and the people of the land, from Yerushalem, and brought them unto Babel.

10 And they said, Behold, we have sent you money to buy you burnt offerings, and sin offerings, and incense, and prepare ye manna, and offer upon the altar of YAHOWAH our ELOHIM;

11 And pray for the life of Nebukad'netzar king of Babel, and for the life of Balshatzar his son, that their days may be upon earth as the days of heaven:

12 And YAHOWAH will give us strength, and lighten our eyes, and we shall live under the shadow of Nebukad'netzar king of Babel, and under the shadow of Balshatzar his son, and we shall serve them many days, and find favour in their sight.

13 Pray for us also unto YAHOWAH our ELOHIM, for we have sinned against YAHOWAH our ELOHIM; and unto this day the fury of YAHOWAH and his wrath is not turned from us.

14 And ye shall read this book which we have sent unto you, to make confession in the house of YAHOWAH, upon the feasts and solemn days.

15 And ye shall say, To YAHOWAH our ELOHIM belongeth righteousness, but unto us the confusion of faces, as it is come to pass this day, unto them of Yehudah, and to the inhabitants of Yerushalem,

16 And to our kings, and to our princes, and to our priests, and to our prophets, and to our fathers:

17 For we have sinned before YAHOWAH,

18 And disobeyed him, and have not hearkened unto the voice of YAHOWAH our ELOHIM, to walk in the commandments that he gave us openly:

19 Since the day that YAHOWAH brought our forefathers out of the land of Mitzraim, unto this present day, we have been disobedient unto YAHOWAH our ELOHIM, and we have been negligent in not hearing his voice.

20 Wherefore the evils cleaved unto us, and the curse, which YAHOWAH appointed by Mosheh his servant at the time that he brought our fathers out of the land of Mitzraim, to give us a land that floweth with milk and honey, like as it is to see this day.

21 Nevertheless we have not hearkened unto the voice of YAHOWAH our ELOHIM, according unto all the words of the prophets, whom he sent unto us:

22 But every man followed the imagination of his own wicked heart, to serve strange elohim, and to do evil in the sight of YAHOWAH our ELOHIM.

2 Therefore YAHOWAH hath made good his word, which he pronounced against us, and against our judges that judged Yisra'EL, and against our kings, and against our princes, and against the men of Yisra'EL and Yehudah,

2 To bring upon us great plagues, such as never happened under the whole heaven, as it came to pass in Yerushalem, according to the things that were written in the Torah of Mosheh;

3 That a man should eat the flesh of his own son, and the flesh of his own daughter.

4 Moreover he hath delivered them to be in subjection to all the kingdoms that are round about us, to be as a reproach and desolation among all the people round about, where YAHOWAH hath scattered them.

5 Thus we were cast down, and not exalted, because we have sinned against YAHOWAH our ELOHIM, and have not been obedient unto his voice.

6 To YAHOWAH our ELOHIM appertaineth righteousness: but unto us and to our fathers open shame, as appeareth this day.

7 For all these plagues are come upon us, which YAHOWAH hath pronounced against us

8 Yet have we not prayed before YAHOWAH, that we might turn every one from the imaginations of his wicked heart.

9 Wherefore YAHOWAH watched over us for evil, and YAHOWAH hath brought it upon us: for YAHOWAH is righteous in all his works which he hath commanded us.

10 Yet we have not hearkened unto his voice, to walk in the commandments of YAHOWAH, that he hath set before us.

11 And now, O YAHOWAH ELOHIM of Yisra'EL, that hast brought thy people out of the land of Mitzraim with a mighty hand, and high arm, and with signs, and with wonders, and with great power, and hast gotten thyself a name, as appeareth this day:

12 O YAHOWAH our ELOHIM, we have sinned, we have done ungodly, we have dealt unrighteously in all thine ordinances.

13 Let thy wrath turn from us: for we are but a few left among the heathen, where thou hast scattered us.

14 Hear our prayers, O YAHOWAH, and our petitions, and deliver us for thine own sake, and give us favour in the sight of them which have led us away:

15 That all the earth may know that thou art YAHOWAH our ELOHIM, because Yisra'EL and his posterity is called by thy name.

16 O YAHOWAH, look down from thine holy house, and consider us: bow down thine ear, O YAHOWAH, to hear us.

17 Open thine eyes, and behold; for the dead that are in the graves, whose souls are taken from their bodies, will give unto YAHOWAH neither praise nor righteousness:

18 But the soul that is greatly vexed, which goeth stooping and feeble, and the eyes that fail, and the hungry soul, will give thee praise and righteousness, O YAHOWAH.

19 Therefore we do not make our humble supplication before thee, O YAHOWAH our ELOHIM, for the righteousness of our fathers, and of our kings.

20 For thou hast sent out thy wrath and indignation upon us, as thou hast spoken by thy servants the prophets, saying,

21 Thus saith YAHOWAH, Bow down your shoulders to serve the king of Babel: so shall ye remain in the land that I gave unto your fathers.

22 But if ye will not hear the voice of YAHOWAH, to serve the king of Babel,

23 I will cause to cease out of the cites of Yehudah, and from without Yerushalem, the voice of mirth, and the voice of joy, the voice of the bridegroom, and the voice of the bride: and the whole land shall be desolate of inhabitants.

24 But we would not hearken unto thy voice, to serve the king of Babel: therefore hast thou made good the words that thou spakest by thy servants the prophets, namely, that the bones of our kings, and the bones of our fathers, should be taken out of their place.

25 And, lo, they are cast out to the heat of the day, and to the frost of the night, and they died in great miseries by famine, by sword, and by pestilence.

26 And the house which is called by thy name hast thou laid waste, as it is to be seen this day, for the wickedness of the house of Yisra'EL and the house of Yehudah.

27 O our ELOHIM, thou hast dealt with us after all thy goodness, and according to all that great mercy of thine,

28 As thou spakest by thy servant Mosheh in the day when thou didst command him to write the Torah before the children of Yisra'EL, saying,

29 If ye will not hear my voice, surely this very great multitude shall be turned into a small number among the nations, where I will scatter them.

30 For I knew that they would not hear me, because it is a stiffnecked people: but in the land of their captivities they shall remember themselves.

31 And shall know that I am YAHOWAH their ELOHIM: for I will give them an heart, and ears to hear:

32 And they shall praise me in the land of their captivity, and think upon my name,

33 And return from their stiff neck, and from their wicked deeds: for they shall remember the way of their fathers, which sinned before YAHOWAH.

34 And I will bring them again into the land which I promised with an oath unto their fathers, Abraham, Yitzkhaq, and Ya'aqob, and they shall be lords of it: and I will increase them, and they shall not be diminished.

35 And I will make an everlasting covenant with them to be their ELOHIM, and they shall be my people: and I will no more drive my people of Yisra'EL out of the land that I have given them.

3 O YAHOWAH of Hosts, ELOHIM of Yisra'EL, the soul in anguish the troubled ruakh, crieth unto thee.

2 Hear, O YAHOWAH, and have mercy; ar thou art merciful: and have pity upon us, because we have sinned before thee.

3 For thou endurest for ever, and we perish utterly.

4 O YAHOWAH of Hosts, thou ELOHIM of Yisra'EL, hear now the prayers of the dead children of Yisra'EL, and of their children, which have sinned before thee, and not hearkened unto the voice of thee YAHOWAH their ELOHIM: for the which cause these plagues cleave unto us.

5 Remember not the iniquities of our forefathers: but think upon thy power and thy name now at this time.

6 For thou art YAHOWAH our ELOHIM, and thee, O YAHOWAH, will we praise.

7 And for this cause thou hast put thy fear in our hearts, to the intent that we should call upon thy name, and praise thee in our captivity: for we have called to mind all the iniquity of our forefathers, that sinned before thee.

8 Behold, we are yet this day in our captivity, where thou hast scattered us, for a reproach and a curse, and to be subject to payments, according to all the iniquities of our fathers, which departed from YAHOWAH our ELOHIM.

9 Hear, Yisra'EL, the commandments of life: give ear to understand wisdom.

10 How happeneth it Yisra'EL, that thou art in thine enemies' land, that thou art waxen old in a strange country, that thou art defiled with the dead,

11 That thou art counted with them that go down into the grave?

12 Thou hast forsaken the fountain of wisdom.

13 For if thou hadst walked in the way of ELOHIM, thou shouldest have dwelled in shalom for ever.

14 Learn where is wisdom, where is strength, where is understanding; that thou mayest know also where is length of days, and life, where is the light of the eyes, and shalom.

15 Who hath found out her place? or who hath come into her treasures?

16 Where are the princes of the heathen become, and such as ruled the beasts upon the earth;

17 They that had their pastime with the fowls of the air, and they that hoarded up silver and gold, wherein men trust, and made no end of their getting?

18 For they that wrought in silver, and were so careful, and whose works are unsearchable,

19 They are vanished and gone down to the grave, and others are come up in their steads.

20 Young men have seen light, and dwelt upon the earth: but the way of knowledge have they not known,

21 Nor understood the paths thereof, nor laid hold of it: their children were far off from that way.

22 It hath not been heard of in Kena'an, neither hath it been seen in Thaiman.

23 The sons of Hagar that seek wisdom upon earth, the merchants of Medan and of Thaiman, the authors of fables, and searchers out of understanding; none of these have known the way of wisdom, or remember her paths.

24 O Yisra'EL, how great is the house of ELOHIM! and how large is the place of his possession!

25 Great, and hath none end; high, and unmeasurable.

26 There were the giants famous from the beginning, that were of so great stature, and so expert in war.

27 Those did not ELOHIM choose, neither gave he the way of knowledge unto them:

28 But they were destroyed, because they had no wisdom, and perished through their own foolishness.

29 Who hath gone up into heaven, and taken her, and brought her down from the clouds?

30 Who hath gone over the sea, and found her, and will bring her for pure gold?

31 No man knoweth her way, nor thinketh of her path.

32 But he that knoweth all things knoweth her, and hath found her out with his understanding: he that prepared the earth for evermore hath filled it with fourfooted beasts:

33 He that sendeth forth light, and it goeth, calleth it again, and it obeyeth him with fear.

34 The stars shined in their watches, and rejoiced: when he calleth them, they say, Here we be; and so with cheerfulness they shewed light unto him that made them.

35 This is our ELOHIM, and there shall none other be accounted of in comparison of him

36 He hath found out all the way of knowledge, and hath given it unto Ya'aqob his servant, and to Yisra'EL his beloved.

37 Afterward did he shew himself upon earth, and conversed with men.

4 This is the book of the commandments of ELOHIM, and the Torah that endureth for ever: all they that keep it shall come to life; but such as leave it shall die.

2 Turn thee, O Ya'aqob, and take hold of it: walk in the presence of the light thereof, that thou mayest be illuminated.

3 Give not thine honour to another, nor the things that are profitable unto thee to a strange nation.

4 O Yisra'EL, happy are we: for things that are pleasing to ELOHIM are made known unto us.

5 Be of good cheer, my people, the memorial of Yisra'EL.

6 Ye were sold to the heathen, not for [your] destruction: but because ye moved ELOHIM to wrath, ye were delivered unto the enemies.

7 For ye provoked him that made you by sacrificing unto devils, and not to ELOHIM.

8 Ye have forgotten the everlasting ELOHIM, that brought you up; and ye have grieved Yerushalem, that nursed you.

9 For when she saw the wrath of ELOHIM coming upon you, she said, Hearken, O ye that dwell about Tzion: ELOHIM hath brought upon me great mourning;

10 For I saw the captivity of my sons and daughters, which the Everlasting brought upon them.

11 With joy did I nourish them; but sent them away with weeping and mourning.

12 Let no man rejoice over me, a widow, and forsaken of many, who for the sins of my children am left desolate; because they departed from the Torah of ELOHIM.

13 They knew not his statutes, nor walked in the ways of his commandments, nor trod in the paths of discipline in his righteousness.

14 Let them that dwell about Tzion come, and remember ye the captivity of my sons and daughters, which the Everlasting hath brought upon them.

15 For he hath brought a nation upon them from far, a shameless nation, and of a strange language, who neither reverenced old man, nor pitied child.

16 These have carried away the dear beloved children of the widow, and left her that was alone desolate without daughters.

17 But what can I help you?

18 For he that brought these plagues upon you will deliver you from the hands of your enemies.

19 Go your way, O my children, go your way: for I am left desolate.

20 I have put off the clothing of shalom, and put upon me the sackcloth of my prayer: I will cry unto the Everlasting in my days.

21 Be of good cheer, O my children, cry unto ELOHIM, and he will deliver you from the power and hand of the enemies.

22 For my hope is in the Everlasting, that he will save you; and joy is come unto me from the Holy One, because of the mercy which shall soon come unto you from the Everlasting our Saviour.

23 For I sent you out with mourning and weeping: but ELOHIM will give you to me again with joy and gladness for ever.

24 Like as now the neighbours of Tzion have seen your captivity: so shall they see shortly your salvation from our ELOHIM which shall come upon you with great glory, and brightness of the Everlasting.

25 My children, suffer patiently the wrath that is come upon you from ELOHIM: for thine enemy hath persecuted thee; but shortly thou shalt see his destruction, and shalt tread upon his neck.

26 My delicate ones have gone rough ways, and were taken away as a flock caught of the enemies.

27 Be of good comfort, O my children, and cry unto ELOHIM: for ye shall be remembered of him that brought these things upon you.

28 For as it was your mind to go astray from ELOHIM: so, being returned, seek him ten times more.

29 For he that hath brought these plagues upon you shall bring you everlasting joy with your salvation.

30 Take a good heart, O Yerushalem: for he that gave thee that name will comfort thee.

31 Miserable are they that afflicted thee, and rejoiced at thy fall.

32 Miserable are the cities which thy children served: miserable is she that received thy sons.

33 For as she rejoiced at thy ruin, and was glad of thy fall: so shall she be grieved for her own desolation.

34 For I will take away the rejoicing of her great multitude, and her pride shall be turned into mourning.

35 For fire shall come upon her from the Everlasting, long to endure; and she shall be inhabited of devils for a great time.

36 O Yerushalem, look about thee toward the east, and behold the joy that cometh unto thee from ELOHIM.

37 Lo, thy sons come, whom thou sentest away, they come gathered together from the east to the west by the word of the Holy One, rejoicing in the glory of ELOHIM.

5 Put off, O Yerushalem, the garment of mourning and affliction, and put on the comeliness of the glory that cometh from ELOHIM for ever.

2 Cast about thee a double garment of the righteousness which cometh from ELOHIM; and set a diadem on thine head of the glory of YAHOWAH.

3 For ELOHIM will shew thy brightness unto every country under heaven.

4 For thy name shall be called of ELOHIM for ever The shalom of righteousness, and The glory of YAHOWAH'S worship.

5 Arise, O Yerushalem, and stand on high, and look about toward the east, and behold thy children gathered from the west unto the east by the word of the Holy One, rejoicing in the remembrance of ELOHIM.

6 For they departed from thee on foot, and were led away of their enemies: but ELOHIM bringeth them unto thee exalted with glory, as children of the kingdom.

7 For ELOHIM hath appointed that every high hill, and banks of long continuance, should be cast down, and valleys filled up, to make even the ground, that Yisra'EL may go safely in the glory of ELOHIM,

8 Moreover even the woods and every sweetsmelling tree shall overshadow Yisra'EL by the commandment of ELOHIM.

9 For ELOHIM shall lead Yisra'EL with joy in the light of his glory with the mercy and righteousness that cometh from him.

EPISTLE OF YIRMEYAHU

6 A copy of an epistle, which YirmeYAHU sent unto them which were to be led captives into Babel by the king of the Babylonians, to certify them, as it was commanded him of ELOHIM.

2 Because of the sins which ye have committed before ELOHIM, ye shall be led away captives into Babel by Nebukad'netzar king of the Babylonians.

3 So when ye be come unto Babel, ye shall remain there many years, and for a long season, namely, seven generations: and after that I will bring you away peaceably from thence.

4 Now shall ye see in Babel elohim of silver, and of gold, and of wood, borne upon shoulders, which cause the nations to fear.

5 Beware therefore that ye in no wise be like to strangers, neither be ye and of them, when ye see the multitude before them and behind them, worshipping them.

6 But say ye in your hearts, O ADONAI, we must worship thee.

7 For mine Angel is with you, and I myself caring for your souls.

8 As for their tongue, it is polished by the workman, and they themselves are gilded and laid over with silver; yet are they but false, and cannot speak.

9 And taking gold, as it were for a virgin that loveth to go gay, they make crowns for the heads of their elohim.

10 Sometimes also the priests convey from their elohim gold and silver, and bestow it upon themselves.

11 Yea, they will give thereof to the common harlots, and deck them as men with garments, [being] elohim of silver, and elohim of gold, and wood.

12 Yet cannot these elohim save themselves from rust and moth, though they be covered with purple raiment.

13 They wipe their faces because of the dust of the temple, when there is much upon them.

14 And he that cannot put to death one that offendeth him holdeth a sceptre, as though he were a judge of the country.

15 He hath also in his right hand a dagger and an ax: but cannot deliver himself from war and thieves.

16 Whereby they are known not to be elohim: therefore fear them not.

17 For like as a vessel that a man useth is nothing worth when it is broken; even so it is with their elohim: when they be set up in the temple, their eyes be full of dust through the feet of them that come in.

18 And as the doors are made sure on every side upon him that offendeth the king, as being committed to suffer death: even so the priests make fast their temples with doors, with locks, and bars, lest their elohim be spoiled with robbers.

19 They light them candles, yea, more than for themselves, whereof they cannot see one.

20 They are as one of the beams of the temple, yet they say their hearts are gnawed upon by things creeping out of the earth; and when they eat them and their clothes, they feel it not.

21 Their faces are blacked through the smoke that cometh out of the temple.

22 Upon their bodies and heads sit bats, swallows, and birds, and the cats also.

23 By this ye may know that they are no elohim: therefore fear them not.

24 Notwithstanding the gold that is about them to make them beautiful, except they wipe off the rust, they will not shine: for neither when they were molten did they feel it.

25 The things wherein there is no breath are bought for a most high price.

26 They are borne upon shoulders, having no feet whereby they declare unto men that they be nothing worth.

27 They also that serve them are ashamed: for if they fall to the ground at any time, they cannot rise up again of themselves: neither, if one set them upright, can they move of themselves: neither, if they be bowed down, can they make themselves straight: but they set gifts before them as unto dead men.

28 As for the things that are sacrificed unto them, their priests sell and abuse; in like manner their wives lay up part thereof in salt; but unto the poor and impotent they give nothing of it.

29 Menstruous women and women in childbed eat their sacrifices: by these things ye may know that they are no elohim: fear them not.

30 For how can they be called elohim? because women set meat before the elohim of silver, gold, and wood.

31 And the priests sit in their temples, having their clothes rent, and their heads and beards shaven, and nothing upon their heads.

32 They roar and cry before their elohim, as men do at the feast when one is dead.

33 The priests also take off their garments, and clothe their wives and children.

34 Whether it be evil that one doeth unto them, or good, they are not able to recompense it: they can neither set up a king, nor put him down.

35 In like manner, they can neither give riches nor money: though a man make a vow unto them, and keep it not, they will not require it.

36 They can save no man from death, neither deliver the weak from the mighty.

37 They cannot restore a blind man to his sight, nor help any man in his distress.

38 They can shew no mercy to the widow, nor do good to the fatherless.

39 Their elohim of wood, and which are overlaid with gold and silver, are like the stones that be hewn out of the mountain: they that worship them shall be confounded.

40 How should a man then think and say that they are elohim, when even the Chaldeans themselves dishonour them?

41 Who if they shall see one dumb that cannot speak, they bring him, and intreat Bel that he may speak, as though he were able to understand.

42 Yet they cannot understand this themselves, and leave them: for they have no knowledge.

43 The women also with cords about them, sitting in the ways, burn bran for perfume: but if any of them, drawn by some that passeth by, lie with him, she reproacheth her fellow, that she was not thought as worthy as herself, nor her cord broken.

44 Whatsoever is done among them is false: how may it then be thought or said that they are elohim?

45 They are made of carpenters and goldsmiths: they can be nothing else than the workmen will have them to be.

46 And they themselves that made them can never continue long; how should then the things that are made of them be elohim?

47 For they left lies and reproaches to them that come after.

48 For when there cometh any war or plague upon them, the priests consult with themselves, where they may be hidden with them.

49 How then cannot men perceive that they be no elohim, which can neither save themselves from war, nor from plague?

50 For seeing they be but of wood, and overlaid with silver and gold, it shall be known hereafter that they are false:

51 And it shall manifestly appear to all nations and kings that they are no elohim, but the works of men's hands, and that there is no work of ELOHIM in them.

52 Who then may not know that they are no elohim?

53 For neither can they set up a king in the land, nor give rain unto men.

54 Neither can they judge their own cause, nor redress a wrong, being unable: for they are as crows between heaven and earth.

55 Whereupon when fire falleth upon the house of elohim of wood, or laid over with gold or silver, their priests will flee away, and escape; but they themselves shall be burned asunder like beams.

56 Moreover they cannot withstand any king or enemies: how can it then be thought or said that they be elohim?

57 Neither are those elohim of wood, and laid over with silver or gold, able to escape either from thieves or robbers.

58 Whose gold, and silver, and garments wherewith they are clothed, they that are strong take, and go away withal: neither are they able to help themselves.

59 Therefore it is better to be a king that sheweth his power, or else a profitable vessel in an house, which the owner shall have use of, than such false elohim; or to be a door in an house, to keep such things therein, than such false elohim. or a pillar of wood in a a palace, than such false elohim.

60 For sun, moon, and stars, being bright and sent to do their offices, are obedient.

61 In like manner the lightning when it breaketh forth is easy to be seen; and after the same manner the wind bloweth in every country.

62 And when ELOHIM commandeth the clouds to go over the whole world, they do as they are bidden.

63 And the fire sent from above to consume hills and woods doeth as it is commanded: but these are like unto them neither in shew nor power.

64 Wherefore it is neither to be supposed nor said that they are elohim, seeing, they are able neither to judge causes, nor to do good unto men.

65 Knowing therefore that they are no elohim, fear them not,

66 For they can neither curse nor bless kings:

67 Neither can they shew signs in the heavens among the heathen, nor shine as the sun, nor give light as the moon.

68 The beasts are better than they: for they can get under a cover and help themselves.

69 It is then by no means manifest unto us that they are elohim: therefore fear them not.

70 For as a scarecrow in a garden of cucumbers keepeth nothing: so are their elohim of wood, and laid over with silver and gold.

71 And likewise their elohim of wood, and laid over with silver and gold, are like to a white thorn in an orchard, that every bird sitteth upon; as also to a dead body, that is east into the dark.

72 And ye shall know them to be no elohim by the bright purple that rotteth upon then and they themselves afterward shall be eaten, and shall be a reproach in the country.

73 Better therefore is the just man that hath none idols: for he shall be far from reproach.

THE PRAYER OF
AZARIAH
ALSO CALLED THE SONG OF THE THREE HOLY CHILDREN

1 And they walked in the midst of the fire, praising ELOHIM, and blessing YAHOWAH.

2 Then AzarYAH stood up, and prayed on this manner; and opening his mouth in the midst of the fire said,

3 Blessed art thou, O YAHOWAH ELOHIM of our fathers: thy name is worthy to be praised and glorified for evermore:

4 For thou art righteous in all the things that thou hast done to us: yea, true are all thy works, thy ways are right, and all thy judgments truth.

5 In all the things that thou hast brought upon us, and upon the holy city of our fathers, even Yerushalem, thou hast executed true judgment: for according to truth and judgment didst thou bring all these things upon us because of our sins.

6 For we have sinned and committed iniquity, departing from thee.

7 In all things have we trespassed, and not obeyed thy commandments, nor kept them, neither done as thou hast commanded us, that it might go well with us.

8 Wherefore all that thou hast brought upon us, and every thing that thou hast done to us, thou hast done in true judgment.

9 And thou didst deliver us into the hands of lawless enemies, most hateful forsakers of ELOHIM, and to an unjust king, and the most wicked in all the world.

10 And now we cannot open our mouths, we are become a shame and reproach to thy servants; and to them that worship thee.

11 Yet deliver us not up wholly, for thy name's sake, neither disannul thou thy covenant:

12 And cause not thy mercy to depart from us, for thy beloved Abraham's sake, for thy servant Yitzkhaq's sake, and for thy holy Yisra'EL's sake;

13 To whom thou hast spoken and promised, that thou wouldest multiply their seed as the stars of heaven, and as the sand that lieth upon the seashore.

14 For we, O YAHOWAH, are become less than any nation, and be kept under this day in all the world because of our sins.

15 Neither is there at this time prince, or prophet, or leader, or burnt offering, or sacrifice, or oblation, or incense, or place to sacrifice before thee, and to find mercy.

16 Nevertheless in a contrite heart and an humble ruakh let us be accepted.

17 Like as in the burnt offerings of rams and bullocks, and like as in ten thousands of fat lambs: so let our sacrifice be in thy sight this day, and grant that we may wholly go after thee: for they shall not be confounded that put their trust in thee.

18 And now we follow thee with all our heart, we fear thee, and seek thy face.

19 Put us not to shame: but deal with us after thy lovingkindness, and according to the multitude of thy mercies.

20 Deliver us also according to thy marvellous works, and give glory to thy name, O YAHOWAH: and let all them that do thy servants hurt be ashamed;

21 And let them be confounded in all their power and might, and let their strength be broken;

22 And let them know that thou art ELOHIM, the only ELOHIM, and glorious over the whole world.

23 And the king's servants, that put them in, ceased not to make the oven hot with rosin, pitch, tow, and small wood;

24 So that the flame streamed forth above the furnace forty and nine cubits.

25 And it passed through, and burned those Chaldeans it found about the furnace.

26 But the Angel of YAHOWAH came down into the oven together with AzarYAH and his fellows, and smote the flame of the fire out of the oven;

27 And made the midst of the furnace as it had been a moist whistling wind, so that the fire touched them not at all, neither hurt nor troubled them.

28 Then the three, as out of one mouth, praised, glorified, and blessed, ELOHIM in the furnace, saying,

29 Blessed art thou, O YAHOWAH ELOHIM of our fathers: and to be praised and exalted above all for ever.

30 And blessed is thy glorious and holy name: and to be praised and exalted above all for ever.

31 Blessed art thou in the temple of thine holy glory: and to be praised and glorified above all for ever.

32 Blessed art thou that beholdest the depths, and sittest upon the Kerubim: and to be praised and exalted above all for ever.

33 Blessed art thou on the glorious throne of thy kingdom: and to be praised and glorified above all for ever.

34 Blessed art thou in the firmament of heaven: and above all to be praised and glorified for ever.

35 O all ye works of YAHOWAH, bless ye YAHOWAH: praise and exalt him above all for ever,

36 O ye heavens, bless ye YAHOWAH: praise and exalt him above all for ever.

37 O ye angels of YAHOWAH, bless ye YAHOWAH: praise and exalt him above all for ever.

38 O all ye waters that be above the heaven, bless ye YAHOWAH: praise and exalt him above all for ever.

39 O all ye powers of YAHOWAH, bless ye YAHOWAH: praise and exalt him above all for ever.

40 O ye sun and moon, bless ye YAHOWAH: praise and exalt him above all for ever.

41 O ye stars of heaven, bless ye YAHOWAH: praise and exalt him above all for ever.

42 O every shower and dew, bless ye YAHOWAH: praise and exalt him above all for ever.

43 O all ye winds, bless ye YAHOWAH: praise and exalt him above all for ever,

44 O ye fire and heat, bless ye YAHOWAH: praise and exalt him above all for ever.

45 O ye winter and summer, bless ye YAHOWAH: praise and exalt him above all for ever.

46 O ye dews and storms of snow, bless ye YAHOWAH: praise and exalt him above all for ever.

47 O ye nights and days, bless ye YAHOWAH: bless and exalt him above all for ever.

48 O ye light and darkness, bless ye YAHOWAH: praise and exalt him above all for ever.

49 O ye ice and cold, bless ye YAHOWAH: praise and exalt him above all for ever.

50 O ye frost and snow, bless ye YAHOWAH: praise and exalt him above all for ever.

51 O ye lightnings and clouds, bless ye YAHOWAH: praise and exalt him above all for ever.

52 O let the earth bless YAHOWAH: praise and exalt him above all for ever.

53 O ye mountains and little hills, bless ye YAHOWAH: praise and exalt him above all for ever.

54 O all ye things that grow in the earth, bless ye YAHOWAH: praise and exalt him above all for ever.

55 O ye mountains, bless ye YAHOWAH: Praise and exalt him above all for ever.

56 O ye seas and rivers, bless ye YAHOWAH: praise and exalt him above all for ever.

57 O ye whales, and all that move in the waters, bless ye YAHOWAH: praise and exalt him above all for ever.

58 O all ye fowls of the air, bless ye YAHOWAH: praise and exalt him above all for ever.

59 O all ye beasts and cattle, bless ye YAHOWAH: praise and exalt him above all for ever.

60 O ye children of men, bless ye YAHOWAH: praise and exalt him above all for ever.

61 O Yisra'EL, bless ye YAHOWAH: praise and exalt him above all for ever.

62 O ye priests of YAHOWAH, bless ye YAHOWAH: praise and exalt him above all for ever.

63 O ye servants of YAHOWAH, bless ye YAHOWAH: praise and exalt him above all for ever.

64 O ye spirits and souls of the righteous, bless ye YAHOWAH: praise and exalt him above all for ever.

65 O ye holy and humble men of heart, bless ye YAHOWAH: praise and exalt him above all for ever.

66 O KhananYAH, AzarYAH, and Misha'EL, bless ye YAHOWAH: praise and exalt him above all for ever: far he hath delivered us from hell, and saved us from the hand of death, and delivered us out of the midst of the furnace and burning flame: even out of the midst of the fire hath he delivered us.

67 O give thanks unto YAHOWAH, because he is gracious: for his mercy endureth for ever.

68 O all ye that worship YAHOWAH, bless the ELOHIM of elohim, praise him, and give him thanks: for his mercy endureth for ever.

THE HISTORY OF
SUSANNA
ALSO CALLED SHOSHANNAH

Set apart from the beginning of Dani'EL, because it is not in the Hebrew, as neither the Narration of Bel and the Dragon.

1 There dwelt a man in Babel, called Yaho'yaqim:
2 And he took a wife, whose name was Shoshannah (Susanna), the daughter of KhilqiYAHU, a very fair woman, and one that feared YAHOWAH.
3 Her parents also were righteous, and taught their daughter according to the Torah of Mosheh.
4 Now Yaho'yaqim was a great rich man, and had a fair garden joining unto his house: and to him resorted the Yehudim; because he was more honourable than all others.
5 The same year were appointed two of the ancients of the people to be judges, such as YAHOWAH spake of, that wickedness came from Babel from ancient judges, who seemed to govern the people.
6 These kept much at Yaho'yaqim's house: and all that had any suits in law came unto them.
7 Now when the people departed away at noon, Shoshannah went into her husband's garden to walk.
8 And the two elders saw her going in every day, and walking; so that their lust was inflamed toward her.
9 And they perverted their own mind, and turned away their eyes, that they might not look unto heaven, nor remember just judgments.
10 And albeit they both were wounded with her love, yet durst not one shew another his grief.
11 For they were ashamed to declare their lust, that they desired to have to do with her.
12 Yet they watched diligently from day to day to see her.
13 And the one said to the other, Let us now go home: for it is dinner time.
14 So when they were gone out, they parted the one from the other, and turning back again they came to the same place; and after that they had asked one another the cause, they acknowledged their lust: then appointed they a time both together, when they might find her alone.
15 And it fell out, as they watched a fit time, she went in as before with two maids only, and she was desirous to wash herself in the garden: for it was hot.
16 And there was no body there save the two elders, that had hid themselves, and watched her.
17 Then she said to her maids, Bring me oil and washing balls, and shut the garden doors, that I may wash me.

18 And they did as she bade them, and shut the garden doors, and went out themselves at privy doors to fetch the things that she had commanded them: but they saw not the elders, because they were hid.
19 Now when the maids were gone forth, the two elders rose up, and ran unto her, saying,
20 Behold, the garden doors are shut, that no man can see us, and we are in love with thee; therefore consent unto us, and lie with us.
21 If thou wilt not, we will bear witness against thee, that a young man was with thee: and therefore thou didst send away thy maids from thee.
22 Then Shoshannah sighed, and said, I am straitened on every side: for if I do this thing, it is death unto me: and if I do it not I cannot escape your hands.
23 It is better for me to fall into your hands, and not do it, than to sin in the sight of YAHOWAH.
24 With that Shoshannah cried with a loud voice: and the two elders cried out against her.
25 Then ran the one, and opened the garden door.
26 So when the servants of the house heard the cry in the garden, they rushed in at the privy door, to see what was done unto her.
27 But when the elders had declared their matter, the servants were greatly ashamed: for there was never such a report made of Shoshannah.
28 And it came to pass the next day, when the people were assembled to her husband Yaho'yaqim, the two elders came also full of mischievous imagination against Shoshannah to put her to death;
29 And said before the people, Send for Shoshannah, the daughter of KhilqiYAHU, Yaho'yaqim's wife. And so they sent.
30 So she came with her father and mother, her children, and all her kindred.
31 Now Shoshannah was a very delicate woman, and beauteous to behold.
32 And these wicked men commanded to uncover her face, (for she was covered) that they might be filled with her beauty.
33 Therefore her friends and all that saw her wept.
34 Then the two elders stood up in the midst of the people, and laid their hands upon her head.
35 And she weeping looked up toward heaven: for her heart trusted in YAHOWAH.
36 And the elders said, As we walked in the garden alone, this woman came in with two maids, and shut the garden doors, and sent the maids away.
37 Then a young man, who there was hid, came unto her, and lay with her.
38 Then we that stood in a corner of the garden, seeing this wickedness, ran unto them.

39 And when we saw them together, the man we could not hold: for he was stronger than we, and opened the door, and leaped out.

40 But having taken this woman, we asked who the young man was, but she would not tell us: these things do we testify.

41 Then the assembly believed them as those that were the elders and judges of the people: so they condemned her to death.

42 Then Shoshannah cried out with a loud voice, and said, O everlasting ELOHIM, that knowest the secrets, and knowest all things before they be:

43 Thou knowest that they have borne false witness against me, and, behold, I must die; whereas I never did such things as these men have maliciously invented against me.

44 And YAHOWAH heard her voice.

45 Therefore when she was led to be put to death, YAHOWAH gave the RUAKH HA QODESH upon a young youth whose name was Dani'EL:

46 Who cried with a loud voice, I am clear from the blood of this woman.

47 Then all the people turned them toward him, and said, What mean these words that thou hast spoken?

48 So he standing in the midst of them said, Are ye such fools, ye sons of Yisra'EL, that without examination or knowledge of the truth ye have condemned a daughter of Yisra'EL?

49 Return again to the place of judgment: for they have borne false witness against her.

50 Wherefore all the people turned again in haste, and the elders said unto him, Come, sit down among us, and shew it us, seeing ELOHIM hath given thee the honour of an elder.

51 Then said Dani'EL unto them, Put these two aside one far from another, and I will examine them.

52 So when they were put asunder one from another, he called one of them, and said unto him, O thou that art waxen old in wickedness, now thy sins which thou hast committed aforetime are come to light.

53 For thou hast pronounced false judgment and hast condemned the innocent and hast let the guilty go free; albeit YAHOWAH saith, The innocent and righteous shalt thou not slay.

54 Now then, if thou hast seen her, tell me, Under what tree sawest thou them companying together? Who answered, Under a mastick tree.

55 And Dani'EL said, Very well; thou hast lied against thine own head; for even now the Angel of ELOHIM hath received the sentence of ELOHIM to cut thee in two.

56 So he put him aside, and commanded to bring the other, and said unto him, O thou seed of Kena'an, and not of Yehudah, beauty hath deceived thee, and lust hath perverted thine heart.

57 Thus have ye dealt with the daughters of Yisra'EL, and they for fear companied with you: but the daughter of Yehudah would not abide your wickedness.

58 Now therefore tell me, Under what tree didst thou take them companying together? Who answered, Under an holm tree.

59 Then said Dani'EL unto him, Well; thou hast also lied against thine own head: for the Angel of YAHOWAH waiteth with the sword to cut thee in two, that he may destroy you.

60 With that all the assembly cried out with a loud voice, and praised ELOHIM, who saveth them that trust in him.

61 And they arose against the two elders, for Dani'EL had convicted them of false witness by their own mouth:

62 And according to the Torah of Mosheh they did unto them in such sort as they maliciously intended to do to their neighbour: and they put them to death. Thus the innocent blood was saved the same day.

63 Therefore KhilqiYAHU and his wife praised ELOHIM for their daughter Shoshannah, with Yaho'yaqim her husband, and all the kindred, because there was no dishonesty found in her.

64 From that day forth was Dani'EL had in great reputation in the sight of the people.

BEL and the DRAGON

The History of the Destruction of Bel and the Dragon, Cut off from the end of Dani'EL.

1 And king Astyages was gathered to his fathers, and Korash of Paras received his kingdom.

2 And Dani'EL conversed with the king, and was honoured above all his friends.

3 Now the Babylonians had an idol, called Bel, and there were spent upon him every day twelve great measures of fine flour, and forty sheep, and six vessels of wine.

4 And the king worshipped it and went daily to adore it: but Dani'EL worshipped YAHOWAH. And the king said unto him, Why dost not thou worship Bel?

5 Who answered and said, Because I may not worship idols made with hands, but the YAHOWAH ELOHIM, who hath created the heaven and the earth, and is Adone over all flesh.

6 Then said the king unto him, Thinkest thou not that Bel is a living ELOHIM? seest thou not how much he eateth and drinketh every day?

7 Then Dani'EL smiled, and said, O king, be not deceived: for this is but clay within, and brass without, and did never eat or drink any thing. But I swear that YAHOWAH is ELOHIM OF ELOHIMS.

8 So the king was wroth, and called for his priests, and said unto them, If ye tell me not who this is that devoureth these expences, ye shall die.

9 But if ye can certify me that Bel devoureth them, then Dani'EL shall die: for he hath spoken blasphemy against Bel. And Dani'EL said unto the king, Let it be according to thy word.

10 Now the priests of Bel were threescore and ten, beside their wives and children. And the king went with Dani'EL into the temple of Bel.

11 So Bel's priests said, Lo, we go out: but thou, O king, set on the meat, and make ready the wine, and shut the door fast and seal it with thine own signet;

12 And to morrow when thou comest in, if thou findest not that Bel hath eaten up all, we will suffer death: or else Dani'EL, that speaketh falsely against us.

13 And they little regarded it: for under the table they had made a privy entrance, whereby they entered in continually, and consumed those things.

14 So when they were gone forth, the king set meats before Bel. Now Dani'EL had commanded his servants to bring ashes, and those they strewed throughout all the temple in the presence of the king alone: then went they out, and shut the door, and sealed it with the king's signet, and so departed.

15 Now in the night came the priests with their wives and children, as they were wont to do, and did eat and drink up all.

16 In the morning betime the king arose, and Dani'EL with him.

17 And the king said, Dani'EL, are the seals whole? And he said, Yea, O king, they be whole.

18 And as soon as he had opened the door, the king looked upon the table, and cried with a loud voice, Great art thou, O Bel, and with thee is no deceit at all.

19 Then laughed Dani'EL, and held the king that he should not go in, and said, Behold now the pavement, and mark well whose footsteps are these.

20 And the king said, I see the footsteps of men, women, and children. And then the king was angry,

21 And took the priests with their wives and children, who shewed him the privy doors, where they came in, and consumed such things as were upon the table.

22 Therefore the king slew them, and delivered Bel into Dani'EL's power, who destroyed him and his temple.

23 And in that same place there was a great dragon, which they of Babel worshipped.

24 And the king said unto Dani'EL, Wilt thou also say that this is of brass? lo, he liveth, he eateth and drinketh; thou canst not say that he is no living elohim: therefore worship him.

25 Then said Dani'EL unto the king, I will worship YAHOWAH my ELOHIM: for he is the living ELOHIM.

26 But give me leave, O king, and I shall slay this dragon without sword or staff. The king said, I give thee leave.

27 Then Dani'EL took pitch, and fat, and hair, and did seethe them together, and made lumps thereof: this he put in the dragon's mouth, and so the dragon burst in sunder : and Dani'EL said, Lo, these are the elohim ye worship.

28 When they of Babel heard that, they took great indignation, and conspired against the king, saying, The king is become a Yehudi, and he hath destroyed Bel, he hath slain the dragon, and put the priests to death.

29 So they came to the king, and said, Deliver us Dani'EL, or else we will destroy thee and thine house.

30 Now when the king saw that they pressed him sore, being constrained, he delivered Dani'EL unto them:

31 Who cast him into the lions' den: where he was six days.

32 And in the den there were seven lions, and they had given them every day two carcases, and two sheep: which then were not given to them, to the intent they might devour Dani'EL.

33 Now there was in Yehudah a prophet, called Khabaquq (Habakkuk), who had made pottage, and had broken bread in a bowl, and was going into the field, for to bring it to the reapers.

34 But the Angel of YAHOWAH said unto Khabaquq, Go, carry the dinner that thou hast into Babel unto

Dani'EL, who is in the lions' den.

35 And Khabaquq said, YAHOWAH, I never saw Babel; neither do I know where the den is.

36 Then the Angel of YAHOWAH took him by the crown, and bare him by the hair of his head, and through the vehemency of his RUAKH set him in Babel over the den.

37 And Khabaquq cried, saying, O Dani'EL, Dani'EL, take the dinner which YAHOWAH ELOHIM hath sent thee.

38 And Dani'EL said, Thou hast remembered me, O YAHOWAH ELOHIM: neither hast thou forsaken them that seek thee and love thee.

39 So Dani'EL arose, and did eat: and the Angel of YAHOWAH set Khabaquq in his own place again immediately. And YAHOWAH remembered Dani'EL.

40 Upon the seventh day the king went to bewail Dani'EL: and when he came to the den, he looked in, and behold, Dani'EL was sitting.

41 Then cried the king with a loud voice, saying, Great art YAHOWAH ELOHIM of Dani'EL, and there is none other beside thee.

42 And he drew him out, and cast those that were the cause of his destruction into the den: and they were devoured in a moment before his face.

THE PRAYER OF
MANASSEH

1 O YAHOWAH, Almighty ELOHIM of our fathers, Abraham, Yitzkhaq, and Ya'aqob, and of their righteous seed;

2 Who hast made heaven and earth, with all the ornament thereof;

3 Who hast bound the sea by the word of thy commandment; who hast shut up the deep, and sealed it by thy terrible and glorious name;

4 Whom all men fear, and tremble before thy power;

5 For the majesty of thy glory cannot be borne, and thine angry threatening toward sinners is importable:

6 But thy merciful promise is unmeasurable and unsearchable;

7 For thou art the Most High YAHOWAH, of great compassion, longsuffering, very merciful, and repentest of the evils of men. Thou, O YAHOWAH, according to thy great goodness hast promised repentance and forgiveness to them that have sinned against thee: and of thine infinite mercies hast appointed repentance unto sinners, that they may be saved.

8 Thou therefore, O YAHOWAH, that art the ELOHIM of the just, hast not appointed repentance to the just, as to Abraham, and Yitzkhaq, and Ya'aqob, which have not sinned against thee; but thou hast appointed repentance unto me that am a sinner:

9 For I have sinned above the number of the sands of the sea. My transgressions, O YAHOWAH, are multiplied: my transgressions are multiplied, and I am not worthy to behold and see the height of heaven for the multitude of mine iniquities.

10 I am bowed down with many iron bands, that I cannot life up mine head, neither have any release: for I have provoked thy wrath, and done evil before thee: I did not thy will, neither kept I thy commandments: I have set up abominations, and have multiplied offences.

11 Now therefore I bow the knee of mine heart, beseeching thee of grace. I have sinned, O YAHOWAH,

12 I have sinned, and I acknowledge mine iniquities:

13 Wherefore, I humbly beseech thee, forgive me, O YAHOWAH, forgive me, and destroy me not with mine iniquites. Be not angry with me for ever, by reserving evil for me; neither condemn me to the lower parts of the earth. For thou art YAHOWAH, even the ELOHIM of them that repent;

14 And in me thou wilt shew all thy goodness: for thou wilt save me, that am unworthy, according to thy great mercy.

15 Therefore I will praise thee for ever all the days of my life: for all the powers of the heavens do praise thee, and thine YAHOWAH is the glory for ever and ever. Amen.

 # Being A HEBREW Israelite

By YaqarYah Yisrael

When you call yourself a HEBREW Israelite, what does that mean? Some say that being a HEBREW Israelite means being the chosen people of the bible. That's only half correct. The other half of being a HEBREW Israelite is knowing HEBREW. Hence the name HEBREW Israelite.

WAIT! HOLD UP!

So you mean we actually should learn HEBREW to be a HEBREW Israelite? HEBREW is a part of our culture. It always has been and always will be. Culture is based on symbols. A symbol is something that stands for something else. Symbols vary cross-culturally and are arbitrary. They only have meaning when people in a culture agree on their use. Language, money, and art are all symbols. Language is the most important symbolic component of culture.

Another definition of culture refers to the pattern of human movement and the symbols that give importance to them. Culture displays itself in the forms of art, literature, clothing, customs, language, and religion.

The Only Reason We Do Not Speak Hebrew Now Is...

We don't speak Hebrew now because it was beaten out of us during slavery. Now most of us speak English. English was never our language. It does not even make sense. It is very inconsistent and full of contradictions. For example, some letters have more than one sound. Some letters have a sound but are silent at random. There are words that are spelled the same but are pronounced differently. There's all types of insanity and instability in the English language, so why cleave to it?

Now It Is Time To Be Reborn!

It is time to bring Yah back into our lives because without Him, we have NO understanding of HEBREW. YAHOWAH, by His RUAKH HA' QODESH (HOLY SPIRIT) reveals all.
If you do not have YAHOWAH. you'll only have a basic understanding of HEBREW, and you'll never grow into more spiritual understandings because it is Yah's language. Anyone can learn HEBREW. Even the devil himself can know HEBREW, but Yah is the one who provides spiritually deeper understandings.

YAHOWAH is The NAME of THE MOST HIGH ELOHIM (GOD) given to the Children of Israel. It is pronounced YA-HO-WAH. His Name means:

HE WAS – HE IS – HE WILL BE
OR
"ETERNAL ONE"

The full revelation of His Set Apart Name is given in the book of Revelation. "Revelation" means to: reveal. Besides revealing His physical appearance (hair like pure wool and feet and skin like unto burnt brass - Rev 1:14-15), The Most High also reveals the mystery of His Name: HE WAS - HE IS -HE WILL BE.

Revelations 1:4
"Yokhanan to the seven Assemblies which are in Asia: Grace be unto you, and shalom, from him WHICH IS, AND WHICH WAS AND WHICH IS TO COME..."

This Scripture reveals YAHOWAH'S Eternal Nature of simultaneously existing within The Past, Present and Future. YAHOWAH'S Name is derived from the Hebrew verb: HAYAH (Strongs H1961).

HAYAH = היה

HAYAH in Hebrew means: "He Was" (past tense). To say "He Is" (present tense) in Hebrew is the word: HOWEH

HOWEH = הוה

Finally, to say "He Will Be" (future tense) in Hebrew is the word: YIHYEH

YIHYEH = יהיה

When The Past, The Present and The Future Are ONE...

When The Eternal Nature of The Most High (Past, Present and Future) are united we have:

YAHOWAH (HAYAH, HOWEH, YIHYEH)

$$\text{יהוה} = \text{היה} + \text{הוה} + \text{יהיה}$$

This Devine Mystery is Revealed 3 More Times...

REVELATION 1:8
"I am Aleph and Taw, saith YAHOWAH, **WHICH IS, AND WHICH WAS AND WHICH IS TO COME**, the Almighty."

REVELATION 4:8
"And the four beasts had each of them six wings about him; and they were full of eyes within: and they rest not day and night, saying, Holy, holy, holy, YAHOWAH ELOHIM Almighty, **WHICH WAS, AND IS, AND IS TO COME**."

REVELATION 11:17
"Saying, We give thee thanks, O YAHOWAH ELOHIM Almighty, **WHICH ART, AND WAST, AND ART TO COME**; because thou hast taken to thee thy great power, and hast reigned.."

Only by understanding the HEBREW language can we receive the full revelation to unlock the SCRIPTURES and the true meaning of YAHOWAH'S NAME!

THE FIRST BOOK OF
MACCABEES

1 And it happened, after that **Aleksandros (Alexander)** son of **Philipos (Philip)**, the Macedonian, who came out of the land of Kittim, had smitten Daryawesh king of the Persians and Medes, that he reigned in his stead, the first over Yawan,

2 And made many wars, and won many strong holds, and slew the kings of the earth,

3 And went through to the ends of the earth, and took spoils of many nations, insomuch that the earth was quiet before him; whereupon he was exalted and his heart was lifted up.

4 And he gathered a mighty strong host and ruled over countries, and nations, and kings, who became tributaries unto him.

5 And after these things he fell sick, and perceived that he should die.

6 Wherefore he called his servants, such as were honourable, and had been brought up with him from his youth, and parted his kingdom among them, while he was yet alive.

7 So Aleksandros reigned twelves years, and then died.

8 And his servants bare rule every one in his place.

9 And after his death they all put crowns upon themselves; so did their sons after them many years: and evils were multiplied in the earth.

10 And there came out of them a wicked root Antiokos surnamed **Ha-Mepho'ar (Epiphanes)**, son of Antiokos the king, who had been an hostage at Rome, and he reigned in the hundred and thirty and seventh year of the kingdom of the Greeks.

11 In those days went there out of Yisra'EL wicked men, who persuaded many, saying, Let us go and make a covenant with the heathen that are round about us: for since we departed from them we have had much sorrow.

12 So this device pleased them well.

13 Then certain of the people were so forward herein, that they went to the king, who gave them licence to do after the ordinances of the heathen:

14 Whereupon they built a place of exercise at Yerushalem according to the customs of the heathen:

15 And made themselves uncircumcised, and forsook the holy covenant, and joined themselves to the heathen, and were sold to do mischief in the eyes of YAHOWAH.

16 Now when the kingdom was established before Antiokos, he thought to reign over Mitzraim that he might have the dominion of two realms.

17 Wherefore he entered into Mitzraim with a great multitude, with chariots, and elephants, and horsemen, and a great navy,

18 And made war against **Talmay (Ptolomy)** king of Mitzraim: but Talmay was afraid of him, and fled; and many were wounded to death.

19 Thus they got the strong cities in the land of Mitzraim and he took the spoils thereof.

20 And after that Antiokos had smitten Mitzraim, he returned again in the hundred forty and third year, and went up against Yisra'EL and Yerushalem with a great multitude,

21 And entered proudly into the sanctuary, and took away the golden altar, and the menorah of light, and all the vessels thereof,

22 And the table of the shewbread, and the pouring vessels, and the vials. and the censers of gold, and the veil, and the crown, and the golden ornaments that were before the temple, all which he pulled off.

23 He took also the silver and the gold, and the precious vessels: also he took the hidden treasures which he found.

24 And when he had taken all away, he went into his own land, having made a great massacre, and spoken very proudly.

25 Therefore there was a great mourning in Yisra'EL, in every place where they were;

26 So that the princes and elders mourned, the virgins and young men were made feeble, and the beauty of women was changed.

27 Every bridegroom took up lamentation, and she that sat in the marriage chamber was in heaviness,

28 The land also was moved for the inhabitants thereof, and all the house of Ya'aqob was covered with confusion.

29 And after two years fully expired the king sent his chief collector of tribute unto the cities of Yehudah, who came unto Yerushalem with a great multitude,

30 And spake peaceable words unto them, but all was deceit: for when they had given him credence, he fell suddenly upon the city, and smote it very sore, and destroyed much people of Yisra'EL.

31 And when he had taken the spoils of the city, he set it on fire, and pulled down the houses and walls thereof on every side.

32 But the women and children took they captive, and possessed the cattle.

33 Then builded they the city of Dawid with a great and strong wall, and with mighty towers, and made it a strong hold for them.

34 And they put therein a sinful nation, wicked men, and fortified themselves therein.

35 They stored it also with armour and victuals, and when they had gathered together the spoils of Yerushalem, they laid them up there, and so they became a sore snare:

36 For it was a place to lie in wait against the sanctuary of YAHOWAH, and an evil adversary to Yisra'EL.

37 Thus they shed innocent blood on every side of the sanctuary, and defiled it:

38 Insomuch that the inhabitants of Yerushalem fled because of them: whereupon the city was made an habitation of strangers, and became strange to those that were born in her; and her own children left her.

39 Her sanctuary was laid waste like a wilderness, her feasts were turned into mourning, her Shabbats into reproach her honour into contempt.

40 As had been her glory, so was her dishonour increased, and her excellency was turned into mourning.

41 Moreover king Antiokos wrote to his whole kingdom, that all should be one people,

42 And every one should leave his Torah: so all the heathen agreed according to the commandment of the king.

43 Yea, many also of the children of Yisra'EL consented to his customs, and sacrificed unto idols, and profaned the Shabbat.

44 For the king had sent letters by messengers unto Yerushalem and the cities of Yehudah that they should follow the strange Torah of the land,

45 And forbid burnt offerings, and sacrifice, and drink offerings, in the temple; and that they should profane the Shabbats and festival days:

46 And pollute the sanctuary and holy people:

47 Set up altars, and groves, and chapels of idols, and sacrifice swine's flesh, and unclean beasts:

48 That they should also leave their children uncircumcised, and make their souls abominable with all manner of uncleanness and profanation:

49 To the end they might forget the Torah, and change all the ordinances.

50 And whosoever would not do according to the commandment of the king, he said, he should die.

51 In the selfsame manner wrote he to his whole kingdom, and appointed overseers over all the people, commanding the cities of Yehudah to sacrifice, city by city.

52 Then many of the people were gathered unto them, to wit every one that forsook the Torah; and so they committed evils in the land;

53 And drove the children of Yisra'EL into secret places, even wheresoever they could flee for succour.

54 Now the fifteenth day of the month Kislew, in the hundred forty and fifth year, they set up the abomination of desolation upon the altar of YAHOWAH, and builded idol altars throughout the cities of Yehudah on every side;

55 And burnt incense at the doors of their houses, and in the streets.

56 And when they had rent in pieces the books of the Torah of YAHOWAH which they found, they burnt them with fire.

57 And whosoever was found with any the book of the covenant of YAHOWAH, or if any committed to the Torah, the king's commandment was, that they should put him to death.

58 Thus did they by their authority unto the children of Yisra'EL every month, to as many as were found in the cities.

59 Now the five and twentieth day of the month they did sacrifice upon the idol altar, which was upon the altar of YAHOWAH.

60 At which time according to the commandment they put to death certain women, that had caused their children to be circumcised.

61 And they hanged the infants about their necks, and rifled their houses, and slew them that had circumcised them.

62 Howbeit many in Yisra'EL were fully resolved in the Torah of YAHOWAH and confirmed in themselves not to eat any unclean thing.

63 Wherefore the rather to die, that they might not be defiled with meats, and that they might not profane the covenant of YAHOWAH: so then they died.

64 And there was very great wrath upon Yisra'EL.

2 In those days arose MattitYAHU the son of Yokhanan, the son of Shimon, a priest of the sons of Yaho'yariv, from Yerushalem, and dwelt in mount Modin.

2 And he had five sons, Yokhanan, called Qadshi:

3 Shimon; called Tassi:

4 Yehudah, who was called Makabi:

5 Eleazar, called Khorani: and Yahonathan, whose surname was Hophsi.

6 And when he saw the blasphemies that were committed in Yehudah and Yerushalem,

7 He said, Woe is me! wherefore was I born to see this misery of my people, and of the holy city, and to dwell there, when it was delivered into the hand of the enemy, and the sanctuary into the hand of strangers?

8 Her temple is become as a man without glory.

9 Her glorious vessels are carried away into captivity, her infants are slain in the streets, her young men with the sword of the enemy.

10 What nation hath not had a part in her kingdom and gotten of her spoils?

11 All her ornaments are taken away; of a free woman she is become a bondslave.

12 And, behold, our sanctuary, even our beauty and our glory, is laid waste, and the Gentiles have profaned it.

13 To what end therefore shall we live any longer?

14 Then MattitYAHU and his sons rent their clothes, and put on sackcloth, and mourned very sore.

15 In the mean while the king's officers, such as compelled the people to transgress the Torah of YAHOWAH, came into the city Modin, to make them sacrifice.

16 And when many of Yisra'EL came unto them, MattitYAHU also and his sons came together.

17 Then answered the king's officers, and said to MattitYAHU on this wise, Thou art a ruler, and an honourable and great man in this city, and strengthened with sons and brethren:

1 MACCABEES

18 Now therefore come thou first, and fulfil the king's commandment, like as all the heathen have done, yea, and the men of Yehudah also, and such as remain at Yerushalem: so shalt thou and thy house be in the number of the king's friends, and thou and thy children shall be honoured with silver and gold, and many rewards.

19 Then MattitYAHU answered and spake with a loud voice, Though all the Gentiles that are under the king's dominion obey him, and fall away every one from the customs of their fathers, and give consent to his commandments:

20 Yet will I and my sons and my brethren walk in the covenant of our fathers.

21 ELOHIM forbid that we should forsake the commandments of YAHOWAH our ELOHIM and for us to break his covenant.

22 We will not hearken to the king's words, to go from our customs, either on the right hand, or the left.

23 Now when he had left speaking these words, there came one of the children of Yisra'EL in the sight of all to sacrifice on the altar which was at Modin, according to the king's commandment.

24 Which thing when MattitYAHU saw, he was inflamed with zeal, and his reins trembled, neither could he forbear to shew his anger according to judgment: wherefore he ran, and slew him upon the altar.

25 Also the king's commissioner, who compelled men to sacrifice, he killed at that time, and the altar he pulled down.

26 Thus dealt he zealously for the Torah of ELOHIM like as Pinkhas did unto Zimri the son of Salu.

27 And MattitYAHU cried throughout the city with a loud voice, saying, Whosoever is zealous of the Torah, and maintaineth the covenant, let him follow me.

28 So he and his sons fled into the mountains, and left all that ever they had in the city.

29 Then many that sought after the Torah of YAHOWAH in their hearts went down into the wilderness, to dwell there:

30 Both they, and their children, and their wives; and their cattle; because afflictions increased sore upon them.

31 Now when it was told the king's servants, and the host that was at Yerushalem, in the city of Dawid, that certain men, who had broken the king's commandment, were gone down into the secret places in the wilderness,

32 They pursued after them a great number, and having overtaken them, they camped against them, and made war against them on the Shabbat day.

33 And they said unto them, Let that which ye have done hitherto suffice; come forth, and do according to the commandment of the king, and ye shall live.

34 But they said, We will not come forth, neither will we do the king's command-

ment, to profane the Shabbat day.

35 So then they gave them the battle with all speed.

36 Howbeit they answered them not, neither cast they a stone at them, nor stopped the places where they lay hid;

37 But said, Let us die all in our innocency: heaven and earth will testify for us, that ye put us to death wrongfully.

38 So they rose up against them in battle on the Shabbat, and they slew them, with their wives and children and their cattle, to the number of a thousand people.

39 Now when MattitYAHU and his friends understood hereof, they mourned for them right sore.

40 And one of them said to another, If we all do as our brethren have done, and fight not for our lives and Torah against the heathen, they will now quickly root us out of the earth.

41 At that time therefore they decreed, saying, Whosoever shall come to make battle with us on the Shabbat day, we will fight against him; neither will we die all, as our brethren that were murdered im the secret places.

42 Then came there unto him a company of Khasidim of the sons of Yisra'EL, which feared YAHOWAH in their hearts, who were mighty men, even all such as were voluntarily devoted unto the Torah.

43 Also all they that fled for persecution joined themselves unto them, and were a stay unto them.

44 So they joined their forces, and smote sinful men in their anger, and wicked men in their wrath: but the rest fled to the heathen for succour.

45 Then MattitYAHU and his friends went round about, and pulled down the altars:

46 And what children soever they found within the coast of Yisra'EL uncircumcised, those they circumcised valiantly.

47 They pursued also after the proud men, and the work prospered in their hand.

48 So they recovered the Torah out of the hand of the Gentiles, and out of the hand of kings, neither suffered they the sinner to triumph.

49 Now when the time drew near that MattitYAHU should die, he said unto his sons, Now hath pride and rebuke gotten strength, and the time of destruction, and the wrath of indignation:

50 Now therefore, my sons, be ye zealous for the Torah, and give your lives for the covenant of your fathers.

51 Call to remembrance what acts our fathers did in their time; so shall ye receive great honour and an everlasting name.

52 Was not Abraham found faithful in temptation, and it was imputed unto him for righteousness?

53 Yoseph in the time of his distress kept the commandment and was made Adon of Mitzraim.

54 Pinkhas our father in being zealous and fervent obtained the covenant of an everlasting priesthood.

55 Yahoshua for fulfilling the word was made a judge in Yisra'EL.

56 Kalaeb for bearing witness before the congregation received the heritage of the land.

57 Dawid for being merciful possessed the throne of an everlasting kingdom.

58 EliYAHU for being zealous and fervent for the Torah was taken up into heaven.

59 KhananYAH, AzarYAH, and Misha'EL, by believing were saved out of the flame.

60 Dani'EL for his innocency was delivered from the mouth of lions.

61 And thus consider ye throughout all ages, that none that put their trust in him shall be overcome.

62 Fear not then the words of a sinful man: for his glory shall be dung and worms.

63 To day he shall be lifted up and to morrow he shall not be found, because he is returned into his dust, and his thought is come to nothing.

64 Wherefore, ye my sons, be valiant and shew yourselves men in the behalf of the Torah; for by it shall ye obtain glory.

65 And behold, I know that your brother Shimon is a man of counsel, give ear unto him alway: he shall be a father unto you.

66 As for Yehudah Makabi, he hath been mighty and strong, even from his youth up: let him be your captain, and fight the battle of the people.

67 Take also unto you all those that observe the Torah, and avenge ye the wrong of your people.

68 Recompense fully the heathen, and take heed to the commandments of the Torah.

69 So he blessed them, and was gathered to his fathers.

70 And he died in the hundred forty and sixth year, and his sons buried him in the sepulchres of his fathers at Modin, and all Yisra'EL made great lamentation for him.

3 Then his son Yehudah, called Makabi, rose up in his stead.

2 And all his brethren helped him, and so did all they that held with his father, and they fought with cheerfulness the battle of Yisra'EL.

3 So he gat his people great honour, and put on a breastplate as a giant, and girt his warlike harness about him, and he made battles, protecting the host with his sword.

4 In his acts he was like a lion, and like a lion's whelp roaring for his prey.

5 For He pursued the wicked, and sought them out, and burnt up those that vexed his people.

6 Wherefore the wicked shrunk for fear of him, and all the workers of iniquity were troubled, because salvation prospered in his hand.

7 He grieved also many kings, and made Ya'aqob glad with his acts, and his memorial is blessed for ever.

8 Moreover he went through the cities of Yehudah, destroying the ungodly out of them, and turning away wrath from Yisra'EL:

9 So that he was renowned unto the utmost part of the earth, and he received unto him such as were ready to perish.

10 Then Aphlonios gathered the Gentiles together, and a great host out of Shomron, to fight against Yisra'EL.

11 Which thing when Yehudah perceived, he went forth to meet him, and so he smote him, and slew him: many also fell down slain, but the rest fled.

12 Wherefore Yehudah took their spoils, and Aphlonios' sword also, and therewith he fought all his life long.

13 Now when Seron, a prince of the army of Aram, heard say that all who feared YAHOWAH had gathered unto Yehudah a multitude and company of the faithful to go out with him to war;

14 He said, I will get me a name and honour in the kingdom; for I will go fight with Yehudah and them that are with him, who despise the king's commandment.

15 So he made him ready to go up, and there went with him a mighty host of the ungodly to help him, and to be avenged of the children of Yisra'EL.

16 And when he came near to the going up of Beth-Khoron, Yehudah went forth to meet him with a small company:

17 Who, when they saw the host coming to meet them, said unto Yehudah, How shall we be able, being so few, to fight against so great a multitude and so strong, seeing we are ready to faint with fasting all this day?

18 Unto whom Yehudah answered, YAHOWAH will shortly give the multitude into the hands of a few; and with the ELOHIM of heaven it is all one, to deliver with a great multitude, or a small company:

19 For to YAHOWAH is the victory, not in the multitude of an host..

20 They come against us in much pride and iniquity to destroy us, and our wives and children, and to spoil us:

21 But we fight for our lives and our Torah.

22 Wherefore YAHOWAH himself will overthrow them before our face: and as for you, be ye not afraid of them.

23 Now as soon as he had left off speaking, he leapt suddenly upon them, and so Seron and his host was overthrown before him.

24 And they pursued them from the going down of Beth-Khoron unto the plain, where were slain about eight hundred men of them; and the residue fled into the land of the Phelishtim.

25 Then began the fear of Yehudah and his brethren, and an exceeding great dread, to fall upon the nations round about them:

26 Insomuch as his fame came unto the king, and all nations talked of the battles of Yehudah.

27 Now when king Antiokos heard these things, he was full of indignation: wherefore he sent and gathered together all the forces of his realm, even a very strong army.

28 He opened also his treasure, and gave his soldiers pay for a year, commanding them to be ready whensoever he should need them.

29 Nevertheless, when he saw that the money of his treasures failed and that the tributes in the country were small, because of the dissension and plague, which he had brought upon the land in taking away the Torah which had been of old time;

30 He feared that he should not be able to bear the charges any longer, nor to have such gifts to give so liberally as he did before: for he had abounded above the kings that were before him.

31 Wherefore, being greatly perplexed in his mind, he determined to go into Paras, there to take the tributes of the countries, and to gather much money.

32 So he left Lizias, a nobleman, and one of the blood royal, to oversee the affairs of the king from the river Perath unto the borders of Mitzraim:

33 And to bring up his son Antiokos, until he came again.

34 Moreover he delivered unto him the half of his forces, and the elephants, and gave him charge of all things that he would have done, as also concerning them that dwelt in Yehudah and Yerushalem:

35 To wit, that he should send an army against them, to destroy and root out the strength of Yisra'EL, and the remnant of Yerushalem, and to take away their memorial from that place;

36 And that he should place strangers in all their quarters, and divide their land by lot.

37 So the king took the half of the forces that remained, and departed from **Antyokya (Antioch)**, his royal city, the hundred forty and seventh year; and having passed the river Perath, he went through the high countries.

38 Then Lizias chose Talmay the son of Dorimon, and **Niqanor (Nikanor)**, mighty men of the king's friends:

39 And with them he sent forty thousand footmen, and seven thousand horsemen, to go into the land of Yehudah, and to destroy it, as the king commanded.

40 So they went forth with all their power, and came and pitched by Ama'os in the plain country.

41 And the merchants of the country, hearing the fame of them, took silver and gold very much, with servants, and came into the camp to buy Hebrew slaves: a power also of Aram and of the land of the Phelishtim joined themselves unto them.

42 Now when Yehudah and his brethren saw that miseries were multiplied, and that the forces did encamp themselves in their borders: for they knew how the king had given commandment to destroy the people, and utterly abolish them;

43 They said one to another, Let us restore the decayed fortune of our people, and let us fight for our people and the sanctuary.

44 Then was the congregation gathered together, that they might be ready for battle, and that they might pray to YAHOWAH, and ask mercy and compassion.

45 Now Yerushalem lay void as a wilderness, there was none of her children that went in or out: the sanctuary of YAHOWAH also was trodden down, and aliens kept the strong hold; the heathen had their habitation in that place; and joy was taken from Ya'aqob, and the pipe with the harp ceased.

46 Wherefore the children of Yisra'EL assembled themselves together, and came to Matzphah, over against Yerushalem; for in Matzphah was the place where they prayed aforetime in Yisra'EL.

47 Then they fasted that day, and put on sackcloth, and cast ashes upon their heads, and rent their clothes,

48 And laid open the book of the Torah of YAHOWAH, wherein the heathen had sought to paint the likeness of their images.

49 They brought also the priests' garments, and the firstfruits, and the tithes: and the Nazarites they stirred up, who had accomplished their days.

50 Then cried they with a loud voice to YAHOWAH ELOHIM, saying, What shall we do with these, and whither shall we carry them away?

51 For thy sanctuary is trodden down and profaned, and thy priests are in heaviness, and brought low.

52 And lo, the heathen are assembled together against us to destroy us: what things they imagine against us, thou knowest.

53 How shall we be able to stand against them, except thou, O ELOHIM, be our help?

54 Then sounded they with trumpets, and cried with a loud voice.

55 And after this Yehudah ordained captains over the people, even captains over thousands, and over hundreds, and over fifties, and over tens.

56 But as for such as were building houses, or had betrothed wives, or were planting vineyards, or were fearful, those he commanded that they should return, every man to his own house, according to the Torah of YAHOWAH.

57 So the camp removed, and pitched upon the south side of Ama'os.

58 And Yehudah said, arm yourselves, and be valiant men, and see that ye be in readiness against the morning, that ye may fight with these heathen, that are assembled together against us to destroy us and our sanctuary:

59 For it is better for us to die in battle, than to behold the calamities of our people and our sanctuary.

60 Nevertheless, as the will of YAHOWAH ELOHIM, so let him do.

4 Then took Gorgias five thousand footmen, and a thousand of the best horsemen, and removed out of the camp by night;

2 To the end he might rush in upon the camp of the Yehudim, and smite them suddenly. And the men of the fortress were his guides.

3 Now when Yehudah heard thereof he himself removed, and the valiant men with him, that he might smite the king's army which was at Ama'os,

4 While as yet the forces were dispersed from the camp.

5 In the mean season came Gorgias by night into the camp of Yehudah: and when he found no man there, he sought them in the mountains: for said he, These fellows flee from us

6 But as soon as it was day, Yehudah shewed himself in the plain with three thousand men, who nevertheless had neither armour nor swords to their minds.

7 And they saw the camp of the heathen, that it was strong and well harnessed, and compassed round about with horsemen; and these were expert of war.

8 Then said Yehudah to the men that were with him, Fear ye not their multitude, neither be ye afraid of their assault.

9 Remember how our fathers were delivered by YAHOWAH in the Red sea, when Pharaoh pursued them with an army.

10 Now therefore let us cry unto heaven, if peradventure YAHOWAH our ELOHIM will have mercy upon us, and remember the covenant of our fathers, and destroy this host before our face this day:

11 That so all the heathen may know that YAHOWAH is the ELOHIM who delivereth and saveth Yisra'EL.

12 Then the strangers lifted up their eyes, and saw them coming over against them.

13 Wherefore they went out of the camp to battle; but they that were with Yehudah sounded their trumpets.

14 So they joined battle, and the heathen being discomfited fled into the plain.

15 Howbeit all the hindmost of them were slain with the sword: for they pursued them unto Uzza, and unto the plains of Edom, and Ashdod, and Yabneh, so that there were slain of them upon a three thousand men.

16 This done, Yehudah returned again with his host from pursuing them,

17 And said to the people, Be not greedy of the spoil inasmuch as there is a battle before us,

18 And Gorgias and his host are here by us in the mountain: but stand ye now against our enemies, and overcome them, and after this ye may boldly take the spoils.

19 As Yehudah was yet speaking these words, there appeared a part of them looking out of the mountain:

20 Who when they perceived that the Yehudim had put their host to flight and were burning the tents; for the smoke that was seen declared what was done:

21 When therefore they perceived these things, they were sore afraid, and seeing also the host of Yehudah in the plain ready to fight,

22 They fled every one into the land of strangers.

23 Then Yehudah returned to spoil the tents, where they got much gold, and silver, and blue silk, and purple of the sea, and great riches.

24 After this they returned to their land and praised YAHOWAH with singing. Thus Yisra'EL had a great deliverance that day

25 And they sung a song of thanksgiving to YAHOWAH, : because it is good, because his mercy endureth forever.

26 Now all the strangers that had escaped came and told Lizias what had happened:

27 Who, when he heard thereof, was confounded and discouraged, because neither such things as he would were done unto Yisra'EL, nor such things as the king commanded him were come to pass.

28 The next year therefore following Lizias gathered together threescore thousand choice men of foot, and five thousand horsemen, that he might subdue them.

29 So they came into Edom, and pitched their tents at Beth-Tzur, and Yehudah met them with ten thousand men.

30 And when he saw that mighty army, he prayed to YAHOWAH and said, Blessed art thou, O YAHOWAH ELOHIM of Yisra'EL, who didst quell the violence of the mighty man by the hand of thy servant Dawid, and gavest the host of strangers into the hands of Yahonathan the son of Saul, and his armourbearer;

31 Shut up this army in the hand of thy people Yisra'EL, and let them be confounded in their power and horsemen:

32 Make them to be of no courage, and cause the boldness of their strength to fall away, and let them quake at their destruction:

33 Cast them down with the sword of them that love thee, and let all those that know thy name praise thee with thanksgiving.

34 So they joined battle; and there were slain of the host of Lizias about five thousand men, even before them were they slain.

35 Now when Lizias saw his army put to flight, and the manliness of Yehudah's soldiers, and how they were ready either to live or die valiantly, he went into Antokyah, and gathered together a company of strangers, and having made his army greater than it was, he purposed to come again into Yehudah.

36 Then said Yehudah and his brethren, Behold, our enemies are discomfited: let us go up to cleanse and dedicate the sanctuary of YAHOWAH.

37 Upon this all the host assembled themselves together, and went up into mount Tzion.

38 And when they saw the sanctuary desolate, and the altar profaned, and the gates burned up, and shrubs growing in the courts as in a forest, or in one of the mountains, yea, and the priests' chambers pulled down;

39 They rent their clothes, and made great lamentation, and cast ashes upon their heads,

40 And fell down flat to the ground upon their faces, and blew an alarm with the trumpets, and cried toward heaven.

41 Then Yehudah appointed certain men to fight against those that were in the fortress, until he had cleansed the sanctuary.

42 So he chose priests of blameless conversation, such as had pleasure in the Torah:

43 Who cleansed the sanctuary, and bare out the defiled stones into an unclean place.

44 And when as they consulted what to do with the altar of burnt offerings, which was profaned;

45 They thought it best to pull it down, lest it should be a reproach to them, because the heathen had defiled it: wherefore they pulled it down,

46 And laid up the stones in the mountain of the temple in a convenient place, until there should come a prophet to shew what should be done with them.

47 Then they took whole stones according to the Torah of YAHOWAH, and built a new altar according to the former;

48 And made up the sanctuary, and the things that were within the temple, and hallowed the courts.

49 They made also new holy vessels, and into the temple they brought the menorah, and the altar of burnt offerings, and of incense, and the table.

50 And upon the altar they burned incense, and the lamps that were upon the menorah they lighted, that they might give light in the temple.

51 Furthermore they set the loaves upon the table, and spread out the veils, and finished all the works which they had begun to make.

52 Now on the five and twentieth day of the ninth month, which is called the month Kislew, in the hundred forty and eighth year, they rose up betimes in the morning,

53 And offered sacrifice according to the Torah upon the new altar of burnt offerings, which they had made.

54 Look, at what time and what day the heathen had profaned it, even in that we praised YAHOWAH with songs, and citherns, and harps, and cymbals.

55 Then all the people fell upon their faces, worshipping and praising YAHOWAH, who had given them good success.

56 And so they kept The Feast of Khanukkah of the altar eight days and offered burnt offerings with gladness, and sacrificed the sacrifice of deliverance and praise.

57 They decked also the forefront of the temple with crowns of gold, and with shields; and the gates and the chambers they renewed, and hanged doors upon them.

58 Thus was there very great gladness among the people, for that YAHOWAH put away the reproach of the heathen.

59 Moreover Yehudah and his brethren with the whole congregation of Yisra'EL ordained, that the days of The Feast of Khanukkah of the altar should be kept in their season from year to year by the space of eight days, from the five and twentieth day of the month Kislew, with mirth and gladness.

60 At that time also they builded up the mount Tzion with high walls and strong towers round about, lest the Gentiles should come and tread it down as they had done before.

61 And they set there a garrison to keep it, and fortified Beth-Tzur to preserve it; that the people might have a defence against Edom.

5 Now when the Gentiles round about heard that the altar was built and the sanctuary renewed as before, it displeased them very much.

2 Wherefore they thought to destroy the generation of Ya'aqob that was among them, and thereupon they began to slay and destroy the people.

3 Then Yehudah fought against the children of Esau in Edom at Aqarbim, because they besieged Gael: and he gave them a great overthrow, and abated their courage, and took their spoils.

4 Also he remembered the injury of the children of Beth-Awon, who had been a snare and an offence unto the people, in that they lay in wait for them in the ways.

5 He shut them up therefore in the towers, and encamped against them, and destroyed them utterly, and burned the towers of that place with fire, and all that were therein.

6 Afterward he passed over to the children of Ammon, where he found a mighty power, and much people, with Timotios their captain.

7 So he fought many battles with them, till at length they were discomfited before him; and he smote them.

8 And when he had taken Yazar, with the towns belonging thereto, he returned into Yehudah.

9 Then the heathen that were at Gil'ad assembled themselves together against the children of Yisra'EL that were in their quarters, to destroy them; but they fled to the fortress of Dathema.

10 And sent letters unto Yehudah and his brethren, The heathen that are round about us are assembled together against us to destroy us:

11 And they are preparing to come and take the fortress whereunto we are fled, Timotios being captain of their host.

12 Come now therefore, and deliver us from their hands, for many of us are slain:

13 Yea, all our brethren that were in the places of Tob are put to death: their wives and their children also they have carried away captives, and borne away their stuff; and they have destroyed there about a thousand men.

14 While these letters were yet reading, behold, there came other messengers from Galilah with their clothes rent, who reported on this wise,

15 And said, They of Ptolemais, and of Tzor, and Tzidon, and all Galilah of the Gentiles, are assembled together against us to consume us.

16 Now when Yehudah and the people heard these words, there assembled a great congregation together, to consult what they should do for their brethren, that were in trouble, and assaulted of them.

17 Then said Yehudah unto Shimon his brother, Choose thee out men, and go and deliver thy brethren that are in Galilah, for I and Yahonathan my brother will go into the country of Gil'ad.

18 So he left Yoseph the son of ZekarYAHU, and AzarYAH, captains of the people, with the remnant of the host in Yehudah to keep it.

19 Unto whom he gave commandment, saying, Take ye the charge of this people, and see that ye make not war against the heathen until the time that we come again.

20 Now unto Shimon were given three thousand men to go into Galilah, and unto Yehudah eight thousand men for the country of Gil'ad.

21 Then went Shimon into Galilah, where he fought many battles with the heathen, so that the heathen were discomfited by him.

22 And he pursued them unto the gate of Ptolemais; and there were slain of the heathen about three thousand men, whose spoils he took.

23 And those that were in Galilah, and in Arpad, with their wives and their children, and all that they had, took he away with him, and brought them into Yehudah with great joy.

24 Yehudah Makabi also and his brother Yahonathan went over Yarden, and travelled three days' journey in the wilderness,

25 Where they met with the Nebo'im, who came unto them in a peaceable manner, and told them every thing that had happened to their brethren in the land of Gil'ad:

26 And how that many of them were shut up in Batzarah, and Batzar, and Almon, Khesbon, Maqed, and Qarnaim; all these cities are strong and great:

27 And that they were shut up in the rest of the cities of the country of Gil'ad, and that against to morrow they had appointed to bring their host against the forts, and to take them, and to destroy them all in one day.

28 Hereupon Yehudah and his host turned suddenly by the way of the wilderness unto Batzarah; and when he had won the city, he slew all the males with the edge of the sword, and took all their spoils, and burned the city with fire,

29 From whence he removed by night, and went till he came to the fortress.

30 And betimes in the morning they looked up, and, behold, there was an innumerable people bearing ladders and other engines of war, to take the fortress: for they assaulted them.

31 When Yehudah therefore saw that the battle was begun, and that the cry of the city went up to YAHOWAH, with trumpets, and a great sound,

32 He said unto his host, Fight this day for your brethren.

33 So he went forth behind them in three companies, who sounded their trumpets, and cried with prayer.

34 Then the host of Timotios, knowing that it was Makabi, fled from him: wherefore he smote them with a great slaughter; so that there were killed of them that day about eight thousand men.

35 This done, Yehudah turned aside to Matzphah; and after he had assaulted it he took and slew all the males therein, and received the spoils thereof and and burnt it with fire.

36 From thence went he, and took Khesbon, Batzarah, Maqedah and the other cities of the country of Gil'ad.

37 After these things gathered Timotios another host and encamped against Raphon beyond the brook.

38 So Yehudah sent men to espy the host, who brought him word, saying, All the heathen that be round about us are assembled unto them, even a very great host.

39 He hath also hired the Arabians to help them and they have pitched their tents beyond the brook, ready to come and fight against thee. Upon this Yehudah went to meet them.

40 Then Timotios said unto the captains of his host, When Yehudah and his host come near the brook, if he pass over first unto us, we shall not be able to withstand him; for he will mightily prevail against us:

41 But if he be afraid, and camp beyond the river, we shall go over unto him, and prevail against him.

42 Now when Yehudah came near the brook, he caused the scribes of the people to remain by the brook: unto whom he gave commandment, saying, Suffer no man to remain in the camp, but let all come to the battle.

43 So he went first over unto them, and all the people after him: then all the heathen, being discomfited before him, cast away their weapons, and fled unto the temple that was at Qarnaim.

44 But they took the city, and burned the temple with all that were therein. Thus was Qarnaim subdued, neither could they stand any longer before Yehudah.

45 Then Yehudah gathered together all the children of Yisra'EL that were in the country of Gil'ad, from the least unto the greatest, even their wives, and their children, and their stuff, a very great host, to the end they might come into the land of Yehudah.

46 Now when they came unto Ephron, (this was a great city in the way as they should go, very well fortified) they could not turn from it, either on the right hand or the left, but must needs pass through the midst of it.

47 Then they of the city shut them out, and stopped up the gates with stones.

48 Whereupon Yehudah sent unto them in peaceable manner, saying, Let us pass through your land to go into our own country, and none shall do you any hurt; we will only pass through on foot: howbeit they would not open unto him.

49 Wherefore Yehudah commanded a proclamation to be made throughout the host, that every man should pitch his tent in the place where he was.

50 So the soldiers pitched, and assaulted the city all that day and all that night, till at the length the city was delivered into his hands:

51 Who then slew all the males with the edge of the sword, and rased the city, and took the spoils thereof, and passed through the city over them that were slain.

1 MACCABEES

52 After this went they over Yarden into the great plain before Bethsan.

53 And Yehudah gathered together those that came behind, and exhorted the people all the way through, till they came into the land of Yehudah.

54 So they went up to mount Tzion with joy and gladness, where they offered to YAHOWAH, because not one of them were slain until they had returned in shalom.

55 Now what time as Yehudah and Yahonathan were in the land of Gil'ad, and Shimon his brother in Galilah before Ptolemais,

56 Yoseph the son of ZekarYAHU, and AzarYAH, captains of the garrisons, heard of the valiant acts and warlike deeds which they had done.

57 Wherefore they said, Let us also get us a name, and go fight against the heathen that are round about us.

58 So when they had given charge unto the garrison that was with them, they went toward Yabneh.

59 Then came Gorgias and his men out of the city to fight against them.

60 And so it was, that Yoseph and Azaras were put to flight, and pursued unto the borders of Yehudah: and there were slain that day of the people of Yisra'EL about two thousand men.

61 Thus was there a great overthrow among the children of Yisra'EL, because they were not obedient unto Yehudah and his brethren, but thought to do some valiant act.

62 Moreover these men came not of the seed of those YAHOWAH chose, by whose hand deliverance was given unto his people.

63 Howbeit the man Yehudah and his brethren were greatly renowned in the sight of all Yisra'EL, and of all the heathen, wheresoever their name was heard of;

64 Insomuch as the the people assembled unto them with joyful acclamations.

65 Afterward went Yehudah forth with his brethren, and fought against the children of Esau in the land toward the south, where he smote Khebron, and the towns thereof, and pulled down the fortress of it, and burned the towers thereof round about.

66 From thence he removed to go into the land of Galilah of the Gentiles, and passed through Shomron.

67 At that time certain priests, desirous to shew their valour, were slain in battle, for that they went out to fight unadvisedly.

68 So Yehudah turned to Ashdod in the land of Galilah of the Gentiles, and when he had pulled down their altars, and burned their carved images with fire, and spoiled their cities, he returned into the land of Yehudah.

6 About that time king Antiokos travelling through the high countries heard say, that Elymais in the country of Paras was a city greatly renowned for riches, silver, and gold;

2 And that there was in it a very rich temple, wherein were coverings of gold, and breastplates, and shields, which Aleksandros, son of Philipos, the Macedonian king, who reigned first among the Grecians, had left there.

3 Wherefore Antiokos came and sought to take the city, and to spoil it; but he was not able, because they of the city, having had warning thereof,

4 Rose up against him in battle: so he fled, and departed thence with great heaviness, and returned to Babel.

5 Moreover there came one who brought him tidings into Paras, that the armies, which went against the land of Yehudah, were put to flight:

6 And that Lizias, who went forth first with a great power was driven away of the Yehudim; and that they were made strong by the armour, and power, and store of spoils, which they had gotten of the armies, whom they had destroyed:

7 Also that they had pulled down the abomination, which he had set up upon the altar in Yerushalem, and that they had compassed about the sanctuary with high walls, as before, and his city Beth-Tzur.

8 Now when the king heard these words, he was astonished and sore moved: whereupon he laid him down upon his bed, and fell sick for grief, because it had not befallen him as he looked for.

9 And there he continued many days: for his grief was ever more and more, and he made account that he should die.

10 Wherefore he called for all his friends, and said unto them, The sleep is gone from mine eyes, and my heart faileth for very care.

11 And I thought with myself, Into what tribulation am I come, and how great a flood of misery is it, wherein now I am! for I was bountiful and beloved in my power.

12 But now I remember the evils that I did at Yerushalem, and that I took all the vessels of gold and silver that were therein, and sent to destroy the inhabitants of Yehudah without a cause.

13 I perceive therefore that for this cause these troubles are come upon me, and, behold, I perish through great grief in a strange land.

14 Then called he for Philipos, one of his friends, who he made ruler over all his realm,

15 And gave him the crown, and his robe, and his signet, to the end he should bring up his son Antiokos, and nourish him up for the kingdom.

16 So king Antiokos died there in the hundred forty and ninth year.

17 Now when Lizias knew that the king was dead, he set up Antiokos his son, whom he had brought up being young, to reign in his stead, and his name he called Eupator.

18 About this time they that were in the tower shut up the children of Yisra'EL round about the sanctuary, and sought always their hurt, and the strengthening of the heathen.

19 Wherefore Yehudah, purposing to destroy them, called all the people together to besiege them.

20 So they came together, and besieged them in the hundred and fiftieth year, and he made mounts for shot against them, and other engines.

21 Howbeit certain of them that were besieged got forth, unto whom some ungodly men of Yisra'EL joined themselves:

22 And they went unto the king, and said, How long will it be ere thou execute judgment, and avenge our brethren?

23 We have been willing to serve thy father, and to do as he would have us, and to obey his commandments;

24 For which cause they of our nation besiege the tower, and are alienated from us: moreover as many of us as they could light on they slew, and spoiled our inheritance.

25 Neither have they stretched out their hand against us only, but also against their borders.

26 And, behold, this day are they besieging the tower at Yerushalem, to take it: the sanctuary also and Beth-Tzur have they fortified.

27 Wherefore if thou dost not prevent them quickly, they will do the greater things than these, neither shalt thou be able to rule them.

28 Now when the king heard this, he was angry, and gathered together all his friends, and the captains of his army, and those that had charge of the horse.

29 There came also unto him from other kingdoms, and from isles of the sea, bands of hired soldiers.

30 So that the number of his army was an hundred thousand footmen, and twenty thousand horsemen, and two and thirty elephants exercised in battle.

31 These went through Edom, and pitched against Beth-Tzur, which they assaulted many days, making engines of war; but they of Beth-Tzur came out, and burned them with fire, and fought valiantly.

32 Upon this Yehudah removed from the tower, and pitched in Beth-Sokherah, over against the king's camp.

33 Then the king rising very early marched fiercely with his host toward Beth-Sokherah, where his armies made them ready to battle, and sounded the trumpets.

34 And to the end they might provoke the elephants to fight, they shewed them the blood of grapes and mulberries.

35 Moreover they divided the beasts among the armies, and for every elephant they appointed a thousand men, armed with coats of mail, and with helmets of brass on their heads; and beside this, for every beast were ordained five hundred horsemen of the best.

36 These were ready at every occasion: wheresoever the beast was, and whithersoever the beast went, they went also, neither departed they from him.

37 And upon the beasts were there strong towers of wood, which covered every one of them, and were girt fast unto them with devices: there were

also upon every one two and thirty strong men, that fought upon them, beside the Indian that ruled him.

38 As for the remnant of the horsemen, they set them on this side and that side at the two parts of the host giving them signs what to do, and being harnessed all over amidst the ranks.

39 Now when the sun shone upon the shields of gold and brass, the mountains glistered therewith, and shined like lamps of fire.

40 So part of the king's army being spread upon the high mountains, and part on the valleys below, they marched on safely and in order.

41 Wherefore all that heard the noise of their multitude, and the marching of the company, and the rattling of the harness, were moved: for the army was very great and mighty.

42 Then Yehudah and his host drew near, and entered into battle, and there were slain of the king's army six hundred men.

43 Eleazar also, surnamed Khorani, perceiving that one of the beasts, armed with royal harness, was higher than all the rest, and supposing that the king was upon him,

44 Put himself in jeopardy, to the end he might deliver his people, and get him a perpetual name:

45 Wherefore he ran upon him courageously through the midst of the battle, slaying on the right hand and on the left, so that they were divided from him on both sides.

46 Which done, he crept under the elephant, and thrust him under, and slew him: whereupon the elephant fell down upon him, and there he died.

47 Howbeit the rest of the Yehudim seeing the strength of the king, and the violence of his forces, turned away from them.

48 Then the king's army went up to Yerushalem to meet them, and the king pitched his tents against Yehudah, and against mount Tzion.

49 But with them that were in Beth-Tzur he made shalom: for they came out of the city, because they had no victuals there to endure the siege, it being a year of rest to the land.

50 So the king took Beth-Tzur, and set a garrison there to keep it.

51 As for the sanctuary, he besieged it many days: and set there artillery with engines and instruments to cast fire and stones, and pieces to cast darts and slings.

52 Whereupon they also made engines against their engines, and held them battle a long season.

53 Yet at the last, their vessels being without victuals, (for that it was the seventh year, and they in Yehudah that were delivered from the Gentiles, had eaten up the residue of the store;)

54 There were but a few left in the sanctuary, because the famine did so prevail against them, that they were fain to disperse themselves, every man to his own place.

55 At that time Lizias heard say, that Philipos, whom Antiokos the king, whiles he lived, had appointed to bring up his son Antiokos, that he might be king,

56 Was returned out of Paras and Madai, and the king's host also that went with him, and that he sought to take unto him the ruling of the affairs.

57 Wherefore he went in all haste, and said to the king and the captains of the host and the company, We decay daily, and our victuals are but small, and the place we lay siege unto is strong, and the affairs of the kingdom lie upon us:

58 Now therefore let us be friends with these men, and make shalom with them, and with all their nation;

59 And covenant with them, that they shall live after their Torah, as they did before: for they are therefore displeased, and have done all these things, because we abolished their Torah.

60 So the king and the princes were content: wherefore he sent unto them to make shalom; and they accepted thereof.

61 Also the king and the princes made an oath unto them: whereupon they went out of the strong hold.

62 Then the king entered into mount Tzion; but when he saw the strength of the place, he broke his oath that he had made, and gave commandment to pull down the wall round about.

63 Afterward departed he in all haste, and returned unto Antokyah, where he found Philipos to be master of the city: so he fought against him, and took the city by force.

7 In the hundred and one and fiftieth year Dimitrios the son of Seliqos departed from Rome, and came up with a few men unto a city of the sea coast, and reigned there.

2 And as he entered into the palace of his ancestors, so it was, that his forces had taken Antiokos and Lizias, to bring them unto him.

3 Wherefore, when he knew it, he said, Let me not see their faces.

4 So his host slew them. Now when Dimitrios was set upon the throne of his kingdom,

5 There came unto him all the wicked and ungodly men of Yisra'EL, having Eliqim, who was desirous to be high priest, for their captain:

6 And they accused the people to the king, saying, Yehudah and his brethren have slain all thy friends, and driven us out of our own land.

7 Now therefore send some man whom thou trustest, and let him go and see what havock he hath made among us, and in the king's land, and let him punish them with all them that aid them.

8 Then the king chose Bakkhides, a friend of the king, who ruled beyond the flood, and was a great man in the kingdom, and faithful to the king,

9 And him he sent with that wicked Eliqim, whom he made high priest, and commanded that he should take vengeance of the children of Yisra'EL.

10 So they departed, and came with a great power into the land of Yehudah, where they sent messengers to Yehudah and his brethren with peaceable words deceitfully.

11 But they gave no heed to their words; for they saw that they were come with a great power.

12 Then did there assemble unto Eliqim and Bakkhides a company of scribes, to require justice.

13 Now the Khasidim were the first among the children of Yisra'EL that sought shalom of them:

14 For said they, One that is a priest of the seed of Aharon is come with this army, and he will do us no wrong.

15 So he spake unto them, peaceably, and sware unto them, saying, As YAHOWAH liveth, if I lie to your people, then let evil befall us.

16 Whereupon they believed him: howbeit he took of them threescore men, and slew them in one day, according to the words which he wrote,

17 The flesh of thy saints have they cast out, and their blood have they shed round about Yerushalem, and there was none to bury them.

18 Wherefore the fear and dread of them fell upon all the people, who said, There is neither truth nor righteousness in them; for they have broken the covenant and oath that they made.

19 After this, removed Bakkhides from Yerushalem, and pitched his tents in Bezeth, where he sent and took many of the men that had forsaken him, and certain of the people also, and when he had slain them, he cast them into the great pit.

20 Then committed he the country to Eliqim, and left with him a power to aid him: so Bakkhides went to the king.

21 But Eliqim contended for the high priesthood.

22 And unto him resorted all such as troubled the people, who, after they had gotten the land of Yehudah into their power, did much hurt in Yisra'EL.

23 Now when Yehudah saw all the mischief that Eliqim and his company had done among the children of Yisra'EL, even above the heathen,

24 He went out into all the coasts of Yehudah round about, and took vengeance of them that had revolted from him, so that they durst no more go forth into the country.

25 On the other side, when Eliqim saw that Yehudah and his company had gotten the upper hand, and knew that he was not able to abide their force, he went again to the king, and said all the worst of them that he could.

26 Then the king sent Niqanor, one of his honourable princes, a man that bare deadly hate unto Yisra'EL, with commandment to destroy the people.

27 So Niqanor came to Yerushalem with a great force; and sent unto Yehudah and his brethren deceitfully with friendly words, saying,

28 Let there be no battle between me and you; I will come with a few men, that I may see you in shalom.

29 He came therefore to Yehudah, and they saluted one another peaceably. Howbeit the enemies were prepared to take away Yehudah by violence.

30 Which thing after it was known to Yehudah, to wit, that he came unto him with deceit, he was sore afraid of him, and would see his face no more.

31 Niqanor also, when he saw that his counsel was discovered, went out to fight against Yehudah beside Capharsalama:

32 Where there were slain of Niqanor's side about five thousand men, and the rest fled into the city of Dawid.

33 After this went Niqanor up to mount Tzion, and there came out of the sanctuary certain of the priests and certain of the elders of the people, to salute him peaceably, and to shew him the burnt sacrifice that was offered for the king.

34 But he mocked them, and laughed at them, and abused them shamefully, and spake proudly,

35 And sware in his wrath, saying, Unless Yehudah and his host be now delivered into my hands, if ever I come again in safety, I will burn up this house: and with that he went out in a great rage.

36 Then the priests entered in, and stood before the altar of YAHOWAH weeping, and saying,

37 Thou, O YAHOWAH ELOHIM, didst choose this house to be called by thy name, and to be a house of prayer and petition for thy people Yisra'EL:

38 I pray thee, I bessech thee O YAHOWAH, Be avenged of this man and his host, and let them fall by the sword: remember their blasphemies, and suffer them not to continue any longer.

39 So Niqanor went out of Yerushalem, and pitched his tents in Beth-Khoron, where an host out of Aram met him.

40 But Yehudah pitched in Adasa with three thousand men, and there he prayed to YAHOWAH, saying,

41 O YAHOWAH ELOHIM, when they that were sent from the king of the Assyrians blasphemed, thine Angel went out, and smote an hundred fourscore and five thousand of them.

42 Even so destroy thou this host before us this day, that the rest may know that he hath spoken blasphemously against thy sanctuary, and judge thou him according to his wickedness.

43 So the thirteenth day of the month Adar the hosts joined battle: but Niqanor's host was discomfited, and he himself was first slain in the battle.

44 Now when Niqanor's host saw that he was slain, they cast away their weapons, and fled.

45 Then they pursued after them a day's journey, from Adasa unto Uzza, sounding an alarm after them with their trumpets.

46 Whereupon they came forth out of all the towns of Yehudah round about, and closed them in; so that they, turning back upon them that pursued them, were all slain with the sword, and not one of them was left.

47 Afterwards they took the spoils, and the prey, and smote off Nikanors head, and his right hand, which he stretched out so proudly, and brought them away, and hanged them up toward Yerushalem.

48 For this cause the people rejoiced greatly, and they kept that day a day of great gladness.

49 Moreover they ordained to keep yearly this day, being the thirteenth of Adar.

50 Thus the land of Yehudah was in rest a little while.

8 Now Yehudah had heard of the the Romans, that they were mighty and valiant men, and such as would lovingly accept all that joined themselves unto them, and make a league of amity with all that came unto them;

2 And that they were men of great valour. It was told him also of their wars and noble acts which they had done among the Galatians, and how they had conquered them, and brought them under tribute;

3 And what they had done in the country of Spain, for the winning of the mines of the silver and gold which is there;

4 And that by their policy and patience they had conquered all the place, though it were very far from them; and the kings also that came against them from the uttermost part of the earth, till they had discomfited them, and given them a great overthrow, so that the rest did give them tribute every year:

5 Beside this, how they had discomfited in battle Philipos, and Perzios, king of the Kittim, with others that lifted up themselves against them, and had overcome them:

6 How also Antiokos the great king of Asia, that came against them in battle, having an hundred and twenty elephants, with horsemen, and chariots, and a very great army, was discomfited by them;

7 And how they took him alive, and covenanted that he and such as reigned after him should pay a great tribute, and give hostages, and that which was agreed upon,

8 And the country of Hodu, and Madai and Lud and of the goodliest countries, which they took of him, and gave to king Eumenes:

9 Moreover how the Grecians had determined to come and destroy them;

10 And that they, having knowledge thereof sent against them a certain captain, and fighting with them slew many of them, and carried away captives their wives and their children, and spoiled them, and took possession of their lands, and pulled down their strong holds, and brought them to be their servants unto this day:

11 It was told him besides, how they destroyed and brought under their dominion all other kingdoms and isles that at any time resisted them;

12 But with their friends and such as relied upon them they kept amity: and that they had conquered kingdoms both far and nigh, insomuch as all that heard of their name were afraid of them:

13 Also that, whom they would help to a kingdom, those reign; and whom again they would, they displace: finally, that they were greatly exalted:

14 Yet for all this none of them wore a crown or was clothed in purple, to be magnified thereby:

15 Moreover how they had made for themselves a senate house, wherein three hundred and twenty men sat in council daily, consulting alway for the people, to the end they might be well ordered:

16 And that they committed their government to one man every year, who ruled over all their country, and that all were obedient to that one, and that there was neither envy nor emmulation among them.

17 In consideration of these things, Yehudah chose Eupoliymos the son of Yokhanan, the son of Haqutz, and Yeshua the son of Eleazar, and sent them to Rome, to make a league of amity and confederacy with them,

18 And to intreat them that they would take the yoke from them; for they saw that the kingdom of the Grecians did oppress Yisra'EL with servitude.

19 They went therefore to Rome, which was a very great journey, and came into the senate, where they spake and said.

20 Yehudah Makabi with his brethren, and the people of the Yehudim, have sent us unto you, to make a confederacy and shalom with you, and that we might be registered your confederates and friends.

21 So that matter pleased the Romans well.

22 And this is the copy of the epistle which the senate wrote back again in tables of brass, and sent to Yerushalem, that there they might have by them a memorial of shalom and confederacy:

23 May YAHOWAH order his blessings and shalom to the people of Rome, and to the people of the Yehudim, by sea and by land for ever: the sword also and enemy be far from them,

24 If there come first any war upon the Romans or any of their confederates throughout all their dominion,

25 The people of the Yehudim shall help them, as the time shall be appointed, with all their heart:

26 Neither shall they give any thing unto them that make war upon them, or aid them with victuals, weapons, money, or ships, as it hath seemed good unto the Romans; but they shall keep their covenants without taking any thing therefore.

27 In the same manner also, if war come first upon the nation of the Yehudim, the Romans shall help them with all their heart, according as the time shall be appointed them:

28 Neither shall victuals be given to them that take part against them, or weapons, or money, or ships, as it hath seemed good to the Romans; but they shall keep their covenants, and that without deceit.

29 According to these articles did the Romans make a covenant with the people of the Yehudim.

30 Howbeit if hereafter the one party or the other shall think to meet to add or diminish any thing, they may do it at their pleasures, and whatsoever they shall add or take away shall be ratified.

31 And as touching the evils that Dimitrios doeth to the Yehudim, we have written unto him, saying, Wherefore thou made thy yoke heavy upon our friends and confederates the Yehudim?

32 If therefore they complain any more against thee, we will do them justice, and fight with thee by sea and by land.

9 Furthermore, when Dimitrios heard the Niqanor and his host were slain in battle, he sent Bakkhides and Eliqim into the land of Yehudah the second time, and with them the chief strength of his host:

2 Who went forth by the way that leadeth to Gilgal, and pitched their tents before Masiyloth, which is in Arbela, and after they had won it, they slew much people.

3 Also the first month of the hundred fifty and second year they encamped before Yerushalem:

4 From whence they removed, and went to Bearoth, with twenty thousand footmen and two thousand horsemen.

5 Now Yehudah had pitched his tents at Belish, and three thousand chosen men with him:

6 Who seeing the multitude of the other army to he so great were sore afraid; whereupon many conveyed themselves out of the host, insomuch as abode of them no more but eight hundred men.

7 When Yehudah therefore saw that his host slipt away, and that the battle pressed upon him, he was sore troubled in mind, and much distressed, for that he had no time to gather them together.

8 Nevertheless unto them that remained he said, Let us arise and go up against our enemies, if peradventure we may be able to fight with them.

9 But they dehorted him, saying, We shall never be able: let us now rather save our lives, and here after we will return with our brethren, and fight against them: for we are but few.

10 Then Yehudah said, ELOHIM forbid that I should do this thing, and flee away from them: if our time be come, let us die manfully for our brethren, and let us not stain our honour.

11 With that the host of Bakkhides removed out of their tents, and stood over against them, their horsemen being divided into two troops, and their slingers and archers going before the host and they that marched in the foreward were all mighty men.

12 As for Bakkhides, he was in the right wing: so the host drew near on the two parts, and sounded their trumpets.

13 They also of Yehudah's side, even they sounded their trumpets also, so that the earth shook at the noise of the armies, and the battle continued from morning till night.

14 Now when Yehudah perceived that Bakkhides and the strength of his army were on the right side, he took with him all the hardy men,

15 Who discomfited the right wing, and pursued them unto the mount Ashdod.

16 But when they of the left wing saw that they of the right wing were discomfited, they followed upon Yehudah and those that were with him hard at the heels from behind:

17 Whereupon there was a sore battle, insomuch as many were slain on both parts.

18 Yehudah also was killed, and the remnant fled.

19 Then Yahonathan and Shimon took Yehudah their brother, and buried him in the sepulchre of

his fathers in Modin.

20 Moreover they bewailed him, and all Yisra'EL made great lamentation for him, and mourned many days, saying,

21 How is the valiant man fallen, that delivered Yisra'EL!

22 As for the other things concerning Yehudah and his wars, and the noble acts which he did, and his greatness, they are not written: for they were very many.

23 Now after the death of Yehudah the wicked began to put forth their heads in all the coasts of Yisra'EL, and there arose up all such as wrought iniquity.

24 In those days also was there a very great famine, by reason whereof the country revolted, and went with them.

25 Then Bakkhides chose the wicked men, and made them lords of the country.

26 And they made enquiry and search for Yehudah's friends, and brought them unto Bakkhides, who took vengeance of them, and used them despitefully.

27 So was there a great affliction in Yisra'EL, the like whereof was not since the time that a prophet was not seen among them.

28 For this cause all Yehudah's friends came together, and said unto Yahonathan,

29 Since thy brother Yehudah died, we have no man like him to go forth against our enemies, and Bakkhides, and against them of our nation that are adversaries to us.

30 Now therefore we have chosen thee this day to be our prince and captain in his stead, that thou mayest fight our battles.

31 Upon this Yahonathan took the governance upon him at that time, and rose up instead of his brother Yehudah.

32 But when Bakkhides gat knowledge thereof, he sought for to slay him

33 Then Yahonathan, and Shimon his brother, and all that were with him, perceiving that, fled into the wilderness of Theqoa, and pitched their tents by the Salt Sea

34 Which when Bakkhides understood, he came near to Yarden with all his host upon the Shabbat day.

35 Now Yahonathan had sent his brother Yokhanan, a captain of the people, to pray his friends the Nebo'im, that they might leave with them their carriage, which was much.

36 But the children of Yambri came out of Medaba, and took Yokhanan, and all that he had, and went their way with it.

37 After this came word to Yahonathan and Shimon his brother, that the children of Yambri made a great marriage, and were bringing the bride from Madaba with a great train, as being the daughter of one of the great princes of Kena'an.

38 Therefore they remembered Yokhanan their brother, and went up, and hid themselves under the covert of the mountain:

39 Where they lifted up their eyes, and looked, and, behold, there was much ado and great carriage: and the bridegroom came forth, and his friends and brethren, to meet them with drums, and instruments of musick, and many weapons.

40 Then Yahonathan and they that were with him rose up against them from the place where they lay in ambush, and made a slaughter of them in such sort, as many fell down dead, and the remnant fled into the mountain, and they took all their spoils.

41 Thus was the marriage turned into mourning, and the noise of their melody into lamentation.

42 So when they had avenged fully the blood of their brother, they turned again to the marsh of Yarden.

43 Now when Bakkhides heard hereof, he came on the Shabbat day unto the banks of Yarden with a great power.

44 Then Yahonathan said to his company, Let us go up now and fight for our lives, for it standeth not with us to day, as in time past:

45 For, behold, the battle is before us and behind us, and the water of Yarden on this side and that side, the marsh likewise and wood, neither is there place for us to turn aside.

46 Wherefore cry ye now unto YAHOWAH, that ye may be delivered from the hand of your enemies.

47 With that they joined battle, and Yahonathan stretched forth his hand to smite Bakkhides, but he turned back from him.

48 Then Yahonathan and they that were with him leapt into Yarden, and swam over unto the other bank: howbeit the other passed not over Yarden unto them.

49 So there were slain of Bakkhides' side that day about a thousand men.

50 Afterward returned Bakkhides to Yerushalem and repaired the strong cites in Yehudah; the fort in Beth-Khoron, and Beth-EL, and Temenah, Paran, and Taphon, these did he strengthen with high walls, with gates and with bars.

51 And in them he set a garrison, that they might work malice upon Yisra'EL.

52 He fortified also the city Beth-Tzur, and Uzza, and the tower, and put forces in them, and provision of victuals.

53 Besides, he took the chief men's sons in the country for hostages, and put them into the tower at Yerushalem to be kept.

54 Moreover in the hundred fifty and third year, in the second month, Eliqim commanded that the wall of the inner court of the sanctuary should be pulled down; he pulled down also the works of the prophets

55 And as he began to pull down, even at that time the hand of YAHOWAH touched Eliqim, and his enterprizes hindered: for his mouth was stopped, and he was taken with a palsy, so that he could no more speak any thing, nor give order concerning his house.

56 So Eliqim died at that time with great torment.

57 Now when Bakkhides saw that Eliqim was

dead, he returned to the king: whereupon the land of Yehudah was in rest two years.

58 Then all the ungodly men held a council, saying, Behold, Yahonathan and his company are at ease, and dwell without care: now therefore we will bring Bakkhides hither, who shall take them all in one night.

59 So they went and consulted with him.

60 Then removed he, and came with a great host, and sent letters privily to his adherents in Yehudah, that they should take Yahonathan and those that were with him: howbeit they could not, because their counsel was known unto them.

61 Wherefore they took of the men of the country, that were authors of that mischief, about fifty persons, and slew them.

62 Afterward Yahonathan, and Shimon, and they that were with him, got them away to Beth-Bashan, which is in the wilderness, and they repaired the decays thereof, and made it strong.

63 Which thing when Bakkhides knew, he gathered together all his host, and sent word to them that were of Yehudah.

64 Then went he and laid siege against Beth-Bashan; and they fought against it a long season and made engines of war.

65 But Yahonathan left his brother Shimon in the city, and went forth himself into the country, and with a certain number went he forth.

66 And he smote Hadar and his brethren, and the children of Pashron in their tent.

67 And when he began to smite them, and came up with his forces, Shimon and his company went out of the city, and burned up the engines of war,

68 And fought against Bakkhides, who was discomfited by them, and they afflicted him sore: for his counsel and travail was in vain.

69 Wherefore he was very wroth at the wicked men that gave him counsel to come into the country, inasmuch as he slew many of them, and purposed to return into his own country.

70 Whereof when Yahonathan had knowledge, he sent ambassadors unto him, to the end he should make shalom with him, and deliver them the prisoners.

71 Which thing he accepted, and did according to his demands, and sware unto him that he would never do him harm all the days of his life.

72 When therefore he had restored unto him the prisoners that he had taken aforetime out of the land of Yehudah, he returned and went his way into his own land, neither came he any more into their borders.

73 Thus the sword ceased from Yisra'EL: but Yahonathan dwelt at Mikmash, and began to govern the people; and he destroyed the ungodly men out of Yisra'EL.

10 In the hundred and sixtieth year Aleksandros, the son of Antiokos surnamed The Magnificent, went up and took Ptolemais: for the people had received him, by means whereof he reigned there,

2 Now when king Dimitrios heard thereof, he gathered together an exceeding great host, and went forth against him to fight.

3 Moreover Dimitrios sent letters unto Yahonathan with loving words, so as he magnified him.

4 For said he, Let us first make shalom with him, before he join with Aleksandros against us:

5 Else he will remember all the evils that we have done against him, and against his brethren and his people.

6 Wherefore he gave him authority to gather together an host, and to provide weapons, that he might aid him in battle: he commanded also that the hostages that were in the tower should be delivered him.

7 Then came Yahonathan to Yerushalem, and read the letters in the audience of all the people, and of them that were in the tower:

8 Who were sore afraid, when they heard that the king had given him authority to gather together an host.

9 Whereupon they of the tower delivered their hostages unto Yahonathan, and he delivered them unto their parents.

10 This done, Yahonathan settled himself in Yerushalem, and began to build and repair the city.

11 And he commanded the workmen to build the walls and the mount Tzion and about with square stones for fortification; and they did so.

12 Then the strangers, that were in the fortresses which Bakkhides had built, fled away;

13 Insomuch as every man left his place, and went into his own country.

14 Only at Beth-Tzur certain of those that had forsaken the Torah and the commandments remained still: for it was their place of refuge.

15 Now when king Aleksandros had heard what promises Dimitrios had sent unto Yahonathan: when also it was told him of the battles and noble acts which he and his brethren had done, and of the pains that they had endured,

16 He said, Shall we find such another man? now therefore we will make him our friend and confederate.

17 Upon this he wrote a letter, and sent it unto him, according to these words, saying,

18 King Aleksandros to his brother Yahonathan sendeth greeting:

19 We have heard of thee, that thou art a man of great power, and meet to be our friend.

20 Wherefore now this day we ordain thee to be the high priest of thy nation, and to be called the king's friend; (and therewithal he sent him a purple robe and a crown of gold:) and require thee to take our part, and keep friendship with us.

21 So in the seventh month of the hundred and sixtieth year, at the feast of the tabernacles, Yahonathan put on the holy robe, and gathered together forces, and provided much armour.

22 Whereof when Dimitrios heard, he was very sorry, and said,

23 What have we done, that Aleksandros hath prevented us in making amity with the Yehudim

to strengthen himself?

24 I also will write unto them words of encouragement, and promise them dignities and gifts, that I may have their aid.

25 He sent unto them therefore to this effect: King Dimitrios unto the people of the Yehudim sendeth greeting:

26 Whereas ye have kept covenants with us, and continued in our friendship, not joining yourselves with our enemies, we have heard hereof, and are glad.

27 Wherefore now continue ye still to be faithful unto us, and we will well recompense you for the things ye do in our behalf,

28 And will grant you many immunities, and give you rewards.

29 And now do I free you, and for your sake I release all the Yehudim, from tributes, and from the customs of salt, and from crown taxes,

30 And from that which appertaineth unto me to receive for the third part or the seed, and the half of the fruit of the trees, I release it from this day forth, so that they shall not be taken of the land of Yehudah, nor of the three governments which are added thereunto out of the country of Shomron and Galilah, from this day forth for evermore.

31 Let Yerushalem also be holy and free, with the borders thereof, both from tenths and tributes.

32 And as for the tower which is at Yerushalem, I yield up authority over it, and give the high priest, that he may set in it such men as he shall choose to keep it.

33 Moreover I freely set at liberty every one of the Yehudim, that were carried captives out of the land of Yehudah into any part of my kingdom, and I will that all my officers remit the tributes even of their cattle.

34 Furthermore I will that all the feasts, and Shabbats, and Renewed Months, and solemn days, and the three days before the feast, and the three days after the feast shall be all of immunity and freedom for all the Yehudim in my realm.

35 Also no man shall have authority to meddle with or to molest any of them in any matter.

36 I will further, that there be enrolled among the king's forces about thirty thousand men of the Yehudim, unto whom pay shall be given, as belongeth to all king's forces.

37 And of them some shall be placed in the king's strong holds, of whom also some shall be set over the affairs of the kingdom, which are of trust: and I will that their overseers and governors be of themselves, and that they live after their own Torah, even as the king hath commanded in the land of Yehudah.

38 And concerning the three governments that are added to Yehudah from the country of Shomron, let them be joined with Yehudah, that they may be reckoned to be under one, nor bound to obey other authority than the high priest's.

39 As for Ptolemais, and the land pertaining thereto, I give it as a free gift to the sanctuary at Yerushalem for the necessary expences of the sanctuary.

40 Moreover I give every year fifteen thousand shekels of silver out of the king's accounts from the places appertaining.

41 And all the overplus, which the officers payed not in as in former time, from henceforth shall be given toward the works of the temple.

42 And beside this, the five thousand shekels of silver, which they took from the uses of the temple out of the accounts year by year, even those things shall be released, because they appertain to the priests that minister.

43 And whosoever they be that flee unto the temple at Yerushalem, or be within the liberties hereof, being indebted unto the king, or for any other matter, let them be at liberty, and all that they have in my realm.

44 For the building also and repairing of the works of the sanctuary expences shall be given of the king's accounts.

45 Yea, and for the building of the walls of Yerushalem, and the fortifying thereof round about, expences shall be given out of the king's accounts, as also for the building of the walls in Yehudah.

46 Now when Yahonathan and the people heard these words, they gave no credit unto them, nor received them, because they remembered the great evil that he had done in Yisra'EL; for he had afflicted them very sore.

47 But with Aleksandros they were well pleased, because he was the first that entreated of true shalom with them, and they were confederate with him always.

48 Then gathered king Aleksandros great forces, and camped over against Dimitrios.

49 And after the two kings had joined battle, Dimitrios' host fled: but Aleksandros followed after him, and prevailed against them.

50 And he continued the battle very sore until the sun went down: and that day was Dimitrios slain.

51 Afterward Aleksandros sent ambassadors to Talmay king of Mitzraim with a message to this effect:

52 Forasmuch as I am come again to my realm, and am set in the throne of my progenitors, and have gotten the dominion, and overthrown Dimitrios, and recovered our country;

53 For after I had joined battle with him, both he and his host was discomfited by us, so that we sit in the throne of his kingdom:

54 Now therefore let us make a league of amity together, and give me now thy daughter to wife: and I will be thy son in law, and will give both thee and her as according to thy dignity.

55 Then Talmay the king gave answer, saying, Happy be the day wherein thou didst return into the land of thy fathers, and satest in the throne of their kingdom.

56 And now will I do to thee, as thou hast written: meet me therefore at Ptolemais, that we may see one another; for I will marry my

daughter to thee according to thy desire.

57 So Talmay went out of Mitzraim with his daughter Qlio'patrah (Cleopatra), and they came unto Ptolemais in the hundred threescore and second year:

58 Where king Aleksandros meeting him, he gave unto him his daughter Qlio'patrah, and celebrated her marriage at Ptolemais with great glory, as the manner of kings is.

59 Now king Aleksandros had written unto Yahonathan, that he should come and meet him.

60 Who thereupon went honourably to Ptolemais, where he met the two kings, and gave them and their friends silver and gold, and many presents, and found favour in their sight.

61 At that time certain pestilent fellows of Yisra'EL, men of a wicked life, assembled themselves against him, to accuse him: but the king would not hear them.

62 Yea more than that, the king commanded to take off his garments, and clothe him in purple: and they did so.

63 And he made him sit by himself, and said into his princes, Go with him into the midst of the city, and make proclamation, that no man complain against him of any matter, and that no man trouble him for any manner of cause.

64 Now when his accusers saw that he was honored according to the proclamation, and clothed in purple, they fled all away.

65 So the king honoured him, and wrote him among his chief friends, and made him a duke, and partaker of his dominion.

66 Afterward Yahonathan returned to Yerushalem with shalom and gladness.

67 Furthermore in the; hundred threescore and fifth year came Dimitrios son of Dimitrios out of Qereti (Crete) into the land of his fathers:

68 Whereof when king Aleksandros heard tell, he was right sorry, and returned into Antyokya.

69 Then Dimitrios made Aphlonios the governor of Aram his general, who gathered together a great host, and camped in Yabneh, and sent unto Yahonathan the high priest, saying,

70 Thou alone liftest up thyself against us, and I am laughed to scorn for thy sake, and reproached: and why dost thou vaunt thy power against us in the mountains?

71 Now therefore, if thou trustest in thine own strength, come down to us into the plain field, and there let us try the matter together: for with me is the power of the cities.

72 Ask and learn who I am, and the rest that take our part, and they shall tell thee that thy foot is not able to to flight in their own land.

73 Wherefore now thou shalt not be able to abide the horsemen and so great a power in the plain, where is neither stone nor flint, nor place to flee unto.

74 So when Yahonathan heard these words of Aphlonios, he was moved in his mind, and choosing ten thousand men he went out of Yerushalem, where Shimon his brother met him for to help him.

75 And he pitched his tents against Yoppa: but; they of Yoppa shut him out of the city, because Aphlonios had a garrison there.

76 Then Yahonathan laid siege unto it: whereupon they of the city let him in for fear: and so Yahonathan won Yoppa.

77 Whereof when Aphlonios heard, he took three thousand horsemen, with a great host of footmen, and went to Ashdod as one that journeyed, and therewithal drew him forth into the plain. because he had a great number of horsemen, in whom he put his trust.

78 Then Yahonathan followed after him to Ashdod, where the armies joined battle.

79 Now Aphlonios had left a thousand horsemen in ambush.

80 And Yahonathan knew that there was an ambushment behind him; for they had compassed in his host, and cast darts at the people, from morning till evening.

81 But the people stood still, as Yahonathan had commanded them: and so the enemies' horses were tired.

82 Then brought Shimon forth his host, and set them against the footmen, (for the horsemen were spent) who were discomfited by him, and fled.

83 The horsemen also, being scattered in the field, fled to Ashdod, and went into Bethdagon, their idol's temple, for safety.

84 But Yahonathan set fire on Ashdod, and the cities round about it, and took their spoils; and the temple of Dagon, with them that were fled into it, he burned with fire.

85 Thus there were burned and slain with the sword well nigh eight thousand men.

86 And from thence Yahonathan removed his host, and camped against Ashqelon, where the men of the city came forth, and met him with great pomp.

87 After this returned Yahonathan and his host unto Yerushalem, having any spoils.

88 Now when king Aleksandros heard these things, he honoured Yahonathan yet more.

89 And sent him a buckle of gold, as the use is to be given to such as are of the king's blood: he gave him also Aqron with the borders thereof in possession.

11 And the king of Mitzraim gathered together a great host, like the sand that lieth upon the sea shore, and many ships, and went about through deceit to get Aleksandros' kingdom, and join it to his own.

2 Whereupon he took his journey into Spain in peaceable manner, so as they of the cities opened unto him, and met him: for king Aleksandros had commanded them so to do, because he was his brother in law.

3 Now as Talmay entered into the cities, he set in every one of them a garrison of soldiers to keep it.

4 And when he came near to Ashdod, they shewed him the temple of Dagon that was burnt, and Ash-

dod and the suburbs thereof that were destroyed, and the bodies that were cast abroad and them that he had burnt in the battle; for they had made heaps of them by the way where he should pass.

5 Also they told the king whatsoever Yahonathan had done, to the intent he might blame him: but the king held his shalom.

6 Then Yahonathan met the king with great pomp at Yoppa, where they saluted one another, and lodged.

7 Afterward Yahonathan, when he had gone with the king to the river called Eleutherus, returned again to Yerushalem.

8 King Talmay therefore, having gotten the dominion of the cities by the sea unto Seluqya upon the sea coast, imagined wicked counsels against Aleksandros.

9 Whereupon he sent ambasadors unto king Dimitrios, saying, Come, let us make a league betwixt us, and I will give thee my daughter whom Aleksandros hath, and thou shalt reign in thy father's kingdom:

10 For I repent that I gave my daughter unto him, for he sought to slay me.

11 Thus did he slander him, because he was desirous of his kingdom.

12 Wherefore he took his daughter from him, and gave her to Dimitrios, and forsook Aleksandros, so that their hatred was openly known.

13 Then Talmay entered into Antyokya, where he set two crowns upon his head, the crown of Asia, and of Mitzraim.

14 In the mean season was king Aleksandros in Qiliqya, because those that dwelt in those parts had revolted from him.

15 But when Aleksandros heard of this, he came to war against him: whereupon king Talmay brought forth his host, and met him with a mighty power, and put him to flight.

16 So Aleksandros fled into Ereb there to be defended; but king Talmay was exalted:

17 For Zabdi'EL the Arabian took off Aleksandros's head, and sent it unto Talmay.

18 King Talmay also died the third day after, and they that were in the strong holds were slain one of another.

19 By this means Dimitrios reigned in the hundred threescore and seventh year.

20 At the same time Yahonathan gathered together them that were in Yehudah to take the tower that was in Yerushalem: and he made many engines of war against it.

21 Then came ungodly persons, who hated their own people, went unto the king, and told him that Yahonathan besieged the tower,

22 Whereof when he heard, he was angry, and immediately removing, he came to Ptolemais, and wrote unto Yahonathan, that he should not lay siege to the tower, but come and speak with him at Ptolemais in great haste.

23 Nevertheless Yahonathan, when he heard this, commanded to besiege it still: and he chose certain of the elders of Yisra'EL and the priests, and put himself in peril;

24 And took silver and gold, and raiment, and divers presents besides, and went to Ptolemais unto the king, where he found favour in his sight.

25 And though certain ungodly men of the people had made complaints against him,

26 Yet the king entreated him as his predecessors had done before, and promoted him in the sight of all his friends,

27 And confirmed him in the high priesthood, and in all the honours that he had before, and gave him preeminence among his chief friends.

28 Then Yahonathan desired the king, that he would make Yehudah free from tribute, as also the three governments, with the country of Shomron; and he promised him three hundred talents.

29 So the king consented, and wrote letters unto Yahonathan of all these things after this manner:

30 King Dimitrios unto his brother Yahonathan, and unto the nation of the Yehudim, sendeth greeting:

31 We send you here a copy of the letter which we did write unto our cousin Lasthenes concerning you, that ye might see it.

32 King Dimitrios unto his father Lasthenes sendeth greeting:

33 We are determined to do good to the people of the Yehudim, who are our friends, and keep covenants with us, because of their good will toward us.

34 Wherefore we have ratified unto them the borders of Yehudah, with the three governments of Apherema and Led and Ramathem, that are added unto Yehudah from the country of Shomron, and all things appertaining unto them, for all such as do sacrifice in Yerushalem, instead of the payments which the king received of them yearly aforetime out of the fruits of the earth and of trees.

35 And as for other things that belong unto us, of the tithes and customs pertaining unto us, as also the saltpits, and the crown taxes, which are due unto us, we discharge them of them all for their relief.

36 And nothing hereof shall be revoked from this time forth for ever.

37 Now therefore see that thou make a copy of these things, and let it be delivered unto Yahonathan, and set upon the holy mount in a conspicuous place.

38 After this, when king Dimitrios saw that the land was quiet before him, and that no resistance was made against him, he sent away all his forces, every one to his own place, except certain bands of strangers, whom he had gathered from the isles of the heathen: wherefore all the forces of his fathers hated him.

39 Moreover there was one Tryphon, that had been of Aleksandros's part afore, who, seeing that all the host murmured against Dimitrios, went to Simalcue the Arabian that brought up Antiokos the young son of Aleksandros,

1 MACCABEES

40 And lay sore upon him to deliver him this young Antiokos, that he might reign in his father's stead: he told him therefore all that Dimitrios had done, and how his men of war were at enmity with him, and there he remained a long season.

41 In the mean time Yahonathan sent unto king Dimitrios, that he would cast those of the tower out of Yerushalem, and those also in the fortresses: for they fought against Yisra'EL.

42 So Dimitrios sent unto Yahonathan, saying, I will not only do this for thee and thy people, but I will greatly honour thee and thy nation, if opportunity serve.

43 Now therefore thou shalt do well, if thou send me men to help me; for all my forces are gone from me.

44 Upon this Yahonathan sent him three thousand strong men unto Antyokya: and when they came to the king, the king was very glad of their coming.

45 Howbeit they that were of the city gathered themselves together into the midst of the city, to the number of an hundred and twenty thousand men, and would have slain the king.

46 Wherefore the king fled into the court, but they of the city kept the passages of the city, and began to fight.

47 Then the king called to the Yehudim for help, who came unto him all at once, and dispersing themselves through the city slew that day in the city to the number of an hundred thousand.

48 Also they set fire on the city, and gat many spoils that day, and delivered the king.

49 So when they of the city saw that the Yehudim had got the city as they would, their courage was abated: wherefore they made supplication to the king, and cried, saying,

50 Grant us shalom, and let the Yehudim cease from assaulting us and the city.

51 With that they cast away their weapons, and made shalom; and the Yehudim were honoured in the sight of the king, and in the sight of all that were in his realm; and they returned to Yerushalem, having great spoils.

52 So king Dimitrios sat on the throne of his kingdom, and the land was quiet before him.

53 Nevertheless he dissembled in all that ever he spake, and estranged himself from Yahonathan, neither rewarded he him according to the benefits which he had received of him, but troubled him very sore.

54 After this returned Tryphon, and with him the young child Antiokos, who reigned, and was crowned.

55 Then there gathered unto him all the men of war, whom Dimitrios had put away, and they fought against Dimitrios, who turned his back and fled.

56 Moreover Tryphon took the elephants, and won Antyokya.

57 At that time young Antiokos wrote unto Yahonathan, saying, I confirm thee in the high priesthood, and appoint thee ruler over the four governments, and to be one of the king's friends.

58 Upon this he sent him golden vessels to be served in, and gave him leave to drink in gold, and to be clothed in purple, and to wear a golden buckle.

59 His brother Shimon also he made captain from the place called The ladder of Tzor unto the borders of Mitzraim.

60 Then Yahonathan went forth, and passed through the cities beyond the water, and all the forces of Aram gathered themselves unto him for to help him: and when he came to Ashqelon, they of the city met him honourably.

61 From whence he went to Azzah, but they of Azzah shut him out; wherefore he laid siege unto it, and burned the suburbs thereof with fire, and spoiled them.

62 Afterward, when they of Azzah made supplication unto Yahonathan, he made shalom with them, and took the sons of their chief men for hostages, and sent them to Yerushalem, and passed through the country unto Dameseq (Dameseq).

63 Now when Yahonathan heard that Dimitrios' princes were come to Qadesh, which is in Galilah, with a great power, purposing to remove him out of the country,

64 He went to meet them, and left Shimon his brother in the country.

65 Then Shimon encamped against Beth-Tzur and fought against it a long season, and shut it up:

66 But they desired to have shalom with him, which he granted them, and then put them out from thence, and took the city, and set a garrison in it.

67 As for Yahonathan and his host, they pitched at the water of Gennesar, from whence betimes in the morning they gat them to the plain of Nasor.

68 And, behold, the host of strangers met them in the plain, who, having laid men in ambush for him in the mountains, came themselves over against him.

69 So when they that lay in ambush rose out of their places and joined battle, all that were of Yahonathan's side fled;

70 Insomuch as there was not one of them left, except MattitYAHU the son of Absalom, and Yehudah the son of Calphi, the captains of the host.

71 Then Yahonathan rent his clothes, and cast earth upon his head, and prayed to YAHOWAH.

72 Afterwards turning again to battle, he put them to flight, and so they ran away.

73 Now when his own men that were fled saw this, they turned again unto him, and with him pursued them to Qadesh, even unto their own tents, and there they camped.

74 So there were slain of the heathen that day about three thousand men: but Yahonathan returned to Yerushalem.

12 Now when Yahonathan saw that time served him, he chose certain men, and sent them to Rome, for to confirm and renew the friendship that they had with them.

2 He sent letters also to the Lacedemonians (Spartans), and to other places, for the same purpose.

3 So they went unto Rome, and entered into the senate, and said, Yahonathan the high priest, and the people of the Yehudim, sent us unto you, to the end ye should renew the friendship, which ye had with them, and league, as in former time.

4 Upon this the Romans gave them letters unto the governors of every place that they should bring them into the land of Yehudah peaceably.

5 And this is the copy of the letters which Yahonathan wrote to the Spartans:

6 Yahonathan the high priest, and the elders of the nation, and the priests, and the other of the Yehudim, unto the Spartans their brethren send greeting:

7 There were letters sent in times past unto Khonaiw the high priest from Daryawesh, who reigned then among you, to signify that ye are our brethren, as the copy here underwritten doth specify.

8 At which time Khonaiw entreated the ambassador that was sent honourably, and received the letters, wherein declaration was made of the league and friendship.

9 Therefore we also, albeit we need none of these things, that we have the Torah of YAHOWAH in our hands to comfort us,

10 Have nevertheless attempted to send unto you for the renewing of brotherhood and friendship, lest we should become strangers unto you altogether: for there is a long time passed since ye sent unto us.

11 We therefore at all times without ceasing, both in our feasts, and other convenient days, do remember you in the sacrifices which we offer, and in our prayers to YAHOWAH, as reason is, until shalom is upon our brethren:

12 And we are right glad of your honour.

13 As for ourselves, we have had great troubles and wars on every side, forsomuch as the kings that are round about us have fought against us.

14 Howbeit we would not be troublesome unto you, nor to others of our confederates and friends, in these wars:

15 For we have help from YAHOWAH ELOHIM that succoureth us, so as we are delivered from our enemies, and our enemies are brought under foot.

16 For this cause we chose Numiniyos the son of Antiokos, and Antipater the son of Yeshua, and sent them unto the Romans, to renew the amity that we had with them, and the former league.

17 We commanded them also to go unto you, and to salute and to deliver you our letters concerning the renewing of our brotherhood.

18 Wherefore now ye shall do well to give us an answer thereto.

19 And this is the copy of the letters which Khonaiw sent.

20 Ariyos king of the Spartans to Khonaiw the high priest, greeting:

21 It is found in Chronicles, that the Spartans and Yehudim are brethren, and that they are of the stock of Abraham:

22 Now therefore, since this is come to our knowledge, ye shall do well to write unto us of your prosperity.

23 We do write back again to you, that your cattle and goods are our's, and our's are your's We do command therefore our ambassadors to make report unto you on this wise.

24 Now when Yahonathan heard that Dimiytriyos' princes were come to fight against him with a greater host than afore,

25 He removed from Yerushalem, and met them in the land of Amathis: for he gave them no respite to enter his country.

26 He sent spies also unto their tents, who came again, and told him that they were appointed to come upon them in the night season.

27 Wherefore so soon as the sun was down, Yahonathan commanded his men to watch, and to be in arms, that all the night long they might be ready to fight: also he sent forth centinels round about the host.

28 But when the adversaries heard that Yahonathan and his men were ready for battle, they feared, and trembled in their hearts, and they kindled fires in their camp.

29 Howbeit Yahonathan and his company knew it not till the morning: for they saw the lights burning.

30 Then Yahonathan pursued after them, but overtook them not: for they were gone over the river Eleutherus.

31 Wherefore Yahonathan turned to the Arabians, who were called Zabadeans, and smote them, and took their spoils.

32 And removing thence, he came to Dameseq, and so passed through all the country,

33 Shimon also went forth, and passed through the country unto Ashqelon, and the holds there adjoining, from whence he turned aside to Yoppa, and won it.

34 For he had heard that they would deliver the hold unto them that took Dimitrios' part; wherefore he set a garrison there to keep it.

35 After this came Yahonathan home again, and calling the elders of the people together, he consulted with them about building strong holds in Yehudah,

36 And making the walls of Yerushalem higher, and raising a great mount between the tower and the city, for to separate it from the city, that so it might be alone, that men might neither sell nor buy in it.

37 Upon this they came together to build up the city, forasmuch as part of the wall toward

the brook on the east side was fallen down, and they repaired that which was called Caphenatha.

38 Shimon also set up Khadidah in Sephela, and made it strong with gates and bars.

39 Now Tryphon went about to get the kingdom of Asia, and to kill Antiokos the king, that he might set the crown upon his own head.

40 Howbeit he was afraid that Yahonathan would not suffer him, and that he would fight against him; wherefore he sought a way how to take Yahonathan, that he might kill him. So he removed, and came to Bethsan.

41 Then Yahonathan went out to meet him with forty thousand men chosen for the battle, and came to Bethsan.

42 Now when Tryphon saw Yahonathan came with so great a force, he durst not stretch his hand against him;

43 But received him honourably, and commended him unto all his friends, and gave him gifts, and commanded his men of war to be as obedient unto him, as to himself.

44 Unto Yahonathan also he said, Why hast thou brought all this people to so great trouble, seeing there is no war betwixt us?

45 Therefore send them now home again, and choose a few men to wait on thee, and come thou with me to Ptolemais, for I will give it thee, and the rest of the strong holds and forces, and all that have any charge: as for me, I will return and depart: for this is the cause of my coming.

46 So Yahonathan believing him did as he bade him, and sent away his host, who went into the land of Yehudah.

47 And with himself he retained but three thousand men, of whom he sent two thousand into Galilah, and one thousand went with him.

48 Now as soon as Yahonathan entered into Ptolemais, they of Ptolemais shut the gates and took him, and all them that came with him they slew with the sword.

49 Then sent Tryphon an host of footmen and horsemen into Galilah, and into the great plain, to destroy all Yahonathan's company.

50 But when they knew that Yahonathan and they that were with him were taken and slain, they encouraged one another; and went close together, prepared to fight.

51 They therefore that followed upon them, perceiving that they were ready to fight for their lives, turned back again.

52 Whereupon they all came into the land of Yehudah peaceably, and there they bewailed Yahonathan, and them that were with him, and they were sore afraid; wherefore all Yisra'EL made great lamentation.

53 Then all the heathen that were round about them sought to destroy them: for said they, They have no captain, nor any to help them: now therefore let us make war upon them, and take away their memorial from among men.

13 Now when Shimon heard that Tryphon had gathered together a great host to invade the land of Yehudah, and destroy it,

2 And saw that the people was in great trembling and fear, he went up to Yerushalem, and gathered the people together,

3 And gave them exhortation, saying, Ye yourselves know what great things I, and my brethren, and my father's house, have done for the Torah of YAHOWAH and the sanctuary, the battles also and troubles which we have seen.

4 By reason whereof all my brethren are slain for Yisra'EL's sake, and I am left alone.

5 Now therefore be it far from me, that I should spare mine own life in any time of trouble: for I am no better than my brethren.

6 Doubtless I will avenge my nation, and the sanctuary of YAHOWAH, and our wives, and our children: for all the heathen are gathered to destroy us of very malice.

7 Now as soon as the people heard these words, their ruakh revived.

8 And they answered with a loud voice, saying, Thou shalt be our leader instead of Yehudah and Yahonathan thy brother.

9 Fight thou our battles, and whatsoever, thou commandest us, that will we do.

10 So then he gathered together all the men of war, and made haste to finish the walls of Yerushalem, and he fortified it round about.

11 Also he sent Yahonathan the son of Absolom, and with him a great power, to Yoppa: who casting out them that were therein remained there in it.

12 So Tryphon removed from Ptolemaus with a great power to invade the land of Yehudah, and Yahonathan was with him in ward.

13 But Shimon pitched his tents at Khadidah, over against the plain.

14 Now when Tryphon knew that Shimon was risen up instead of his brother Yahonathan, and meant to join battle with him, he sent messengers unto him, saying,

15 Whereas we have Yahonathan thy brother in hold, it is for money that he is owing unto the king's treasure, concerning the business that was committed unto him.

16 Wherefore now send an hundred talents of silver, and two of his sons for hostages, that when he is at liberty he may not revolt from us, and we will let him go.

17 Hereupon Shimon, albeit he perceived that they spake deceitfully unto him yet sent he the money and the children, lest peradventure he should procure to himself great hatred of the people:

18 Who might have said, Because I sent him not the money and the children, therefore is Yahonathan dead.

19 So he sent them the children and the hundred talents: howbeit Tryphon dissembled neither would he let Yahonathan go.

20 And after this came Tryphon to invade the land, and destroy it, going round about by the way

that leadeth unto Adora: but Shimon and his host marched against him in every place, wheresoever he went.

21 Now they that were in the tower sent messengers unto Tryphon, to the end that he should hasten his coming unto them by the wilderness, and send them victuals.

22 Wherefore Tryphon made ready all his horsemen to come that night: but there fell a very great snow, by reason whereof he came not. So he departed, and came into the country of Gil'ad.

23 And when he came near to Bascama he slew Yahonathan, who was buried there.

24 Afterward Tryphon returned and went into his own land.

25 Then sent Shimon, and took the bones of Yahonathan his brother, and buried them in Modin, the city of his fathers.

26 And all Yisra'EL made great lamentation for him, and bewailed him many days.

27 Shimon also built a monument upon the sepulchre of his father and his brethren, and raised it aloft to the sight, with hewn stone behind and before.

28 Moreover he set up seven pyramids, one against another, for his father, and his mother, and his four brethren.

29 And in these he made cunning devices, about the which he set great pillars, and upon the pillars he made all their armour for a perpetual memory, and by the armour ships carved, that they might be seen of all that sail on the sea.

30 This is the sepulchre which he made at Modin, and it standeth yet unto this day.

31 Now Tryphon dealt deceitfully with the young king Antiokos, and slew him.

32 And he reigned in his stead, and crowned himself king of Asia, and brought a great calamity upon the land.

33 Then Shimon built up the strong holds in Yehudah, and fenced them about with high towers, and great walls, and gates, and bars, and laid up victuals therein.

34 Moreover Shimon chose men, and sent to king Dimitrios, to the end he should give the land an immunity, because all that Tryphon did was to spoil.

35 Unto whom king Dimitrios answered and wrote after this manner:

36 King Dimitrios unto Shimon the high priest, and friend of kings, as also unto the elders and nation of the Yehudim, sendeth greeting:

37 The golden crown, and the scarlet robe, which ye sent unto us, we have received: and we are ready to make a stedfast shalom with you, yea, and to write unto our officers, to confirm the immunities which we have granted.

38 And whatsoever covenants we have made with you shall stand; and the strong holds, which ye have builded, shall be your own.

39 As for any oversight or fault committed unto this day, we forgive it, and the crown tax also, which ye owe us: and if there were any other tribute paid in Yerushalem, it shall no more be paid.

40 And look who are meet among you to be in our court, let then be enrolled, and let there be shalom betwixt us.

41 Thus the yoke of the heathen was taken away from Yisra'EL in the hundred and seventieth year.

42 Then the people of Yisra'EL began to write in their instruments and contracts, In the first year of Shimon the high priest, the governor and leader of the Yehudim.

43 In those days Shimon camped against Azzah and besieged it round about; he made also an engine of war, and set it by the city, and battered a certain tower, and took it.

44 And they that were in the engine leaped into the city; whereupon there was a great uproar in the city:

45 Insomuch as the people of the city rent their clothes, and climbed upon the walls with their wives and children, and cried with a loud voice, beseeching Shimon to grant them shalom.

46 And they said, Deal not with us according to our wickedness, but according to thy mercy.

47 So Shimon was appeased toward them, and fought no more against them, but put them out of the city, and cleansed the houses wherein the idols were, and so entered into it with songs and thanksgiving.

48 Yea, he put all uncleanness out of it, and placed such men there as would keep the Torah of YAHOWAH, and made it stronger than it was before, and built therein a dwellingplace for himself.

49 They also of the tower in Yerushalem were kept so strait, that they could neither come forth, nor go into the country, nor buy, nor sell: wherefore they were in great distress for want of victuals, and a great number of them perished through famine.

50 Then cried they to Shimon, beseeching him to be at one with them: which thing he granted them; and when he had put them out from thence, he cleansed the tower from pollutions:

51 And entered into it the three and twentieth day of the second month in the hundred seventy and first year, and they praised YAHOWAH with branches of palm trees, and with harps, and cymbals, and with viols, and hymns, and songs: because there was destroyed a great enemy out of Yisra'EL.

52 He ordained also that that day should be kept every year with gladness. Moreover the hill of the temple that was by the tower he made stronger than it was, and there he dwelt himself with his company.

53 And when Shimon saw that Yokhanan his son was a valiant man, he made him captain of all the hosts; and he dwelt in Uzza.

14 Now in the hundred threescore and twelfth year king Dimitrios gathered his forces together, and went into Madai to get him help to fight against Tryphone.

2 But when Arshaqeh, the king of Paras and Madai, heard that Dimitrios was entered within his borders, he sent one of his princes to take him alive:

3 Who went and smote the host of Dimitrios, and took him, and brought him to Arshaqeh, by whom he was put in ward.

4 As for the land of Yehudah, that was quiet all the days of Shimon; for he sought the good of his nation in such wise, as that evermore his authority and honour pleased them well.

5 And as he was honourable in all his acts, so in this, that he took Yoppa for an haven, and made an entrance to the isles of the sea,

6 And enlarged the bounds of his nation, and recovered the country,

7 And gathered together a great number of captives, and had the dominion of Uzza, and Beth-Tzur, and the tower, out of the which he took all uncleaness, neither was there any that resisted him.

8 Then did they till their ground in shalom, and the earth gave her increase, and the trees of the field their fruit.

9 The ancient men sat all in the streets, communing together of good things, and the young men put on glorious and warlike apparel.

10 He provided victuals for the cities, and set in them all manner of munition, so that his honourable name was renowned unto the end of the world.

11 He made shalom in the land, and Yisra'EL rejoiced with great joy:

12 For every man sat under his vine and his fig tree, and there was none to fray them:

13 Neither was there any left in the land to fight against them: yea, the kings themselves were overthrown in those days.

14 Moreover he strengthened all those of his people that were brought low: the Torah he searched out; and every contemner of the Torah of YAHOWAH and wicked person he took away.

15 He beautified the sanctuary of YAHOWAH, and multiplied vessels of the temple.

16 Now when it was heard at Rome, and as far as Sparta, that Yahonathan was dead, they were very sorry.

17 But as soon as they heard that his brother Shimon was made high priest in his stead, and ruled the country, and the cities therein:

18 They wrote unto him in tables of brass, to renew the friendship and league which they had made with Yehudah and Yahonathan his brethren:

19 Which writings were read before the congregation at Yerushalem.

20 And this is the copy of the letters that the Spartans sent; The rulers of the Spartans, with the city, unto Shimon the high priest, and the elders, and priests, and residue of the people of the Yehudim, our brethren, send greeting:

21 The ambassadors that were sent unto our people certified us of your glory and honour: where-

fore we were glad of their coming,

22 And did register the things that they spake in the council of the people in this manner; Numiniyos son of Antiokos, and Antipater son of Yeshua, the Yehudim'ss ambassadors, came unto us to renew the friendship they had with us.

23 And it pleased the people to entertain the men honourably, and to put the copy of their ambassage in publick records, to the end the people of the Spartans might have a memorial thereof: furthermore we have written a copy thereof unto Shimon the high priest.

24 After this Shimon sent Numiniyos to Rome with a great shield of gold of a thousand pound weight to confirm the league with them.

25 Whereof when the people heard, they said, What thanks shall we give to Shimon and his sons?

26 For he and his brethren and the house of his father have established Yisra'EL, and chased away in fight their enemies from them, and confirmed their liberty.

27 So then they wrote it in tables of brass, which they set upon pillars in mount Tzion: and this is the copy of the writing; The eighteenth day of the month Elul, in the hundred threescore and twelfth year, being the third year of Shimon the high priest,

28 At Modin in the great congregation of the priests, and people, and rulers of the nation, and elders of the country, were these things notified unto us.

29 Forasmuch as oftentimes there have been wars in the country, wherein for the maintenance of their sanctuary, and the Torah of YAHOWAH, Shimon the son of MattitYAHU, of the posterity of Yahoyarib, together with his brethren, put themselves in jeopardy, and resisting the enemies of their nation did their nation great honour:

30 (For after that Yahonathan, having gathered his nation together, and been their high priest, was added to his people,

31 Their enemies prepared to invade their country, that they might destroy it, and lay hands on the Torah of YAHOWAH and his sanctuary:

32 At which time Shimon rose up, and fought for his nation, and spent much of his own substance, and armed the valiant men of his nation and gave them wages,

33 And fortified the cities of Yehudah, together with Beth-Tzur, that lieth upon the borders of Yehudah, where the armour of the enemies had been before; but he set a garrison of Yehudim there:

34 Moreover he fortified Yoppa, which lieth upon the sea, and Uzza, that bordereth upon Ashdod, where the enemies had dwelt before: but he placed Yehudim there, and furnished them with all things convenient for the reparation thereof.)

35 The people therefore sang the acts of Shimon, and unto what glory he thought to bring his nation, made him their governor and chief priest, because he had done all these things, and for the

justice and faith which he kept to his nation, and for that he sought by all means to exalt his people.

36 And YAHOWAH was with his people in all that was done, YAHOWAH delivered the heathen into their hand, from our land and from the city of Dawid and from the fortresses that were fortified. For from it the heathen surrounded and breached the sanctuary and they defiled it, and stopped the service of YAHOWAH.

37 But he placed Yehudim therein. and fortified it for the safety of the country and the city, and raised up the walls of Yerushalem.

38 King Dimitrios also confirmed him in the high priesthood according to those things,

39 And made him one of his friends, and honoured him with great honour.

40 For he had heard say, that the Romans had called the Yehudim their friends and confederates and brethren; and that they had entertained the ambassadors of Shimon honourably;

41 Also that the Yehudim and priests were well pleased that Shimon should be their governor and high priest for ever, until there should arise a faithful prophet in Yisra'EL;

42 Moreover that he should be their captain, and should take charge of the sanctuary of YAHOWAH, to set them over their works, and over the country, and over the armour, and over the fortresses, that, I say, he should take charge of the sanctuary;

43 Beside this, that he should be obeyed of every man, and that all the writings in the country should be made in his name, and that he should be clothed in purple, and wear gold:

44 Also that it should be lawful for none of the people or priests to break any of these things, or to gainsay his words, or to gather an assembly in the country without him, or to be clothed in purple, or wear a buckle of gold;

45 And whosoever should do otherwise, or break any of these things, he should be punished.

46 Thus it liked all the people to deal with Shimon, and to do as hath been said.

47 Then Shimon accepted hereof, and was well pleased to be high priest, and captain and governor of the Yehudim and priests, and to defend them all.

48 So they commanded that this writing should be put in tables of brass, and that they should be set up within the compass of the sanctuary in a conspicuous place;

49 Also that the copies thereof should be laid up in the treasury, to the end that Shimon and his sons might have them.

15 Moreover Antiokos son of Dimitrios the king sent letters from the isles of the sea unto Shimon the priest and prince of the Yehudim, and to all the people;

2 The contents whereof were these: King Antiokos to Shimon the high priest and prince of his nation, and to the people of the Yehudim, greeting:

3 Forasmuch as certain pestilent men have usurped the kingdom of our fathers, and my purpose is to challenge it again, that I may restore it to the old estate, and to that end have gathered a multitude of foreign soldiers together, and prepared ships of war;

4 My meaning also being to go through the country, that I may be avenged of them that have destroyed it, and made many cities in the kingdom desolate:

5 Now therefore I confirm unto thee all the oblations which the kings before me granted thee, and whatsoever gifts besides they granted.

6 I give thee leave also to coin money for thy country with thine own stamp.

7 And as concerning Yerushalem and the sanctuary, let them be free; and all the armour that thou hast made, and fortresses that thou hast built, and keepest in thine hands, let them remain unto thee.

8 And if anything be, or shall be, owing to the king, let it be forgiven thee from this time forth for evermore.

9 Furthermore, when we have obtained our kingdom, we will honour thee, and thy nation, and thy temple, with great honour, so that your honour shall be known throughout the world.

10 In the hundred threescore and fourteenth year went Antiokos into the land of his fathers: at which time all the forces came together unto him, so that few were left with Tryphon.

11 Wherefore being pursued by king Antiokos, he fled unto Dora, which lieth by the sea side:

12 For he saw that troubles came upon him all at once, and that his forces had forsaken him.

13 Then camped Antiokos against Dora, having with him an hundred and twenty thousand men of war, and eight thousand horsemen.

14 And when he had compassed the city round about, and joined ships close to the town on the sea side, he vexed the city by land and by sea, neither suffered he any to go out or in.

15 In the mean season came Numiniyos and his company from Rome, having letters to the kings and countries; wherein were written these things:

16 Lucius, consul of the Romans unto king Talmay, greeting:

17 The Yehudim'ss ambassadors, our friends and confederates, came unto us to renew the old friendship and league, being sent from Shimon the high priest, and from the people of the Yehudim:

18 And they brought a shield of gold of a thousand pound.

19 We thought it good therefore to write unto the kings and countries, that they should do them no harm, nor fight against them, their cities, or countries, nor yet aid their enemies against them.

20 It seemed also good to us to receive the shield of them.

21 If therefore there be any pestilent fellows, that have fled from their country unto you, deliver

them unto Shimon the high priest, that he may punish them according to their own Torah.

22 The same things wrote he likewise unto Dimitrios the king, and Attalus, to Aritah, and Arshaqeh,

23 And to all the countries and to Zamshaqi, and the Spartans, and to Dilos, and Mindos, and Shiqon, and Qariah, and Zamos, and also the inhabitants of Pamphilah, and Liqiya, and Haliq'ranse, and Rodesh, and Pezilos, and Qu. And the men of Zidosh, and Hardon, and Qorthina, and Genidos, and Qiphros (Cyprus), and Qurini (Cyrene).

24 And the copy hereof they wrote to Shimon the high priest.

25 So Antiokos the king camped against Dora the second day, assaulting it continually, and making engines, by which means he shut up Tryphon, that he could neither go out nor in.

26 At that time Shimon sent him two thousand chosen men to aid him; silver also, and gold, and much armour.

27 Nevertheless he would not receive them, but brake all the covenants which he had made with him afore, and became strange unto him.

28 Furthermore he sent unto him Athinobios, one of his friends, to commune with him, and say, Ye withhold Yoppa and Uzza; with the tower that is in Yerushalem, which are cities of my realm.

29 The borders thereof ye have wasted, and done great hurt in the land, and got the dominion of many places within my kingdom.

30 Now therefore deliver the cities which ye have taken, and the tributes of the places, whereof ye have gotten dominion without the borders of Yehudah:

31 Or else give me for them five hundred talents of silver; and for the harm that ye have done, and the tributes of the cities, other five hundred talents: if not, we will come and fight against you

32 So Athinobios the king's friend came to Yerushalem: and when he saw the glory of Shimon, and the cupboard of gold and silver plate, and his great attendance, he was astonished, and told him the king's message.

33 Then answered Shimon, and said unto him, We have neither taken other men's land, nor holden that which appertaineth to others, but the inheritance of our fathers, which our enemies had wrongfully in possession a certain time.

34 Wherefore we, having opportunity, hold the inheritance of our fathers.

35 And whereas thou demandest Yoppa and Uzza, albeit they did great harm unto the people in our country, yet will we give thee an hundred talents for them. Hereunto Athinobios answered him not a word;

36 But returned in a rage to the king, and made report unto him of these speeches, and of the glory of Shimon, and of all that he had seen: whereupon the king was exceeding wroth.

37 In the mean time fled Tryphon by ship unto Arthushah.

38 Then the king made Qandibios captain of the sea coast, and gave him an host of footmen and horsemen,

39 And commanded him to remove his host toward Yehudah; also he commanded him to build up Qedron, and to fortify the gates, and to war against the people; but as for the king himself, he pursued Tryphon.

40 So Qandibios came to Yabneh and began to provoke the people and to invade Yehudah, and to take the people prisoners, and slay them.

41 And when he had built up Qedron, he set horsemen there, and an host of footmen, to the end that issuing out they might make outroads upon the ways of Yehudah, as the king had commanded him.

16 Then came up Yokhanan from Uzza, and told Shimon his father what Qandibios had done.

2 Wherefore Shimon called his two eldest sons, Yehudah and Yokhanan, and said unto them, from our youth unto now, I and my brethren, and my father's house, have fought against the enemies of Yisra'EL; and YAHOWAH has prospered our ways, to delivered Yisra'EL from their hands.

3 But now I am old, and ye, by ELOHIM'S mercy, are of a sufficient age: be ye instead of me and my brother, and go and fight for our nation, and the help from heaven be with you.

4 So he chose out of the country twenty thousand men of war with horsemen, who went out against Qandibios, and rested that night at Modin.

5 And when as they rose in the morning, and went into the plain, behold, a mighty great host both of footmen and horsemen came against them: howbeit there was a water brook betwixt them.

6 So he and his people pitched over against them: and when he saw that the people were afraid to go over the water brook, he went first over himself, and then the men seeing him passed through after him.

7 That done, he divided his men, and set the horsemen in the midst of the footmen: for the enemies' horsemen were very many.

8 Then sounded they with the holy trumpets: whereupon Qandibios and his host were put to flight, so that many of them were slain, and the remnant gat them to the strong hold.

9 At that time was Yehudah Yokhanan's brother wounded; but Yokhanan still followed after them, until he came to Qedron, which Qandibios had built.

10 So they fled even unto the towers in the fields of Ashdod; wherefore he burned it with fire: so that there were slain of them about two thousand men. Afterward he returned into the land of Yehudah in shalom.

11 Moreover in the plain of Yerikho was Ptolemeus the son of Khagav made captain, and he had abundance of silver and gold:

12 For he was the high priest's son in law.

13 Wherefore his heart being lifted up, he thought to get the country to himself, and thereupon con-

sulted deceitfully against Shimon and his sons to destroy them.

14 Now Shimon was visiting the cities that were in the country, and taking care for the good ordering of them; at which time he came down himself to Yerikho with his sons, Mat-titYAHU and Yehudah, in the hundred three-score and seventeenth year, in the eleventh month, called Sabat:

15 Where the son of Khagav receiving them deceitfully into a little hold, called Doek, which he had built, made them a great banquet: howbeit he had hid men there.

16 So when Shimon and his sons had drunk largely, Talmay and his men rose up, and took their weapons, and came upon Shimon into the banqueting place, and slew him, and his two sons, and certain of his servants.

17 In which doing he committed a great treachery, and recompensed evil for good.

18 Then Talmay wrote these things, and sent to the king, that he should send him an host to aid him, and he would deliver him the country and cities.

19 He sent others also to Uzza to kill Yokhanan: and unto the tribunes he sent letters to come unto him, that he might give them silver, and gold, and rewards.

20 And others he sent to take Yerushalem, and the mountain of the temple.

21 Now one had run afore to Uzza and told Yokhanan that his father and brethren were slain, and, quoth he, Talmay hath sent to slay thee also.

22 Hereof when he heard, he was sore astonished: so he laid hands on them that were come to destroy him, and slew them; for he knew that they sought to make him away.

23 As concerning the rest of the acts of Yokhanan, and his wars, and worthy deeds which he did, and the building of the walls which he made, and his doings,

24 Behold, these are written in the chronicles of his priesthood, from the time he was made high priest after his father.

THE SECOND BOOK OF
MACCABEES

1 The brethren, the Yehudim that be at Yerushalem and in the land of Yehudah, wish unto the brethren, the Yehudim that are throughout Mitzraim health and shalom:

2 ELOHIM be gracious unto you, and remember his covenant that he made with Abraham, Yitzkhaq, and Ya'aqob, his faithful servants;

3 And give you all an heart to serve him, and to do his will, with a good courage and a willing mind;

4 And YAHOWAH open your hearts in his Torah and commandments, and send you shalom,

5 And YAHOWAH hear your prayers, and be at one with you, and never forsake you in time of trouble.

6 And now we be here praying for you.

7 What time as Dimitrios reigned, in the hundred threescore and ninth year, we the Yehudim wrote unto you in the extremity of trouble that came upon us in those years, from the time that Yeshua and his company revolted from the holy land and kingdom,

8 And burned the porch, and shed innocent blood: then we prayed unto YAHOWAH, and were heard; we offered also sacrifices and fine flour, and lighted the lamps, and set forth the loaves on the table of YAHOWAH.

9 And now see that ye keep The Feast of Khanukkah of the Altar in the month Kislew.

10 In the hundred fourscore and eighth year, the people that were at Yerushalem and in Yehudah, and the council, and Yehudah, sent greeting and health unto Aristobulus, king Ptolemeus' master, who was of the stock of the anointed priests, and to the Yehudim that were in Mitzraim:

11 Insomuch as YAHOWAH ELOHIM hath delivered us from great perils, we thank him highly, as having been in battle against a king.

12 For YAHOWAH cast them out that fought within the holy city.

13 For when the leader was come into Paras, and the army with him that seemed invincible, they were slain in the temple of Nanea by the deceit of Nanea's priests.

14 For Antiokos, as though he would marry her, came into the place, and his friends that were with him, to receive money in name of a dowry.

15 Which when the priests of Nanea had set forth, and he was entered with a small company into the compass of the temple, they shut the temple as soon as Antiokos was come in:

16 And opening a privy door of the roof, they threw stones like thunderbolts, and struck down the captain, hewed them in pieces, smote off their heads and cast them to those that were without.

17 Thanksgiving and praise be to YAHOWAH in all things, who hath delivered up the ungodly.

18 Therefore whereas we are now purposed to keep The Feast of Khanukkah of the Altar upon the five and twentieth day of the month Kislew, we thought it necessary to certify you thereof, that ye also might keep it, as The Feast of Sukkot, and of the fire, which was given us when NekhemYAH offered sacrifice, after that he had builded the temple and the altar.

19 For when our fathers were led into Paras, the priests that were then devout took the fire of the altar privily, and hid it in an hollow place of a pit without water, where they kept it sure, so that the place was unknown to all men.

20 Now after many days, when it pleased YAHOWAH, NekhemYAH (Nehemiah), being sent from the king of Paras, did send of the posterity of those priests that had hid it to the fire: but when they told us they found no fire, but thick water;

21 Then commanded he them to draw it up, and to bring it; and when the sacrifices of YAHOWAH were laid on, NekhemYAH commanded the priests to sprinkle the wood and the things laid thereupon with the water.

22 When this was done, and the time came that the sun shone, which afore was hid in the cloud, there was a great fire kindled, so that every man marvelled.

23 And the priests made a prayer to YAHOWAH whilst the sacrifice was consuming, I say, both the priests, and all the rest, Yahonathan beginning, and the rest answering thereunto, as NekhemYAH did.

24 And the prayer was after this manner; O YAHOWAH ELOHIM, Creator of all things, who art fearful and strong, and righteous, and merciful, and the only and gracious King,

25 YAHOWAH the Righteous One, who opens his hand wide to all the living, and everlasting, thou that deliverest Yisra'EL from all trouble, and didst choose the fathers, and sanctify them:

26 Receive the sacrifice for thy whole people Yisra'EL, and preserve thine own portion, and sanctify it.

27 Gather those together that are scattered from us, deliver them that serve among the heathen, look upon them that are despised and abhorred, and let the heathen know that thou art YAHOWAH our ELOHIM.

28 Punish them that oppress us, and with pride do us wrong.

29 Plant thy people again in thy holy place, as Mosheh hath spoken.

30 And the priests sung psalms of thanksgiving to YAHOWAH.

31 Now when the sacrifice was consumed, NekhemYAH commanded the water that was left to be poured on the great stones.

32 When this was done, there was kindled a flame: but it was consumed by the light that shined from the altar.

33 So when this matter was known, it was told the king of Paras, that in the place, where the priests that were led away had hid the fire, there appeared water, and that NekhemYAH had purified the sacrifices therewith.

34 Then the king, inclosing the place, made it holy, after he had tried the matter.

35 And the king took many gifts, and bestowed thereof on those whom he would gratify.

36 And NekhemYAH called this thing Haphtar, which is as much as to say, a cleansing: but many men call it Nephtar.

2 It is also found in the records, that YirmeYA-HU the prophet commanded them that were carried away to take of the fire, as it hath been signified:

2 And how that the prophet, having given them the Torah, charged them not to forget the Torah of YAHOWAH, and that they should not err in their minds, when they see images of silver and gold, with their ornaments.

3 And with other such speeches exhorted he them, that the Torah of YAHOWAH should not depart from their hearts.

4 It was also contained in the same writing, that the prophet, from the mouth of YAHOWAH, commanded the tabernacle and the ark to go with him, as he went forth into the mountain, where Mosheh climbed up, and saw the heritage of ELOHIM.

5 And when YirmeYAHU came thither, he found an hollow cave, wherein he laid the tabernacle, and the ark, and the altar of incense, and so stopped the door.

6 And some of those that followed him came to mark the way, but they could not find it.

7 Which when YirmeYAHU perceived, he blamed them, saying, As for that place, it shall be unknown until the time that YAHOWAH gather his people again together, and receive them unto mercy.

8 Then shall YAHOWAH shew them these things, and the glory of YAHOWAH shall appear, and the cloud also, as it was shewed under Mosheh, and as when Shelomoh desired that the place might be honourably sanctified to YAHOWAH.

9 It was also declared, that he being wise offered the sacrifice of Khanukkah, and of the finishing of the temple of YAHOWAH.

10 And as when Mosheh prayed unto YAHOWAH, the fire came down from heaven, and consumed the sacrifices: even so prayed Shelomoh also, and the fire came down from heaven, and consumed the burnt offerings.

11 And Mosheh said, Because the sin offering was not to be eaten, it was consumed.

12 So Shelomoh kept the sacrifice to YAHOWAH those eight days.

13 The same things also were reported in the writings and commentaries of NekhemYAH; and how

he founding a library gathered together the acts of the kings, and the prophets, and of Dawid, and the epistles of the kings concerning the holy gifts.

14 In like manner also Yehudah gathered together all those things that were lost by reason of the war we had, and they remain with us,

15 Wherefore if ye have need thereof, send some to fetch them unto you.

16 Whereas we then are about to celebrate the purification, we have written unto you, and ye shall do well, if ye keep the same days.

17 We hope also, that YAHOWAH our ELOHIM, that delivered all his people, and gave them all an heritage, and the kingdom, and the priesthood, and the sanctuary,

18 As he promised in the Torah, will shortly have mercy upon us, and gather us together out of every land under heaven into the holy place: for he hath delivered us out of great troubles, and hath purified the place.

19 Now as concerning Yehudah Makabi, and his brethren, and the purification of the great temple, and the dedication of the altar,

20 And the wars against Antiokos Epiphanes (The Magnificent), and Eupator his son,

21 And the manifest signs that came from heaven unto those that behaved themselves manfully to their honour for Yehudism: so that, being but a few, they overcame the whole country, and chased barbarous multitudes,

22 And recovered again the temple renowned all the world over, and freed the city, and upheld the Torah which were going down, YAHOWAH being gracious unto them with all favour:

23 All these things, I say, being declared by Yeshua of Qurini in five books, we will assay to abridge in one volume.

24 For considering the infinite number, and the difficulty which they find that desire to look into the narrations of the story, for the variety of the matter,

25 We have been careful, that they that will read may have delight, and that they that are desirous to commit to memory might have ease, and that all into whose hands it comes might have profit.

26 Therefore to us, that have taken upon us this painful labour of abridging, it was not easy, but a matter of sweat and watching;

27 Even as it is no ease unto him that prepareth a banquet, and seeketh the benefit of others: yet for the pleasuring of many we will undertake gladly this great pains;

28 Leaving to the author the exact handling of every particular, and labouring to follow the rules of an abridgement.

29 For as the master builder of a new house must care for the whole building; but he that undertaketh to set it out, and paint it, must seek out fit things for the adorning thereof: even so I think it is with us.

30 To stand upon every point, and go over things at large, and to be curious in particulars, belongeth

to the first author of the story:

31 But to use brevity, and avoid much labouring of the work, is to be granted to him that will make an abridgment.

32 Here then will we begin the story: only adding thus much to that which hath been said, that it is a foolish thing to make a long prologue, and to be short in the story itself.

3 Now when the holy city was inhabited with all shalom, and the Torah of YAHOWAH were kept very well, because the heart of Khonaiw was whole with YAHOWAH our ELOHIM, and his hatred of wickedness,

2 It came to pass that even the kings themselves did honour the place, and magnify the temple of YAHOWAH with their best gifts;

3 Insomuch that Seliqos of Asia of his own revenues bare all the costs belonging to the service of the sacrifices in the house of YAHOWAH.

4 But one Shimon of the tribe of Benyamin, who was made governor of the temple, fell out with the high priest about disorder in the city.

5 And when he could not overcome Khonaiw, he gat him to Aphlonios the son of Thraseas, who then was governor of Aram and Kena'an,

6 And told him that the treasury in Yerushalem was full of infinite sums of money, so that the multitude of their riches, which did not pertain to the account of the sacrifices, was innumerable, and that it was possible to bring all into the king's hand.

7 Now when Aphlonios came to the king, and had shewed him of the money whereof he was told, the king chose out Hiliodoros his treasurer, and sent him with a commandment to bring him the foresaid money.

8 So forthwith Hiliodoros took his journey; under a colour of visiting the cities of Aram and Kena'an, but indeed to fulfil the king's purpose.

9 And when he was come to Yerushalem, and had been courteously received of the high priest of the city, he told him what intelligence was given of the money, and declared wherefore he came, and asked if these things were so indeed.

10 Then the high priest told him that there was such money laid up for the relief of widows and fatherless children:

11 And that some of it belonged to TobiYAH son of Horqenos, a man of great dignity, and not as that wicked Shimon had misinformed: the sum whereof in all was four hundred talents of silver, and two hundred of gold:

12 And that it was altogether impossible that such wrongs should be done unto them, that had committed it to the holiness of the place, and to the majesty and inviolable sanctity of the temple of YAHOWAH, honoured over all the world.

13 But Hiliodoros, because of the king's commandment given him, said, That in any wise it must be brought into the king's treasury.

14 So at the day which he appointed he entered in to order this matter: wherefore there was no small agony throughout the whole city.

15 But the priests, prostrating themselves before the altar of YAHOWAH in their priests' vestments, called unto YAHOWAH upon him that made a Torah concerning things given to be kept, that they should safely be preserved for such as had committed them to be kept.

16 Then whoso had looked the high priest in the face, it would have wounded his heart: for his countenance and the changing of his colour declared the inward agony of his mind.

17 For the man was so compassed with fear and horror of the body, that it was manifest to them that looked upon him, what sorrow he had now in his heart.

18 Others ran flocking out of their houses to the general supplication to YAHOWAH, because the house of YAHOWAH was like to come into contempt of the Heathen.

19 And the women, girt with sackcloth under their breasts, abounded in the streets, and the virgins that were kept in ran, some to the gates, and some to the walls, and others looked out of the windows.

20 And all, holding their hands toward heaven, made supplication to YAHOWAH.

21 Then it would have pitied a man to see the falling down of the multitude of all sorts, and the fear of the high priest crying out to YAHOWAH for deliverance.

22 They then called upon YAHOWAH to keep the things committed of trust safe and sure for those that had committed them.

23 Nevertheless Hiliodoros executed that which was decreed.

24 Now as he was there present himself with his guard about the treasury, YAHOWAH ELOHIM of RUKHOTH caused a great apparition, so that all that presumed to come in with him were astonished at the power of ELOHIM, and fainted, and were sore afraid.

25 For there appeared unto them an horse with a terrible rider upon him, and adorned with a very fair covering, and he ran fiercely, and smote at Hiliodoros with his forefeet, and it seemed that he that sat upon the horse had complete harness of gold.

26 Moreover two other young men appeared before him, notable in strength, excellent in beauty, and comely in apparel, who stood by him on either side; and scourged him continually, and gave him many sore stripes.

27 And Hiliodoros fell suddenly unto the ground, and was compassed with great darkness: but they that were with him took him up, and put him into a litter.

28 Thus him, that lately came with a great train and with all his guard into the treasury of YAHOWAH, they carried out, being unable to help himself with his weapons: and manifestly they acknowledged the power of ELOHIM.

29 For he by the hand of YAHOWAH was cast down, and lay speechless without all hope of life.

30 But they praised YAHOWAH, that had miraculously honoured his own place: for the temple of YAHOWAH; which a little afore was full of fear

and trouble, when YAHOWAH appeared, was filled with joy and gladness.

31 Then straightways certain of Hiliodoros' friends prayed Khonaiw, that he would call upon the Presence of YAHOWAH to grant him his life, who lay ready to die.

32 So the high priest, suspecting lest the king should misconceive that some treachery had been done to Hiliodoros by the Yehudim, offered a sacrifice for the health of the man.

33 Now as the high priest was making an atonement, the same young men in the same clothing appeared and stood beside Hiliodoros, saying, Give Khonaiw the high priest great thanks, in somuch as for his sake YAHOWAH hath granted thee life:

34 And seeing that the hand of YAHOWAH hast scourged thee from heaven, declare unto all men the mighty power of our ELOHIM. And when they had spoken these words, they appeared no more.

35 So Hiliodoros, after he had offered sacrifice unto YAHOWAH, and made great vows unto him that had saved his life, and saluted Khonaiw, returned with his host to the king.

36 Then testified he to all men the works of the great YAHOWAH, which he had seen with his eyes.

37 And when the king Hiliodoros, who might be a fit man to be sent yet once again to Yerushalem, he said,

38 If thou hast any enemy or traitor, send him thither, and thou shalt receive him well scourged, if he escape with his life: for in that place, no doubt; there is an especial power of ELOHIM.

39 For he that dwelleth in heaven hath his eye on that place, and defendeth it; and he beateth and destroyeth them that come to hurt it.

40 And the things concerning Hiliodoros, and the keeping of the treasury, fell out on this sort.

4 This Shimon now, of whom we spake afore, having been a betrayer of the money, and of his country, slandered Khonaiw, as if he had terrified Hiliodoros, and been the worker of these evils.

2 Thus was he bold to call him a traitor, that had deserved well of the city, and tendered his own nation, and was so zealous of the Torah of YAHOWAH.

3 But when their hatred went so far, that by one of Shimon's faction murders were committed,

4 Khonaiw seeing the danger of this contention, and that Aphlonios, as being the governor of Aram and Kena'an, did rage, and increase Shimon's malice,

5 He went to the king, not to be an accuser of his countrymen, but seeking the good of all, both publick and private:

6 For he saw that it was impossible that the state should continue quiet, and Shimon leave his folly, unless the king did look thereunto.

7 But after the death of Seliqos, when Antiokos, called The Magnificent, took the kingdom, Yeshua the brother of Khonaiw laboured underhand to be high priest,

8 Promising unto the king by intercession three hundred and threescore talents of silver, and of another revenue eighty talents:

9 Beside this, he promised to assign an hundred and fifty more, if he might have licence to set him up a place for exercise, and for the training up of youth in the fashions of the heathen, and to write them of Yerushalem by the name of Antiochians.

10 Which when the king had granted, and he had gotten into his hand the rule he forthwith brought his own nation to Greekish fashion.

11 And the royal privileges granted of special favour to the Yehudim by the means of Yokhanan the father of Eupoliymos, who went ambassador to Rome for amity and aid, he took away; and putting down the governments which were according to the Torah of YAHOWAH, he brought up new customs against the Torah:

12 For he built gladly a place of exercise under the tower itself, and brought the chief young men under his subjection, and made them wear a hat.

13 Now such was the height of Greek fashions, and increase of heathenish manners, through the exceeding profaneness of Yeshua, that ungodly wretch, and no high priest;

14 That the priests had no courage to serve any more at the altar, but despising the temple, and neglecting the sacrifices, hastened to be partakers of the unlawful allowance in the place of exercise, after the game of Discus called them forth;

15 Not setting by the honours of their fathers, but liking the glory of the Grecians best of all.

16 By reason whereof YAHOWAH sent sore calamity upon them: for they had them to be their enemies and avengers, whose custom they followed so earnestly, and unto whom they desired to be like in all things.

17 For it is not a light thing to do wickedly against the word of YAHOWAH: but the time following shall declare these things.

18 Now when the game that was used every faith year was kept at Tzor, the king being present,

19 This ungracious Yeshua sent special messengers from Yerushalem, who were Antiochians, to carry three hundred drachms of silver to the sacrifice of Hercules, which even the bearers thereof thought fit not to bestow upon the sacrifice, because it was not convenient, but to be reserved for other charges.

20 This money then, in regard of the sender, was appointed to Hercules' sacrifice; but because of the bearers thereof, it was employed to the making of gallies.

21 Now when Aphlonios the son of Menestheus was sent into Mitzraim for the coronation of king Ptolemeus Philometor, Antiokos, understanding him not to be well affected to his affairs, provided for his own safety: whereupon he came to Yoppa, and from thence to Yerushalem:

22 Where he was honourably received of Yeshua, and of the city, and was brought in with torch alight, and with great shoutings: and so afterward went with his host unto Kena'an.

23 Three years afterward Yeshua sent Minylaos, the aforesaid Shimon's brother, to bear the money unto the king, and to put him in mind of certain necessary matters.

24 But he being brought to the presence of the king, when he had magnified him for the glorious appearance of his power, got the priesthood to himself, offering more than Yeshua by three hundred talents of silver.

25 So he came with the king's mandate, bringing nothing worthy the high priesthood, but having the fury of a cruel tyrant, and the rage of a savage beast.

26 Then Yeshua, who had undermined his own brother, being undermined by another, was compelled to flee into the country of the Ammonim.

27 So Minylaos got the principality: but as for the money that he had promised unto the king, he took no good order for it, albeit Sostratis the ruler of the castle required it:

28 For unto him appertained the gathering of the customs. Wherefore they were both called before the king.

29 Now Minylaos left his brother Lizimakos in his stead in the priesthood; and Sostratus left Crates, who was governor of the Cyprians.

30 While those things were in doing, they of Tarsi (Tarsus) and Mallos made insurrection, because they were given to the king's concubine, called Antiokos.

31 Then came the king in all haste to appease matters, leaving Androniqos, a man in authority, for his deputy.

32 Now Minylaos, supposing that he had gotten a convenient time, stole certain vessels of gold out of the temple, and gave some of them to Androniqos, and some he sold into Tzor and the cities round about.

33 Which when Khonaiw knew of a surety, he reproved him, and withdrew himself into a sanctuary at Daphne, that lieth by Antokyah.

34 Wherefore Minylaos, taking Androniqos apart, prayed, him to get Khonaiw into his hands; who being persuaded thereunto, and coming to Khonaiw in deceit, gave him his right hand with oaths; and though he were suspected by him, yet persuaded he him to come forth of the sanctuary: whom forthwith he shut up without regard of justice.

35 For the which cause not only the Yehudim, but many also of other nations, took great indignation, and were much grieved for the unjust murder of the man.

36 And when the king was come again from the places about Qiliqya, the Yehudim that were in the city, and certain of the Greeks that abhorred the fact also, complained because Khonaiw was slain without cause.

37 Therefore Antiokos was heartily sorry, and moved to pity, and wept, because of the sober and modest behaviour of him that was dead.

38 And being kindled with anger, forthwith he took away Androniqos his purple, and rent off his clothes, and leading him through the whole city unto that very place, where he had committed impiety against Khonaiw, there slew he the cursed murderer. Thus YAHOWAH rewarded him his punishment, as he had deserved.

39 Now when many sacrileges had been committed in the city by Lizimakos with the consent of Minylaos, and the fruit thereof was spread abroad, the multitude gathered themselves together against Lizimakos, many vessels of gold being already carried away.

40 Whereupon the common people rising, and being filled with rage, Lizimakos armed about three thousand men, and began first to offer violence; one Auranus being the leader, a man far gone in years, and no less in folly.

41 They then seeing the attempt of Lizimakos, some of them caught stones, some clubs, others taking handfuls of dust, that was next at hand, cast them all together upon Lizimakos, and those that set upon them.

42 Thus many of them they wounded, and some they struck to the ground, and all of them they forced to flee: but as for the churchrobber himself, him they killed beside the treasury.

43 Of these matters therefore there was an accusation laid against Minylaos.

44 Now when the king came to Tzor, three men that were sent from the senate pleaded the cause before him:

45 But Minylaos, being now convicted, promised Talmay the son of Dorimon to give him much money, if he would pacify the king toward him.

46 Whereupon Talmay taking the king aside into a certain gallery, as it were to take the air, brought him to be of another mind:

47 Insomuch that he discharged Minylaos from the accusations, who notwithstanding was cause of all the mischief: and those poor men, who, if they had told their cause, yea, before the Scythians, should have been judged innocent, them he condemned to death.

48 Thus they that followed the matter for the city, and for the people, and for the holy vessels, did soon suffer unjust punishment.

49 Wherefore even they of Tzor, moved with hatred of that wicked deed, caused them to be honourably buried.

50 And so through the covetousness of them that were of power Minylaos remained still in authority, increasing in malice, and being a great traitor to the citizens.

5 About the same time Antiokos prepared his second voyage into Mitzraim:

2 And then it happened, that through all the city, for the space almost of forty days, there were seen horsemen running in the air, in cloth of gold, and armed with lances, like a band of soldiers,

3 And troops of horsemen in array, encountering and running one against another, with shaking

of shields, and multitude of pikes, and drawing of swords, and casting of darts, and glittering of golden ornaments, and harness of all sorts.

4 Wherefore every man prayed to YAHOWAH that that apparition might turn to good.

5 Now when there was gone forth a false rumour, as though Antiokos had been dead, Yeshua took at the least a thousand men, and suddenly made an assault upon the city; and they that were upon the walls being put back, and the city at length taken, Minylaos fled into the castle:

6 But Yeshua slew his own citizens without mercy, not considering that to get the day of them of his own nation would be a most unhappy day for him; but thinking they had been his enemies, and not his countrymen, whom he conquered.

7 Howbeit for all this he obtained not the principality, but at the last received shame for the reward of his treason, and fled again into the country of the Ammonim.

8 In the end therefore he had an unhappy return, being accused before Aretas the king of the Arabians, fleeing from city to city, pursued of all men, hated as a forsaker of the Torah, and being had in abomination as an open enemy of his country and countrymen, he was cast out into Mitzraim.

9 Thus he that had driven many out of their country perished in a strange land, retiring to the Spartans, and thinking there to find succour by reason of his kindred:

10 And he that had cast out many unburied had none to mourn for him, nor any solemn funerals at all, nor sepulchre with his fathers.

11 Now when this that was done came to the king's car, he thought that Yehudah had revolted: whereupon removing out of Mitzraim in a furious mind, he took the city by force of arms,

12 And commanded his men of war not to spare such as they met, and to slay such as went up upon the houses.

13 Thus there was killing of young and old, making away of men, women, and children, slaying of virgins and infants.

14 And there were destroyed within the space of three whole days fourscore thousand, whereof forty thousand were slain in the conflict; and no fewer sold than slain.

15 Yet was he not content with this, but presumed to go into the most holy temple of all the world; Minylaos, that traitor to the Torah of YAHOWAH, and to his own country, being his guide:

16 And taking the holy vessels with polluted hands, and with profane hands pulling down the things that were dedicated by other kings to the augmentation and glory and honour of the place, he gave them away.

17 And so haughty was Antiokos in mind, that he considered not that YAHOWAH was angry for a while for the sins of them that dwelt in the city, and therefore his eye was not upon the place.

18 For the anger of YAHOWAH was on the people for their sins were like dung, this man, as soon as he had come, the hand of YAHOWAH had af-

flicted him, and put back from his presumption, as Hiliodoros was, whom Seliqos the king sent to view the treasury.

19 Nevertheless YAHOWAH did not choose the people for the place's sake, but the place far the people's sake.

20 And therefore the place itself, that was partaker with them of the adversity that happened to the nation, did afterward communicate in the benefits sent from YAHOWAH: and as it was forsaken in the wrath of the Almighty, so again, the great YAHOWAH being reconciled, it was set up with all glory.

21 So when Antiokos had carried out of the temple a thousand and eight hundred talents, he departed in all haste unto Antokyah, weening in his pride to make the land navigable, and the sea passable by foot: such was the haughtiness of his mind.

22 And he left governors to vex the nation: at Yerushalem, Philipos, for his country a Phrygian, and for manners more barbarous than he that set him there;

23 And at mount Garizim, Androniqos; and besides, Minylaos, who worse than all the rest bare an heavy hand over the citizens, having a malicious mind against the Assembly of YAHOWAH.

24 He sent also that detestable ringleader Aphlonios with an army of two and twenty thousand, commanding him to slay all those that were in their best age, and to sell the women and the younger sort:

25 Who coming to Yerushalem, and pretending shalom, did forbear till the holy day of the Shabbat, when taking the Yehudim keeping holy day, he commanded his men to arm themselves.

26 And so he slew all them that were gone to the celebrating of the Shabbat, and running through the city with weapons slew great multitudes.

27 But Yehudah Makabi with nine others, or thereabout, withdrew himself into the wilderness, and lived in the mountains after the manner of beasts, with his company, who fed on herbs continually, lest they should be partakers of the pollution.

6 Not long after this the king sent an old man of Athinas (Athens) to compel the Yehudim to depart from the Torah of their fathers, and not to live after the Torah of YAHOWAH:

2 And to pollute also the temple in Yerushalem, and to call it the temple of Jupiter Olympius; and that in Garizim, of Jupiter the Defender of strangers, as they did desire that dwelt in the place.

3 The coming in of this mischief was sore and grievous to the people:

4 For the temple was filled with riot and revelling by the Gentiles, who dallied with harlots, and had to do with women within the circuit of the holy places, and besides that brought in things that were not lawful.

5 The altar of YAHOWAH also was filled with profane things, which the Torah forbiddeth.

6 Neither was it lawful for a man to keep Shabbat days or ancient fasts, or to profess himself at all to be a Yehudi.

7 And in the day of the king's birth every month they were brought by bitter constraint to eat of the sacrifices; and when the fast of Bacchus was kept, the Yehudim were compelled to go in procession to Bacchus, carrying ivy.

8 Moreover there went out a decree to the neighbour cities of the heathen, by the suggestion of Talmay, against the Yehudim, that they should observe the same fashions, and be partakers of their sacrifices:

9 And whoso would not conform themselves to the manners of the Gentiles should be put to death. Then might a man have seen the present misery.

10 For there were two women brought, who had circumcised their children; whom when they had openly led round about the city, the babes hanging at their breasts, they cast them down headlong from the wall.

11 And others, that had run together into caves near by, to keep the Shabbat day secretly, being discovered by Philipos, were all burnt together, because they made a conscience to help themselves for the honour of the most sacred day.

12 Now I beseech those that read this book, that they be not discouraged for these calamities, but that they judge those punishments not to be for destruction, but for a chastening of our nation.

13 For it is a token of his great goodness, when wicked doers are not suffered any long time, but forthwith punished.

14 For not as with other nations, whom YAHOWAH patiently forbeareth to punish, till they be come to the fulness of their sins, so dealeth he with us,

15 Lest that, being come to the height of sin, afterwards he should take vengeance of us.

16 And therefore ELOHIM never withdraweth his mercy from us: and though he punish with adversity, yet doth YAHOWAH never forsake his people.

17 But let this that we at spoken be for a warning unto us. And now will we come to the declaring of the matter in a few words.

18 Eleazar, one of the principal scribes, an aged man, and of a well favoured countenance, was constrained to open his mouth, and to eat swine's flesh.

19 But he, choosing rather to die gloriously, than to live stained with such an abomination, spit it forth, and came of his own accord to the torment,

20 As it behoved them to come, that are resolute to stand out against such things, as are not lawful for love of YAHOWAH to be tasted.

21 But they that had the charge of that wicked feast, for the old acquaintance they had with the man, taking him aside, besought him to bring flesh of his own provision, such as was lawful for him to use, and make as if he did eat of the flesh taken from the sacrifice commanded by the king;

22 That in so doing he might be delivered from death, and for the old friendship with them find favour.

23 But he began to consider discreetly, and as became his age, and the excellency of his ancient years, and the honour of his gray head, whereon was come, and his most honest education from a child, or rather the holy Torah made and given by YAHOWAH: therefore he answered accordingly, and willed them straightways to send him to the grave.

24 For it becometh not our age, said he, in any wise to dissemble, whereby many young persons might think that Eleazar, being fourscore years old and ten, were now gone to a strange customs;

25 And so they through mine hypocrisy, and desire to live a little time and a moment longer, should be deceived by me, and I get a stain to mine old age, and make it abominable.

26 For though for the present time I should be delivered from the punishment of men: yet should I not escape the hand of YAHOWAH, neither alive, nor dead.

27 Wherefore now, manfully changing this life, I will shew myself such an one as mine age requireth,

28 And leave a notable example to such as be young to die willingly and courageously for the honourable and holy Torah. And when he had said these words, immediately he went to the torment:

29 They that led him changing the good will they bare him a little before into hatred, because the foresaid speeches proceeded, as they thought, from a desperate mind.

30 But when he was ready to die with stripes, he groaned, and said, It is manifest unto YAHOWAH, that hath the holy knowledge, that whereas I might have been delivered from death, I now endure sore pains in body by being beaten: but in soul am well content to suffer these things, because I fear him.

31 And thus this man died, leaving his death for an example of a noble courage, and a memorial of virtue,for the Torah of YAHOWAH not only unto young men, but unto all his nation.

7 It came to pass also, that seven brethren with their mother were taken, and compelled by the king against the Torah to taste swine's flesh, and were tormented with scourges and whips.

2 But one of them that spake first said thus, What wouldest thou ask or learn of us? we are ready to die, rather than to transgress the Torah of our fathers.

3 Then the king, being in a rage, commanded pans and caldrons to be made hot:

4 Which forthwith being heated, he commanded to cut out the tongue of him that spake first, and to cut off the utmost parts of his body, the rest of his brethren and his mother looking on.

5 Now when he was thus maimed in all his members, he commanded him being yet alive to be brought to the fire, and to be fried in the pan: and as the vapour of the pan was for a good space dispersed, they exhorted one another with the mother to die manfully, saying thus,

6 The Kherub of YAHOWAH looketh upon us, and in truth hath comfort in us, as Mosheh the servant of YAHOWAH in his song, which witnessed to their faces, declared, saying, And he shall be comforted in his servants.

7 So when the first was dead after this number, they brought the second to make him a mocking stock: and when they had pulled off the skin of his head with the hair, they asked him, Wilt thou eat, before thou be punished throughout every member of thy body?

8 But he answered in his own language, and said, No. Wherefore he also received the next torment in order, as the former did.

9 And when he was at the last gasp, he said, Thou like a fury takest us out of this present life, but the King of the world shall raise us up, who have died for his Torah, unto everlasting life.

10 After him was the third made a mocking stock: and when he was required, he put out his tongue, and that right soon, holding forth his hands manfully.

11 And said courageously, These I had from heaven; and for his Torah I despise them; and from him I hope to receive them again.

12 Insomuch that the king, and they that were with him, marvelled at the young man's courage, for that he nothing regarded the pains.

13 Now when this man was dead also, they tormented and mangled the fourth in like manner.

14 So when he was ready to die he said thus, It is good, being put to death by men, to look for hope from YAHOWAH to be raised up again by him: as for thee, thou shalt have no resurrection to life.

15 Afterward they brought the fifth also, and mangled him.

16 Then looked he unto the king, and said, Thou hast power over men, thou art corruptible, thou doest what thou wilt; yet think not that our nation is forsaken of YAHOWAH;

17 But abide a while, and behold his great power, how YAHOWAH will torment thee and thy house.

18 After him also they brought the sixth, who being ready to die said, Be not deceived without cause: for we suffer these things for ourselves, having sinned against YAHOWAH our ELOHIM: therefore marvellous things are done unto us.

19 But think not thou, that takest in hand to strive against YAHOWAH, that thou shalt escape unpunished.

20 But the mother was marvellous above all, and worthy of honourable memory: for when she saw her seven sons slain within the space of one day, she bare it with a good courage, because of the hope that she had in YAHOWAH.

21 Yea, she exhorted every one of them in her own language, filled with courageous spirits; and stirring up her womanish thoughts with a manly stomach, she said unto them,

22 I cannot tell how ye came into my womb: for I neither gave you breath nor life, neither was it I that formed the members of every one of you;

23 But doubtless YAHOWAH the Creator of the world, who formed the generation of man, and found out the beginning of all things, will also of his own mercy give you breath and life again, as ye now regard not your own selves for his Torah' sake.

24 Now Antiokos, thinking himself despised, and suspecting it to be a reproachful speech, whilst the youngest was yet alive, did not only exhort him by words, but also assured him with oaths, that he would make him both a rich and a happy man, if he would turn from the Torah of his fathers; and that also he would take him for his friend, and trust him with affairs.

25 But when the young man would in no case hearken unto him, the king called his mother, and exhorted her that she would counsel the young man to save his life.

26 And when he had exhorted her with many words, she promised him that she would counsel her son.

27 But she bowing herself toward him, laughing the cruel tyrant to scorn, spake in her country language on this manner; O my son, have pity upon me that bare thee nine months in my womb, and gave thee such three years, and nourished thee, and brought thee up unto this age, and endured the troubles of education.

28 I beseech thee, my son, look upon the heaven and the earth, and all that is therein, and consider that ELOHIM made them of things that were not; and so was mankind made likewise.

29 Fear not this tormentor, but, being worthy of thy brethren, take thy death that YAHOWAH ELOHIM may receive thee again in mercy with thy brethren.

30 Whiles she was yet speaking these words, the young man said, Whom wait ye for? I will not obey the king's commandment: but I will obey the commandment of the Torah of YAHOWAH that was given unto our fathers by Mosheh.

31 And thou, that hast been the author of all mischief against the Hebrews, shalt not escape the hand of YAHOWAH.

32 For we suffer because of our sins.

33 And though the living YAHOWAH be angry with us a little while for our chastening and correction, yet shall he be at one again with his servants.

34 But thou, O godless man, and of all other most wicked, be not lifted up without a cause, nor puffed up with uncertain hopes, lifting up thy hand against the servants of YAHOWAH:

2 MACCABEES

35 For thou hast not yet escaped the judgment of Almighty ELOHIM, who seeth all things.

36 For our brethren, who now have suffered a short pain, are dead under ELOHIM'S covenant of everlasting life: but thou, through the judgment of YAHOWAH, shalt receive just punishment for thy pride.

37 But I, as my brethren, offer up my body and life for the Torah of our fathers, beseeching YAHOWAH that he would speedily be merciful unto our nation; and that thou by torments and plagues mayest confess, that he alone is YAHOWAH;

38 And that in me and my brethren the wrath of YAHOWAH, which is justly brought upon our nation, may cease.

39 Than the king' being in a rage, handed him worse than all the rest, and took it grievously that he was mocked.

40 So this man died undefiled, and put his whole trust in ELOHIM.

41 Last of all after the sons the mother died.

42 Let this be enough now to have spoken concerning the idolatrous feasts, and the extreme tortures.

8 Then Yehudah Makabi, and they that were with him, went privily into the towns, and called their kinsfolks together, and took unto them all such as continued in the Torah of YAHOWAH, and assembled about six thousand men.

2 And they called upon YAHOWAH their ELOHIM, that YAHOWAH would look upon the people that was trodden down of all; and also pity the temple profaned of ungodly men;

3 And that he would have compassion upon the city, sore defaced, and ready to be made even with the ground; and hear the blood that cried unto him,

4 And remember the wicked slaughter of harmless infants, and the blasphemies committed against his name; and that he would shew his hatred against the wicked.

5 Now when Makabi had his company about him, he could not be withstood by the heathen: for the wrath of YAHOWAH was turned into mercy.

6 Therefore he came at unawares, and burnt up towns and cities, and got into his hands the most commodious places, and overcame and put to flight no small number of his enemies.

7 But specially took he advantage of the night for such privy attempts, insomuch that the fruit of his holiness was spread every where.

8 So when Philipos saw that this man increased by little and little, and that things prospered with him still more and more, he wrote unto Ptolemeus, the governor of Aram and Kena'an, to yield more aid to the king's affairs.

9 Then forthwith choosing Niqanor the son of Patroclus, one of his special friends, he sent him with no fewer than twenty thousand of all nations under him, to root out the whole generation of the Yehudim; and with him he joined also Gorgias a captain, who in matters of war had great experience.

10 So Niqanor undertook to make so much money of the captive Yehudim, as should defray the tribute of two thousand talents, which the king was to pay to the Romans.

11 Wherefore immediately he sent to the cities upon the sea coast, proclaiming a sale of the captive Yehudim, and promising that they should have fourscore and ten bodies for one talent, not expecting the vengeance that was to follow upon him from YAHOWAH.

12 Now when word was brought unto Yehudah of Niqanor's coming, and he had imparted unto those that were with him that the army was at hand,

13 They that were fearful, and distrusted the justice of ELOHIM, fled, and conveyed themselves away.

14 Others sold all that they had left, and withal besought YAHOWAH to deliver them, sold by the wicked Niqanor before they met together:

15 And if not for their own sakes, yet for the covenants he had made with their fathers, and for his holy and glorious name's sake, by which they were called.

16 So Makabi called his men together unto the number of six thousand, and exhorted them not to be stricken with terror of the enemy, nor to fear the great multitude of the heathen, who came wrongly against them; but to fight manfully,

17 And to set before their eyes the injury that they had unjustly done to the holy place of YAHOWAH, and the cruel handling of the city, whereof they made a mockery, and also the taking away of the government of their forefathers:

18 For they, said he, trust in their weapons and boldness; but our confidence is in the name of YAHOWAH our ELOHIM who at a beck can cast down both them that come against us, and also all the world.

19 Moreover, he recounted unto them what deliverance YAHOWAH did to their forefathers, and how they were delivered, when under Sanchaerib an hundred fourscore and five thousand perished.

20 And he told them of the battle that they had in Babel with the Galatians, how they came but eight thousand in all to the business, with four thousand Macedonians, and that the Macedonians being perplexed, the eight thousand destroyed an hundred and twenty thousand because of the help that they had from the hand of YAHOWAH from heaven, and so received a great booty.

21 Thus when he had made them bold with these words, and ready to die for the Torah and the country, he divided his army into four parts;

22 And joined with himself his own brethren, leaders of each band, to wit Shimon, and Yoseph, and Yahonathan, giving each one fifteen hundred men.

23 Also he appointed Eleazar to read the Torah of YAHOWAH: and when he had given them this watchword, The help of YAHOWAH; himself leading the first band,

24 And by the help of YAHOWAH ELOHIM they slew above nine thousand of their enemies, and wounded and maimed the most part of Niqanor's host, and so put all to flight;

25 And took their money that came to buy them, and pursued them far: but lacking time they returned:

26 For it was the day before the Shabbat, and therefore they would no longer pursue them.

27 So when they had gathered their armour together, and spoiled their enemies, they occupied themselves about the Shabbat, yielding exceeding praise and thanks to YAHOWAH their ELOHIM, who had preserved them unto that day, which was the beginning of mercy distilling upon them.

28 And after the Shabbat, when they had given part of the spoils to the maimed, and the widows, and orphans, the residue they divided among themselves and their servants.

29 When this was done, and they had made a common supplication to YAHOWAH ELOHIM, they besought the merciful YAHOWAH to be reconciled with his servants for ever.

30 Moreover of those that were with Timotios and Bakkhides, who fought against them, they slew above twenty thousand, and very easily got high and strong holds, and divided among themselves many spoils more, and made the maimed, orphans, widows, yea, and the aged also, equal in spoils with themselves.

31 And when they had gathered their armour together, they laid them up all carefully in convenient places, and the remnant of the spoils they brought to Yerushalem.

32 They slew also Philarches, that wicked person, who was with Timotios, and had annoyed the Yehudim many ways.

33 Furthermore at such time as they kept the feast for the Victory of YAHOWAH in Yerushalem they burnt Qalistines, that had set fire upon the holy gates, who had fled into a little house; and so he received a reward meet for his wickedness.

34 As for that most ungracious Niqanor, who had brought a thousand merchants to buy the Yehudim,

35 He was through the help of YAHOWAH brought down by them, of whom he made least account; and putting off his glorious apparel, and discharging his company, he came like a fugitive servant through the midland unto Antyokya having very great dishonour, for that his host was destroyed.

36 Thus he, that took upon him to make good to the Romans their tribute by means of captives in Yerushalem, told abroad, that the Yehudim had ELOHIM to fight for them, and therefore they could not be hurt, because they followed the Torah that he gave them.

9 About that time came Antiokos with dishonour out of the country of Paras

2 For he had entered the city called Persepolis, and went about to rob the temple, and to hold the city; whereupon the multitude running to defend themselves with their weapons put them to flight; and so it happened, that Antiokos being put to flight of the inhabitants returned with shame.

3 Now when he came to Ecbatane, news was brought him what had happened unto Niqanor and Timotios.

4 Then swelling with anger. he thought to avenge upon the Yehudim the disgrace done unto him by those that made him flee. Therefore commanded he his chariotman to drive without ceasing, and to dispatch the journey, the judgment of YAHOWAH now following him. For he had spoken proudly in this sort, That he would come to Yerushalem and make it a common burying place of the Yehudim.

5 But YAHOWAH Almighty, the ELOHIM of Isreal, smote him with an incurable and invisible plague: or as soon as he had spoken these words, a pain of the bowels that was remediless came upon him, and sore torments of the inner parts;

6 And that most justly: for he had tormented other men's bowels with many and strange torments.

7 Howbeit he nothing at all ceased from his bragging, but still was filled with pride, breathing out fire in his rage against the Yehudim, and commanding to haste the journey: but it came to pass that he fell down from his chariot, carried violently; so that having a sore fall, all the members of his body were much pained.

8 And thus he that a little afore thought he might command the waves of the sea, (so proud was he beyond the condition of man) and weigh the high mountains in a balance, was now cast on the ground, and carried in an horselitter, shewing forth unto all the manifest power of YAHOWAH.

9 So that the worms rose up out of the body of this wicked man, and whiles he lived in sorrow and pain, his flesh fell away, and the filthiness of his smell was noisome to all his army.

10 And the man, that thought a little afore he could reach to the stars of heaven, no man could endure to carry for his intolerable stink.

11 Here therefore, being plagued, he began to leave off his great pride, and to come to the knowledge of himself by the scourge of ELOHIM, his pain increasing every moment.

12 And when he himself could not abide his own smell, he said these words, It is meet to be subject unto ELOHIM, and that a man that is mortal should not proudly think of himself if he were ELOHIM.

13 This wicked person prayed also unto YAHOWAH, who now YAHOWAH would no more hear his voice, he vowed a vow unto YAHOWAH saying thus,

14 That the holy city (to the which he was going in haste to lay it even with the ground, and to make it

a common buryingplace,) he would set at liberty:

15 And as touching the Yehudim, whom he had judged not worthy so much as to be buried, but to be cast out with their children to be devoured of the fowls and wild beasts, he would make them all equals to the citizens of Athinas:

16 And the temple of YAHOWAH, which before he had spoiled, he would garnish with goodly gifts, and restore all the holy vessels with many more, and out of his own revenue defray the charges belonging to the sacrifices:

17 Yea, and that also he would become a Yehudi himself, and go through all the world that was inhabited, and declare the power of ELOHIM.

18 But for all this his pains would not cease: for the just judgment of YAHOWAH was come upon him: therefore despairing of his health, he wrote unto the Yehudim the letter underwritten, containing the form of a supplication, after this manner:

19 Antiokos, king and governor, to the good Yehudim his citizens wisheth much joy, health, and prosperity:

20 If ye and your children fare well, and your affairs be to your contentment, I give very great thanks to YAHOWAH, having my hope in heaven.

21 As for me, I was weak, or else I would have remembered kindly your honour and good will returning out of Paras, and being taken with a grievous disease, I thought it necessary to care for the common safety of all:

22 Not distrusting mine health, but having great hope in the salvation of YAHOWAH to escape this sickness.

23 But considering that even my father, at what time he led an army into the high countries. appointed a successor,

24 To the end that, if any thing fell out contrary to expectation, or if any tidings were brought that were grievous, they of the land, knowing to whom the state was left, might not be troubled:

25 Again, considering how that the princes that are borderers and neighbours unto my kingdom wait for opportunities, and expect what shall be the event. I have appointed my son Antiokos king, whom I often committed and commended unto many of you, when I went up into the high provinces; to whom I have written as followeth:

26 Therefore I pray and request you to remember the benefits that I have done unto you generally, and in special, and that every man will be still faithful to me and my son.

27 For I am persuaded that he understanding my mind will favourably and graciously yield to your desires.

28 Thus the murderer and blasphemer having suffered most grievously, as he entreated other men, so died he a miserable death in a strange country in the mountains.

29 And Philipos, that was brought up with him, carried away his body, who also fearing the son of Antiokos went into Mitzraim to Ptolemeus Philometor.

10 Now Makabi and his company, the RUAKH of YAHOWAH guiding them, recovered the temple and the city:

2 But the altars which the heathen had built in the open street, and also the chapels, they pulled down.

3 And having cleansed the temple they made another altar, and striking stones they took fire out of them, and offered a sacrifice to YAHOWAH after two days, and set forth incense, and lights, and shewbread on the table of YAHOWAH.

4 When that was done, they fell flat down, and besought YAHOWAH ELOHIM saying, We beseech thee YAHOWAH that you might keep us from such troubles; but if we sinned any more against thee, that thou would chasten us with mercy, and that we might not be delivered unto the blasphemous and barbarous Gentiles.

5 Now it was from YAHOWAH upon the same day that the strangers profaned the temple, on the very same day it was cleansed again, even the five and twentieth day of the same month, which is Kislew.

6 And they kept the feast of YAHOWAH eight days with gladness, like unto the feast of Sukkot, remembering that not long afore they had held The Feast of Sukkot, when as they wandered in the mountains and dens like beasts.

7 Therefore they bare branches, and fair boughs, and palms also, and sang psalms unto YAHOWAH that had given them good success in cleansing his place.

8 They ordained also by a common statute and decree, That every year those days should be kept of the whole nation of the Yehudim.

9 And this was the end of Antiokos, called The Magnificent.

10 Now will we declare the acts of Antiokos Eupator, who was the son of this wicked man, gathering briefly the calamities of the wars.

11 So when he was come to the crown, he set one Lizias over the affairs of his realm, and appointed him his chief governor of Aram and Kena'an.

12 For Ptolemeus, that was called Macron, choosing rather to do justice unto the Yehudim for the wrong that had been done unto them, endeavoured to continue shalom with them.

13 Whereupon being accused of the king's friends before Eupator, and called traitor at every word because he had left Qiphros, that Philometor had committed unto him, and departed to Antiokos The Magnificent, and seeing that he was in no honourable place, he was so discouraged, that he poisoned himself and died.

14 But when Gorgias was governor of the holds, he hired soldiers, and nourished war continually with the Yehudim:

15 And therewithall the Edomim, having gotten into their hands the most commodious holds, kept the Yehudim occupied, and receiving those

that were banished from Yerushalem, they went about to nourish war.

16 Then they that were with Makabi made supplication, and besought YAHOWAH that he would be their helper; and so they ran with violence upon the strong holds of Edom,

17 And assaulting them strongly, they won the holds, and kept off all that fought upon the wall, and slew all that fell into their hands, and killed no fewer than twenty thousand.

18 And because certain, who were no less than nine thousand, were fled together into two very strong castles, having all manner of things convenient to sustain the siege,

19 Makabi left Shimon and Yoseph, and Zakkai also, and them that were with him, who were enough to besiege them, and departed himself unto those places which more needed his help.

20 Now they that were with Shimon, being led with covetousness, were persuaded for money through certain of those that were in the castle, and took seventy thousand drachms, and let some of them escape.

21 But when it was told Makabi what was done, he called the governors of the people together, and accused those men, that they had sold their brethren for money, and set their enemies free to fight against them.

22 So he slew those that were found traitors, and immediately took the two castles.

23 And having good success with his weapons in all things he took in hand, he slew in the two holds more than twenty thousand.

24 Now Timotios, whom the Yehudim had overcome before, when he had gathered a great multitude of foreign forces, and horses out of Asia not a few, came as though he would take Yehudah by force of arms.

25 But when he drew near, they that were with Makabi turned themselves to pray unto YAHOWAH, and sprinkled earth upon their heads, and girded their loins with sackcloth,

26 And fell down at the foot of the altar of YAHOWAH, and besought YAHOWAH saying, YAHOWAH be merciful to us, and to be an enemy to our enemies, and an adversary to our adversaries, as thy holy Torah declareth.

27 So after the prayer they took their weapons, and went on further from the city: and when they drew near to their enemies, they kept by themselves.

28 Now the sun being newly risen, they joined both together; the one part having together with their virtue their refuge also unto YAHOWAH their ELOHIM for a pledge of their success and victory: the other side making their rage leader of their battle

29 But when the battle waxed strong, there appeared unto the enemies from heaven five comely men upon horses, with bridles of gold, and two of them led the Yehudim,

30 And took Makabi betwixt them, and covered him on every side weapons, and kept him safe, but

shot arrows and lightnings against the enemies: so that being confounded with blindness, and full of trouble, they were killed.

31 And there were slain of footmen twenty thousand and five hundred, and six hundred horsemen.

32 As for Timotios himself, he fled into a very strong hold, called Gawra, where Khereas was governor.

33 But they that were with Makabi laid siege against the fortress courageously four days.

34 And they that were within, trusting to the strength of the place, blasphemed exceedingly, and uttered wicked words.

35 Nevertheless upon the fifth day early twenty young men of Makabi's company, inflamed with anger because of the blasphemies, assaulted the wall manly, and with a fierce courage killed all that they met withal.

36 Others likewise ascending after them, whiles they were busied with them that were within, burnt the towers, and kindling fires burnt the blasphemers alive; and others broke open the gates, and, having received in the rest of the army, took the city,

37 And killed Timotios, that was hid in a certain pit, and Khereas his brother, with Apollophanes.

38 When this was done, they praised YAHOWAH with psalms and thanksgiving, who had done so great things for Yisra'EL, and given them the victory.

11 Not long after the, Lizias the king's protector and cousin, who also managed the affairs, took sore displeasure for the things that were done.

2 And when he had gathered about fourscore thousand with all the horsemen, he came against the Yehudim, thinking to make the city an habitation of the Gentiles,

3 And to make a gain of the temple, as of the other chapels of the heathen, and to set the high priesthood to sale every year:

4 Not at all considering the power of YAHOWAH but puffed up with his ten thousands of footmen, and his thousands of horsemen, and his fourscore elephants.

5 So he came to Yehudah, and drew near to Beth-Tzur, which was a strong town, but distant from Yerushalem about five furlongs, and he laid sore siege unto it.

6 Now when they that were with Makabi heard that he besieged the holds, they and all the people with lamentation and tears besought YAHOWAH that he would send a good Angel to deliver Yisra'EL.

7 Then Makabi himself first of all took weapons, exhorting the other that they would jeopard themselves together with him to help their brethren: so they went forth together with a willing mind.

8 And as they were at Yerushalem, there appeared before them on horseback one in white clothing,

shaking his armour of gold.

9 Then they praised the merciful ELOHIM all together, and took heart, insomuch that they were ready not only to fight with men, but with most cruel beasts, and to pierce through walls of iron.

10 Thus they marched forward in their armour, having an Angel sent before them: for YAHOWAH was merciful unto them

11 And giving a charge upon their enemies like lions, they slew eleven thousand footmen, and sixteen hundred horsemen, and put all the other to flight.

12 Many of them also being wounded escaped naked; and Lizias himself fled away shamefully, and so escaped.

13 Who, as he was a man of understanding, casting with himself what loss he had had, and considering that the Hebrews could not be overcome, because YAHOWAH ELOHIM helped them, he sent unto them,

14 And persuaded them to agree to all reasonable conditions, and promised that he would persuade the king that he must needs be a friend unto them.

15 Then Makabi consented to all that Lizias desired, being careful of the common good; and whatsoever Makabi wrote unto Lizias concerning the Yehudim, the king granted it.

16 For there were letters written unto the Yehudim from Lizias to this effect: Lizias unto the people of the Yehudim sendeth greeting:

17 Yokhanan and Absolom, who were sent from you, delivered me the petition subscribed, and made request for the performance of the contents thereof.

18 Therefore what things soever were meet to be reported to the king, I have declared them, and he hath granted as much as might be.

19 And if then ye will keep yourselves loyal to the state, hereafter also will I endeavour to be a means of your good.

20 But of the particulars I have given order both to these and the other that came from me, to commune with you.

21 Fare ye well. The hundred and eight and fortieth year, the four and twentieth day of the month Dioscorinthius.

22 Now the king's letter contained these words: King Antiokos unto his brother Lizias sendeth greeting:

23 Since our father is translated unto the elohim, our will is, that they that are in our realm live quietly, that every one may attend upon his own affairs.

24 We understand also that the Yehudim would not consent to our father, for to be brought unto the custom of the Gentiles, but had rather keep their own manner of living: for the which cause they require of us, that we should suffer them to live after their own Torah.

25 Wherefore our mind is, that this nation shall be in rest, and we have determined to restore them their temple, that they may live according to the customs of their forefathers.

26 Thou shalt do well therefore to send unto them, and grant them shalom, that when they are certified of our mind, they may be of good comfort, and ever go cheerfully about their own affairs.

27 And the letter of the king unto the nation of the Yehudim was after this manner: King Antiokos sendeth greeting unto the council, and the rest of the Yehudim:

28 If ye fare well, we have our desire; we are also in good health.

29 Minylaos declared unto us, that your desire was to return home, and to follow your own business:

30 Wherefore they that will depart shall have safe conduct till the thirtieth day of Xanthicus with security.

31 And the Yehudim shall use their own kind of meats and Torah, as before; and none of them any manner of ways shall be molested for things ignorantly done.

32 I have sent also Minylaos, that he may comfort you.

33 Fare ye well. In the hundred forty and eighth year, and the fifteenth day of the month Xanthicus.

34 The Romans also sent unto them a letter containing these words: Quintus Memmius and Titus Manlius, ambassadors of the Romans, send greeting unto the people of the Yehudim.

35 Whatsoever Lizias the king's cousin hath granted, therewith we also are well pleased.

36 But touching such things as he judged to be referred to the king, after ye have advised thereof, send one forthwith, that we may declare as it is convenient for you: for we are now going to Antyokya.

37 Therefore send some with speed, that we may know what is your mind.

38 Farewell. This hundred and eight and fortieth year, the fifteenth day of the month Xanthicus.

12 When these covenants were made, Lizias went unto the king, and the Yehudim were about their husbandry.

2 But of the governours of several places, Timotios, and Aphlonios the son of Genneus, also Hieronymus, and Demophon, and beside them Niqanor the governor of Qiphros, would not suffer them to be quiet and live in shalom.

3 The men of Yoppa also did such an ungodly deed: they prayed the Yehudim that dwelt among them to go with their wives and children into the boats which they had prepared, as though they had meant them no hurt.

4 Who accepted of it according to the common decree of the city, as being desirous to live in shalom, and suspecting nothing: but when they were gone forth into the deep, they drowned no less than two hundred of them.

5 When Yehudah heard of this cruelty done unto his countrymen, he commanded those that were with him to make them ready.

6 And calling upon YAHOWAH the righteous Judge, he came against those murderers of his

brethren, and burnt the haven by night, and set the boats on fire, and those that fled thither he slew.

7 And when the town was shut up, he went backward, as if he would return to root out all them of the city of Yoppa.

8 But when he heard that the inhabitants of Yabnah (Jamnites) were minded to do in like manner unto the Yehudim that dwelt among them,

9 He came upon the inhabitants of Yabnah (Yabnah (Jamnites)) also by night, and set fire on the haven and the navy, so that the light of the fire was seen at Yerushalem two hundred and forty furlongs off.

10 Now when they were gone from thence nine furlongs in their journey toward Timotios, no fewer than five thousand men on foot and five hundred horsemen of the Arabians set upon him.

11 Whereupon there was a very sore battle; but Yehudah's side by the help of YAHOWAH got the victory; so that the Nomades of Ereb, being overcome, besought Yehudah for shalom, promising both to give him cattle, and to pleasure him otherwise.

12 Then Yehudah, thinking indeed that they would be profitable in many things, granted them shalom: whereupon they shook hands, and so they departed to their tents.

13 He went also about to make a bridge to a certain strong city, which was fenced about with walls, and inhabited by people of divers countries; and the name of it was Caspis.

14 But they that were within it put such trust in the strength of the walls and provision of victuals, that they behaved themselves rudely toward them that were with Yehudah, railing and blaspheming, and uttering such words as were not to be spoken.

15 Wherefore Yehudah with his company, calling upon the great YAHOWAH ELOHIM of Hosts, who without rams or engines of war did cast down Yerikho in the time of Yahoshua son of Nun, gave a fierce assault against the walls,

16 And took the city by the will of ELOHIM, and made unspeakable slaughters, insomuch that a lake two furlongs broad near adjoining thereunto, being filled full, was seen running with blood.

17 Then departed they from thence seven hundred and fifty furlongs, and came to Kharaca unto the Yehudim that are called Tubieni.

18 But as for Timotios, they found him not in the places: for before he had dispatched any thing, he departed from thence, having left a very strong garrison in a certain hold.

19 Howbeit Dozitios and Zozipater, who were of Makabi's captains, went forth, and slew those that Timotios had left in the fortress, above ten thousand men.

20 And Makabi ranged his army by bands, and set them over the bands, and went against Timotios, who had about him an hundred and twenty thousand men of foot, and two thousand and five hundred horsemen.

21 Now when Timotios had knowledge of Yehudah's coming, he sent the women and children and the other baggage unto a fortress called Carnion: for the town was hard to besiege, and uneasy to come unto, by reason of the straitness of all the places.

22 But when Yehudah his first band came in sight, the enemies, being smitten with fear and terror through the appearing of the Angel of YAHOWAH who seeth all things, fled amain, one running into this way, another that way, so as that they were often hurt of their own men, and wounded with the points of their own swords.

23 Yehudah also was very earnest in pursuing them, killing those wicked wretches, of whom he slew about thirty thousand men.

24 Moreover Timotios himself fell into the hands of Dozitios and Zozipater, whom he besought with much craft to let him go with his life, because he had many of the Yehudim'ss parents, and the brethren of some of them, who, if they put him to death, should not be regarded.

25 So when he had assured them with many words that he would restore them without hurt, according to the agreement, they let him go for the saving of their brethren.

26 Then Makabi marched forth to Carnion, and to the temple of Atargatis, and there he slew five and twenty thousand persons.

27 And after he had put to flight and destroyed them, Yehudah removed the host toward Ephron, a strong city, wherein Lizias abode, and a great multitude of divers nations, and the strong young men kept the walls, and defended them mightily: wherein also was great provision of engines and darts.

28 But when Yehudah and his company had called upon YAHOWAH ELOHIM of Hosts, who with his power breaketh the strength of his enemies, they won the city, and slew twenty and five thousand of them that were within,

29 From thence they departed to Scythopolis, which lieth six hundred furlongs from Yerushalem,

30 But when the Yehudim that dwelt there had testified that the Scythopolitans dealt lovingly with them, and entreated them kindly in the time of their adversity;

31 They gave them thanks, desiring them to be friendly still unto them: and so they came to Yerushalem, the feast of the weeks approaching.

32 And after the feast, called Shebuot, they went forth against Gorgias the governor of Edom,

33 Who came out with three thousand men of foot and four hundred horsemen.

34 And it happened that in their fighting together a few of the Yehudim were slain.

35 At which time Dozitios, one of Bacenor's company, who was on horseback, and a strong man, was still upon Gorgias, and taking hold of his coat drew him by force; and when he would have tak-

2 MACCABEES

en that cursed man alive, a horseman of Thracia coming upon him smote off his shoulder, so that Gorgias fled unto Marisa.

36 Now when they that were with Gorgias had fought long, and were weary, Yehudah called upon YAHOWAH, that he would shew himself to be their helper and leader of the battle.

37 And with that he began in his own language, and sung psalms to YAHOWAH with a loud voice, and rushing unawares upon Gorgias' men, he put them to flight.

38 So Yehudah gathered his host, and came into the city of Odollam, And when the seventh day came, they purified themselves, as the custom was, and kept the Shabbat in the same place.

39 And upon the day following, as the use had been, Yehudah and his company came to take up the bodies of them that were slain, and to bury them with their kinsmen in their fathers' graves.

40 Now under the coats of every one that was slain they found things consecrated to the idols of the inhabitants of Yabnah (Jamnites), which is forbidden the Yehudim by the Torah. Then every man saw that this was the cause wherefore they were slain.

41 All men therefore praising YAHOWAH, the righteous Judge, who had opened the things that were hid,

42 Betook themselves unto prayer, and besought him that the sin committed might wholly be put out of remembrance. Besides, that noble Yehudah exhorted the people to keep themselves from sin, forsomuch as they saw before their eyes the things that came to pass for the sins of those that were slain.

43 And when he had made a gathering throughout the company, to YAHOWAH for the sum of two thousand drachms of silver, he sent it to Yerushalem to offer a sin offering to YAHOWAH, doing therein very well and honestly, in that he was mindful of the resurrection:

44 For if he had not hoped that they that were slain should have risen again, it had been superfluous and vain to pray for the dead.

45 And also in that he perceived that there was great favour laid up of YAHOWAH for those that died godly, it was an holy and good thought. Whereupon he made a reconciliation for the dead, that they might be delivered from sin.

13 In the hundred forty and ninth year it was told Yehudah, that Antiokos Eupator was coming with a great power into Yehudah,

2 And with him Lizias his protector, and ruler of his affairs, having either of them a Grecian power of footmen, an hundred and ten thousand, and horsemen five thousand and three hundred, and elephants two and twenty, and three hundred chariots armed with hooks.

3 Minylaos also joined himself with them, and with great dissimulation encouraged Antiokos, not for the safeguard of the country, but because he thought to have been made governor.

4 But the King of kings moved Antiokos' mind against this wicked wretch, and Lizias informed the king that this man was the cause of all mischief, so that the king commanded to bring him unto Bearoth, and to put him to death, as the manner is in that place.

5 Now there was in that place a tower of fifty cubits high, full of ashes, and it had a round instrument which on every side hanged down into the ashes.

6 And whosoever was condemned of sacrilege, or had committed any other grievous crime, there did all men thrust him unto death.

7 Such a death it happened that wicked man to die, not having so much as burial in the earth; and that most justly:

8 For inasmuch as he had committed many sins about the altar of YAHOWAH, whose fire and ashes were holy, he received his death in ashes.

9 Now the king came with a barbarous and haughty mind to do far worse to the Yehudim, than had been done in his father's time.

10 Which things when Yehudah perceived, he commanded the multitude to call upon YAHOWAH night and day, that if ever at any other time, he would now also help them, being at the point to be put from the Torah of YAHOWAH, from their country, and from the holy temple:

11 And that he would not suffer the people, that had even now been but a little refreshed, to be in subjection to the blasphemous Gentiles.

12 So when they had all done this together, and besought the merciful YAHOWAH with weeping and fasting, and lying flat upon the ground three days long, Yehudah, having exhorted them, commanded they should be in a readiness.

13 And Yehudah, being apart with the elders, determined, before the king's host should enter into Yehudah, and get the city, to go forth and try the matter in fight by the help of YAHOWAH.

14 So when he had committed all to YAHOWAH, and exhorted his soldiers to fight manfully, even unto death, for the Torah, the temple of YAHOWAH, the city, the country, and the commonwealth, he camped by Modin:

15 And having given the watchword to them that were about him, To YAHOWAH is the Victory; with the most valiant and choice young men he went in into the king's tent by night, and slew in the camp about four thousand men, and the chiefest of the elephants, with all that were upon him.

16 And at last they filled the camp with fear and tumult, and departed with good success.

17 This was done in the break of the day, because the protection of YAHOWAH did help him.

18 Now when the king had taken a taste of the manliness of the Yehudim, he went about to take the holds by policy,

19 And marched toward Beth-Tzur, which was a strong hold of the Yehudim: but he was put to flight, failed, and lost of his men:

20 For Yehudah had conveyed unto them that were in it such things as were necessary.

21 But Rhodocus, who was in the Yehudim'ss host, disclosed the secrets to the enemies; therefore he was sought out, and when they had gotten him, they put him in prison.

22 The king treated with them in Bethsum the second time, gave his hand, took their's, departed, fought with Yehudah, was overcome;

23 Heard that Philipos, who was left over the affairs in Antyokya, was desperately bent, confounded, intreated the Yehudim, submitted himself, and sware to all equal conditions, agreed with them, and offered sacrifice to YAHOWAH, honoured the temple, and dealt kindly with the place,

24 And accepted well of Makabi, made him principal governor from Ptolemais unto the Gerrhenians;

25 Came to Ptolemais: the people there were grieved for the covenants; for they stormed, because they would make their covenants void:

26 Lizias went up to the judgment seat, said as much as could be in defence of the cause, persuaded, pacified, made them well affected, returned to Antyokya. Thus it went touching the king's coming and departing.

14 After three years was Yehudah informed, that Dimitrios the son of Seliqos, having entered by the haven of Tripolis with a great power and navy,

2 Had taken the country, and killed Antiokos, and Lizias his protector.

3 Now one Eliqim, who had been high priest, and had defiled himself wilfully in the times of their mingling with the Gentiles, seeing that by no means he could save himself, nor have any more access to the holy altar,

4 Came to king Dimitrios in the hundred and one and fiftieth year, presenting unto him a crown of gold, and a palm, and also of the boughs which were used solemnly in the temple: and so that day he held his shalom.

5 Howbeit having gotten opportunity to further his foolish enterprize, and being called into counsel by Dimitrios, and asked how the Yehudim stood affected, and what they intended, he answered thereunto:

6 Those of the Yehudim that he called Khasidim, whose captain is Yehudah Makabi, nourish war and are seditious, and will not let the rest be in shalom.

7 Therefore I, being deprived of mine ancestors' honour, I mean the high priesthood, am now come hither:

8 First, verily for the unfeigned care I have of things pertaining to the king; and secondly, even for that I intend the good of mine own countrymen: for all our nation is in no small misery through the unadvised dealing of them aforersaid.

9 Wherefore, O king, seeing knowest all these things, be careful for the country, and our nation, which is pressed on every side, according to the clemency that thou readily shewest unto all.

10 For as long as Yehudah liveth, it is not possible that the state should be quiet.

11 This was no sooner spoken of him, but others of the king's friends, being maliciously set against Yehudah, did more incense Dimitrios.

12 And forthwith calling Niqanor, who had been master of the elephants, and making him governor over Yehudah, he sent him forth,

13 Commanding him to slay Yehudah, and to scatter them that were with him, and to make Eliqim high priest of the great temple.

14 Then the heathen, that had fled out of Yehudah from Yehudah, came to Niqanor by flocks, thinking the harm and calamities ot the Yehudim to be their welfare.

15 Now when the Yehudim heard of Niqanor's coming, and that the heathen were up against them, they cast earth upon their heads, and made supplication to YAHOWAH that had established his people for ever, and who always helpeth his portion with manifestation of his presence.

16 So at the commandment of the captain they removed straightways from thence, and came near unto them at the town of Dessau.

17 Now Shimon, Yehudah's brother, had joined battle with Niqanor, but was somewhat discomfited through the sudden silence of his enemies.

18 Nevertheless Niqanor, hearing of the manliness of them that were with Yehudah, and the courageousness that they had to fight for their country, durst not try the matter by the sword.

19 Wherefore he sent Posidonius, and Theodotus, and MattitYAHU, to make shalom.

20 So when they had taken long advisement thereupon, and the captain had made the multitude acquainted therewith, and it appeared that they were all of one mind, they consented to the covenants,

21 And appointed a day to meet in together by themselves: and when the day came, and stools were set for either of them,

22 Ludas placed armed men ready in convenient places, lest some treachery should be suddenly practised by the enemies: so they made a peaceable conference.

23 Now Niqanor abode in Yerushalem, and did no hurt, but sent away the people that came flocking unto him.

24 And he would not willingly have Yehudah out of his sight: for he love the man from his heart

25 He prayed him also to take a wife, and to beget children: so he married, was quiet, and took part of this life.

26 But Eliqim, perceiving the love that was betwixt them, and considering the covenants that were made, came to Dimitrios, and told him that Niqanor was not well affected toward the state; for that he had ordained Yehudah, a traitor to his realm, to be the king's successor.

27 Then the king being in a rage, and provoked with the accusations of the most wicked man, wrote to Niqanor, signifying that he was much displeased with the covenants, and commanding

2 MACCABEES

him that he should send Makabi prisoner in all haste unto Antyokya.

28 When this came to Niqanor's hearing, he was much confounded in himself, and took it grievously that he should make void the articles which were agreed upon, the man being in no fault.

29 But because there was no dealing against the king, he watched his time to accomplish this thing by policy.

30 Notwithstanding, when Makabi saw that Niqanor began to be churlish unto him, and that he entreated him more roughly than he was wont, perceiving that such sour behaviour came not of good, he gathered together not a few of his men, and withdrew himself from Niqanor.

31 But the other, knowing that he was notably prevented by Yehudah's policy, came into the great and holy temple of YAHOWAH, and commanded the priests, that were offering their usual sacrifices, to deliver him the man.

32 And when they sware that they could not tell where the man was whom he sought,

33 He stretched out his right hand toward the temple, and made an oath in this manner: If ye will not deliver me Yehudah as a prisoner, I will lay this temple of ELOHIM even with the ground, and I will break down the altar, and erect a notable temple unto Bacchus.

34 After these words he departed. Then the priests lifted up their hands toward YAHOWAH ELOHIM, and besought him that was ever a defender of their nation, saying in this manner;

35 Thou, O YAHOWAH ELOHIM of all things, who hast need of nothing, wast pleased that the temple of thine habitation should be among us:

36 Therefore now, O holy FATHER of all holiness, keep this house ever undefiled, which lately was cleansed, and stop every unrighteous mouth.

37 Now was there accused unto Niqanor one Razis, one of the elders of Yerushalem, a lover of his countrymen, and a man of very good report, who for his kindness was called a father of the Yehudim.

38 For in the former times, when they mingled not themselves with the Gentiles, he had been accused of a troubler of the Yehudim, and did boldly jeopard his body and life with all vehemency for the Torah of his ELOHIM.

39 So Niqanor, willing to declare the hate that he bare unto the Yehudim, sent above five hundred men of war to take him:

40 For he thought by taking him to do the Yehudim much hurt.

41 Now when the multitude would have taken the tower, and violently broken into the outer door, and bade that fire should be brought to burn it, he being ready to be taken on every side fell upon his sword;

42 Choosing rather to die manfully, than to come into the hands of the wicked, to be abused otherwise than beseemed his noble birth:

43 But missing his stroke through haste, the multitude also rushing within the doors, he ran boldly up to the wall, and cast himself down manfully among the thickest of them.

44 But they quickly giving back, and a space being made, he fell down into the midst of the void place.

45 Nevertheless, while there was yet breath within him, being inflamed with anger, he rose up; and though his blood gushed out like spouts of water, and his wounds were grievous, yet he ran through the midst of the throng; and standing upon a steep rock,

46 When as his blood was now quite gone, he plucked out his bowels, and taking them in both his hands, he cast them upon the throng, and calling upon YAHOWAH ELOHIM, ELOHIM of life and RUAKH to restore him those again, he thus died.

15 But Niqanor, hearing that Yehudah and his company were in the strong places about Shomron, resolved without any danger to set upon them on the Shabbat day.

2 Nevertheless the Yehudim that were compelled to go with him said, O destroy not so cruelly and barbarously, but give honour to that day, which he, that seeth all things, hath honoured with holiness above all other days.

3 Then the most ungracious wretch demanded, if there were a Mighty one in heaven, that had commanded the Shabbat day to be kept.

4 And when they said, He is the ELOHIM, ELOHIM of Heaven a living, and mighty, who commanded the seventh day to be kept:

5 Then said the other, And I also am mighty upon earth, and I command to take arms, and to do the king's business. Yet he obtained not to have his wicked will done.

6 So Niqanor in exceeding pride and haughtiness determined to set up a publick monument of his victory over Yehudah and them that were with him.

7 But Yehudah had ever sure confidence that the name of ELOHIM would help him:

8 Wherefore he exhorted his people not to fear the coming of the heathen against them, but to remember the salvation of YAHOWAH which in former times they had received from heaven, and now to expect the victory and aid, which should come unto them from the Almighty.

9 And so comforting them out of the word of YAHOWAH and the prophets, and withal putting them in mind of the battles that they won afore, he made them more cheerful.

10 And when he had stirred up their minds, he gave them their charge, shewing them therewithall the falsehood of the heathen, and the breach of oaths.

11 Thus he armed every one of them, not so much with defence of shields and spears, as with comfortable and good words: and beside that, he told them a dream worthy to be believed, as if it had been so indeed, which did not a little rejoice them.

12 And this was his vision: That Khonaiw, who had been high priest, a virtuous and a good man, reverend in conversation, gentle in condition, well spoken also, and exercised from a child in all points of virtue, holding up his hands prayed to YAHOWAH for the whole body of the Yehudim.

13 This done, in like manner there appeared a man with gray hairs, and exceeding glorious, who was of a wonderful and excellent majesty.

14 Then Khonaiw answered, saying, This is a lover of the brethren, who prayeth much for the people, and for the holy city, to wit, YirmeYAH the prophet of ELOHIM.

15 Whereupon YirmeYAH holding forth his right hand gave to Yehudah a sword of gold, and in giving it spake thus,

16 Take this holy sword, a gift from ELOHIM, with the which thou shalt wound the adversaries.

17 Thus being well comforted by the words of Yehudah, which were very good, and able to stir them up to valour, and to encourage the hearts of the young men, they determined not to pitch camp, but courageously to set upon them, and manfully to try the matter by conflict, because the city and the sanctuary and the temple were in danger.

18 For the care that they took for their wives, and their children, their brethren, and folks, was in least account with them: but the greatest and principal fear was for the House of YAHOWAH their ELOHIM.

19 Also they that were in the city took not the least care, being troubled for the conflict abroad.

20 And now, when as all looked what should be the trial, and the enemies were already come near, and the army was set in array, and the beasts conveniently placed, and the horsemen set in wings,

21 Makabi seeing the coming of the multitude, and the divers preparations of armour, and the fierceness of the beasts, stretched out his hands toward heaven, and called upon ELOHIM that worketh wonders, knowing that victory cometh not by arms, but even as it seemeth good to him, he giveth it to such as are worthy:

22 Therefore in his prayer he said after this manner; O YAHOWAH ELOHIM, thou didst send thine Angel in the time of ChizqiYAHU king of Yehudah, and didst slay in the host of Sanchaerib an hundred fourscore and five thousand:

23 Wherefore now also, O ELOHIM of Heaven, send an Angel before us for a fear and dread unto them;

24 And through the might of thine arm let those be stricken with terror, that come against thy holy people to blaspheme. And he ended thus.

25 Then Niqanor and they that were with him came forward with trumpets and songs.

26 But Yehudah and his company encountered the enemies with invocation and prayer to YAHOWAH.

27 So that fighting with their hands, and praying unto YAHOWAH with their hearts, they slew no less than thirty and five thousand men: for through the appearance of YAHOWAH was a wonderful victory.

28 Now when the battle was done, returning again with joy, they knew that Niqanor lay dead in his harness.

29 Then they made a great shout and a noise, praising YAHOWAH ELOHIM of Hosts in their own language.

30 And Yehudah, who was ever the chief defender of the citizens both in body and mind, and who continued his love toward his countrymen all his life, commanded to strike off Niqanor's head, and his hand with his shoulder, and bring them to the temple of YAHOWAH.

31 So when he was there, and called them of his nation together, and set the priests before the altar, he sent for them that were of the tower,

32 And shewed them vile Niqanor's head, and the hand of that blasphemer, which with proud brags he had stretched out against the holy temple of the Almighty.

33 And when he had cut out the tongue of that ungodly Niqanor, he commanded that they should give it by pieces unto the fowls, and hang up the reward of his madness before the temple.

34 So every man praised toward YAHOWAH ELOHIM of heaven, saying, Blessed be YAHOWAH that hath kept his own place undefiled.

35 He hanged also Niqanor's head upon the tower, an evident and manifest sign unto all of the help of YAHOWAH.

36 And they ordained all with a common decree in no case to let that day pass without solemnity, but to celebrate the thirtieth day of the twelfth month, which in the Syrian tongue is called Adar, the day before Mordekai's day.

37 Thus went it with Niqanor: and from that time forth the Hebrews had the city in their power. And here will I make an end.

38 And if I have done well, and as is fitting the story, it is that which I desired: but if slenderly and meanly, it is that which I could attain unto.

39 For as it is hurtful to drink wine or water alone; and as wine mingled with water is pleasant, and delighteth the taste: even so speech finely framed delighteth the ears of them that read the story. And here shall be an end.

NOTES

KNOWING OUR H.I.S.TORY

The Hebrew Israelite Story

The Hebrew Israelite Story, H.I.S.tory, is rooted deep in the unspoken and under documented history of the so called Black/Afro-Latino/Native American.

There were many slaves who knew who they were and tried to maintain their heritage in a land that was not theirs. They demonstrated this through artifacts such as the Cursive Hebrew writings on the pews of the First African Baptist Church in Savannah, GA and by leading rebellions with the Bible as their foundation of "Truth."

We Must Remember Our Hebrew Israelite Story And Pass It Down To Future Generations.

Some of the early slaves who possessed the strength of our ancestors were Gabriel Prosser and Nat Turner. They each are reported in history as standing on the word of YAH and using HIS WORD to lead rebellions against those who were the oppressors of our people.

Psalms 9:9
"YAHOWAH also will be a refuge for the oppressed,
a refuge in times of trouble."

These gentlemen were some of the first stones of the foundation for those who followed and continued in the study and dissemination of HIS WORD; bringing forth the "TRUTH."

As we continue our journey, though the Hebrew Israelite Story, H.I.S.tory, we enter the era of the Israelites being birthed in America. Some of the first men to acknowledge the so called Black/Afro-Latino/Native American were the Israelites of the Bible were F. S. Cherry, William Saunders Crowdy, Wentworth A. Mathews, Israel ben Newman, Mordecai Herman, and Arnold Josiah Ford Moshe Ben Kareem (MaShah), and Yaiqab Ben Gad. Each of these men started congregations to teach the lost sheep of Israel who they were according the Bible. They are a part of the next level of foundational stones in the Hebrew Israelite Story which paved the way for our current Lions of Judah who are continuing to teach the lost sheep of Israel (Banging on Esau) across the four corners of the earth.

NOTE: "The Mystery Stone" has the 10 Commandments inscribed in Ancient Paleo Hebrew on a stone found by the local native indians in New Mexico at that time. "Though people were aware of the rock when New Mexico became a territory in 1850, no one could read it. Local Indians told the owner of the land in 1871 that the rock predated their tribes coming to the area". http://www.legendsofamerica.com/nm-riopuercovalley.html

We Can All Agree On Keeping The Laws, Statutes, and Commandments of YAHOWAH.

Though all of these groups may have differences in doctrine, we can all agree on keeping the Laws, Statutes, and Commandments of YAHOWAH.

Isaiah 11: 12

And he shall set up an ensign for the nations, and shall assemble the outcasts of Yisra'EL, and gather together the dispersed of Yehudah from the four corners of the earth.

This just a small list of all the Israelites awakened in the last days.

Ambassadors of Christ (AOC)
Army of Israel (AOI)
B'nai Adath
B'nai Zaqen
Banya Yasharahla
Beth ELOHIM
Beth Shalom
Brazilian Israelites
Commandment Keepers
Dimona Israelites
Dominican Israelites
Ethiopian Israelites
For Our People Edification (F.O.P.E.)
Ha'Shabbah
Haitian Israelites
House of David (HOD)
House of Israel (HOI)
I AM ISRAEL (IAI)
Igbo Israelites
Israelite Heritage
Israelite Preparatory Institute (I.P.I.)
Israelite School of Universal Practical Knowledge (ISUPK)
Israelites Scattered in Africa
Israelites Scattered in Asia
Israelites Scattered in Europe
Israelites Scattered in South America
Israelites United in Christ (IUIC)
Jamaican Israelites

KHAIYASHUA
Kol Sheariyth
Light of Zion
Lions of Israel
MYMG
Mexican Israelites
Nation of Israel (NOI)
Native American Israelites
NCCI
NCCI Sanctioned Body
Puerto Rican Israelites
Qahal
Saints of Christ (England)
Sh'ma Yisrael
Shield of Wisdom
Shomrey Ha'Torah
Sicarii
Sounds of Sinai (Tabernacle of ELOHIM)
South American Israelites
Strong Tower
Sword of Zion
Tabernacles of Israel (Jamaica)
The House of the Redeemed Servants
The Path to YAHUAH
United Congregation of Israel
United Kingdom Israelites
United Kingdom of Israel Congregation (UKOIC)
YAH'S House
YAHAWAH'S Camp

Double Honor to all the Israelite Assemblies, Camps, and Congregations spreading the truth throughout the four corners of the earth. Shalom to All of Israel from Brother JediYah Melek

NOTES

NOTES

JediYAH Melek Ben Dani'EL

Khasidah KhaniYAH Melek

YaqarYAH Bat JediYAH Ben Dani'EL

GadelYAH Ben Manassheh Ephraim

CPSIA information can be obtained
at www.ICGtesting.com
Printed in the USA
BVHW01s2357160518
516455BV00005B/13/P

9 780999 631416